International Banking
and
Financial Systems:
A Comparison

International Banking
and
Financial Systems:

A Comparison

Andrew Mullineux, Ph D

NatWest Lecturer in Money and Banking
Department of Economics, University of Birmingham

Graham & Trotman

A member of the Kluwer Academic Publishers Group

LONDON/DORDRECHT/BOSTON

First published 1987 by
Graham & Trotman Ltd
Sterling House
66 Wilton Road
London SW1V 1DE

Graham & Trotman Inc
Kluwer Academic Publishers Group
101 Philip Drive
Assinippi Park
Norwell, MA 02061
USA

British Library Cataloguing in Publication Data
Mullineux, A.W.
   International banking and financial systems: A comparison
   1. Banks and banking
      I. Title
      332.1   HG1601
ISBN 0-86010-916-X

Library of Congress Cataloguing-in-Publication Data
   Mullineux, A.W.
      International banking and financial systems.
      Bibliography: p.
      Includes index.
         1. Banks and banking. 2. Banks and banking, International. 3. Finance. 4. International finance
      I. Title.
      HG1573.M84 1987 332.1   87-23605
      ISBN 0-86010-916-X

Typeset by Electronic Village Editorial Services, Richmond, Surrey
Printed and Bound in Great Britain at the Alden Press, Oxford

Contents

To Joan and Harry

Preface

This book is largely based on a series of lectures given to students taking Money, Banking and Finance degrees at the University of Birmingham. The lectures are attended by undergraduate students, for whom the "Comparative Banking" course is compulsory in the third year of their programme, and by students taking the course as an option on the Masters degree programme. The students have shown a great deal of interest in the subject-matter and have contributed to the book by asking searching questions and submitting thorough essays. I must thank them for this.

It is hoped that this book will serve as a text not only for future students at this University but also for people studying banking in connection with degree programmes at other higher educational institutions or in pursuit of professional qualifications.

Furthermore, with its international comparisons and analyses it is hoped that the book will also be a useful guide to professional bankers working in today's increasingly international markets.

I thank Judith for her support, despite the competing claim of her studies upon her time. I also thank our children, Ruth (6) and Joe (3), for indulging us in our preoccupations, despite the fact that Ruth pulled the plug on the word processor one morning as I was completing a chapter and caused some of the text to be lost. I hope the revised version is acceptable and must bear full responsibility for any inaccuracies.

A. Mullineux
March, 1987
University of Birmingham, England.

1

The UK Banking System

1.1 Introduction

The 1970s was a period in which there was a rapid internationalisation of banking. Because of the colonial pasts of their country of incorporation many European banks already had overseas branches and representative offices and had developed correspondent relationships with overseas banks by the early 1970s. The major US banks had already built up overseas networks to service the needs of US based multinational corporations and European and Japanese banks followed this trend in the 1970s as major domestic companies became increasingly international in outlook. The process accelerated following the massive oil price rise engineered by the Organisation of Petroleum Exporting Countries (OPEC) in 1973.[1] The OPEC countries, especially the major Middle Eastern countries, developed large balance of trade surpluses as a result and tended to place them with the large international banks dealing in the Eurodollar market, the price of oil being denominated in dollars. The Eurodollar market had grown in the 1960s as a result of a series of US balance of trade deficits.[2] The consequent outflow of dollars found a home in the Eurodollar market based in London. After the Vietnam war and following the move to floating exchange rates in the early 1970s the US deficit declined and the Eurodollar market was expected to decline with it. The OPEC I oil price shock in 1973, however, provided a major new source of funds for the market which subsequently grew rapidly. The floating exchange rate system having replaced the dollar exchange standard, the currencies of other major economies began to be adopted as international reserves and the Eurocurrency market developed, although the Eurodollar market remains the largest sector. The Eurocurrency market also spread beyond Europe to become an international market. The major trading centres are offshore banking centres which offer relatively lax regulatory and tax regimes to attract international business. The London based Euromarkets can be regarded as offshore markets because they have received favourable tax treatment and have been virtually free from regulation.

The major international banks, especially the US and European ones,[3] became involved in the lucrative business of recycling the deposits of the OPEC countries. They formed syndicates to lend to countries with balance of trade deficits. Some of the East European, South East Asian, and African countries became significant borrowers but by far the most voracious were the Latin American (LA) countries. The business appeared to be relatively safe because countries were not expected to default and the major LA borrowers were judged to have sound economic prospects. Towards the end of the 1970s a number of countries began to dismantle their exchange controls,[4] and the process continued into the 1980s.[5] This development partly explains why the 1980s has become a period of globalisation, following the period of internationalisation of banking[6] in the 1970s.

In 1979 OPEC engineered a second major oil price[7] rise and the syndicated loan market looked set to grow further. Oil prices, however, began to fall again, in both nominal and real terms, in the early 1980s as new supplies[8] came on tap and oil conservation measures promoted in many countries began to have an effect. The surpluses of the OPEC countries began to decline and, ironically, oil producing lesser developed countries (LDCs) began to find it difficult to service their debt payments. The problems first emerged amongst some of the East European debtors, especially Poland, however. The debtors' problems were compounded by the fact that many of the major industrial countries responded to OPEC II by imposing restrictive fiscal and monetary policy designed to contain the inflationary impact of the oil price shock in the light of their experiences following OPEC I. Growth in world trade slowed, making it difficult for LDCs to export a sufficient quantity of goods to raise revenue to service their debts. Interest rates also rose. This increased the cost of servicing their debt because the practice of charging variable interest rates[9] had become widespread in the 1970s.[10] Mexico, a major oil producer which relies heavily on exports to the US, was forced to default on its interest payments in 1982[11] and the Latin American debt crisis, later to become more widespread and known as the 'third world' debt problem was born.

With the supply of OPEC funds declining dramatically and syndicated loans to third world borrowers suddenly more risky, the international banks had to rethink their strategies rapidly. Many of them, especially the US and UK banks, began to look more carefully at their domestic markets as an alternative source of growth. They found that they had lost considerable ground in the retail banking sector to mutual savings banks[12] and that investment banks in the US and merchant banks in the UK were making inroads into their corporate business. In the US the process of securitisation gathered pace in the early 1980s. The large investment banks began packaging loan assets such as mortgages and selling them to investors. Meanwhile the corporate sector was increasingly raising funds by issuing commercial paper and bonds, rather than by borrowing from banks. The major corporations moved first but the smaller corporations, with no standard credit rating, later began to raise funds through so called 'junk bonds'. This process of securitisation caught on in Europe in the first half of the 1980s as major multinational corporations began to raise substantial quantities of money through Eurobond and Eurorate issues. By virtue of their strong credit standing, many of them being more credit worthy than banks especially in the light of their heavy 'third world' debt exposures, large corporations found that securities based finance had become cheaper than bank finance. Meanwhile, investors discovered that they could obtain higher yields on the securities markets than they could by leaving money on deposit with banks. The banks themselves were keen to support the securitisation process because it enabled them to keep in touch with their corporate clients and earn fee income from placing paper, notes and bonds issued by the companies. They also found that the growth of the Eurobond market provided them with the opportunity of buying securities to hold as assets in place of loans. The advantage was that the securities could be sold whereas loans could not, unless they themselves were repackaged as securities. As mentioned above, the process of securitisation in the US has encompassed repackaging, but this has not become widespread in Europe and elsewhere yet. The banks have been loath to repackage their Third World debt because they fear that it would sell at such a discount that the size of their provisioning against this debt would be seen to be inadequate.[13] Securitisation thus involves the process of replacing traditional loans with tradeable securities. This process involves not just the displacement of loans by securities but also the repackaging of loans into securities. Displacement has been prevalent in Europe and is reflected by the fact that the Eurobond market has grown more rapidly than the Eurocurrency market in the 1980s.

Under pressure from their supervisors, banks around the world were encouraged to raise their capital ratios, which had, in many cases, fallen to historically low levels by the beginning of the 1980s, in the light of the greater risks associated with country loans following the Mexican crisis. Many of the industrialised countries also experienced recessions as a result of restrictive policies adopted in the wake of OPEC II and this exposed the banks to problem loans to their domestic corporate sectors as well. The supervisory authorities in many countries eventually allowed banks to raise capital by issuing perpetual floating rate notes (FRNs)[14] in the early 1980s. This gave banks an even greater interest in the Eurobond market. It also meant that major international banks, already exposed to each other through the Eurocurrency market which had become an international interbank market, also began to hold each others debt. As a consequence a failure of a major bank in any one country could have substantial knock-on or domino effects on the wider international banking system. It, therefore, became necessary for the bank supervisors in the major industrial countries to allocate supervisory responsibilities. They responded to the internationalisation of banking by reaching an agreement in 1975 called the Basle Concordat.[15] This was revised in 1983[16] in the light of experiences that had shown up its deficiencies. Globalisation and the rapid development of securitisation have made it difficult for the supervisors to keep pace with developments. Globalisation involves the creation of global markets and, as a result of securitisation, banking and capital markets have converged towards a global financial pool. The erosion of exchange controls has permitted this development. International money flows are now far larger than those required solely to finance trade and meet trade deficits. Globalisation raises the issue of fairness of competition. Banks from countries with more liberal regulatory and tax regimes can underprice those from less liberal countries in the global markets. The Japanese banks, which have grown most rapidly in the 1980s, have been doing particularly well in the Eurocurrency and Eurobond markets and banks from other countries[17] have complained that this is due to an unfair competitive advantage. In particular, the Japanese banks appear to be allowed to have very low capital bases. The Japanese banks argue that they have substantial hidden reserves so that their capital base is larger than it appears. Nevertheless, the Japanese authorities responded to criticism in 1986 by requiring Japanese to raise their capital ratios toward the international average, allowing them to achieve this by running down hidden reserves to some extent. The supervisors are, therefore, exerting pressure on each other to create a 'level playing field' to ensure fair competition. Their power to do so is limited to their influence over the regulatory regimes in their countries. It is up to governments to complete the process through tax reform and this might take longer to achieve. Securitisation has also caused concern amongst the supervisors[18] as off balance sheet risks have grown. Through notes issuance facilities (NIFs) and similar instruments, banks make commitments to buy new securities from their clients when they cannot sell the full amount in the market. These and other contingent liabilities expose banks to risks that are not reflected in their balance sheets. The supervisors[19] have recommended that these off balance sheet risks should also be backed by capital and a number of countries, including Japan, Germany, the US and the UK, have subsequently imposed requirements on domestic banks to hold capital to back these liabilities. A significant development in international banking supervisory coordination occurred in January 1987. The UK and US supervisors issued joint proposals on capital adequacy using standardised measures of capital and imposing uniform requirements on US and UK banks to cover both balance sheet and off balance sheet risks. They hope to persuade the supervisory authorities in other countries to adopt similar standards and thus to make them internationally applicable.

The extent of the change that has taken place in the 1980s is illustrated by the fact that in the first half of the decade the volume of international loans fell from about %100bn a year to %25bn a year whilst issues of bonds and notes rose from %50bn to nearly %200bn a year. The growth in the Eurobond market has been encouraged by a substantial amount of financial innovation designed to provide hedges against risks emanating from exchange and interest rate fluctuations; and by a fall in inflation that has encouraged a switch out of real and into financial assets at a time of positive real interest rates. Nominal rates also fell substantially in the mid 1980s, making it more profitable for banks to carry securities on their books and increasing the liquidity of the markets, making it easier to sell securities when desired. A change in the world economic climate could conceivably reverse the trend towards securitisation, especially if it caused a substantial fall in securities prices. Innovations are not likely to be abandoned, however, and exchange and interest rate risks will remain in the absence of a substantial reform of the international monetary system. Even inflation can be fairly easily dealt with by the index linking of securities, as the UK Government showed in the early 1980s.[20] Many analysts and practitioners see securitisation as a natural evolution of the banking system, rather than a response to economic conditions peculiar to the 1980s. The globalisation of financial markets also seems to be a natural compliment to the growing interdependence of world economies. This trend is, therefore, unlikely to be reversed.

Amongst all this change, London has become a major attraction to foreign banks. It is the major centre of the Euromarkets and its monetary authorities have been keen to promote London as a major financial centre in the emerging global markets. The City has made a substantial contribution to the UK economy through its invisible earnings in the past and the government clearly wants this to continue. The Bank of England had, until the mid 1980s when new supervisory arrangements were introduced,[21] adopted the role of overseeing not only the banks but also the wider financial system. In this role it became concerned about the relative decline of the Stock Exchange, over which it had no formal supervisory authority, since the removal of UK exchange controls in 1979. The erosion of exchange controls worldwide had encouraged the development of global trading in the equities of major multinationals. The UK brokers were not sufficiently well capitalised to make large block deals in these equities but the participants in the Eurobond market, the major international banks and securities houses, were. Apart from losing international equities business to the Eurobond traders it became likely that the Stock Exchange would lose out to securities exchanges abroad. The emerging global equities market seemed likely to revolve around Tokyo, New York and a European exchange; so that the three exchanges, positioned in key time zones, could provide for twenty-four hour trading in international equities akin to the twenty-four hour trading that had developed in the foreign exchange markets. London was a key centre in the latter and the Bank wanted it to have a similar position in the former. When the Office of Fair Trading (OFT) threatened to take the Stock Exchange to court over its restrictive practices and a deal was struck between the Secretary of State for Trade and Industry and the Chairman of the Stock Exchange in 1983, the Bank saw its opportunity. The deal involved dropping the OFT case in return for the Stock Exchange's agreement to abandon fixed commissions, charged by brokers, in favour of negotiated commissions. The change, scheduled for the 27 October 1986, became known as the 'big bang'. In order to achieve its objectives, of reforming the Stock Exchange and creating large well-capitalised UK investment banks capable of competing in the emerging global securities markets, the Bank encouraged UK banks to form alliances with stock exchange member firms. It also took the opportunity to reform the gilt-edged market in parallel with the Stock Exchange equity market, modelling it on the US Treasury Bonds market. It was opportunities in the gilts market in particular that attracted an influx of US and other foreign banks and securities houses to London in the 1980s. Many foreign banks, especially those from the US, also bought participation in Stock Exchange member firms to build up their investment banking capabilities.

The 'big bang' involved more than the replacement of fixed commissions with negotiable commissions. The members of the Stock Exchange also decided to do away with the traditional dual-capacity system, under which jobber and brokers had well defined and separate tasks, in favour of single capacity and to computerise the dealing and information systems. Meanwhile the major UK commercial banks built up investment banking divisions and some of the merchant banks also converted themselves into investment banks. Finally, just prior to the 'big bang', the Stock Exchange members joined forces with the major Eurobond market participants and formed a joint self regulatory organisation for securities business called The Securities Association. International equity trading was thereby brought back within the Stock Exchange but the Eurobond market was kept separate. The 'big bang' consequently achieved a reform of the Stock Exchange akin to the changes that had been introduced to the New York Stock Exchange on May Day 1975, and also achieved an effect equivalent to the abolition of the US Glass-Steagall Act and similar Japanese legislation discussed in chapter 2. The US and Japanese legislation prevents commercial banks from participating in certain securities business, particularly the underwriting of corporate securities, in those countries. UK legislation has not enforced the division between commercial banking and securities business but the restrictive practices operated by the Stock Exchange provided an effective barrier to banks.

The 'big bang', therefore, rendered London one of the most liberal financial centres in the world and added to its appeal to foreign banks. French, German and Swiss banks act as universal banks in their domestic markets. The equity markets in their country of origin are relatively underdeveloped, however, and they have been attracted by the new opportunities in London. Their governments and those of other European countries, especially Holland, have responded to the deregulation of the Stock Exchange by engaging in a competitive liberalisation of their own securities markets. They are clearly unwilling to see London emerge as the dominant financial centre in Europe.

The attraction of London to the Japanese and US banks is the opportunity to engage in securities business from which they are prohibited at home. Apart from the opportunity of making profits, they probably hope to build up a good track record in the securities markets to enable them to persuade their domestic authorities to relax the restrictive legislation at home. The Japanese and US securities houses have also been attracted by new opportunities. The US investment banks seem to be particularly interested in the gilts-market but the Japanese securities houses were, surprisingly, not amongst the first group of institutions that applied to the Bank for authorisation to join the market. They perhaps felt that they would be rebuffed because of the dearth of reciprocal opportunities open to UK institutions at the time. Alternatively, they may feel, as most analysts do, that the market is insufficiently large to support the current number of authorised applicants. They are perhaps waiting for the post 'big bang' dust to settle before applying for authorisation. The liberal London environment also provided an opportunity for securities houses from the US and Japan to enter into banking business, from which they are barred at home. Whilst some of the US investment banks have taken advantage of this opportunity, Nomura Securities[22] became the first Japanese securities house to be granted a banking licence by the Bank in 1986. The other major Japanese securities houses are likely to be granted licences providing the Japanese authorities continue to open up access to the financial markets to UK institutions. Until restrictive legislation is removed in New York and Tokyo, London seems likely to remain the centre of the emerging global markets in which banks and securities houses compete most freely. The other European financial centres have some catching up to do. Competition for business will be intense. It is generally expected that there will be some casualties and it is unclear as yet whether the new self regulatory arrangements,[23] designed to protect investors, will cope in the presence of major international companies. US institutions in particular have shown themselves willing to fight expensive legal battles at home. The emergence of so many financial conglomerates will create a number of conflicts of interest and numerous opportunities for insider dealing, which is illegal in the UK under the 1985 Company Securities (Insider Dealing) Act. Rigorous policing will be needed to prevent abuses.

With the major players assembled, the game commenced following the 'big bang'. The overseas banks are likely to compete actively in the corporate financial services market as well as the securities markets. They are not expected to take much interest in the retail market because the major UK banks are already entrenched and competition, already intense, is set to increase following liberalising building society legislation in 1986. Some have, however, participated in the explosion of home loan finance that has occurred in the UK in the 1980s. Only Citicorp has made a serious attempt to break into the retail banking market but it is believed to be reconsidering this strategy. The merchant banks have already discovered that the US investment banks are interested in business related to merger activity. Despite their expertise they lack the capital backing that the new investment banking subsidiaries of the major UK clearing banks and their foreign competitors have. Instead of arranging mergers in the future they could become the subject of hostile bids themselves, although the Bank is trying to avoid this possibility by promoting an amendment to the Banking Bill which was passing through parliament in 1987. Only time will tell whether the major UK clearing banks will find their equities and gilt-edged businesses profitable. It will depends on how well their hastily assembled investment banking teams can fare against more experienced rivals.

The major clearers may eventually decide to concentrate on the retail, rather than the dealing, side of the business; distributing stocks and shares through their branches as part of a strategy of establishing financial supermarkets capable of offering a full array of financial services to their household customers. The domestic retail market has itself become more competitive in the 1980s. It has also been highly profitable because of the large spread between lending and borrowing rates. The 'big four' clearing banks[24] controlled about 40% of domestic banking deposits and 50% of domestic banking lending in 1985 and have numerous other interests, including credit card businesses. The other nine clearing banks are smaller in terms of balance sheet size and number of operating branches. Competition in this sector was heightened by the privatisation of TSB in 1986. With its substantial injection of capital and a branch network of a similar size to Barclays Bank it is now appropriate to talk about the 'big five'. The high margins and other lucrative domestic business allowed the banks to return to high profits in the mid 1980s, following a couple of lean years in which they had been required to raise their capital ratios and increase their provisions.

Their most formidable competitors in the retail banking sector have been the building societies. Whilst the major banks were concentrating on building up their international business in the 1970s the building societies raised their share of Great Britain's personal sector liquid assets dramatically, from 38% in 1974 to 51.4% in 1985, largely at the expense of banks. When the banks renewed their interest in the domestic markets in the 1980s they tried to reverse the trend. They also launched an offensive into the home loans market, the traditional preserve of the building societies. By 1983, 16% of their loans outstanding were home loans, compared to 6% in 1974. Building societies, however, remained market leaders with a 76% share. A tax reform in 1985, putting banks and societies on a more equal footing, allowed banks to start to increase their share of retail deposits, at the expense of societies. The extent of the banks' change of emphasis is illustrated by the fact that in 1984 personal loans accounted for 35.1% of total domestic loans, compared to 20.4% in 1980. Retail lending had grown 229% whilst total UK loans had grown 91%. The building societies were allowed to enter the personal loan market in 1987 and as a result margins may well be squeezed as competition for loans forces down loan rates whilst competition for savings continues to raise deposit rates. A lengthy consumer boom, following the recession of the early 1980s, has created favourable market conditions so far. With growth continuing, the boom looks set to run for some time yet but in 1986 the governor of the Bank of England and the chairman of Barclays Bank saw fit to warn institutions about the risk of overindulging in the binge. Consumer indebtedness was rising and there was evidence that a growing number of households were unable to service their debts. Banks were warned not to allow the quality of their assets to deteriorate. A crisis seems unlikely in the absence of a house price collapse. This would reduce the value of the collateral on which many of the loans are implicitly or explicitly based and some analysts are not ruling out this possibility in the next recession. It also seems unlikely that the demand for personal and home loans will continue to grow indefinitely at the rate witnessed in the mid 1980s. When the growth declines or stops, pressure on margins will begin to tell. Many analysts expect a merger wave to result as weaker building societies seek mergers with their stronger brethren . Additionally, the 1986 building society legislation permits mergers between banks and building societies before the end of the decade. Some of the larger societies may eventually convert themselves into public companies to give themselves greater freedom to compete with banks over a broader spectrum of business than allowed under the more permissive 1986 building society legislation.

Competition for corporate business is also set to increase. The UK banks traditionally lent working capital whilst the merchant banks provided a whole array of other services. With the corporate sector increasingly funding itself through the securities markets the major clearing banks have sought to win placement business through their merchant banking subsidiaries in order to maintain contact with corporate clients and cross-sell other services. Not only do the merchant banks face greater competition from the subsidiaries of the major UK clearing banks but they have also experienced heightened competition in the venture capital field from a number of specialist institutions that have emerged in the 1980s. The smaller clearing banks and the TSB also intend to build up their corporate business and the foreign-owned investment banks are also seeking a slice of the merchant banking business. Whilst some of the larger merchant banks have transformed themselves into investment banks, the smaller ones seem more likely to prosper by specialising in selected merchant banking activities and converting themselves into financial boutiques.

The longer run outlook for the UK banking sector is hard to gauge until the post 'big bang' shake up in the capital, and especially the gilts, market is over. Mergers are expected, as mentioned above, between the weaker merchant banks and building societies and stronger institutions. The trend toward financial conglomerates probably has some way to go but it may well be that, in the longer run, financial firms will start to divest subsidiaries because they find conglomerates unwieldy, in the way that major corporate sector firms have done. If the new self regulatory system does not provide adequate investor protection, a stronger supervisory agency, with substantial statutory powers, may be needed. The opposition parties have promised stricter supervision of firms involved in investment business. The Conservative government[25] became concerned about 'short-termism' in 1986. This is the tendency of institutional investors, such as pension and insurance fund managers, to take a short term view. Too much of their investment is aimed at making short term capital gains and too little is made with a view to promoting the long term prospects of industrial and commercial companies. The Labour Party has been concerned about 'short-termism' for a long time, although it has primarily criticised banks for not advancing long term loans to industry. It feels that the UK would benefit from the establishment of a state backed National Investment Bank (NIB) and perhaps a number of Regional Development Banks. The contributions of the French and Japanese state backed industrial investment banks, to their countries' economic development, are held up as examples of the benefits of having such state backed specialised institutions. The Labour Party has also proposed a merger between the National Girobank and the National Savings Bank, and perhaps also the TSBs, in the past. The aim was to create a People's Bank to increase competition in the retail banking sector. This no longer seems necessary in the light of the heightened competition provided by the privatisation of the TSB and the legislation allowing building societies to diversify further into retail banking business. The UK banking system is relatively devoid of specialised institutions, with the purpose of servicing the needs of particular sectors of industry or agriculture. The only significant institution is Investors in Industry (3i), which was formed by merging two specialist institutions[26] that had been created following the Macmillan Committee Report[27] on the financial system. The report had identified a gap in the financial system, called the Macmillan Gap. This was the lack of short and medium term finance for small businesses. The specialised institutions were established to plug this gap. 3i has now effectively become a venture capital institution. It is owned by the 'big four' clearing banks and the Bank of England (referred to simply as the Bank in the remainder of this chapter). The Wilson Committee's Report on financial institutions[28] also identified a gap, the Wilson Gap, and it too concerned small business finance. It judged the creation of an NIB to be unnecessary, although there was a sizeable group of committee members dissenting from this view. Since the 1980 Wilson Report, the Conservative government, which gained power in 1979, has introduced a series of measures, many of them consistent with the proposals contained in the Report, to improve the flow of funds to small businesses, such as the Business Expansion Scheme and the Loan Guarantee Scheme.[29] The creation of the Unlisted Securities Market in 1980 and the Third Market in 1987 has also made it easier for small and medium sized businesses to raise capital. A National Economic Development Council[30] Committee also formulated proposals for NIB in 1985. The Conservative government[31] is unlikely to sanction such proposals but a Labour government may well establish an NIB if it regains power.[32]

1.2 The Banking System

The banking sector was traditionally taken to comprise: the central bank, the Bank, the commercial banks; the merchant banks; the overseas banks; the Trustee Savings Banks (TSBs); the National Girobank (NG); the National Savings Bank (NSB); and the Finance Houses. The banking system, however, also includes a number of secondary banks which have, since the 1979 Banking Act, become known as licensed deposit takers (LDTs) and the building societies, which are mutual savings institutions that have traditionally specialised in mortgage finance for house purchases but have increasingly become involved in retail banking by extending their involvement in the provision of money transmission services (MTSs).   Legislation in the mid 1980s, discussed further in the next section, has rendered the separation of the traditional banking sector from the wider banking system anachronistic. The TSBs of England, Scotland and Wales have been reorganised to form the TSB group which was privatised in September 1986 to form a large clearing bank, making it more appropriate to talk about the 'big five' clearing banks than the 'big four'; the National Westminster (NatWest), Barclays, Midlands and Lloyds banks. The Building Societies Act, passed in the summer of 1986, allowed the building societies to diversify further into retail banking and other financial business with effect from January 1987. They are, for example, permitted to extend loans to their customers for purposes other than house purchase or home improvement and as a consequence they can issue cheque guarantee cards for the first time, increasing their ability to provide a comprehensive MTS and enhancing the attractiveness of the interest bearing cheque accounts that many of them had begun to offer in the first half of the 1980s. They are not, however, permitted to make loans to the corporate sector in the way that their cousins in the US, the savings and loan associations and mutual savings banks, are now allowed to do. Forthcoming legislation on bank regulation will also remove the distinction between recognised banks and LDTs introduced by the 1979 Banking Act.

Various retail concerns have also begun to offer banking and other financial services to their customers through their stores. These are usually associated with the provision of charge and credit cards. The financial subsidiary of Marks and Spencer, Britain's biggest retailer, was granted a licence to take deposits in January 1987, for example. Burton's associate company, Wellbeck Finance, also holds a deposit taker's licence. Finally, the home loans market has attracted a number of new participants which raise funds on the wholesale money markets rather than the retail savings markets, as the building societies have traditionally done. The insurance companies have also become more active in the provision of home loans finance, often bypassing the building societies through which they traditionally provided funds for endowment mortgages.[33]

The Bank is the banker of both the government and the banks. It also has supervisory responsibilities and acts as the government's agent for carrying out monetary policy. The latter roles will be discussed further in the next section. As bankers' bank it lies at the centre of the clearing system. The clearing banks hold accounts with it and these are adjusted at the end of each day's clearing once net positions have been calculated. It is also involved in day to day transactions between the government and the banks. These fluctuate considerably and as a result there can be sizeable net flows into or out of the banks. The Bank does not deal directly with the banks but operates in the money markets using discount houses as intermediaries. Through its open market operations in the short term securities, such as Treasury and commercial bills, which the banks hold as liquid reserves it can smooth out these flows and implement monetary policy. The rate of interest at which the Bank is willing to discount and sell bills, offered to it or brought from it by the discount houses, can influence money market rates generally.

The discount houses are all recognised banks under the 1979 Act and are members of the London Discount Market Association (LDMA). They are unique to the London money market and are viewed by many as being anachronistic. By taking secured call deposits, or 'money at call', they provide a remunerative outlet for banks' surplus funds. These funds are used to purchase a variety of short term assets the most important of which are : Treasury bills, commercial bills, and short dated gilt-edged securities. The discount houses have traditionally been the principal market-makers in bills and because of their role as a buffer between the banks and the Bank they have enjoyed a protected status. Their number has, however, dwindled and many have diversified into other securities business, exploiting their expertise as market-makers. The new monetary control arrangements introduced in August 1981[34] bolstered their position by requiring banks whose bills were recognised as 'eligible'[35] to maintain minimum and average ratios of their eligible liabilities[36] as money at call with members of the LDMA. This became known as the 'club money' requirement and it is to be terminated in 1987 and replaced with an alternative liquidity requirement on banks.[37] This led to speculation that the Bank might be considering the possibility of dealing directly with banks in the future.

Some of the members of the LDMA were taken over by banks during the merger wave involving commercial banks, merchant banks, stock brokers and stock jobbers that preceded the 'big bang' in October 1986.[38] The Bank has, however, required them to be operated, by their new parents, as separately capitalised subsidiaries and has sought assurances that they will not be absorbed into the investment banking departments of the emerging financial conglomerates. The Bank, in parallel with the reform of the equity market, has revised the gilt-edged market arrangements.[39] Under the new arrangements the discount houses are allowed to diversify into market making activities in the longer term gilt-edged securities whilst retaining sole right to market making in the securities in which they traditionally deal. The Bank has declared that this arrangement is temporary but for the time being their protected position remains. The discount houses cover the full weekly Treasury bill tender, which provides the major source of the government's short term funding, and they are active dealers in short dated government stocks and local authority stocks and bonds. They discount bills of exchange, thereby facilitating borrowing by the corporate sector to which they also offer various forms of short term investments for company treasuries. They also provide a secondary market for negotiable dollar and sterling certificates of deposit (CDs) which has contributed to the success of this investment instrument in the UK. In a similar manner, they hope to contribute to the success of the nascent sterling commercial paper instrument, which was permitted by the monetary authorities in 1986.[40] The discount houses' trading activities are regulated by the Bank which, in consultation with them, has established a complex system for gauging their capital requirements in relation to the risks associated with their various assets.

The terms commercial and clearing banks are now virtually synonymous in the UK. Clearing banks are commercial banks which, as a group, handle the bulk of the country's cheque and credit clearing. The payments system has recently been re-organised and will be discussed in more detail below. The major banks all now participate directly in one or more of the clearing systems. Because the clearing systems are privately owned, however, they were dominated by the London Clearing Banks which consisted of the aforementioned 'big four', Coutts and Co., which is owned by Natwest, and Williams and Glyn's, which became part of the Royal Bank of Scotland Group in 1985. The chairman of these six banks formed the Committee of London Clearing Bankers (CLCB). The Scottish Clearing Banks[41] and the Northern Ireland Banks were also included amongst the so called clearing banks. Since the re-organisation of the clearing systems the Committee of London and Scottish Bankers (CLSB)[42] has replaced the CLCB and other banks have become more actively involved in the clearing systems.

The 'big four' commercial banks have extensive nationwide branch networks. The TSB also has a nationwide network, although it is much better represented in Scotland, the North and the Midlands, than in the South. The Yorkshire Bank, which is owned by three of the 'big four'[43] has a network that is concentrated in its domestic and neighbouring counties. The Co-operative Bank has a relatively small but expanding branch network and operates mainly through the retail outlets of the co-operative movement nationwide. The major Scottish banks all have the bulk of their branches in their native country, as do the Northern Ireland banks. The NG, which is state owned, offers services through the nationwide network of post offices. The 'big four' have been reducing the size of their networks whilst expanding their Automated Teller Machine (ATM) networks. The TSB is seeking to expand its presence in the south of England whilst the Royal Bank of Scotland (RBS) and the Bank of Scotland are seeking ways of expanding their share of the market south of the border with England. The RBS is believed to be seeking a merger partner, possibly a building society, whilst the Bank of Scotland has been exploring home banking opportunities and offering services through building societies.

The 'big four' have diversified considerably since the early 1970s as traditional demarcations between the activities of clearing banks and other financial institutions have been progressively eroded. The TSB has also diversified rapidly in this period, converting itself first from a savings bank to a retail bank and then into a commercial bank by developing the range of services it offers to the corporate sector. It is expected to use its privatisation proceeds to extend its geographic coverage and to expand its corporate business. The latter remains a smaller proportion of its total business than is typical amongst the 'big four'. The Yorkshire and Co-operative banks and the NG also tend to be more highly oriented towards retail banking business than the 'big four'.

As a result of their diversification, which continued in the 1980s when they moved into the home loans market and developed investment banking capabilities in preparation for the 'big bang', the 'big four' have become 'universal banks'. They offer a wide range of financial services in both the domestic and international markets and are well represented in the major onshore and offshore financial centres. As a result of the UK's colonial past they also have overseas subsidiaries in foreign banking markets. Apart from providing MTSs, the clearing banks seek both retail and wholesale deposits of various maturities in various currencies and supply various types of finance. In the early 1980s they responded to growing competition for deposits from the building societies, merchant banks and other institutions, by introducing interest bearing current accounts,[44] and 'free banking'[45] and offering a wider variety of savings accounts. Their share of aggregate deposits had been eroded in the 1970s and early 1980s, with the building societies the major beneficiaries. When the 'big four' re-examined their strategies following the Mexican debt crisis in 1982 they clearly decided to pay more attention to developing their domestic business than they had in the 1970s; when there was a rapid internationalisation of banking as a result of the opportunities provided by the need to recycle the OPEC surpluses.[46]

On the lending side, again in response to growing competition, the major event in the first half of the 1980s has been the clearing banks' rapid build up of secured home loans, or mortgage, business. The 'big four' moved first but the retail oriented Yorkshire and TSB banks soon followed suit and in 1986 NG also announced that it would be offering mortgages. The 'big four' started on the road to becoming 'universal banks' in 1958, when they acquired stakes in leading finance companies. Since then they have entered numerous banking related services, usually through subsidiaries, including : merchant banking, factoring, leasing, company registrar services, computer payroll services, unit trusts, and credit cards. Most recently they have added securities dealing and broking capabilities to their merchant banking subsidiaries to form investment banking capabilities. Unlike the German universal banks, the major UK commercial banks do not hold major share stakes in industrial companies; although they are increasingly putting up capital for small and new companies through venture capital divisions and in response to various government schemes.[47] In the March 1986 Budget various financial institutions were permitted to offer Personal Equity Plans (PEPs)[48] and the major banks plan to open 'share shops' to provide a discount broking service to the public through their branches. The major banks also offer executor and trustee services, taxation advice and insurance broking services. Lloyds offers a full estate agency service and other banks and many building societies are also developing capabilities in this area. On the retail banking side the objective of the major banks is to develop 'financial supermarkets' at which their household customers can gain access to the whole array of financial services being marketed. Many areas into which they have diversified may not be particularly profitable but they give them the opportunity to cross-sell other products to interested customers. Involvement in home loans and perhaps estate agency is seen as a key to cross-selling various services in connection with the largest transactions that most households make. Although their international expansion has decelerated, the big banks make a significant proportion of their earnings overseas; where a presence is necessary to service the needs of their internationally oriented corporate customers and to take advantage of new opportunities in the increasingly globalised banking and capital markets, which themselves have been merging.

The merchant banks have their origins in merchant houses which traded in various areas of the world. They tended, therefore, to be located in the major ports. As they grew they found a remunerative source of business in accepting bills of exchange. In return for a fee they would add their name to bills issued by lesser known traders to finance their activities. The representative body of the 16 leading merchant banks, which are not subsidiaries of the major UK commercial banks,[49] became known as the Accepting Houses Committee. They now all have their head offices in the City of London but may have opened branches in provincial cities and overseas in recent years. The finance of international trade remains an important activity but other business is now more important than their traditional accepting business. They have diversified into corporate finance, investment management, foreign exchange, finance and corporate advisory services, including that relating to mergers and acquisitions and Euromarket business. Through subsidiaries many are also involved in leasing, hire purchase, factoring, insurance broking, shipping and property development and management. In preparation for the 'big bang' some of them transformed themselves into investment banks by merging with brokers and jobbing firms. In the 1980s some began to offer cash management accounts, which are current accounts with chequing facilities offering money market related interest rates, to large private depositors. This brought them into competition with the commercial banks which responded by introducing similar accounts. Their main source of funds, however, remains the wholesale money markets, in which they participate actively and have contributed to the success of negotiable CDs. They lend mainly to the corporate sector; concentrating on medium term loans, finance for exports backed by ECGD[50] guarantee; and eurocurrency loans. They play an important role in providing finance for small companies. They also function as issuing houses, sponsoring capital issues on behalf of their clients on the Stock Exchange, the Unlisted Securities Market[51] (USM) and the Third Market.[52]

Additionally they act as intermediaries between capital users and capital providers in the domestic and international capital markets. Apart from the members of the Acceptance Houses Committee and the subsidiaries of the major UK commercial banks, there are a number of merchant banks which are subsidiaries of US and other foreign banks.

London rivals New York as the financial centre in which the most overseas banks are established. The majority of the foreign banks have established branches or offices since the beginning of the 1960s but some have been present for over a century. Others have achieved representation through stakes in jointly owned consortium banks. The attraction, particularly in the 1970s, was the rapid growth in the Eurocurrency markets. In the 1980s their numbers increased further, due to the growth in the Eurobond markets and the opportunities, especially in the reorganised gilts market, offered by the 'big bang'. London is the the most important Euromarket centre. The number of consortium banks began to fall in the 1980s as a number of their participants established branches or representative offices instead, to heighten their profile in the City. US banks are the most prevalent, followed by Japanese, Italian, French, Swiss, West German and Spanish banks. Some of the banks also maintain branches in provincial cities where they normally perform special functions, such as catering for the North Sea Oil industry or for the ethnic groups. Only Citicorp, the largest US bank holding company, has attempted to break into the retail banking market through its Citibank Savings branches and by offering home loans. It has also taken over a discount house and broking and jobbing firms and become the first foreign bank to join one of the clearing systems. Citibank is, however, rethinking its strategies and seems likely to concentrate more on the wholesale and securities markets, rather than the retail banking market, in the future. American Express and Sears, through its UK retail subsidiaries, have, however, been actively marketing credit and charge cards respectively; an activity which brings them into competition with UK banks and retailers. The majority of overseas banks operating branches in the UK are recognised banks.

Banks opening representative offices do not require licences but must assure the Bank that they are not taking deposits in the UK. They are usually established to build up business contacts prior to the opening of branches. Overseas banks, especially the American, Japanese and Swiss ones, are prominent in the Euromarkets. Some of the overseas banks are operated by Japanese and US investment banks or securities houses. In 1986 Nomura[53] became the first Japanese Securities house to be granted a banking licence in the UK and licences are expected to be granted to the other large Japanese securities houses before the end of the 1980s.

The TSB movement originated in the nineteenth century. Savings deposited with TSBs were managed by unpaid trustees and invested in public sector debt. They spread rapidly throughout most of the UK and even reached the Channel Islands. Until their privatisation in September 1986, they were governed by a series of TSB Acts. The 1985 Act, provided for their reorganisation, into the TSB Group and the TSB Channel Islands (TSB(CI)), and their privatisation. During the 1960s they diversified away from being small personal savings banks towards retail banking. Cheque accounts were introduced in 1965 and the TSB Unit Trust, now one of the largest in the UK, was launched in 1968. The Central Trustee Savings Bank (CTSB) was incorporated in 1973 to act as banker to the TSBs and their subsidiaries. In 1975 it became a member of the London Bankers' Clearing House. Government control over the TSBs was relaxed in 1976 when restrictive statutory limitations on their activities were removed. They were permitted to lend to the public, for example. There then followed a period of rationalisation and by December 1983 there were only four TSBs : TSB England and Wales; TSB Scotland; TSB Northern Ireland; and TSB(CI). Diversification also continued with the TSB Trustcard Ltd being established in 1978, to provide credit card services and, along with the TSB Trust Company Ltd, to provide life assurance and unit trust services. United Dominions Trust Ltd, a finance house, was purchased in 1981. They were not recognised banks under the 1979 Banking Act, being subject to Treasury control instead. After the 1985 TSB Act the TSBs and their associated companies were reorganised to form the TSB Group PLC, a holding company. TSB(CI), which was separately floated on the stock exchange in 1986, after the September flotation of the TSB Group, is a separately capitalised, wholly owned, subsidiary. The TSB Group is now a recognised bank.

The National Giro was established in 1968, by the Post Office, to provide a simple money transmission service operated through the postal system. It was renamed the National Girobank (NG) in 1978 in an attempt to break into retail banking business. Its MTSs are mainly used by local authorities and government departments. It introduced a personal loans service in 1975 and began to offer mortgages for house purchasers in 1986. It also offers corporate loans but has not made a major impact in this field and the business sector does not make extensive use of its MTS. It joined the London Bankers' Clearing House in 1981 and became a fully operational member in 1983, when it began to offer chequing accounts. Like the TSBs, it was included in the monetary sector which was redefined in August 1981[54] and because of its public sector status it was excluded from the licensing provisions of the 1979 Banking Act.

The National Savings Bank (NSB) was established in 1861 as the Post Office Savings Bank (POSB). It collects deposits through ordinary and investment accounts offered through Post Offices. Withdrawals from the latter are subject to one month's notice and consequently pay higher interest than the former, from which small withdrawals can be made on demand. These accounts have, since composite rate tax[55] was extended to banks as well as building societies by the 1985 budget, been the only ones[56] paying interest gross. This should have made them particularly attractive to non-tax payers but there has not so far been a marked inflow of deposits as a result. The deposits they attract are lodged with the National Debt Commisssioners and invested in government securities. The NSB also offers various savings certificates and bonds, some of which are index-linked. In the early 1980s these were particularly successful and the NSB was given a heightened role in the funding of the Public Sector Borrowing Requirement.

The Finance House Association (FHA) was established in 1945 and has 43 members which control 80% of instalment credit business in the UK. The majority of them are owned by banks[57] or other financial institutions. Many of them became LDTs under the 1979 Banking Act and consequently they are included in the monetary sector and must conform to the monetary control arrangements introduced in 1981. The bulk of their funds are derived from their parent institutions, although they also raise funds from other banks and financial institutions and corporate treasuries. The majority of the funds are used to finance the purchase of cars and commercial vehicles. They also finance hire purchase agreements involving other consumer durables and their corporate sector business includes equipment leasing, factoring, insurance, industrial finance and property bonds. They have tended to diversify in the 1980s and the FHA became critical of the distinction drawn under the 1979 Act between LDTs and recognised banks; arguing that it had become outmoded and conferred an unwarranted higher status upon recognised banks. In the wake of the Johnson Matthey Bank (JMB) affair in 1985, the provisions of the 1979 Act were reviewed[58] and a uniform licensing system is to be introduced following new legislation expected in 1987.

The building societies were not included in the UK monetary sector and are not subject to the 1979 Banking Act. Because of their mutual status they were, until the provisions of the 1986 Building Societies Act became effective on 1 January 1987, supervised by the Chief Registrar of Friendly Societies. They are now supervised by the Building Societies Commission (BSC) instead[59] but remain outside monetary sector and are not to be subject to the forthcoming banking legislation. They are, however, major deposit taking institutions and they offer a wide range of financial services. They provide numerous savings schemes and MTSs, including cheque books. They compete strongly with the commercial banks and the NG and the NSB. In 1984 the 190 building societies held 50% of personal sector liquid assets, whilst the monetary sector's share was 34% and that of the Department of National Savings was 16%. Since then the banks have managed to increase their share at the expense of the building societies which have turned increasingly to the wholesale markets, including the Eurobond market, for funds. The top five societies account for 55% of the total assets of the movement and a series of mergers is expected following the 1986 legislation which empowered them to diversify further into retail banking and related financial business. Prior to the Act they specialised in home loans; a low risk business by virtue of the fact that their long term loans were secured against property which is normally an appreciating asset. They have traditionally held a high proportion of liquid assets and until 1984 they operated an interest rate cartel through the Building Societies Association (BSA). This broke up following Abbey National's[60] decision to withdraw from the arrangement. Since then they have competed more actively on savings and lending rates.

Competition has been heightened as banks have attempted to increase their share of deposits in the mid 1980s and have moved into the home loans business in the first half of the 1980s. A number of foreign banks, insurance companies and specialist, wholesale funded, loan institutions have also either entered or stepped up their activity in the market. With mortgage demand rampant and savings inflows declining, in 1986 the societies ran down their liquidity to the minimum levels accepted by Registrar. New capital and liquidity requirements were proposed by the BSC toward the end of 1986. The capital requirement proposals were based on the risk asset ratio approach adopted by the Bank, and applied to banks, and were regarded by the BSA to be very restrictive. The BSA complained that they would inhibit their ability to diversify under the new regime introduced by the 1986 Act. Revised requirements were expected to be published in 1987. Under the Act they are empowered to diversify into retail banking and related financial services and to raise a larger proportion of funds on the wholesale markets. The extent of their diversification is limited although the BSC is empowered to relax some of the restrictions. They are to be allowed to make personal loans not associated with house purchase and improvement and issue cheque guarantee cards, extending their ability to compete in the provision of MTSs. The restrictions, however, ensure that their main activity will still be to extend home loans. They are protected from hostile takeover bids, from banks especially, for a period and they require the consent of a substantial majority of their shareholders, who are also their depositors, prior to going public. Some have expressed a desire to go public in the future. Those that choose to do so will come under the supervisory wing of the Bank.

The larger societies are expected to exploit their new freedom to diversify most fully and a series of mergers is expected; because the smaller societies will find it advantageous to merge with the larger ones, which will be seeking to extend their geographic coverage and asset base. Overlapping branch networks would then be rationalised. With deposits harder to come by, interest rates deregulated,[61] and only the larger ones having access to the UK wholesale markets and the Euromarkets, the smaller societies are expected to feel the pinch at an early stage. The larger societies, if they go public, are likely to become more like commercial banks. Some of the smaller societies may eventually be absorbed into the TSB and the Scottish banks, which are seeking to make the coverage of their UK branch networks more comprehensive. The Hong Kong and Shanghai Banking Corporation[62] has also been seeking ways of expanding into the European markets and had its proposed merger with the Royal Bank of Scotland turned down[63] in 1982. The larger societies have already increased the proportion of funds they derive from the wholesale market by issuing floating rate notes on the Eurobond market. Until the 1985 budget they had been precluded from doing so because they were required to pay interest net, rather than gross, on all funds raised. This was not the practice in the Euromarkets. They are still subject to a composite rate tax (CRT) on retail deposits and continue to pay net interest. The banks had long complained that this put them at a competitive advantage and they had campaigned for the removal of CRT. Instead the banks were also subject to a CRT following the provisions of the 1986 budget. This created a more level playing field as did an earlier decision to subject the capital gains derived by building societies from their gilts portfolio dealings to capital gains tax in line with the treatment of banks.

The general picture of the domestic banking and financial system is, therefore, one of increasing diversification by various institutions into wider financial services and growing competition in the retail banking, home loans, corporate lending and securities markets. The process of securitisation is blurring the distinction between the money and banking markets and the capital markets. The banks have been forced to get involved in domestic and Euro-securities markets in order to service the increasingly sophisticated needs of their major corporate clients. Growth of the nascent UK commercial paper markets[64] on anything like the scale of the US market will reinforce this process.

The sterling money markets consist of the discount market and the parallel money markets, which have developed since the late 1950s as a result of growing demand for short term funds by banks, local authorities, and other financial intermediaries, especially finance houses. The banks' needs have grown as they have engaged more extensively in liability management; the practice of seeking out profitable loan and other investment opportunities and then arranging funding. This has increased their demand for short term wholesale funding. Previously they had tended to collect retail deposits and then seek profitable uses for them.

The discount market revolves around the LDMA, a number of money broking firms and the money trading departments of a number of banks. It is the market through which the government meets its short term financing needs by issuing Treasury bills. It is also a market for other bills, which are issued to raise short term funds. It allows the banks to regulate their liquidity by placing surplus funds as 'money at call' with the discount houses. When operational deposits at the Bank get too low these funds can be drawn at short notice. The market is also used by the Bank to smooth out fluctuations in transactions between banks and the government and to exert an influence on interest rates in connection with its monetary policy goals. Its liquidity function has been increasingly shared by parallel markets, especially the inter bank and certificate of deposit (CD) markets.

The role of the parallel markets is to allow financial institutions, corporations and local authorities to raise or place short term deposits to maintain desired levels of liquidity. These markets compete for deposits, which are liquid and interest bearing, with the discount market. Partly because of the heightened competition, the latter's position was protected by the 'club money' requirement introduced in August 1981 under the new monetary control arrangements. Sterling CDs were first issued by banks in October 1968, to attract funds from commercial and industrial depositors which might otherwise have been deposited outside the UK banking system. They are now principally used as a means of interbank financing. CDs are issued in multiples of £10,000, with a minimum value of £50,000. Their term to maturity varies from 3 months to 5 years and they are issued at face value on an interest bearing basis. Their attraction is that they can be sold prior to maturity in the secondary market, in which the discount houses are the main dealers. Their introduction, therefore, marked an early step on the road to securitisation, which caught on rapidly following the 1982 Mexican debt crisis. CDs may be issued by banks or building societies as an alternative to borrowing on the interbank market. They may be purchased by banks, in preference to making interbank loans; discount houses, as traders; and by non bank, especially corporate, investors. The majority of them are held by banks and discount houses.

The interbank market facilitates the taking and placing of sterling deposits between banks in London. Lending is unsecured and transactions are arranged, through money brokers, by telephone. The market is predominantly short term and the amounts involved can be very large. Most of the banking sector participates in this wholesale market and so too do non-banks such as pension funds, insurance companies and finance houses and large corporations. Other sterling money markets include the local authority market and the inter-company market. The latter could grow rapidly following the introduction of commercial paper in 1986.

The Eurocurrency market, of which London is the most important centre, is effectively an international multi-currency interbank market. A Eurocurrency is one that is held on deposit with a bank outside the country which issues the currency. The market originated in Europe, and especially London, which attracted substantial dollar deposits. Although the Eurodollar market is still by far the largest, there are now substantial markets in other major currencies, such as the yen, the Deutschemark and sterling. The markets are no longer restricted to Europe either. They revolve around a number of offshore centres; such as Singapore and Hong Kong in the Far East and Bahrain in the Middle East and have become the largest international financial markets.

London's attraction as a financial centre owes a lot to its hosting the Euromarkets which have been left largely free from tax liabilities and, until 1987, unregulated. London is, therefore, an offshore banking centre[65] and depositors and borrowers are attracted by interest rates which are more competitive than those available in corresponding domestic markets. The main suppliers of funds are: commercial corporations; official institutions, such as central banks, governments, and international agencies; and commercial banks. Much of the business involves banks on-lending primary deposits to other banks. The ultimate borrowers are predominantly large multinational corporations, governments or government agencies, and international monetary organisations such as the World Bank.

The Eurocurrency markets played an important role in the recycling of the surpluses accruing to the OPEC countries following the 1973 oil price rise. As a result a number of major international banks developed large exposures to developing countries. These 'country risks' were initially judged to be small because, unlike companies, governments could not go into liquidation. The lending, often involving large sums, was syndicated by lead banks and numerous banks participated. The recycling was not only to oil importing countries but also to countries such as Mexico and Venezuela which, as major oil producers, appeared to be particularly safe borrowers. Following the 1982 Mexican debt crisis country risks had to be re-assessed and as a result the syndicated loan market has ceased to grow rapidly. The major borrowers in this market became industrial countries such as France and Sweden. Attention began to switch from the Eurocurrency to the Eurobond markets, also centred in London, as banks attempted to securitise their loans by making them tradeable. It had become a widespread practice to advance variable rate loans through the syndicated loan markets.

After the Mexican crisis the floating rate note (FRN) market grew rapidly, largely at the expense of the securitised loan markets. FRNs combine some of the attributes of variable rate loans with those of traditional bond finance. Banks buying FRNs, which are normally underwritten by syndicates of banks formed by a lead manager, can trade them on the secondary markets. They are not forced to carry them on their balance sheets as they were when they participated in syndicated loans. FRNs also attracted investment funds from other sources, predominantly the major participants in the Eurocurrency markets which also raised finance by issuing FRNs. The market became even more active in the mid 1980s when banks, under pressure from supervisory authorities, began to build up their capital bases. Some authorities counted perpetual FRNs as capital and banks, therefore, took the opportunity of issuing them to raise capital more cheaply than they could on the equity markets. The Bank did not count debt acquired through the issue of FRNs as capital until 1985 when Lloyds Bank issued perpetual FRNs which were convertible into preference shares. Since then the major clearing banks have all raised capital by issuing convertible perpetual FRNs. A similar ruling by the US Authorities toward the end of 1986 opened the way for US banks to raise capital in this way. Unfortunately at the end of 1986 the market suffered a setback as demand for perpetual FRNs relative to their supply declined. The future of the market remained uncertain in early 1987. One reason for this was probably the rapid growth of the Euro commercial paper market. It seemed probable that the latter would continue to grow, satisfying the needs of the corporate sector for raising and placing short term funds, whilst the traditional Eurobond market would re-assert itself.

The Eurobond market, like the Eurocurrency market, was unregulated and enjoyed certain tax advantages. It is now, however, subject to the regulatory provisions of the 1986 Financial Services Act. The market had grown to be London's premier securities market by the early 1980s and its participants, the major international banks and securities houses, had begun to trade in the equities of major international companies, by-passing the Stock Exchange. The major borrowers are the same as those involved in the Eurocurrency market. The realisation that trade in major international equities could be lost spurred the Stock Exchange Council (SEC) to sponsor reforms going well beyond the removal of the restrictive practice[66] operated by stockbrokers, of charging fixed commissions. The SEC allowed UK banks and foreign institutions to acquire limited stakes and then full participations in broking and jobbing firms, in order to increase their capitalisation and allow them to compete with the major international banks and securities houses. In the end even this was not enough and the SEC had to merge with the International Securities Regulatory Organisation (Isro)[67] to bring all international equity trading within the Stock Exchange. The Eurobond market is to remain separate and seemed likely become a Recognised Investment Exchange (RIE),[68] overseen by the Association of International Brokers and Dealers, under the new regulatory arrangements for the securities industry introduced in the 1986 Financial Services Act.

The gilt-edged securities market is to remain within the Stock Exchange and so too is the domestic corporate bond market. The latter, however, has lain virtually dormant for a number of years despite the efforts of the Treasury and the Bank to encourage its revitalisation. This may be because major UK corporations have ready access to the Eurobond markets and have found an ample demand for bank backed commercial bills. One reason for this is that the Bank pursued monetary control through a method known as 'overfunding' following the introduction of the new monetary control arrangements in 1981. The Bank adopted the practise of selling more bonds than required to fund the PSBR, replacing the previous practice of over issuing Treasury bills but having the same effect of soaking up bank liquidity. Liquidity shortages were then relieved by buying bills. With Treasury bills in relatively short supply, commercial bills were purchased leaving the Bank sitting on what became known as the 'bill mountain'. 'Overfunding' was abandoned following an announcement by the Chancellor of the Exchequer at the annual Mansion House Speech in October 1986. It had produced a situation in which the Bank was effectively lending to the corporate sector which was believed to be issuing more bills than strictly required to meet working capital needs. It was, therefore, distorting financial flows whilst only having cosmetic effects on money supply growth. Its major impact was to inhibit the growth of sterling M3. Since then this monetary aggregate has been dropped as a monetary target and reverted to the status of an indicator of monetary conditions. The reduction of the 'bill mountain' is expected to make way for growth in the commercial paper market, rather than to contribute to the revitalisation of the UK corporate bond market, however.

The Stock Exchange (SE) has also introduced two new markets to enable smaller companies to raise capital without having to comply with the requirements of a full Stock Exchange (SE) listing. The Unlisted Securities Market (USM) was opened in 1980 to allow medium sized businesses to raise capital and grow to the point where they could graduate to a full SE listing. It has proved successful and, contrary to expectations, suffered no set back immediately after the October 1986 'big bang'. On the contrary, it emerged as a more liquid market. In January 1987 the Third Market was opened to provide a forum for trading shares in small companies. These companies may eventually move onto the USM if they prove successful. It is expected to attract issues under the aegis of the Business Expansion Scheme (BES).[69] The SEC hopes that it will also attract companies which have so far raised capital through the 'over the counter' (OTC) market, which has developed out-side the SE. Trade in this market is primarily concluded via telephone links. The SE is, therefore, attempting to bring all equities trading under one roof.

The SE also offers various stock options and is forging international links with other exchanges dealing in futures and options, such as the Philidelphia Stock Exchange. The London International Financial Futures Exchange (Liffe) also trades in futures and options contracts and is forging international links. It is to become an Recognised Investment Exchange (RIE) under the new investor protection legislation and has entered into discussions with the SE. A merger between the exchanges is not expected but some agreement to specialise in certain types of contracts could be reached. London is also a major commodities and metals trading centre. The London Commodities Exchange (LCE) is relatively well organised but the trading practices of the London Metal Exchange (LME) have been called into question and are likely to be reformed so that it can qualify as an RIE. London is a particularly important centre for precious metals, especially gold, trading.

The non-cash payments systems in the UK revolves around the clearing banks. Cash payments predominate but cheques, credit and charge cards, standing orders and direct credits and debits are widely used. There was a distinction between the CLCB, which has been replaced by the CLSB, and the members of the London Bankers' Clearing House (BCH), which was responsible for operating the clearing system in England and Wales. Its operational members were the six London Clearing Banks (LCBs), the Bank, the Co-operative Bank, and the CTSB, which both joined in December 1975, and the NG, which joined in February 1983. The LCBs were required to drop their interest setting agreement in 1971, following the introduction of 'Competition and Credit Control' (CCC). CCC introduced new monetary control arrangements which were replaced by alternative arrangements in August 1981. They had, however, been accused of retaining a cartel-like arrangement concerning the provision of MTS by virtue of their ownership of the clearing systems. This arrangement was subject to a number of investigations[70] and generally found not to be against the public interest. Some criticisms were, however, voiced and the National Consumer Council (NCC) Report[71] suggested some reforms. Subsequent to the NCC report Standard Chartered, a UK based international bank, and Citibank applied to join the BCH. The BCH asked these banks to give it time to review the organisation, membership and control of the clearing systems and requested other banks to defer applications until after the review. A committee was established under the Chairmanship of Mr D M Child of NatWest Bank and the Child Report[72] was published in December 1984. The proposed new arrangements will be discussed after a brief review of the clearing systems.

Two cheque clearings take place each business day. Town Clearing allows cheques of high denominations to be cleared on the same day. General clearing involves cheques of lower denominations and takes up to three days. Non-clearing banks and building societies have agency arrangements with BCH members and inter-branch clearings are dealt with separately by each bank. There is also a credit clearing operation. A growing proportion of clearing is done through the Bankers Automated Clearing System (BACS). Prior to the new arrangements, the shareholders in BACS were the 'big four' clearing banks and Williams and Glyn's. At the centre of the paper and automated clearings is the Bank which holds the settlement accounts of the clearing banks. As with paper clearings, non clearing banks and other financial institutions had agency arrangements with BACS, through which customers of banks and nonbanks are able to initiate computerised payments by presenting magnetic tapes. The number of nonbank users had increased rapidly since the early 1970s. The Clearing House Automated Payments System (CHAPS) was introduced in 1984 to enable participating banks to provide guaranteed same day payments nationwide. It is a nationwide inter-bank system which augments the existing clearing systems.

The Child Report proposed to open up the clearing system and attempted to meet previous criticisms. A supervisory body or 'umbrella organisation', the Association for Payment Clearing Services (APCS), was established to oversee the development of the payments system as a whole. Additionally, three operating companies were established which will own and operate the clearing systems. These will be responsible for: high volume paper clearings, i.e. the general cheque and credit clearing business; high value clearings, i.e. Town Clearing and CHAPS; and electronic high volume clearings. Membership of the various companies will be opened to banks and other financial institutions willing to pay an entry fee, designed to compensate the original owners for their costs of setting up the systems, and able to meet certain volume and other requirements. Members, those using the systems on an agency basis, and the Bank, which will also be a member of each of the companies, will all be represented in the APCS. The principal of separate clearings is designed to allow financial institutions to participate only in those clearing operations that suit their own business needs. It is too early to tell whether the new arrangements will prove satisfactory given the building societies' intention to build up their involvement in the provision of MTSs.

The Child Report also discussed plans to establish a fourth company to cover electronic funds transfer at point of sale (EFTPOS). The major banks have experimented with a number of EFTPOS systems but have found it difficult to agree on mutually acceptable arrangements for a nationwide system, either amongst themselves or with the major retail concerns with which they were negotiating. In January 1986 plans to develop a nationwide system were announced and a working party was established. Its proposals for a system involving unified terminals were not accepted by the major banks, which announced towards the end of 1986, that they would proceed to develop a system in which banks would supply customised terminals which could link into a common infrastructure. The major banks have also developed extensive ATM networks and some have formed agreements with other banks to allow reciprocal usage.[73] Meanwhile the building societies have been developing ATM networks. Halifax, the largest, has developed its own network. Others are participating in shared networks such as Matrix and LINK. The latter also includes the Co-operative bank, the NG, Citibank and American Express amongst its participants. The machines to be installed are advanced and capable of linking into an EFTPOS system. One building society[74] has launched its own EFTPOS experiment in Northampton whilst another[75] has been participating in home banking with the Bank of Scotland. Meanwhile major retail chains and stores, including petrol companies, are developing their own electronic payments systems.

The proposal to create a fourth company to cover EFTPOS was designed to allow the major clearing banks to charge entry fees to recover the cost of developing their system to its current stage. Unless membership is thrown open to other financial institutions at an early stage, and entry fees are kept low, there is a risk that competing networks might be established. This would be inefficient, because of the economies of scale involved in the development of electronically based payments systems, and it would lead to a further proliferation of plastic cards. After a series of fits and starts it seems that one or more nationwide EFTPOS systems could be developed by the early 1990s. The pace of introduction depends not only on the extent to which retailers are willing to share the costs but also on the consumers' willingness to use the system. There are a number of legal issues concerning the consumers position in electronic transactions to be tidied up. The National Consumer Council has drawn attention to some of these[76] and in January 1987 a committee was established[77] to consider their implications. Militating against rapid introduction of EFTPOS is the fact that most banks now offer MTS free to customers with non-negative current account balances. It will, therefore, be difficult for banks to persuade consumers of the benefits of an electronic payments system when they are providing paper based services free. The banks and retailers will, therefore, have to shoulder not only the set up costs but also the running costs unless a more rational charging system, which clearly reflects the lower long run costs to the banks of moving from electronic to paper based transfers, for MTSs is introduced. Nationwide EFTPOS would, therefore, be achieved sooner if banks moved to full charging for MTSs and offered interest on positive balances held in current accounts; replacing the current system of paying implicit interest by not recovering the costs of providing MTS.[78] To prevent a wasteful proliferation of EFTPOS systems it might be appropriate for the Bank, given its responsibility for overseeing the functioning of, though not regulating, the payments system, to ensure that an efficient nationwide EFTPOS system, to which both banks and building societies have equal access, is developed. Monetary authorities in other countries, such as France and Singapore, have taken such an initiative; facilitating rapid introduction of EFTPOS systems.

1.3 Regulation and Supervision

Prior to the 1979 Banking Act deposit taking institutions were regulated and supervised under a variety of statutes by a number of different official bodies. The Treasury was responsible for the TSBs, the NG, and the NSB; the Registrar of Friendly Societies supervised the building societies; the Bank of England supervised the banking sector, and the Department of Trade and Industry was responsible, under the Companies Act, for the activities of various secondary or near banks which were not recognised by the Bank to be part of the banking sector. Separate legislation covered the NSB, the NG, the TSBs, the building societies and banks. The secondary banking crisis,[79] which originated in 1973, forced the Bank, in conjunction with the major clearing banks, to launch a rescue operation. It subsequently became clear that the DTI was ill-equipped to supervise the secondary banks. As a result of this realisation and in order to comply with the 1977 EC Banking Directive[80] legislation was passed in 1979.

The main provisions of the 1979 Banking Act were: to introduce a new authorisation procedure, covering both banks and secondary banks; to regulate the use of banking names and descriptions; to introduce a registration scheme for representative offices established by overseas banks; and to introduce a deposit protection scheme.

The Act also gave statutory force to the Bank of England's regulatory and supervisory responsibilities and its ultimate purpose was to protect depositors against losses. It prohibited the acceptance of deposits by institutions other than recognised banks, licensed deposit takers (LDTs), and specified institutions, such as TSBs, the NSB, the NG and the building societies, already subject to separate statutory regulation. Recognised status is granted by the Bank to institutions which, in its view, provide a wide range of banking services or a highly specialised banking service and which enjoyed a high reputation and standing in the financial community, such as clearing and merchant banks. Other deposit taking institutions, including the finance houses and secondary banks, were required to apply for licences which were granted by the Bank subject to satisfactory fulfilment of prudential and financial criteria laid down by the Bank. The Bank has stressed that licensed status should not be regarded as reflecting adversely on reputation and standing. The Bank is empowered to withdraw recognition or licences and amend the authorisation criteria subject to the approval of the Chancellor of the Exchequer. By the end of February 1985 there were 285 recognised banks and 320 LDTs. These institutions are not exempt from other legislation relating to particular banking activities; the most important of which are contained in the 1958 Prevention of Fraud (Investments) Act, which covers dealings in securities, the 1974 Consumer Credit Act, which controls the provision of consumer credit and related activities, and various Companies Acts. In addition, by virtue of their diversification, they are also subject to the provisions of the 1986 Financial Services Act and the 1985 Company Securities (Insider Dealing) Act which outlaws insider dealing.

The 1979 Banking Act provided for the establishment of a Deposit Protection Fund (DPF). Both recognised banks and LDTs are required to contribute to the DPF in proportion to the size of their deposit base subject to a minimum level of contribution. It is designed to protect small depositors against loss; the maximum protected deposit for each depositor being £10,000. If institutions become insolvent depositors will be paid out an amount equal to 75% of their individual protected deposits. Contributions to the fund are tax deductible.

The Bank, as supervisor of the banking system, has historically issued quantitative and qualitative guidelines. Since the 1979 Act these have carried more authority and, in the wake of the Act, it initiated a wide ranging discussion with banking institutions concerning capital and liquidity adequacy and foreign currency exposure by publishing three papers containing draft proposals.[81]

Capital adequacy was subsequently gauged by monitoring two ratios : the gearing ratio, which is the ratio of deposits to capital; and the risk-assets ratio (RAR), which applies risk weights to each type of asset and relates the result to the capital base of a bank. The definition of capital has been revised since the original proposals to include : equity, which comprises of share capital, reserves, and general loan loss provisions; term subordinated debt; and perpetual subordinated debt. Specific loan loss provisions are excluded and each type of capital is subject to a number of adjustments, when calculating the ratio, and an overall limit to the amount of non-equity capital included has been established. Equity must account for at least half and term debt may not exceed a third of total capital whilst perpetual debt must not exceed half of equity. Perpetual debt includes securities with an unlimited life that can be automatically converted to the equivalent of equity if a bank encounters serious operating difficulties. The specifically designed perpetual FRNs issued by the major clearing banks and discussed in section 1.2 fall into this category. Fixed ratios are not set, the Bank establishing the appropriate ratios for each institution following regular prudential interviews.

The liquidity proposals laid down guidelines designed to ensure that: banks hold sufficient cash or liquid assets; match appropriately the profiles of assets or liabilities; and maintain and adequately diversified deposit base. No prudential ratios were set, the adequacy of liquidity being monitored through bank returns and prudential interviews. Procedures were also laid down to monitor banks' foreign currency exposure and guidelines were set to limit the extent of these exposures. In April 1983 the Bank also issued guidelines with respect to single borrower credit exposure. It required that all individual exposures to nonbanks above 10% of a bank's capital base should be reported and that exposures in excess of 10% would require higher capital ratios to be maintained.

A number of these requirements and guidelines and the 1979 Banking Act itself are to be revised and given statutory backing in a new Banking Act in mid-1987. These changes were prompted by the Johnson Matthey Bank (JMB) affair in October 1984.[82] The Bank, with the help of a number of other banks,[83] rescued JMB, which was a recognised bank. It had substantial problem loans and had exceeded the lending exposure guidelines. Further, it had been audited only three months earlier and been given a clean bill of health. The affair brought into question: the adequacy of bank supervisory procedures; the usefulness of distinguishing between recognised banks and LDTs and subjecting the latter to more rigorous supervision than the former; the lending exposure guidelines; and the relationship of auditors and supervisors. In December 1984 a joint Treasury-Bank Committee was established to conduct a wide ranging inquiry into banking supervision. It reported in June 1985 and a subsequent White Paper in December 1985,[84] on which the forthcoming legislation is to be based, adopted and embellished its proposals. As a result the two-tier authorisation system is expected to be replaced by a single licensing system with the Bank's supervisory powers broadened and strengthened. Additionally, provisions will be made for a regular dialogue between the Bank and a bank's auditors; statutory loan exposure limits will be established; the staff of the Bank's Banking Supervision Department will be increased and given better training; and the Bank will have new powers to obtain information. Prior to the White Paper, in September 1985, the Bank strengthened the management of its Supervisory department by establishing a Bank Supervisory Committee consisting of senior directors. The White Paper also proposed the establishment of a Board of Banking Supervision. In May 1986 the Chancellor approved five nominations by the Bank for membership of the Board, which is to advise the Governor of the Bank and report separately to the Chancellor annually. The Governor is free to ignore its advice but must report to the Treasury if it does so. The statutory basis of bank regulation and the Bank's supervisory responsibility is, therefore, to be strengthened by forthcoming legislation, which will also make the relationship between the Treasury and the Bank concerning bank supervision clearer. There was some friction following the JMB affair, with the Treasury claiming that it had not been kept adequately informed about the Bank's actions.

In 1986 the TSBs were privatised and also came under the Bank's supervisory wing, having previously been supervised by the Treasury by virtue of their anomalous status. As a result of legislation covering TSBs prior to the 1985 TSB Act, which provided for their reorganisation and privatisation, they were not state owned institutions but they were not public companies or mutual organisations either.[85] In 1986, there was further significant legislation relating to the banking system. The Building Societies Act[86] provided for building societies to diversify further into personal banking and related services with effect from January 1987 and the establishment of the Building Societies Commission (BSC) to take over supervisory responsibilities from the Registrar. The BSC is required to ensure adherence to the provisions of the Act and is given discretion to relax some of the limits set on the extent of allowable diversification. It has attempted to make the supervision and regulation of building societies consistent with the arrangements likely to be applied to banks following the forthcoming banking legislation. In this connection it has been discussing capital and liquidity requirements with the members of the BSA and has been establishing provisions for a freer exchange of information with auditors. Both the Bank and the BSC will have to pursue their supervisory roles in the light of the 1986 Financial Services Act (FSA).

The FSA aims to improve investor protection and provides for the DTI to delegate its supervisory responsibilities to the Securities and Investments Board (SIB). The DTI has been given greater investigative powers and the SIB will authorise Self Regulatory Organisations (SROs) and Recognised Investment Exchanges (RIEs). The new supervisory arrangements are expected to be in place by the Autumn of 1987. SROs will supervise the activities of businesses that register with them in accordance with rule books and procedures approved by the SIB. RIEs will provide for the scrutiny of market trading activities. The Stock Exchange for example is to become a RIE and has devised a new trading system, which was introduced in October 1986, to allow the monitoring of all transactions on the market by The Securities Association (TSA), which is expected to become the SRO. TSA was formed in 1986, following the merger of the Stock Exchange Council (SEC) and the International Securities Regulatory Organisation (ISRO), which was previously expected to be the SRO for the Eurobond market. TSA will authorise traders on both the Stock Exchange and the Eurobond markets, which is expected to become a separate RIE under the auspices of the Association of International Bond Dealers (AIBD). A number of other SROs and RIEs are to be authorised to cover all sectors of investment business and the various securities and commodities markets. The London International Financial Futures Exchange (Liffe), the London Commodity Exchange (LCE) and the London Metal Exchange (LME) are all, for example, expected to become RIEs. Life assurance, unit trust, investment management, and futures broking and dealing business will all have to register with SROs, of which there will probably be five, or the SIB.

With banks, building societies and other institutions having already diversified or being in the process of diversification, many institutions will have to register with more than one SRO. This will bring banks, and increasingly building societies, under the purview of new supervisory authorities. To take account of this complication a practice of electing a lead supervisor, chosen by considering an institution's main line of business, is to be adopted. The lead supervisor for banks will clearly be the Bank and for building societies it will be the BSC. The Bank or the BSC will then be required to open up a dialogue with the SIB and the SROs with which the institutions they supervise are registered. The aim is to ensure that all the activities of their supervisees are adequately and consistently supervised. In this connection the SIB and the Bank have worked closely together to devise a basic set of rules, including those relating to capital adequacy, to apply to investment businesses. The SIB has also been seeking to persuade the accounting profession, whose various associations will also have to seek recognition, to come to an agreement over the conditions under which auditors and supervisors can open up a dialogue. The SIB is also making arrangements for the establishment of an investor protection fund. Initially separate funds were expected to be established by each SRO but now a pooled fund seems more likely, despite opposition from TSA which is expected to be the largest contributor.

The FSA also provided for the DTI to apply the principle of reciprocity in considering the access of foreign institutions to UK financial markets. This has been used to put pressure on the Japanese authorities to open access to UK banking and financial institutions to Japanese markets. The provisions permit the authorities to refuse licences to institutions from countries not offering reciprocal access to UK institutions and allow for licences to be revoked in some cases where reciprocity is not forthcoming. Insider dealing being prohibited by the 1985 Company Securities (Insider Dealing) Act, institutions are expected to establish 'chinese walls' between various departments to prevent the exploitation by dealing departments of sensitive information gleaned from clients by advisory departments. Authorised businesses are expected to establish their own internal policing arrangements and licences can be revoked if these prove to be inadequate. In February 1985 the UK Banking Ombudsman, whose activities are funded by the recognised banks, began work. The Ombudsman will consider the claims of dissatisfied customers and will be empowered to make substantial awards to settle customers' complaints. Dissatisfied customers retain their right to go to court if they choose. Although bank funded, the Ombudsman is expected to act impartially. Awards to consumers are payable by the bank concerned and binding. The building societies and other groups of intermediaries seem likely to follow suit by establishing Ombudsmen to deal with consumer complaints impartially without precluding access to the courts.

The new supervisory arrangements, based on self-regulation with statutory backing, have yet to be tried. Many practitioners[87] and opposition party politicians feel that they will eventually have to be replaced by an agency, akin to the US Securities Exchange Commission, with more substantial statutory powers relating to investigation and prosecution. The Government has argued that the new system, with its inherent flexibility, should first be given a try. It hopes that the increased investigatory powers of the DTI and the establishment of the Fraud Investigation Group (FIG)[88] in 1985 will improve fraud and insider trading detection and prosecution. It is also considering the proposals of the Roskill Committee,[89] which are designed to increase the chances of successful prosecution in cases of financial fraud, and has introduced stiffer penalties for offenders.

The Bank has also been involved in the development of supervisory arrangements and procedures to cover international banking activities; through EC Committees and the Basle Committee,[90] which is traditionally chaired by one of the Bank's directors. In January 1987 the Bank and the US banking supervisors issued joint proposals for assessing capital adequacy. They came to an agreement on the definition of capital, broadly adopting the previous one employed by the Bank, and proposed a more detailed application of the RAR approach. More weighting categories were introduced and off balance sheet risks were to be provisioned for more comprehensively than in previous guidelines issued by the Bank in April 1985. These had applied to note insurance facilities (Nifs)[91] and similar standby credit facilities. These contingent liabilities were given a weighting of 50% of that applying to drawn loans when calculating the RAR. The new proposals reduced the weighting on Nifs to 25% in line with recently introduced US practices. The Bank and the US authorities hope to persuade other central banks and monetary authorities to adopt similar guidelines in order to promote a 'level playing field' for international banks.

The activities of the banks, especially the clearing banks, have been heavily influenced by government monetary policy and the Bank's chosen method of monetary control. The government is responsible for formulating monetary policy and the Bank acts as its agent in implementing it. Major changes in methods of monetary control must be sanctioned by the Treasury, however. Competition and Credit Control (CCC)[92] introduced new methods of monetary control which became operative in September 1971. It aimed to reduce reliance on direct credit controls and the Bank Rate[93] and to rely on open market operations (OMOs) instead. Quantitative lending ceilings were abolished and the London and Scottish clearing banks' collective agreement on interest rates was terminated. The cash and liquidity ratios that had previously prevailed were replaced by the Reserve Asset Ratio (RAR), which applied to all banks in the main banking system, rather than just the major clearing banks as had been the case with the cash and liquidity ratios. Finance houses and discount houses were subject to similar controls. The RAR was to be rendered variable by calls by the Bank for special deposits which would bear interest. In 1972 the Bank Rate was replaced by the Minimum Lending Rate (MLR),[94] which was related to market rates and not set completely at the discretion of the Bank, as the Bank Rate had been. Qualitative controls over lending, established by Bank directives, remained in force. Broadly they aimed to encourage a flow of funds to finance exports and industry rather than consumer expenditure. There were also controls over hire purchase (HP) agreements, which set minimum down payments and the maximum repayment periods.

By the end of 1973, it became clear that the policy was not working, despite the fact that interest rates were at record levels. Direct controls over bank lending were reintroduced in the form of the Supplementary Special Deposit Scheme (SSDS) or 'corset'. Guidelines were set on interest bearing deposits which, if exceeded, would trigger a call by the Bank for SSDS, which, as a penalty, would bear no interest. The SSDS was abandoned and re-imposed on a number of occasions until it was finally abandoned in June 1980. It was not markedly successful in restricting bank lending and on occasions banks chose to incur penalties. Further, it distorted financial flows by encouraging them to by-pass their traditional intermediaries, the banks. 'Bill-leak'[95] was a major source of disintermediation. The clearing banks complained[96] that the SSDS and the requirement on them to hold 1% of their eligible liabilities in the form of cash with the Bank, to facilitate clearing and fund the activities of the Bank, were unfair.

The Chancellor of the newly elected Conservative government set in motion a joint Bank-Treasury review of the methods of controlling the money supply in November 1979 and in March 1980 a Consultative Green Paper[97] advocated dropping the MLR and RAR. The 1½% cash requirement had become the fulcrum of OMOs so that the RAR had become redundant and the Green Paper proposed that the cash requirement should be extended to all banks. It also discussed the merits of various monetary base control and monetary base indicator systems. The Bank had, however, previously[98] made its opposition to monetary base control clear.

Following consultations, a new system of monetary control was introduced in August 1981.[99] It applied to the monetary sector which was redefined to include: recognised banks, LDTs, the NG, the TSBs and the Bank's banking department. Building societies were excluded. MLR ceased to be posted continuously and it has since only been introduced temporarily on one occasion, as part of an attempt to halt the rapid fall in sterling in January 1985. To increase the supply of bills eligible for discounting at the Bank, in order to facilitate OMOs, the Bank extended its list of banks eligible to accept bills. It also required eligible banks to place 'club money'[100] with the members of the LDMA. The 1% cash ratio requirement, applying to the London clearing banks, was dropped in favour of a cash ratio requirement on all institutions in the new monetary sector. They were required to hold ½% of their eligible liabilities in non-operating, non-interest bearing deposits with the Bank. In addition the clearing banks maintain ordinary current accounts with the Bank for clearing purposes.

The government adopted a monetary policy designed to reduce the rate of growth of sterling M3, called the Medium Term Financial Strategy, in its 1980 Budget. This was to be achieved by progressively reducing the PSBR. The re-intermediation that followed the removal of the 'corset' distorted sterling M3 growth and since 1980 various monetary aggregates, including PSL2[101] which includes building societies deposits, have been used as targets alongside sterling M3. As mentioned in section 1.2, the 'overfunding' technique was used to exert control over sterling M3 growth. This also proved to be distortionary and the spread of the practice of paying interest on demand deposits had made the implications of sterling M3 growth increasingly hard to interpret by the mid 1980s.[102] The overfunding technique was dropped in 1986 and it seems unlikely that sterling M3 will be targeted after the 1987 budget. A narrow money aggregate M0[103] has also been targeted since 1985 and its targeting is likely to continue beyond the 1987 budget. Despite the Bank's reservations, it remains a possibility that the Treasury might encourage it to adopt a monetary base control or indicator system in the future. A more likely outcome is that the authorities will concentrate on controlling interest rates through OMOs in short term securities and join the Exchange Rate Mechanism of the European Monetary System following the general election expected in 1987. This would replace monetary targeting with formal exchange rate targeting, informal exchange rate targeting having apparently been adopted in 1985.

The monetary control arrangements introduced in 1981 abandoned reserve requirements and no standard minimum prudential liquidity requirements were subsequently introduced. In July 1986, however, the bank issued proposals to replace the 'club money' arrangement. Following discussions with the banks, the Bank is likely to introduce a primary liquid asset requirement. Banks will have to hold a certain proportion of their liabilities in the form of highly liquid sterling assets, including cash and eligible bills. A two-tier system has been proposed. The eleven main clearing banks, to be called the primary liquidity banks, will be obliged to hold their own liquid assets, whilst secondary banks will be allowed either to hold their own liquid assets or to hold liquid assets in the form of deposits with the primary liquid banks.

Qualitative controls on lending have been relaxed in the 1980s. Term controls on hire purchase (HP) agreements were lifted in July 1982 and similar controls on bank lending have also been removed. Banks no longer have to restrict their loans to 75% of the value of a car purchase, for example, and can extend 100% mortgages if they wish. Restrictions on repayment periods have also been lifted. The result has been a rapid build up of consumer lending and credit extended by finance houses and credit card companies. Additionally, freed from the 'corset' and qualitative credit controls, the major banks were able to move into the home loan market in the 1980s. A new directive concerning lending for house purchases, known as the O'Brien rule after the Governor at the time , was issued in January 1982, however. Its aims were: to prevent home owners from realising the equity in their houses when they sold them at a capital gain and intended to purchase another house; and to prevent homeowners from raising mortgages for purposes other than house purchase or improvements. The rules also effectively prevented homeowners from using their houses as security for loans unrelated to buying. They were far from watertight and many homeowners were effectively financing consumption using supplementary home loans, which were supposedly being used for home improvements, and some of the proceeds of house sales to buy furnishings and consumer durables. They also became anomalous in the light of the new powers granted to building societies in 1986 to extend both home loans and ordinary consumer loans and the entry of banks, with similar powers, into the home loan market. The Bank consequently eased them in December 1986, allowing houses to be used as security for a wide range of loans.

1.4 Deregulation

As the previous section indicates, the UK banking and financial system has experienced a considerable amount of regulatory reform, a widening of the supervisory net, and increased statutory backing for supervision. Prior to the 1979 Banking Act, the Bank supervised the wider financial system whilst concentrating primarily on the major banks in what has been described as a club-like arrangement. The DTI, the Treasury and the Registrar of Friendly Societies also had supervisory responsibilities over well defined groups of institutions. The Treasury's wider responsibilities were largely delegated to the Bank.[104] Elsewhere, such as in the Lloyds Insurance Market, and the Stock Exchange, self-regulatory arrangements of a club-like nature were in operation. A series of frauds involving losses to investors prompted the Lloyds Act in 1982, which was supposed to tighten regulation of the market whilst retaining the principle of self-regulation, and prompted the DTI to commission, in July 1981, an investigation into investor protection by Professor Jim Gower, its advisor on company law. The Gower Report,[105] published in January 1984, recommended a system, based on self-regulatory organisations overseen by a statutorily backed body and formed the basis of the proposals contained in the FSA. Lloyds was excluded from the FSA because it had already been covered by the 1982 Act, but further incidences of bad practices prompted both internal and external inquiries into its regulatory structure. In January 1987 an external inquiry[106] recommended various additional changes and the Secretary of State for Trade and Industry threatened further legislation unless Lloyds put its house in order. The FSA will extended supervision to previously unregulated areas, such as the Eurobond markets. Meanwhile the Bank and the BSC have more extensive and formal supervisory powers. The previous 'club like' arrangements appear to be a thing of the past and practitioners will probably only enjoy self-regulatory powers as long as they use them professionally.

The regulatory reform can be seen as a necessary response to the deregulation that had already occurred and was accelerating. It was designed to improve depositor and investor protection. It also aimed to bring UK practices into line with a series of EC Directives relating to the banking and other financial institutions.

Deregulation in the UK has not involved just removal of regulations. It also covers financial innovations, the removal of restrictive practices, and product diversification by the major financial intermediaries. The first significant development was probably the abolition of the interest setting cartel operated by the clearing banks in 1971. Banks, and building societies to a lesser extent, began to diversify rapidly in the 1970s. The banks expanded both their international and their domestic retail and corporate activities whilst the building societies moved into the provision of MTS. This process continued into the 1980s as banks, freed from the SSDS and qualitative credit controls, moved into the home loans market and building societies, often in conjunction with the smaller clearing banks which offered them clearing facilities and cheque guarantee cards, expanded their MTS activities and began to establish ATM networks. Competition in the domestic savings and home loans markets increased following the collapse of the BSA's interest setting arrangement in 1985, when Abbey National, the second largest society, dropped out. Since then a number of specialist home loan companies, which raise their funds on the wholesale markets, were established. As a result competition in the retail banking and home loans markets has increased considerably. This has been heightened by series of tax changes, discussed in section 1.2, which have ensured that banks and building societies are treated more comparably by the Inland Revenue. The privatisation of the TSBs and the provisions of the 1986 Building Societies Act, which allows building societies to diversify further into retail banking, will reinforce these developments.

The deal, struck in 1983, between the Secretary of State for Trade and Industry and the Chairman of the Stock Exchange, to end the practice of setting minimum commissions, combined with the removal of exchange controls in 1979, led to a build up of pressure for a substantial reform of the Stock Exchange culminating in the October 1986 'big bang'. The removal of exchange controls had allowed a more rapid growth in the London based Eurocurrency and Eurobond markets. The major UK banks benefited from their increased ability to participate in foreign exchange business and the process of securitisation sparked the rapid growth of the Eurobond market, particularly following the 1982 Mexican debt crisis. Many foreign banks and securities houses were attracted to London to participate in the offshore markets. In the first half of the 1980s the Eurobond market began to rival the Stock Exchange as London's major securities market and its participants had begun to trade in international equities as well. Major companies were increasingly able to by-pass both the Stock Exchange and the banks by issuing Eurobonds. The Stock Exchange Council (SEC) realised that a more comprehensive reform would be required to stop the loss of further international securities business. Toward this end: new computerised information and trading systems were devised; the dual capacity system, involving the separation of broking and jobbing functions, was abandoned in favour of a system based on broker-dealers and market makers; and increased participation in member firms, to enable the injection of capital to allow them to compete with the major international securities houses and banks, was sanctioned. Until March 1986 the participations were limited to 29.9%. After that date full participations were allowed.

The new market practices and dealing and information systems came into operation with the 'big bang' on 27 October 1986. The Bank allowed merchant and commercial banks to participate in broking and jobbing firms in order to create investment banking subsidiaries and the major clearing banks completed their conversion to universal banks as a result. In September 1986, just prior to the 'big bang', the SEC and Isro issued joint proposals, subsequently approved by their memberships, to merge. This widened membership of the Stock Exchange, achieving the objective of the AIBD to secure membership for its members, whilst bringing all UK based international equities trading within the Stock Exchange, achieving the SEC's objective. It meant that many foreign institutions, especially from Japan, had gained membership of the Stock Exchange whilst their countries of origin were not offering reciprocal access to UK institutions. The DTI did not oppose the Isro-SEC merger on these grounds but can exploit powers, granted under the FSA, to withdraw licences if anomalies concerning reciprocity prevail.

Other deregulatory developments of the innovatory kind have been occurring as the UK financial markets adopt ideas developed in the US, where the process of securitisation is furthest advanced. In May 1986 the first sterling commercial paper was issued. This complemented the rapid growth of the Euro-commercial paper market, which is winning business from the Euronote market. Despite its slow start,[107] the sterling market is expected to take off at the expense of commercial bills and corporate loans. The banks, therefore, stand to lose some of the business they do with their most creditworthy corporate customers. They hope to gain some compensation by earning fee income from placing the paper. An active secondary market in CP had not developed by the first quarter of 1987, however, and the banks themselves remained the main holders of the paper. With the corporate bond market still dormant, the UK seems unlikely to see the explosion of 'junk bond'[108] issues that the US has witnessed in the 1980s. It might, however, witness the development of a secondary mortgage market. Such a market, in which the major US federal mortgage agencies,[109] banks, savings and loan associations, and securities houses participate, has grown explosively in the US in the 1980s.

In January 1987, National Home Loans (NHL), a wholesale funded UK mortgage investment company, sold about 1250 mortgages to a separate UK incorporated company, NHL First Funding, which will use the proceeds of a £50m FRN issue to purchase them. NHL will, thereby, remove the loans from its balance sheet and free its capital for further lending. If other specialist companies, banks, and building societies follow suit a secondary market could eventually develop. This would benefit the building societies by giving them flexibility to adjust the size of their home loans portfolios to gain maximum benefits from their new freedoms to diversify whilst adhering to the portfolio guidelines laid down in the 1986 Building Society Act. The societies may, however, prove unwilling to participate in the secondary market initially, fearing that by making it liquid they will allow the specialist, wholesale funded, home loan companies to compete with them more effectively. The development of a secondary market in mortgage backed securities also raises questions concerning the protection of the interests of homeowners whose mortgages are sold by one lender to another. A working party has been set up by the Department of the Environment to look into the implications for the consumer of securitising mortgages. Some guidelines and perhaps legislation is expected in the future. The building societies are still the major lenders in the home loans market but the banks and the specialised institutions are also major players. With the BSC supervising the societies, the Bank supervising the banks and the status of the wholesale funded specialist institutions, which do not take retail deposits, unclear, no one supervisor is directly responsible for all the institutions trading in the home loans market. It might prove desirable for the authorities to require the formation of a RIE to cover the home loans market in the future.

1) Sometimes called the OPEC I shock.
2) Often attributed, at least in part, to the Vietnam War.
3) Although the Japanese Banks joined in later.
4) The UK and Switzerland removed them in 1979 and Japan followed suit in 1980
5) See White and Vittas (1986).
6) See Pecchioli (1983) for further discussion of the internationalisation of banking.
7) Often called the OPEC II shock.
8) Including North Sea oil.
9) Calculated as a mark-up over the London inter-bank offer rate (Libor).
10) See Lever and Huhne (1985) for further discussion.
11) See Kraft (1984) for an account of of the Mexican rescue.
12) Building societies in the UK and 'thrifts' in the US.
13) With the possible exception of the Swiss and German banks.
14) With certain special characteristics, particularly convertibility into preference shares.
15) See Committee on Banking Regulations and Supervisory Practices (1975).
16) See Committee on Banking Regulations and Supervisory Practices (1983).
17) The chairman of Barclays Bank, for example, has complained strongly.
18) See Bank for International Settlements (1986) and Committee on Banking Regulations and Supervisory Practices (1986).
19) See Committee on Banking Regulations and Supervisory Practices (1986).
20) When index-linked gilt-securities proved to be very successful.
21) Particularly the Financial Services Act, see Section 1.3.
22) The largest Japanese securities house.
23) Discussed in section 1.3.
24) Barclays, National Westminster, Midland, and Lloyds.
25) Particularly, the Chancellor, Nigel Lawson.
26) 3i was previously known as Finance For Industry (FFI), which had been formed in 1973 as a holding for the Industrial and Commercial Finance Company (ICFC) and the Finance Corporation for Industry (FCI).
27) See Committee on Finance and Industry (1931).
28) See Committee to Review the Functioning of the Financial System (1980).
29) The Loan Guarantee Scheme aims to encourage banks to lend to small businesses by providing a government guarantee on 70% of the loan. A 2 1/2% premium on the guaranteed portion of the loan is paid by the borrower. The Business Expansion Scheme encourages independent investors to help small businesses by giving top rate tax relief on equity investments in unquoted companies.
30) The NEDC is a forum in which representatives of the government, trades unions and industry meet to discuss industrial and economic issues.
31) 1979-1983, 1983 to date.
32) The Conservative Party won the 1987 election.

33) Mortgages linked to life assurance which provide for the repayment of the money advanced in a lump sum at the end of the life of the policy and the loan. Ordinary repayment mortgages, in contrast, provide for the repayment of both the principal and the interest over an agreed period of time.

34) See Bank of England (1981).

35) Eligible bills are bank acceptances which the Bank is prepared to rediscount.

36) Broadly these are banks' sterling deposit liabilities, excluding deposits whose original maturity is over two years, and any sterling resources obtained by switching foreign currencies into sterling, see Brown (1982, Appendices II and III) for further details.

37) Discussed in sections 1.2 and 1.3.

38) The 'big bang' was the name given to the reform of the Stock Exchange discussed in subsequent sections of this chapter.

39) See Bank of England (1985).

40) See sections 1.2 and 1.4.

41) The Bank of Scotland, the Royal Bank of Scotland, and the Clydesdale Bank, which is owned by the Midland Bank.

42) The CLSB consists of the former members of the CLCB plus the chairmen of the Bank of Scotland, the Royal Bank of Scotland (RBS), the Standard Chartered Bank and the TSB. The members of the CLCB were the chairmen of the 'big four' clearing banks and those of Coutts & Co and Williams and Glyn's. The latter is not separately represented in the CLSB because it merged with the RBS in 1985.

43) Barclays, Lloyds and NatWest.

44) To customers that maintain a pre-set minimum balance, which is often quite large.

45) Which is the practice of not charging for money transmission services if the balance remains positive. Previously charges were waived for customers maintaining pre-set minimum balances of around £250.

46) Which accrued after the OPEC I shock.

47) Such as the Business Expansion Scheme. The Loan Guarantee Scheme has also encouraged more bank lending to small businesses.

48) PEPs aim to encourage wider share ownership by allowing a tax free build up of investment in equities through special accounts at financial institutions such as banks and building societies.

49) With the exception of Samuel Montagu & Co Ltd.

50) The Export Credit Guarantee Department, which is a government backed agency which insures loans extended to facilitate UK trade with the rest of the world.

51) The USM is used by companies not large enough to seek a full Stock Exchange listing.

52) The Third Market is for companies which are too small to raise capital on the USM.

53) The largest Japanese securities house.

54) Under the new monetary control arrangements entitled: 'Monetary Control - Provisions', see Bank of England (1981).

55) Composite rate tax is deducted from interest payments at source. It is a common rate applying to all savers regardless of their tax coding.

56) Apart from those offered by banks with branches in the UK offshore centres; the Isle of Man and the Channel Islands.

57) All the London Clearing Banks own one, for example.

58) See section 2.3.

59) See section 2.3.

60) Abbey National is the second largest building society.

61) Following the collapse of the interest cartel in 1985.

62) See chapter 6.

63) On the recommendation of the Monopolies Commission, see Command Paper 8472.

64) See also section 1.4.

65) See chapter 6.

66) See also section 1.4.
67) See also section 1.4.
68) See also sections 1.3 and 1.4.
69) See note 29.
70) See Price Commission (1978), Committee to Review the Functioning of the Financial System (1980) and National Consumer Council (1983).
71) See National Consumer Council (1983).
72) Members of the Bankers' Clearing House (1985).
73) E.g. Midland and NatWest, which are to share with the TSB in the future. 74) The Anglia Building Society.
75) The Nottingham Building Society.
76) See National Consumer Council (1983) and Goode (1985) for further discussion.
77) By the government. The independent review committee is to be chaired by Professor R. Jack, a part time professor of mercantile law.
78) See Mullineux (1987a, Chapter 3) for further discussion.
79) See Reid (1982) for a detailed account.
80) See European Communities (1977).
81) See Bank of England (1980, 1981, 1982).
82) See Mullineux (1987b, Appendix B) for further discussion.
83) Including the major clearing banks and the accepting and gold bullion houses.
84) Command Paper 9695.
85) Their status was, however, a matter of substantial debate. Some savers claimed that the TSBs were mutual organisations and the Labour Party claimed that they were government owned.
86) Which received Royal Ascent in 1986.
87) Deliotte, Haskins and Sells, a major accountancy firm, sponsored a survey in 1986 which found considerable doubt amongst practitioners about the prospects of the new supervisory arrangements. The findings are published in a paper entitles: 'Regulation and the Financial Services Bill, a City Research Associates Survey'.
88) The FIG aims to coordinate efforts on major fraud cases by using lawyers and accountants from the Department of Trade and Industry to help the City Police Fraud Squad in its investigations.
89) See Roskill Committee (1986).
90) The Committee on Banking Regulations and Supervisory Practises that meets at the Bank for International Settlements in Basle and is also known as the Cooke Committee because it is chaired by Mr W.P.Cooke of the Bank of England.
91) Note issuance facilities (Nifs) enable borrowers to issue short term paper on a regular basis because the issues are underwritten by syndicates of banks which guarantee the availibility of funds to purchase unsold notes at each roll-over date.
92) Bank of England (1971).
93) Which was the minimum rate at which the Bank would normally lend to the discount houses.
94) Which was the minimum rate at which the Bank would normally lend to the discount houses. Between October 1982, when it replaced Bank Rate, and May 1978 it was usually fixed by a formula linking it to the Treasury bill tender rate. Thereafter, like Bank Rate it was fixed at the discretion of the Bank until the practice of setting MLR was abandoned in 1981.
95) The holding of bankers' acceptances outside the banking system.
96) See Committee of London Clearing Bankers (1978), for example.
97) Command Paper 7858.
98) See Bank of England (1979).
99) See Bank of England (1981).
100) See above.

101) PSL stands for Public Sector Liquidity.

102) See Bank of England (1987).

103) It consists of notes and coins in public circulation, banks' till money and bankers' balances with the Bank.

104) See Committee to Review the Functioning of Financial Institutions (1980, Chapter 3 and Appendix 4) and Select Committee on Nationalised Industries (1976).

105) See Command Paper 9125.

106) The Committee of Inquiry was established by the Trade and Industry Secretary in 1986 and was chaired by Sir Patrick Neill, see Neill Report (1987).

107) See section 1.2 for further discussion.

108) 'Junk bonds' are bonds issued in the US by corporations which are not rated by the major US credit rating agencies, Standard and Poor's and Moody's.

109) The Federal Home Loan Banks and the Federal National Mortgage Association (Fannie Mae).

2

Banking in the USA and Japan

2.1 Introduction

The US and Japanese banking systems differ from those of most OECD countries[1] because legislation attempts to maintain a strict separation between commercial banking and some securities business; especially the underwriting of corporate equities. The relevant legislation, in the US and Japan respectively, is the Glass-Steagall Act and Article 65 of the Banking Act. It prevents banks from developing into universal banks on the Swiss or German models.

In both Japan and the US banks are also heavily restricted in a number of other respects. In some states, US banks have faced severe branching restrictions and, until the 1980s, interstate branching was prohibited. Banks have also been prevented from investing significantly in commerce and industry, in the way that German and Japanese banks have done.[2] They are also prevented from forging links with the nonbank corporate sector through holding companies, a practice common in Japan. US commercial banks are, therefore, prohibited from undertaking investment banking business, in the sense of securities underwriting and investment through equity participation. Conformably, securities houses in the US are not allowed to take deposits or extend commercial loans. They are commonly called investment banks but they are mainly engaged in primary and secondary securities market trading and do not hold major participations in commercial enterprises in the way that the French investment banks do.

In Japan banks can and do hold large equity portfolios but they are not allowed to underwrite share issues, although they may join government bond syndicates. US banks are also active in their domestic government bond market, the US Treasury bond market. Unlike the US banks, the Japanese banks have specialised by function. At the beginning of the 1980s there were three distinct groups; the long term credit banks; the trust banks; and the commercial banks, which concentrate on short term loans and deposits, cannot issue debentures, and do not normally engage in trust business. There are also a number of important government sponsored financial institutions in Japan. Such institutions are not prevalent in the US, where they normally have supervisory roles. In the US, not only are there no long term credit banks but long term bank lending is rare. The volume of long term bank lending is much greater in France, Germany and Japan than in the UK and US. This is sometimes attributed to the existence of more highly developed capital markets in the US and the UK. UK banks have been criticised for their lack of long term

37

lending and it has been argued[3] that the country would benefit from the existence of a development bank like the French or Japanese ones. It is, however, evident that German and Japanese corporations have, in the 1980s, decided to reduce their reliance on long term bank finance and to raise more capital and funds through the securities markets instead. In both the UK and the US, the capital markets are dominated by institutional investors, such as insurance companies and pension funds, although private share ownership is more widespread in the US and increasing in the UK.

There are, therefore, a number of differences but also some essential similarities between the US and Japanese banking systems. This is attributable to the fact that the occupying US authorities imposed some changes on the Japanese banking system after World War Two. Overseas branches were closed, state owned banks were privatised, the central bank was made more independent of government influence, and Article 65, with its striking similarities to the Glass-Steagall Act, was introduced. The Japanese authorities also adopted the US practice of interest rate control, paying particular attention to rates on short term deposits. The government successfully adapted the system to serve their post- war reconstruction programme and the subsequent rapid industrial development. It served them well until the 1973 oil price shock after which pressures for change began to build up. There was some liberalisation in the late 1970s and the early 1980s but since then outside and internal pressure for change has accumulated.

In the US, the pressure for deregulation built up in the 1970s and deregulation has proceeded rapidly in the 1980s. Whilst branching restrictions have been weakened in one way or another, the Glass-Steagall Act remains in force, although its influence has been eroded by innovations and the exploitation of loopholes in the legislation.

International Banking Facilities (IBFs)[4] were permitted to open in New York in 1981, establishing it as an offshore banking centre. Liberalisation has not, however, gone as far in New York as in London. Japan has looked toward New York, rather than London, as a model and it permitted offshore banking facilities, similar to New York's IBFs, to open in Tokyo towards the end of 1986. Whilst interest rate deregulation had been completed by March 1986 in the US, the Japanese authorities were proceeding cautiously towards a similar deregulation. Given the relatively more cautious approach, Japanese deregulation continue to lag behind US deregulation. It is uncertain whether New York will close the deregulatory gap with London in the future. In both Japan and the US there are significant lobby groups counselling caution and some re-regulation in the US remains a possibility, especially following the dominance of Congress achieved by the Democrats following their successes in the 1986 mid term elections.

With the US experiencing record bank failures in the mid 1980s there seems to be room for an increase in concentration in the US banking system. The rise in the failure rate started in the 1970s as competition in the banking sector began to increase and margins were squeezed. There are a large number of small banking institutions in Japan whose prospects could be impaired by a liberalisation of interest rates and a narrowing of margins as a result of increased competition. It seems likely that the Japanese authorities will have to encourage mergers and allow an increase in banking concentration if, as seems likely,[5] they want to avert a rash of bank failures. The future of Article 65 and the Glass-Steagall Act is debatable given that banking and capital markets are becoming increasingly globalised and Japanese and

US banks and other financial institutions, particularly securities houses, can operate as universal banks in London and elsewhere in Europe.

2.2 The US Banking System

i) Introduction

In the mid 1980s the US banking system presented a strange picture. In aggregate banks and 'thrifts'[6] were doing well. Profits were healthy and capital and loan loss provisions had been boosted since the 1982 Mexican debt crisis[7] and the 1984 Continental Illinois crisis.[8] The share prices of the major money centre and the large regional banks were strong. Failures amongst banks and thrifts, however, hit record post war levels in the mid 1980s. The failure rate in fact started to rise at the beginning of the 1970s but it hit levels in the 1980s not seen since the late 1930s. In 1986 record failures were recorded for the fifth year running. 138 banks were merged or liquidated in 1986. 120 had failed in 1985 and 79 in 1984. During the latter half of the 1930s an average of 67 banks failed a year. This was small, however, compared to the post 1929 Great Crash depression years, 1930-1933, when an average of 2,227 banks failed a year and 4,000 failed in 1933. In this period deposits were uninsured and rumours sparked 'runs' on banks. The establishment of the Federal Deposit Insurance Corporation (FDIC) in 1934 seemed to have an immediate beneficial impact. The existence of the FDIC and a relatively conservative attitude to banking until the 1970s[9] seem to explain the low failure rate in the 1940 to 1970 period. The number of banks on the FDIC's troubled list has also risen progressively. In December 1986 about 10% of the country's banks were on the troubled list. That number has grown more rapidly than the number of failures, however, because supervisors have subjected banks to closer scrutiny and placed them on the list more readily. The failure rate and number of troubled banks are now at the highest levels since the FDIC was created. Additionally, the supervisory authority for the savings and loan associations (SLAs), the Federal Home Loan Bank Board (FHLBB), declared that 21 SLAs had been closed in 1986, whilst 46 had been ordered to change their management and 22 had been forced to merge with stronger partners. A further 250 of the 3,250 thrifts insured by the Federal Savings and Loan Insurance Corporation (FSLIC) were on the troubled list. Ten SLAs had collapsed in 1985, nine in 1984 and six in 1983. The 1986 failure level was also a modern record.

The US banking system has a low concentration in comparison with banking systems in other OECD countries and also when compared to the commercial and industrial sectors of the US economy. The market capitalisation of the largest US bank, Citicorp, which was the second largest bank in the world in 1986, is small relative to that of International Business Machines (IBM) or General Motors, for example. In most industrial countries the larger banks have capitalisations roughly on a par with their major domestic corporate clients. There are over 14,000 commercial banks and over 4,700 near banks or 'thrifts', excluding credit unions of which there are 21,000, in the US. 9,000 of the banks are unit banks, which are banks with only one office. The US has more banks per head of the population than any other country, although a few countries[10] have more bank offices or branches per head of the population. The fifteen largest banks held only about 30%

of the banking system's assets in the early 1980s, whilst the ten largest held only about 20% of total domestic deposits. Such concentrations are small compared to European systems, where commonly five or less banks dominate, and the Japanese system. It is the banking system in which unit banks are most prevalent but it is clearly a hybrid system, mixing branch and unit banking. Over time the number of unit banks has declined as a proportion of the total number of banks. The US system is also described as a dual banking system because of the alternative, state and federal, authorisation routes. This authorisation procedure, combined with the desire to maintain state autonomy, has restricted interstate branching and led to a wide variation in the extent of intrastate branching permitted.

The rising trend in failures in the 1970s is hard to account for but appears, at least in part, to be attributable to financial innovation and growing competition between thrifts, commercial banks and investment banks. The causes of these changes have been hotly debated and cannot be assessed in detail here. Increased variability in inflation and interest rates, however, seem to have provided an incentive for financial innovation whilst technical innovations in the fields of data processing and communications have enhanced opportunities for those with the capital to invest in modernisation. The acceleration of financial innovation in the 1980s and the increased exploitation of loopholes in legislation have brought thrifts, commercial banks and investment banks into closer competition at a time when interest rates have been formally deregulated in a phased manner since the Depository Institutions Deregulation and Monetary Control Act (1980).[11] Margins between lending and borrowing rates have been cut as competition for savings has increased deposit rates. The interest rate deregulation was started in the 1970s and completed in the mid 1980s. A shake out may have been caused by interest rate deregulation which might account for the increase in failures since the early 1970s. Its effects may take until the end of the 1980s, and perhaps longer, to unwind but may be a temporary phenomenon. The acceleration in the failure rate in the first half of the 1980s can probably be attributed to the fact that a number of shocks have hit specific groups of banks, supplementing the effects of interest rate deregulation. The falling oil prices in the first half of the 1980s brought problems for the energy banks.[12] They were exacerbated by the rapid fall in oil prices in 1986, following an abrupt change in OPEC policy.[13] The problems of the oil sector, to which the energy banks are heavily exposed, have been alleviated somewhat following a further revision in the OPEC policy, towards the end of 1986, designed to push oil prices back up to $18 a barrel, well above the $10 a barrel level hit earlier in the year and above the $15 barrel level at which the problem of the energy banks was judged to be containable. The farm banks,[14] which prior to the 1986 troubles amongst the energy banks had been the major problem group, have suffered from weak agricultural prices in the early 1980s and continue to cause concern.[15] The real estate market also took a tumble in the early 1980s, hitting the SLAs particularly hard. Falling real estate values in the farming belt and the energy states, such as Texas, Oklahoma and Louisiana, have exacerbated the bank's problems by reducing the value of the security underlying the loans. Small branch or unit banks in areas where farming or oil and gas extraction are the major industries naturally have heavy exposures to problem clients because of the industrial specialisation in their locality. Hence most of the failures have been amongst small banks. Nevertheless the accumulated cost to the FDIC has been large. Bigger banks have also hit trouble but they have generally been treated differently.[16] The crisis at Continental Illinois, a Chicago based money centre bank, in 1984 demonstrated the risk of relying on wholesale markets for funds. Because of very strict intrastate branching regulations, Continental Illinois had no branch network and, therefore, lacked a sound retail base. Rumours, which were supposedly unfounded, about its liquidity position rapidly generated a crisis requiring a costly, Treasury sponsored, bail-out by the FDIC. As a rule, the supervisory authorities prefer to arrange mergers. Larger banks have, given the opportunity to circumvent intrastate or interstate branching restrictions, usually proved willing to absorb smaller troubled banks. Mergers involving larger troubled banks take longer to arrange. In the case of Continental Illinois, which was amongst the top ten US banks by asset value at the time, no white knight could be found. The authorities were forced to effectively nationalise it. New management was installed, and its loan book thinned down. By 1987 it was back in profit and the authorities had begun to sell off their holdings in the bank.

Most of the larger, especially the money centre, banks were relatively healthy in the mid 1980s although their exposure to third world, and especially Latin American, debtors was still a cause for concern and their provisions against this debt had not been as extensive as those made by many European commercial banks, especially the Swiss and German ones. In the mid 1980s the only major bank causing any difficulties was Bank America. It had been overtaken in the early 1980s by Citicorp as the world's and the US's largest bank. Bank America has heavy exposure to the third world debtor countries and a number of domestic problem loans, especially in the energy sector. A major crisis seems unlikely to result, however, because the bank has a sound retail base in California and has been the subject of takeover offers. The second largest Californian bank, First Interstate, has made a takeover bid for example, and Citicorp is rumoured to be interested. Bank America does, however, seem determined to retain its independence and has been raising capital by selling subsidiaries. If either of the mergers transpire, however, a new megabank would be created. The First Interstate-Bank America merger would create a bank able to dominate the Californian market and attract the interest of anti-trust authorities, however, and a Citicorp-Bank America merger would probably attract the interest of the Federal anti-trust authorities and be opposed by the Federal Reserve Board (FRB).[17] Following a couple of Supreme Court rulings on bank mergers in the early 1980s, the FRB has been inhibited in its opposition to mergers but it is likely to ensure that a merger between Citicorp and Bank America is cleared by the anti-trust authorities.

De facto deregulation has been in process since the early 1970s when thrifts effectively offered interest bearing current accounts, which were prohibited by the FRB's Regulation Q and complimentary regulations applying to other banks and the thrifts, through financial innovations.[18] Interest rates were formally deregulated following the 1980 DIDMC Act, which provided for interest rate controls to be phased out. This Act, along with the Garn-St Germain Act in 1982, allowed thrifts to offer additional retail and corporate banking services. Alongside the growing competition from thrifts for their traditional banking business, commercial banks have also faced increasing competition from investment banks, which began to offer Cash Management Accounts (CMAs) in the late 1970s.[19] These accounts try to match the mix of banking services commonly offered by the commercial banks and have been offered by an increasing number of investment banks in the 1980s.

Retail chains and stores have also become significant competitors in the retail banking market. Facing an assault from a number of sources in their traditional markets and with margins squeezed through growing competition and interest rate deregulation, the commercial banks have sought to diversify. They are particularly attracted by the opportunities for fee earning in the securities markets that have arisen in connection with the process of securitisation which has taken hold in the 1980s. The commercial paper (CP) market has grown significantly since the 1960s but its growth has accelerated in the 1980s. This development is particularly worrying for banks since it allows their corporate clients, especially those with the best credit ratings, to raise money more cheaply directly from each other, by-passing the banks. The banks have, therefore, sought compensation by seeking permission to distribute CP. This was granted by the supervisors but their ruling has been challenged by the investment banks who feel that they should be the sole dealers in CP by virtue of the Glass-Steagall (G-S) Act. In 1986 the legal battle was still being waged.[20]

Although there has been a considerable amount of deregulation since the beginning of the 1970s the G-S Act and branching restrictions remain. The official interest rate deregulation followed de facto deregulation. Branching deregulation appears to be following a similar route. Many states have already passed more liberal intrastate regulations concerning bank branching and mergers and acquisitions and groups of them have also passed reciprocal agreements allowing regional interstate mergers. A few have opened their doors completely to out of state banks without requiring reciprocity and others have provided for freedom of entry following a fixed period in which regional interstate mergers will be permitted. The money centre banks have largely been left out in the cold whilst regional banking groups of a size capable of rivalling them are formed. The money centre banks have not, however, been standing idly by. They have engaged in de facto branching. This has been achieved through a number of routes including : the establishment of Bank Holding Companies (BHCs);[21] chain banking;[22] extending Automated Teller Machine (ATM) networks; acquiring troubled thrifts and banks; and establishing 'non-bank' banks or limited service banks[23]

The key to reducing the number of failures appears to be to permit the absorption of smaller banks into larger regional and national networks. This would reduce the extent to which small banks were exposed to particular industries because larger banks, with more extensive networks, have a greater geographical spread and are able to reduce risk by holding larger and more diversified portfolios. If the process of increasing concentration is controlled under the watchful eye of the supervisors, who have recourse to anti-trust legislation, a number of sizeable regional banks are likely to emerge. Such banks would be able to compete with the major money centre banks and competition in banking may well be increased rather than reduced. Many of the smaller banks have local monopolies and increased competition would reduce the incidence of this. In some cases consumers would be offered a wider range of services as a result and obtain basic banking services more cheaply. It should be stressed, however, that many of the smaller banks are able to offer a wider range of services than one would expect because they maintain correspondent relationships [24] with other commercial banks and the Federal Reserve Banks[25] .

Product deregulation currently relies heavily on financial innovation and the exploitation of loopholes in the G-S Act. But, like the Japanese banks, the US banks have exploited opportunities to diversify into new business abroad, especially in London, Switzerland and various offshore banking centres. They have gained experience in securities business and become major players and innovators, along with the securities houses, in both the London based Eurocurrency and Eurobond markets[26] and in the Swiss Bond market. Meanwhile the investment banks have been able to gain experience in commercial banking business. The US banks, given domestic restrictions and growing opportunities[27] following the 1973 oil price shock, turned their attention increasingly toward international banking in the 1970s. The major banks extended their representation in Europe and the major offshore centres. The regional and medium sized banks also became keen to participate in the loan syndicates formed to lend to Third World, and especially Latin American, countries and led by the major banks. In the early 1980s the major banks were also attracted by the growth prospects in the Asian-Pacific region. By 1982 the US banks were the best represented abroad and had built up a considerable exposure to the Latin American debtors. Since the Mexican Debt Crisis broke in 1982 the US banks have tended to increase their emphasis on domestic business and to pay more attention to the growing competition for their traditional business, from 'thrifts' and investment banks, in the new environment of deregulated interest rates.

The US banking system has good prospects provided the Latin American debt problem does not generate a crisis. It is unlikely that the US monetary authorities and the IMF and the World Bank would allow the debt problem to reach crisis conditions again. The US banks are now better prepared to weather any storms and should grow around the problem, which will decline in significance as their portfolios of other assets grow and they become less reliant on interest income and more reliant on fee income. This process could be aided by allowing the banks greater freedom to diversify into securities business. The problems of the energy banks are likely to decline if oil prices hold at around the $18 per barrel achieved in early 1987. The farm banks are likely to remain a longer term problem which will have to be dealt with in the light of developments in US farm policy. World overproduction of a number of agricultural products has depressed prices and caused trade disputes, between the US and the EEC for example, raising the threat of protectionist measures in 1987.

In the absence of Congressional legislation, deregulation is likely to proceed in a piecemeal manner through financial innovations and the exploitation of loopholes. The supervisors have repeatedly requested legislation designed to regulate the pace of deregulation. In March 1987, however, legislation which aimed to clear up some of the issues concerning what did and did not constitute securities business was shelved. It would have allowed banks to diversify into areas which the investment banks have claimed is securities business. The proposed legislation ran into substantial opposition. Alternative legislation has been proposed by the chairman of the Senate banking committee, Mr William Proxmore. It aims to bar the FRB from using its discretion to approve new securities related ventures by Federally chartered banks for one year. The FRB has allowed significant de facto deregulation and this has increasingly attracted criticism from Congress. By curtailing the FRB's powers temporarily, Mr Proxmore hopes to prompt Congress into legislative action. The newly proposed legislation also intends to ban 'non-bank' banks.

Legislation is required to deal with the issues of product deregulation, branching, the proliferation of 'nonbank' banks and record bank failures. Inaction has inhibited the supervisors' ability to do their job and may have increased the risk of future failures. If an economic recession occurs prior the end of the 1980s, an increase in the number of bank failures could again occur, bringing with it the possibility of tougher regulation, rather than deregulation.

The above interpretation of the prospects for the US banking systen could be over optimistic. It could be that interest rate deregulation has encouraged banks to take more risks. In order to grow around problem loans banks may have to continually seek more risky, and potentially more profitable, loans, given the growing competition for business. Because their retail bases are often restricted and competition for deposits has increased, there is a greater chance that they will overstretch themselves. A more liberal approach to branching and to product diversification would clearly help offset these tendencies. Additionally, the moves toward risk related capital requirements and deposit insurance premiums,[28] will help to restrain excesses and a more permissive attitude towards the absorption of weaker institutions, by stronger ones, would facilitate a rationalisation of the system.

ii) The Banking System

Banks are defined under the 1956 Bank Holding Company (BHC) Act as institutions that both accept demand deposits and make corporate and consumer loans. The only major government banks are the twelve Federal Reserve Banks whose stock is held by the private member banks of the Federal Reserve System (FRS), which are required to purchase shares. There are three broad categories of private sector banks : commercial banks; 'thrifts'; and investment banks or securities houses. Historically these institutions have specialised in particular types of business and their specialisation was reinforced by legislation. As loopholes in the legislation have been exploited since the early 1970s and regulations have been changed, they have increasingly encroached upon each others territory. A dual authorisation system is in operation and there are numerous unit banks amongst the 14,700 or so banks which were operating in 1986. Around 3,300 of the banks are subsidiaries of nearly 800 multi-BHCs. A BHC is a holding company that owns the controlling interest in one or more banks and a multi-BHC is a holding company that owns a controlling interest in two or more banks. Federal law does not prohibit BHCs from acquiring banks across state lines. It does, however, restrict the activity and requires the permission of state governments to be sought. As with branching, regulation of BHCs varies between states. The BHC movement has grown rapidly since 1970. Banks are also interrelated through chain banking, which does not use the holding company device. Instead the interrelationship results through ownership of two or more banks by individuals or families, or through interlocking directorships or other arrangements. Most chain banking groups appear to be rather small, involving only two or three banks. The banking system is interconnected through correspondent relationships which allow banks to widen the range of services they offer. They play a particularly important role in the payments system discussed below.

The other major groups of deposit taking institutions are the savings and loan associations (SLAs), the credit unions (CUs) and the mutual savings banks (MSBs). As a group they are known as 'thrifts' and they have traditionally concentrated on providing services to the retail sector. They neither provided chequing accounts nor in corporate lending. They have been permitted to diversify in the 1980s and have become more direct competitors with commercial banks.

SLAs are similar in some respects to UK building societies. Traditionally they have collected savings through passbook accounts and advanced home loans in the form of fixed rate mortgages. In the 1970s they started to offer negotiable order of withdrawal (NOW) accounts, which were effectively interest bearing current accounts on which cheques could be drawn. They can only hold personal, as opposed to business, accounts but they can sell fixed period certificates of deposit (CDs).

Like Commercial banks, SLAs can be chartered by state or federal governments. In the early 1980s there were over 4,300 SLAs in the US. About 44 % of them were federally chartered. This group held about 62 % of aggregate SLA deposits. They are required to be mutual organisations, which means that they must be owned by their savings account holders. State chartered institutions may be mutual organisations or joint stock companies, owned by shareholders rather than depositors. Whilst their proportion of the total remains small, the number of SLAs operating as public companies has been increasing as some SLAs have converted from mutual organisations to stock companies. By going public, 'thrifts' can raise additional capital and this increases their capacity to diversify.In addition to offering saving, time and chequing accounts and making loans and investments, SLAs have, since the DIDMC Act, been allowed to issue credit cards and manage trust accounts for customers. Such business was previously the preserve of the commercial banks.

The SLAs ran into trouble in the mid 1970s as interest rates started to rise whilst their deposit rates were fixed by the FHLBB in relation to the rates set by the FRB for the commercial bank deposits.[29] This led to a decline in their deposits as savers sought higher returns by investing in Treasury bills and Money Market Mutual Funds (MMMFs).[30] The supervisors could not simply allow deposit rate ceilings to rise because this would have raised the cost of funds whilst the returns from fixed interest rate mortgages would have remained virtually static. The regulators responded by encouraging SLAs to issue variable rate mortgages and, through the DIDMC Act, they provided for the phasing out of interest rate ceilings and the diversification of SLAs into other retail business to reduce their reliance on the property market.

Mutual savings banks (MSBs) also offer interest bearing NOW and savings accounts and their assets also consist largely of residential mortgages. The distinction between MSBs and SLAs is a technical one rather than a matter of substance. MSBs are normally chartered by one of 18 states, most of which are in the north eastern section of the US. Although organised as mutuals, they are managed by a self perpetuating board of trustees. The final distinction is that they have been allowed to hold specified amounts of demand deposits and to make a limited amount of loans to incorporated businesses. There were around 450 MSBs in the mid 1980s, about a third of which had elected to join the FHLB system. Like the SLAs, they are subject to the uniform reserve requirements set by the FRB under the 1980 Monetary Control Act. They may belong to state based private insurance schemes, where these are available, or to the FDIC's scheme, which covers the commercial banks, rather than the FSLIC's scheme, which covers the federally chartered SLAs and state chartered SLAs that elect to join it in preference to state schemes. There is also a trend amongst MSBs to convert from mutual to public status. By the mid-1980s 155 of the top 300 US savings institutions were publically owned, a much higher proportion than a decade earlier. The MSBs have also been allowed to diversify as a result of the DIDMC and the Garn-St Germain (G-SG) Acts.

Credit Unions (CUs) can also be state or federally chartered. In the mid 1980s there were about 21,500 of them. They are normally small non profit making institutions which accept deposits from, or sell shares to, their memberships and make loans, usually for the purchase of consumer durables, to their members. Unlike European co-operative banks, they are generally organised around a common bond of membership, such as having a common employer or belonging to a club. Employers often provide office facilities on their premises, thereby reducing their costs and allowing them to extend loans at relatively low interest rates. Although small individually and in aggregate, they have become the fastest growing group of deposit taking institutions. This is attributable to the introduction of deposit insurance through the National Credit Union Insurance Fund in 1970 and liberalisation through the DIDMC and G-SG Acts, which has allowed them to diversify and has loosened the 'common bond' requirement enabling more people to join credit unions and making them more like cooperative banks serving local communities.[31]

Investment banks dominate the primary securities markets in corporate stocks and bonds, state and local government securities and government bonds. They issue and underwrite securities, selling and distributing them to their original purchasers. Brokers and dealers are primarily involved in the secondary securities markets. The larger investment banks are also active in the secondary markets; providing brokerage services and dealing and trading on their own accounts. They began to diversify into commercial banking related services in the late 1970s even though they are barred from taking deposits by the Glass-Steagall Act. In 1977 Merrill Lynch took the initiative by introducing cash management accounts (CMAs),[33] which consist of a personal banking package, including: a credit card, instant loans, investment in a money market mutual fund (MMMF), a cheque-book facility and record keeping, including a monthly statement. Other investment banks subsequently offered similar services. MMMFs collect money from private investors and invest it in large amounts in high yielding short term money market instruments such as Treasury bills. The interest is collected by the MMMF and passed to depositors, net of a fee, in the form of a monthly 'dividend' which clearly resembles interest paid on a deposit. MMMFs can be established by companies other than investment banks and can be regarded as non bank depository institutions. Investments in MMMF 'accounts' are not, however, deposits under current legislation. Consequently, they are unregulated in the sense that they are not subject to the FRB's reserve requirements. They were not subject to the interest rate controls on commercial bank or 'thrift' deposits. Their attractiveness may decline now that interest rate controls have been removed and banks and 'thrifts' can offer competitive interest rates because they are not insured and, unless they are backed by chequing facilities, they are less liquid than accounts offered by banks and 'thrifts'.

By exploiting a loophole in the BHC Act, which defines a bank, a number of limited service or 'nonbank' banks have been established by banks wishing to extend their branch networks and other financial institutions and corporations eager to gain an entry into the financial services industry. They do not combine the extension of commercial loans, the provision of payments services, and the taking of deposits and are not, therefore, banks under the BHC Act. Instead they specialise. ATMs supply payments services and cash credits and are not classed as banks, especially if they don't receive deposits. Loan production offices specialise in loans to the corporate and consumer sectors and do not take deposits. Consumer banks take deposits and extend payments services but do not advance loans.

Non deposit taking financial institutions include insurance companies, which are regulated by state governments, private pension funds, and investment companies. They are the major institutional investors in the equity and bond markets. Insurance companies are also significant investors in mortgages. There are also a number of finance companies which generally extend relatively small loans or instalment credits on the basis of large scale borrowing on the wholesale money markets and the capital markets.

A number of federal agencies with distinct financial purposes have been established. Typically, they do not lend directly to ultimate borrowers. They normally guarantee loans made by private sector institutions or, alternatively, lend to such institutions enabling them to relend to the final borrowers. They have been used to further government policy concerning small businesses, agriculture, and home ownership.

The Federal Housing Administration (FHA) insures mortgages against loss to the lender and, by establishing standardised terms, it has helped to create a national home loan market. The Federal National Mortgage Association (Fannie Mae) operates a secondary market for mortgages. It is allowed to sell its own short term notes and to buy government guaranteed mortgages, thereby redirecting funds toward home loans. It has been instrumental in rescheduling and repackaging fixed rate mortgages to give troubled SLAs the opportunity to re-arrange their portfolios and increase the proportion of variable rate mortgages in them.

The farming sector has considerable political power and most of the financial requirements of the agricultural sector are covered by government sponsored programmes. The Farm Credit System (FCS) comprises a set of institutions which provide short, medium and long term farm credit to farmers and agricultural businesses. It is presided over by an independent government agency, the Federal Credit Administration (FCA) and also includes the Federal Land Bank System (FLBS), the Production Credit System (PCS) and the Banks for Cooperatives. The FLBS consists of twelve Federal Land Banks (FLBs), which are the main suppliers of long term credit to farmers in their districts. They do not lend directly to farmers but instead make funds available through FLB Associations, which are owned by the borrowers. The FLBs acquire their funds through the FCS, which issues securities in the money and capital markets. The PCS extends short and medium term credit through twelve Federal Intermediate Credit Banks (FICBs), which do not lend directly but instead make funds available through locally owned and controlled Produce Credit Associations. Additionally, there are numerous farmers' cooperatives created for the purposes of marketing agricultural produce and purchasing inputs. To finance such activities, twelve Banks for Cooperatives have been established within the FCS, which funds them.

In 1958 the Small Business Administration (SBA) was established as a federal agency with the purpose of providing help and guidance to small business firms. Various programmes have been devised, including credit programmes which involve either direct loans or partial guarantees of long term loans made by banks.

The non cash payment system in the US relies heavily on cheques and is highly fragmented. Wages and salaries are commonly paid by cheque and cheques are used extensively to pay bills because standing orders and direct debits are not widely available. There is no nationwide cheque guarantee system and consequently credit cards and travellers cheques are frequently used because of their wide acceptability. Over 70% of households have one or more credit cards. The postal service plays a minor role in the payments system, which has been dominated by banks although 'thrifts' are playing an increasingly important role. ATMs are widely distributed and shared networks are becoming more common. EFTPOS is at an early stage. There have been many pilot and local schemes. It is expected to grow rapidly following the adoption of 'chip' cards in place of magnetic stripe cards.

The federal government is the sole issuer of notes and coins which the twelve Federal Reserve Banks (FRBs) store and distribute to depository institutions. Cheque clearing is undertaken by both private and public sector banks. The FRBs provide the basic infrastructure and operate 48 cheque clearing houses. The Federal Reserve System (FRS) is required to monitor developments in the payments system and to ensure nationwide availability of services. The FRS thus both participates in and regulates the payments system. Prior to the 1980 DIDMC Act, small banks tended to clear cheques through correspondent banks and large banks cleared through the FRBs, which provided services free of charge. The Act required the FRS to recover its costs and ensure the provision of an efficient nationwide service. This requires it to cross-subsidise unprofitable business and allows private banks to compete successfully for profitable business. In the mid 1980s about 30% of cheques were cleared internally by the depository institutions on which they were drawn. The FRS cleared about 35% of cheques and the bank operated clearing houses and correspondent banks cleared the remaining 35%. The FRS thus plays a major role in the clearing system and acts as clearer of last resort. Since the DIDMC Act it has offered its services to all depository institutions, including 'thrifts'.

The banks and the FRBs also compete in the provision of non paper based payments services. Automated Clearing Houses (ACHs) transfer funds electronically. Thirty- three Federal Reserve offices were processing ACH transactions in the mid 1980s and there were three privately operated ACHs; the New York Clearing House Association (NYCHA) and the local Arizona and Hawaii ACHs. The FRS service was introduced in 1973 and initially concentrated on interbank transactions. Since then the ACHs have become more widely used for salary payments and for regular payments involving insurance premiums and mortgages and, after 1983, corporations began to use ACHs for trade payments. The FRS dominates the ACH system which many believe to be a natural monopoly. The FRS is required to cover its cost. It has adopted a long run pricing policy designed to encourage usage to enable the provision of services to move toward the minimum efficient scale. This pricing policy has tended to discourage competition from private sector correspondent banks because of the high entry costs.

The ACH system concentrates mainly on retail payments. There are a number of interbank communications networks which are used for high value wholesale transfers and interbank payments. Fed Wire links all the FRS offices and handles transfers of account balances between member banks. Bankwire is a private communications system serving a number of major North American banks. Its net settlement system, Cashwire, offers settlement through the FRS. CHIPS is an interbank funds transfer system operated by the NYCHA. CHESS is a Chicago based system similar to CHIPS. SWIFT, the international bank communications network based in Belgium and owned by member banks throughout the world, is also used quite extensively by US banks for domestic interbank transactions.

iii) Regulation and Supervision

Before getting to grips with the complex supervisory structure it is helpful to review briefly the major US banking legislation.

The 1863 National Bank Act (NBA), which was significantly amended in 1864, lays down the law for federally chartered banks. Charters are granted by the Comptroller of Currency, who is the Chief Officer of the Office of the Comptroller of Currency (OCC) within the Treasury Department and is in charge of administering the national banking system.

The 1913 Federal Reserve Act created the Federal Reserve System (FRS) to serve as the central bank of the US. It was not the first central bank in US history and the country's banking system had operated for a lengthy period without a central bank.[34] The law was later refined by the 1933 and 1935 Banking Acts, in the wake of the Great Crash in 1929 and the ensuing banking crisis. The 1913 Act details the principal functions of the FRS. It is required to: regulate the money supply; hold the legal reserves of member banks; meet demands for currency; effect nationwide funds transfers and promote and facilitate cheque clearing; examine and supervise member banks chartered by various states and obtain periodic reports from them; collect and interpret economic information with a bearing on credit problems; and act as fiscal agent and custodian of government funds as well as legal depository for the US Treasury and all other government departments.

The FRS fulfils these requirements through its Board of Governors, the Federal Reserve Board (FRB), and the Federal Open Market Committee (FOMC), the Federal Advisory Council (FAC), the Federal Reserve Banks and their branches and member banks.

The 1927 McFadden Act permitted national banks to establish intrastate branches in order to allow them to compete with state-chartered banks that were allowed to branch statewide. It did not, however, permit national banks to cross state lines. In conjunction with the Douglas amendment to the 1956 Bank Holding Company (BHC) Act, the McFadden Act attempts to prohibit interstate branching by banks.

The 1933 Glass-Steagall (G-S) Act, which is a subsection of the 1933 Banking Act, and its amending legislation, the 1935 Banking Act, prevented the speculative use of bank credit and provided for the separation of banking and securities business. It prohibited banks from acting as agents in securities transactions with brokers and dealers and from directly underwriting corporate securities. In addition the 1933 Banking Act created the Federal Open Market Committee (FOMC), to formulate and oversee the execution of monetary policy, and the Federal Deposit Insurance Corporation (FDIC), which was dealt with more fully in the Federal Deposit Insurance Act. The FDIC is managed by a board of directors and is a government corporation that insures individual deposits up to a preset value.[35] National banks are required to subscribe to the FDIC and state chartered banks may elect to do so. Federally chartered SLAs and MSBs belong to a similar scheme administered by the FSLIC.

The 1956 BHC Act and its amendments limit the activities of BHCs to areas of bank management and control. They require divestiture of non banking interests that have no close relationship to banking, which is defined to include deposit taking, commercial lending and the provision of payments services. BHCs are required to register with the FRS and are regulated by the provisions of its regulation Y.

The 1919 Edge Act authorised the federal chartering of corporations, known as Edge Act Corporations (EACs), for the express purpose of engaging in international or foreign banking or other international or foreign financial operations. Fund raising and lending activities of EACs must be related to the financing of international trade. Regulation K of the FRS governs their activities and they are permitted to be established by national or state banks nationwide.

Prior to the 1978 International Banking Act (IBA) there was no general banking legislation applying to foreign bank operations in the US. It put foreign and domestic banks on a more equal footing.

The 1980 Monetary Control Act (MCA) gave the FRS broader authority to set reserve requirements. It applies to all FDIC insured banks, MSBs, insured CUs, federally chartered SLAs, EACs, International Banking Facilities (IBFs)[36] and foreign bank branches and agencies where the foreign bank has consolidated worldwide assets in excess of $1bn. It effectively gave the FRB authority to set reserve requirements for all sizeable deposit taking institutions. In return they were given access to the services provided by the FRS. As a result of the MCA, virtually all time and deposit accounts are subject to reserve requirements.

The 1980 Depository Institutions Deregulation Act (DIDA) was passed in tandem with the MCA. It provided for the phasing out of regulations on rates of interest and dividends payable on deposits over a six year period. The process was completed in March 1986 and was overseen by the DID Committee (DIDC) which consisted of : the Secretary of the Treasury; the Chairmen of the Federal Reserve Board, the FDIC, the FHLBB, and the National Credit Union Board (NCUB); and the Comptroller of Currency. It had the effect of eliminating administered interest rate differentials between commercial banks and 'thrifts'.

The 1982 Garn-St Germain Depository Institutions Act (GSGA) aimed to revitalise the housing market by modifying regulations applying to 'thrifts' to give them greater scope to diversify.[37]

The Federal Reserve Board permitted the establishment of IBFs from December 1981 to allow banks to win back offshore business, especially from the Eurodollar market. IBFs are offshore banking facilities operated by federally or state chartered banks. They are exempt from the reserve requirements set by the FRB and enjoy varying degrees of relief from taxation according to the state or city in which they are located. They are, however, subject to federal taxation. IBFs have proved attractive to foreign depositors because they are protected by US banking laws and they have been successful in attracting offshore funds back to the US.[38] They are not subject to interstate branching restrictions but they must concentrate on international business, although this need not be related to international trade as is the case for EACs.

The supervisory structure is rather complex in the US because regulation is shared between a number of agencies. This is partly because of the dual authorisation system which leads to both state and federal bank regulation. The National Bank Act had vested supervisory responsibility over federally chartered banks in the OCC. The OCC is headed by the Comptroller, who is nominated by the Secretary of the Treasury and appointed by the President, subject to Senate approval, for a five year term. The OCC is legally subject to the general direction of the Secretary of the Treasury but it traditionally operates autonomously. It is required to submit reports to Congress but is financially independent.

The central banking system was established in 1913, following a major banking crisis, in order to regulate the flow of money and bank credit and to provide liquidity to banks in distress. In order to maintain decentralisation twelve Federal Reserve Banks were established. These were to be subject to co-ordination, regulation and supervision by a Board of Governors in Washington DC. The FRB has in practice adopted the major policy making role with the Federal Reserve Banks playing a supervisory role in their regions and supplying money transmission services.[39] The FRB was rather passive until the bank failures of the 1930s, after which its control over interest rates was increased and it was empowered to impose interest rate ceilings. Membership of the FRS is compulsory for national banks and optional for state banks. The FRS is an independent agency in the sense that it is not attached to any other bureau, department or agency in the federal government. The seven person ruling Board of Governors is appointed by the President. Appointments are long term[40] and cannot be revoked. Nevertheless, there is some debate about its true degree of independence from White House influence.[41] Its chairman has to report bi-annually to the Congressional and Senate Banking Committees. The FOMC's monetary policy is supposed to be consistent with the government's economic objectives and consequently its chairman is required to report to other Congressional committees concerning the role of monetary and exchange rate policy in general economic policy.

In addition to having responsibility for the conduct of monetary policy, the FRB has wide supervisory powers over its member banks. It does not grant charters but it does conduct bank examinations and grant permission for mergers, branching, and holding company acquisitions. Additionally, it sets reserve requirements for all depository institutions that handle transactions accounts. The formation of the FRS, therefore, led to the FRB sharing supervisory duties with the OCC and the state regulators. The responsibilities were divided as follows : the OCC regulated national banks whilst the FRB concentrated on state banks which had elected to join the FRS; non members being the responsibility of state authorities. Also, under the BHC Act, the FRB has responsibility for regulating and supervising BHCs and for monitoring mergers and takeovers concerning BHCs.

The establishment of the FDIC in 1934 added another regulatory tier. All members of the FRS were required to participate in the deposit insurance scheme and non members were allowed to join on a voluntary basis provided that they were willing to accept the requirements laid down by the FDIC. The vast majority of commercial banks have joined, membership being virtually a competitive necessity. The FDIC, therefore, extends supervisory authority over virtually all US banks. It is financed by annual insurance premiums paid by member banks.[42] In line with its responsibility for protecting deposits it conducts bank examinations and supervision in order to prevent bank failures. When failures do occur, however, it makes prompt payments to holders of protected accounts, by drawing on the protection fund. The FDIC has been fairly successful in imposing uniform standards of sound management throughout the banking system and in so doing it has been able to influence the behaviour of small state chartered banks that do not belong to the FRS. It is also empowered to facilitate mergers between troubled insured banks and sound insured banks, provided that branching restrictions are not violated. This is done by lending funds to or buying some assets from the distressed bank to make a merger attractive to the other party. It is also authorised to lend to or buy assets from insured banks in danger of failing if the failure would have damaging consequences for the local or national banking system. In the early 1980s, with the number of bank failures rising, it was allowed to authorise interstate mergers of failing and healthy insured banks where local merger partners could not be found.

The formation of the FDIC meant that state banks were subject to both state and FDIC regulation, if they were not members of the FRS, and subject to regulation by the FDIC and the FRB, if they were members of the FRS. National banks meanwhile were regulated by both the OCC and the FDIC and, in some respects, by the FRB, which also regulates the BHCs. Banks can and do switch between federal and state charters according to perceived costs and benefits.

Each state in the union has some supervisory authority over banks chartered by it. Their duties are broadly analogous to those of the OCC concerning national banks. They grant charters, conduct examinations, promulgate regulations, rule on mergers and acquisitions and so on. They frequently also regulate and supervise other state chartered financial institutions, particularly 'thrifts'.

Apart from the three federal agencies and the state authorities the Department of Justice (DoJ) and the Securities and Exchange Commission (SEC) also exert a regulatory influence. The DoJ monitors and controls the expansion and merger of banks and 'thrifts' to enforce general anti-trust laws and also plays a role in detecting and prosecuting fraud. The SEC, which was established in 1943, has the task of supervising the securities markets and it imposes statutory controls for the protection of investors. This means that it can and does exercise a healthy interest in the capitalisation of banks quoted on the Stock Exchange and in their attempts to participate in the securities markets. It takes a particular interest in the activities of BHCs.

SLAs may be state or federally chartered. The latter are subject to regulation by the FHLBB. Membership of the FHLB system is mandatory for federally chartered SLAs and optional for state chartered SLAs. Nearly 90% of SLAs belong to the system and these SLAs have about 98% of all SLA deposits. The FHLBB is empowered to examine member associations. Through its twelve regional offices, it may extend loans to individual associations. Short term loans are made to enable SLAs to meet deposit withdrawals and long term loans are designed to allow them to purchase additional mortgages if local sources of funds are inadequate. The FHLBB obtains its funds by selling securities in the capital market. Branching restrictions on SLAs are considerably more liberal than those applied to commercial banks and state laws do not take precedence. SLA deposits may be insured by the FSLIC, which all federally chartered SLAs are required to join. Membership is optional for state chartered SLAs and some states[43] have their own private SLA deposit insurance schemes. Like other 'thrifts', SLAs have been subject to FRS reserve requirements since the 1980 MCA. Since then they have also had access to the FRS's discount window for short term loans and access to the FRS's cheque clearing operations for their NOW accounts.

Most MSBs are regulated by the states in which they do business but they may be insured by the FDIC, rather than the FSLIC. They are subject to the provisions of the MCA and they may join the FHLB system, but less than half have chosen to do so. CUs may be chartered either by state or federal governments under the 1934 Federal Credit Union Act. Since 1970 deposits have been insured by the National Credit Union Share Insurance Fund, which is comparable to the FDIC and the FSLIC. CUs are also subject to the provisions of the MCA.

The wider banking system, consisting of 'thrifts' and banks, is, therefore, regulated by four federal agencies,[44] as well as state authorities, the SEC and the DoJ. Some rationalisation would appear to be possible and a White House Committee chaired by Vice President George Bush, called the Bush Taskforce, was established to consider ways of simplifying the supervisory system. At one stage it wanted to upgrade the OCC to create a new federal banking agency which would have taken over the FRB's responsibilities concerning nationally chartered banks. The FRB opposed such a development[45] and eventually gained support for its case from the Treasury Department. The Chairman of the FRB, Paul Volcker, argued that the FRB's intimate knowledge of the banking system, gleaned from its participation in bank supervision, was essential to its effective functioning in its roles of formulating and executing monetary policy. The final proposals, published in 1984, had not led to any legislation by 1987. The three federal bank regulators seem, however, to have worked together more closely since 1984, following the Bush Task Force Report and the Continental Illinois crisis. They have jointly imposed minimum capital requirements and have lobbied Congress for new banking legislation: to regulate the pace of the de facto deregulation that has been going on; and to help deal with the problem energy and farm banks and 'thrifts'. In order to deal with the problem banks the supervisory authorities need flexibility. This was threatened in April 1986 when the Office of Management and Budget (OMB) asserted its jurisdiction over the FDIC, the OCC, and the FHLBB. Given their financial independence these regulatory agencies believed the OMB's claims were unfounded.

Following the 1982 Mexican Crisis the bank supervisors encouraged banks to increase their capital ratios and loan loss provisions. Prior to 1982 there was no uniform policy on capital adequacy amongst the three federal banking regulators. Following the 1984 Continental Illinois crisis the three agencies announced yet higher minimum capital requirements entailing a 5.5% primary capital to total assets ratio and a 6% total capital to total assets ratio. In 1986 the FRB issued proposals for risk related capital requirements. These were similar to those adopted by the Bank of England and recommended by the Basle Committee on bank supervision.[46] Risk based ratios had been abandoned in the 1960s in favour of more flexible controls. Following consultations the guidelines were finalised. They are to work in tandem with the minimum guidelines announced in 1985 and will apply to all banks with assets greater than $1bn and take account of off balance sheet risks for the first time. Nifs required capital backing of 30% of a standard loan, compared with the 50% weight given by the Bank of England. These guidelines were further modified in 1987 following the issue in January 1987 of joint proposals, by the Bank of England and the three US federal banking supervisory agencies, to create a common system for measuring the capital strength of banks in the two countries. The risk asset ratio approach was applied more rigorously, especially to off balance sheet items, and the requirements on Nifs were more in line with those previously introduced in the US. The two countries hoped that other banking authorities, especially the Japanese ones, would adopt similar arrangements. Otherwise commercial bank cooperation could not be counted upon because the US and UK commercial banks felt that Japanese banks were already operating with more liberal capital requirements and would be at a further advantage if the US and UK banks alone were subject to the proposed requirements.

The major problem facing the regulators in the mid 1980s was the record number of failures amongst both banks and 'thrifts'. In 1986 the energy banks took over from the farm banks as the major problem group. The three federal bank regulatory agencies announced a plan to ease the crisis facing banks with heavy loan exposure to the farming sector. They also hinted that, if necessary, it would be applied to banks with heavy exposures to Latin American debtors and the energy sector. The plan permitted banks to slip below their minimum capital requirements in the medium term and relaxed reporting rules; so that restructured loans were not automatically classified as non performing.

The adoption of the risk asset ratio approach to capital adequacy should restrict the rate of bank diversification into more risky assets. Reinforcing this approach was the decision of the FDIC, in March 1986, to double the premium for federal deposit insurance charged to more risky banks. The two tier system will require risky banks to pay $\frac{2}{12}$ of 1% of their domestic deposits to the FDIC instead of the normal $\frac{1}{12}$ of 1%, The aim is to make it harder for risky banks to expand at the rate of healthy banks. The problem of reforming the FDIC's scheme is another of the major concerns of the bank regulators. The large banks have frequently complained that because premia do not vary with size and because larger banks are normally safer than smaller ones, by virtue of having larger and often more diversified portfolios, they are effectively subsidising smaller banks which should pay relatively larger premiums. The larger banks, however, tend to have a larger proportion of uninsured deposits[47] and, as the Continental Illinois rescue[48] demonstrated, these are insured de facto. The debate about the appropriate way of setting premia has dragged on for years but recently proposals for a risk based insurance scheme[49] have gained wider acceptance. The FDIC's decision to introduce a two tier system can be interpreted as a step in the direction of a risk based scheme. The FDIC can only take over the running of a bank once it has been closed by the regulators. It was seeking power from Congress in 1986 to allow it to intervene prior to closure; to enable it to manage the affairs of troubled banks for a limited period whilst it sought a suitable merger partner. In 1986 the FDIC also sanctioned the transfer of its responsibilities for regulating the registration, disclosure and reporting of publically owned banks to the SEC. This had been recommended by the Bush Task Force.

With failures rising, the FDIC was experiencing a major drain on its resources and in April 1986 the bank regulators requested Congress to pass a law allowing the interstate acquisition of banks in difficulty, in order to make it easier to find buyers. The existing law permitting acquisitions of medium sized troubled banks expired in that month. The regulators wanted the law to be renewed and extended to cover smaller banks. The aim was to deal with the problems amongst energy and farming banks at minimum cost on the FDIC. In the absence of legislation the state regulators were forced to take matters into their own hands. In September 1986, for example, Texas, a unit bank state hit particularly hard by the oil price fall, relaxed its banking law to allow out of state rescues of banks and SLAs. It was also considering a constitutional amendment to allow statewide banking.

The federal bank regulators have lobbied consistently, through reports to Congressional committees and other channels, for comprehensive banking legislation to cover both product and geographic deregulation. They are concerned at the pace of the piecemeal de facto deregulation occurring through the exploitation of loopholes in existing legislation. Increasingly they are facing applications from banks to undertake new business and from other business to open limited service banks and their rulings are being challenged with a growing frequency by disappointed banks or by the Securities and Investments Association. The SIA represents the firms in the securities industry. They wish to maintain the current arrangements excluding banks from various securities business in order to protect their market positions. In October 1986 the Comptroller went further by calling for a change in the law to allow US banks to compete effectively in the rapidly growing global financial markets. He felt that the current laws contradicted their purpose, which was to reinforce the stability of the banking system. Instead of doing this they weakened the banks by restricting their ability to diversify and spread risks. He also expressed his concern that there was only one US bank in the world's top ten and drew attention to the facts that US banks could do things in London and Tokyo that they could not do in New York and that foreign banks were forming relationships with US securities houses whilst US banks were severely limited in the types of business they could engage in.

In January 1987 the president of the New York Federal Reserve Bank, Mr Gerald Corrigan, suggested that reforms should be introduced to ensure the separation of banking and commerce. Large commercial companies such as Sears Roebuck and the Ford motor company, which had expanded rapidly into the financial services industry, should be forced to dispose of their banking operations. In addition, most of the legal barriers preventing some classes of financial institutions from engaging in certain types of financial activity should be removed. Common corporate ownership of banks, 'thrifts' and insurance and securities companies should be permitted and so too should combinations of commercial companies and non-bank financial institutions. The resulting financial conglomerates would need to be subject to consolidated supervision by the authorities. Mr Corrigan's proposals would generate a financial environment akin to the post 'big bang' London one. UK commercial banks have not traditionally held equity stakes in non-financial companies but they have evolved into financial conglomerates. In both Germany and Japan banks have traditionally held sizeable equity stakes in non-financial companies and this has been increasingly criticised because of its potential for creating conflicts of interest. In both countries there are moves to reduce such equity holdings, see sections 2.2 and 3.2. Mr Corrigan's proposals are, therefore, consistent with international trends. In March 1987, however, proposed banking legislation was stalled, as mentioned at the end of the previous section. It is, therefore, possible that more comprehensive legislation consistent with Mr Corrigan's proposals can now be considered.

The SLAs have been another problem group. The record failures in the mid 1980s had severely drained the resources of the FSLIC. The Continental Illinois crisis had reminded the regulators that, despite deposit insurance, panic can spread rapidly. Runs on the privately insured SLAs in Maryland and Ohio in 1985 provided a similar warning for the FHLBB. Many of the privately insured SLAs have since been encouraged to join the FSLIC. The FSLIC is, however, severely undercapitalised and various schemes have been proposed to bolster its funding. In order to take some pressure off the FSLIC the FHLBB has lobbied for legislation to allow greater freedom to arrange mergers between troubled SLAs and out of state banks. In line with the FDIC's treatment of troubled banks, the FSLIC has decided to charge higher premia to troubled 'thrifts' in order to curb their ability to expand. As 1986 wore on and the list of failed SLAs continued to grow whilst the number of SLAs virtually insolvent remained large, the FHLBB repeatedly warned of the rapid decline in the FSLIC's resources. The FHLBB gained some support from the FRB, which decided to waive the requirement on BHCs to operate acquired 'thrifts' as separately capitalised subsidiaries. Citicorp had applied to the FRB, in May 1986, for permission to sell banking services through acquired 'thrifts'. The FRB's aim was to increase the attractiveness of failing 'thrifts' to BHCs and and to make it easier for the FHLBB to arrange mergers without having to close 'thrifts' and draw on the funds of the FSLIC. In early 1986 the FHLBB also took the precaution of requiring marginal 'thrifts' to boost their capital bases. They complained that this amounted to back door re-regulation because it inhibited their ability to exploit the opportunity to diversify granted by the DIDMC Act and the G-SG Act.

Toward the end of 1986 Congress came to the rescue of the troubled SLAs and farm banks. Two separate bills were introduced to Congress in October 1986. One contained proposals to recapitalise the FSLIC by setting up an organisation to use the retained earnings of the twelve regional FHLBs as a base for borrowing in the capital markets. The funds raised would then be passed to the FSLIC in order to allow it to continue to meet its obligations towards the depositors of failed 'thrifts'. The scheme aims to keep the FSLIC afloat without an injection of Treasury funds. The latter may eventually prove necessary, however, because over a third of the 3,200 or so SLAs insured by the FSLIC are judged to be close to insolvency because they have to pay above market rates to attract deposits. The other bill, which concerned the FCS, was an amendment to legislation, passed in 1985, which had sought to put off a Treasury rescue. The 1985 legislation had required a pooling of FCS assets to shore up weaker lenders. It was successfully opposed by the more profitable members of the FCS and a Treasury bail out was eventually required. The new legislation allows the FCS to reschedule some of the debt over a twenty year period. Many analysts expect that the Treasury will again be required to inject funds.

iv) Deregulation

A distinction is often drawn in the US between geographic, interest rate, and product deregulation. Geographic deregulation covers the breakdown of branching restrictions imposed by state banking supervisory authorities and through the McFadden Act and the Douglas amendment to the BHC Act. Interest rate deregulation relates to the removal of the FRB's regulation Q and related restrictions, imposed by the other regulatory authorities, on interest rates paid on deposits. Product deregulation entails both financial instrument innovation and product diversification which leads groups of financial institutions to offer services previously associated by other groups of institutions. Deregulation, therefore, encompasses not only the liberalisation of banking regulations but also de facto deregulation, which entails the exploitation of loopholes in existing regulations, and financial innovation.

Financial innovation was a response to the high inflation rates of the 1970s and increased volatility in exchange and interest rates. Interest rates have both risen and become more variable in countries that have attempted to reduce inflation by controlling the rate of growth of the money supply. This approach to monetary policy was adopted by most of the larger OECD countries in the late 1970s. Whilst some of these countries have dropped or downgraded the formal targeting of monetary aggregates, interest rates have been retained as the prime monetary policy instrument. Following the breakdown of the Smithsonian Agreement[50] in the early 1970s there was a widespread adoption of floating exchange rates. Subsequently, exchange rates have become more volatile. In the mid 1980s a number of countries, including the UK, came to regard exchange rate targeting as a viable alternative anti-inflationary policy to monetary targeting. Because central banks' reserves had become small relative to international monetary flows it was virtually impossible to hit exchange rate targets without supportive interest rate movements. Interest rates were the only policy instrument capable of responding rapidly to changes in currency market sentiment. Consequently they became the most important monetary policy instrument to countries adopting exchange rate targets. Although inflation had been reduced in the mid 1980s, the continuing volatility of exchange and interest rates, in the absence of a new international monetary agreement, was likely to encourage further innovation. Much of the innovation has been designed to attract business by offering instruments which provide hedges against inflation and interest and exchange rate risks. The financial innovation has itself been made possible by technological innovations in the fields of telecommunications and data processing which have, since the 1970s, been widely adopted by the international banking community in which US banks figure prominently.

In the US, interest rate deregulation was completed in March 1986 under the guidance of the DIDC, which was established by the 1980 DIDMC Act. This provided for the phased removal of regulation Q and other interest rate restrictions and the widespread introduction of new financial instruments, such as NOW accounts and MMMFs.[51] The interest rate restrictions had prohibited interest payments on demand deposits and set maximum rates on time and savings deposits. They were designed to protect the market position of the 'thrifts' because of their mutual status and special role in the provision of home loans. Pressure for the deregulation of interest rates had built up in the 1970s. Accelerating inflation had led to a rise in market related interest rates and this provided investors with the opportunity to earn higher returns outside the banks and 'thrifts'. The SLAs responded by offering NOW accounts, which were effectively interest bearing cheque accounts, in the mid 1970s, whilst the investment banks and other institutions began to offer MMMFs towards the end of the 1970s to attract deposits that would normally have gone to commercial banks or 'thrifts'. 'Thrifts' were, therefore, diversifying into retail banking business whilst other institutions were beginning to make inroads into the traditional deposit taking business of the banks and the 'thrifts'. The DIDMC Act responded to the de facto deregulation by providing for the removal of interest rate restrictions and, therefore, the favoured position of the 'thrifts' in the deposit taking market. In return for the loss of privilege they were allowed to diversify further into retail banking business and to extend corporate loans. This process was reinforced by the 1982 G-SG Act. The 1971 Hunt Commission Report had advocated freer competition between banks and other deposit taking institutions. This had occurred de facto in the 1970s and was ratified in the 1980s. The effect was to increase competition for deposits and raise the return to investors in depository institutions, reinforcing the rise in real interest rates.

The banks also faced stiffer competition in the retail banking sector from other sources in the 1980s. The investment banks, for example, having already introduced MMMFs began to offer Cash Management Accounts (CMAs), which added current account facilities to the MMMF facility. Meanwhile the banks' corporate business had also begun to be squeezed in the 1970s by the growth in the commercial paper market (CP), through which corporate treasuries can lend and borrow without bank intermediation. Its growth accelerated in the 1980s when interest in securities became more widespread. This trend has allowed investment banks to attract fee earning corporate business. They have proved particularly adept at devising new instruments to serve the increasingly sophisticated needs of their growing number of corporate clients. Faced with the loss of high quality corporate business at a time when they were nursing problem loans to Latin American countries, the major money centre banks have tried to latch on to the trend towards securitisation in order to boost their fee earning business. They have also been providing discount broking services through their branches since the New York Stock Exchange reform on May Day 1975. They have stepped up their activity in this area in the 1980s because they have concentrated more on domestic, rather than international, markets following the 1982 Mexican crisis. Their moves into discount broking and CP distribution and other securities business, whilst sanctioned by the regulators, have not gone unchallenged by the securities industry, which is represented by the Securities and Investments Associations (SIA).

The SIA has claimed that many of the banks' activities violate the Glass-Steagall (G-S) Act. Through the courts the SIA has challenged a number of the liberalising rulings of the regulatory agencies. The regulators are in a difficult position because they feel that banks need to diversify to spread risk, especially following interest rate deregulation and in the light of the international trend towards securitisation. They have, therefore, been disposed to allowing de facto deregulation, by permitting the exploitation of loopholes in the existing legislation, whilst lobbying for a major reform in banking legislation. Understandably the securities industry has sought to protect its interests whilst exploiting loopholes allowing entry into banking business and opportunities to diversify into banking business in more liberal centres such as London. The banks meanwhile regard the development of their securities business to be essential if they are to keep contacts with corporate clients and cross sell other products. They are driven, therefore, not just by a desire to add to profits by winning fee earning business but as a defensive measure to protect the flow of profits from other sources.

The G-S Act prohibits commercial banks from dealing in and underwriting corporate securities. Interpretations of the terms dealing, underwriting and securities are matters for debate, however, in the financial markets of the 1980s. Further, banks cannot own companies that are primarily engaged in proscribed securities business. Commercial banks are, however, allowed to deal in a number of public sector securities alongside investment banks, including Treasury Bonds. The US Treasury Bonds market had become the world's largest financial market by the mid 1980s. The intepretation of the term dealing was crucial to the decision to allow banks to offer discount broking services. The banks argued that by simply selling shares to the public, whilst not offering advice, they were merely acting as agents rather than dealers. The Supreme Court finally ruled against the SIA in January 1986, permitting banks to offer discount brokerage services through subsidiaries. The case dated back to 1983 when the Comptroller approved requests by banks to establish discount broking subsidiaries. With the banks still prohibited from dealing in equities on their own account there seems little reason to prevent banks from offering full broking services incorporating research and advice. This is because conflicts of interest and the potential for insider dealing would be limited. In June 1986 the investment banking arm of NatWest became the first foreign bank to be allowed, by the FRB, to offer investment banking services, including both broking and research facilities. It was, however, barred from underwriting. This ruling set a precedent and is likely to be challenged by the SIA.

The case regarding the distribution of CP was still under consideration in 1986. Banks had moved into the business as a result of a long standing ruling that CP was not a security. This was reversed in 1984. The case then revolved around whether or not CP dealing constituted underwriting. The FRB ruled that it did not. This was challenged by the SIA, which received a favourable ruling, from a district court in February 1986, concerning its suit against Bankers Trust, the commercial bank that had moved into the market most aggressively. The matter will probably have to be resolved by the Supreme Court in the absence of Congressional legislation. A favourable ruling is expected on the grounds that the banks are acting solely as agents. In other areas of securitisation, First Boston, which in partnership with Credit Suisse owns an affiliate, Credit Suisse-First Boston (CFSB), which is a leading firm in the Eurobond market, has been highly innovative.[52] The trend towards securitisation has been encouraged not only by the desire to reduce the risks inherent in loans by making them effectively tradeable but also by a switch out of tangible assets into securities. The latter has been encouraged by the fall in inflation, against which tangible assets, especially houses and precious metals, have been a traditional hedge, and the rise in real interest rates. Falls in the prices of tangible assets, such as real estate, have also increased the risks involved in loans by reducing the value of collateral.

The G-S Act's provisions, like the interest rate regulations, are coming under increasing pressure as more and more loopholes are exploited and de facto deregulation proceeds. The entry into US investment banking by Nat West's subsidiary and the partnership formed by Goldman Sachs, one of the larger US investment banks, and Sumitomo Bank, one of Japan's larger commercial banks, call into question the future of separating investment and commercial banking in the US. Meanwhile US commercial and investment banks are allowed to provide universal banking services through offices and subsidiaries abroad, especially in London. By allowing the commercial banks to participate in securities business abroad the FRB presumably hopes that they can build up a track record in the securities business that will make the G-S Act an anachromism.

Geographic deregulation has also accelerated in the 1980s, again largely de facto in the absence of Congressional legislation. There has also been a considerable amount of state deregulation in the 1980s. Most of this provides for interstate branching in the limited sense that 'out of state' banks from states with reciprocal legislation can establish branches. Groups of states have participated in regional agreements and other states have provided for reciprocal agreements with any other state.[53]

Money centre banks are often excluded and Citicorp consequently challenged the legality of the regional banking pacts. The Supreme Court ruled against Citicorp in June 1985, declaring regional interstate merger pacts constitutional. Many states, such as California, have provided for a move to full interstate branching in the early 1990s. The aim is to allow the formation of large regional banks capable of competing with the money centre banks when full interstate banking becomes a reality in the early 1990s. In the interim the money centre banks are likely to continue to build up their nationwide presence by extending their ATM networks, acquiring failing banks and 'thrifts', and establishing 'non bank' or limited service banks. Citicorp, for example, operates in one way or another in 41 states and can accept deposits in seventeen of them. This has been achieved largely by acquiring failing institutions and by taking advantage of the opportunity to move into states offering nationwide rather than regional reciprocal agreements. The proliferation of limited service banks in a country already regarded as overbanked is causing the regulators concern. It is leading to unregulated branching and allowing companies with substantial non banking interests to enter into banking business in an unregulated manner. The regulators have been requesting legislation on 'nonbank' banks since 1984, when the OCC ruled that they were legal and was subsequently swamped by applications for authorisation. It declared a six month moratorium to allow it to process existing applications[54] and in the hope that Congress would legislate. With no legislation forthcoming, it was forced to lift the moratorium in October 1984. De facto branching has also been occurring for some time through the development of BHCs. If ATMs, which are not currently regarded as branches because of the limited services they offer, are eventually allowed to take deposits and provide other services, in addition to granting withdrawals, interstate banking could effectively develop quite rapidly. The general development in electronic banking makes nationwide branching a practical proposition and when it is eventually formally permitted the clearing system will have to adapt accordingly. Even the last bastions of unit banking are beginning to fall. Following the Continental Illinois crisis in 1984, Illinois has taken a more liberal approach to intrastate branching and, faced with problems amongst banks exposed to the energy sector, Texas also took action. In September 1986 Texas relaxed its banking law to allow out of state banks to rescue failing banks and SLAs and a bill proposing a constitutional amendment to allow statewide branching was also under consideration. There were about 1,500 banks in Texas at the time and, once opened up, Texas is expected to become the second largest[55] banking market in the US.

Geographic deregulation has been proceeding by both branching, or de novo entry, and mergers. Merger activity has accelerated since 1981 when two Supreme Court rulings made it clear that horizontal, as opposed to conglomerate, bank mergers that did not violate federal or state banking legislation could only be stopped if they were against the public interest, as defined under general anti-trust legislation. Since then there has been a wave of mergers because the FRB was forced to take a more liberal approach to them. It had previously barred mergers which it deemed to be against the public interest even where there was no clear anti-trust law violation. The court effectively ruled that the bank regulators were not empowered to do this. Since the rulings, both the number and the size of bank mergers have increased. As a result of the later ruling on the legality of regional interstate banking pacts, a second merger wave is expected with a number of large regional banks emerging as a result. There has also been an increase in merger activity amongst BHCs. This activity is likely to be monitored more closely because a single merger can simultaneously reduce competition in a number of different markets. As product deregulation proceeds many feel that conglomerate mergers will become more common. These may be difficult to prevent because they are not obviously anti-competitive. If such a tendency develops universal banking will be brought much closer and the traditional separation between banks and non-financial corporations may also disappear.

Geographic expansion and product diversification both absorb bank capital and both can potentially contribute to the reduction of risks incurred by banks. The regulators are keen to ensure that risks are reduced as far as possible by guiding the banks towards the correct mix of product and geographic extension.[56] Reduced fragmentation can ensure that a larger proportion of banks have sound retail bases. Product diversification can spread risks but it can also increase risks if not regulated because it allows banks to move into business where they face more experienced competitors. The regulators seem to have adopted the view that product diversification is desirable in the longer term but should go hand in hand with geographic extension to ensure that banks can absorb the short term risks incurred by moving into new business.

Another significant deregulatory development was the FRB's decision in 1981 to permit the establishment of IBFs. Like the Edge Act, this allowed banks to establish specialised offices nationwide. The FRB took this action to allow US depository institutions to become more competitive in conducting business with non US residents. Through IBFs, foreign institutions can conduct banking transactions in the US free from reserve requirements and without the cost of insurance by the FDIC. Additionally, some states have granted IBFs exemptions from locally imposed taxes. IBF transactions take place almost exclusively with non-residents and their assets and liabilities are denominated almost entirely in dollars. The IBFs have been successful in winning back business lost to the Eurodollar market and other offshore centres, especially in the Caribbean. They introduced offshore banking facilities to the US whilst keeping the offshore business separate from the domestic markets. Similar facilities were introduced in Japan in 1986 and will be discussed in the next section. In other centres, such as London, it has not been deemed necessary to segregate offshore and domestic business. With deregulation and globalisation proceeding apace the segregation may disappear in the future.

In the light of the rapid de facto deregulation and the lobbying from the regulators, US banking legislation is likely to be revised before the end of the decade . In March 1987, however, not only was the proposed legislation shelved, at least temporarily, but the FRB seems likely to be prevented from exploiting its discretionary powers to permit de facto deregulation, for at least a year, whilst a new banking bill is formulated that has a greater chance of being passed by Congress. If the regulators get their way, the legislation will be generally liberalising but will empower them to regulate deregulation in order to maintain standards of depositor and, more generally, investor protection. Diversification makes provisions for investor protection necessary, as the UK authorities have acknowledged, because of the conflicts of interest that are created.

The insider dealing scandals,[57] involving Dennis Levine and Ivan Boesky, that erupted towards the end of 1986 and eventually led the SEC to uncover further cases of insider dealing in early 1987, demonstrated that investment banks are not immune from conflicts of interest. The separation of their brokerage and dealing activities has been inadequately policed by their compliance officers. A more rigorous application of self regulation seems, therefore, to be required to assure adequate investor protection. The implications of the episode will not be ignored by the UK supervisory authorities. Insider dealing has been rife despite the existence of the SEC, which has more substantial investigatory powers and greater statutory backing than the UK's nascent SIB. 'Chinese walls' and compliance officers have not been able to prevent it. One answer seems to lie in extending the powers and improving the training of compliance officers and perhaps increasing their number, in line with the growing volume of securities trading, and make them more independent of the firms in which they work, which currently employ them.

The elimination of the separation of commercial and investment banking would possibly increase the incidence of of conflicts of interest and the potential for insider dealing and one might, therefore, expect the scandals to have have reduced the chance of legislation to remove the G-S Act. They have, however, demonstrated that the G-S Act does not eliminate the potential for insider dealing and have damaged the standing of investment banks and weakened their lobbying power. As the president of the New York Federal Reserve Bank suggested, in January 1987, an alternative solution might lie in repealing the G-S Act and requiring the banks to form holding companies with subsidiaries specialising in financial activities between which 'Chinese walls' would have to be erected in more integrated financial conglomerates. The various subsidiaries would be regulated separately and supervised by the appropriate authorities.

2.3 The Japanese Banking System

i) Introduction

The Japanese banking system has been marked by its segmentation. Various types of banks are authorised to pursue well defined business and barred from securities underwriting by Article 65. The banks can broadly be divided into long term and short term credit institutions, the former being allowed to raise funds by issuing debentures and the latter relying on retail and wholesale deposits.

Throughout the post war period the authorities have kept interest rates low. Despite this, the household sector has displayed a high propensity to save and has invested a smaller proportion of its income in housing than is common in the major western industrialised economies. The banking system has proved to be a highly effective vehicle for channelling the household sector's financial surplus into the corporate sector; which, until the 1970s, had an avaricious appetite for these cheap funds. This arrangement sponsored a rapid post war reconstruction followed by rapid economic growth in the 1950s and 1960s. Because banks lent so cheaply the corporate sector became highly geared. It relied primarily on indirect bank finance for both working and investment capital. Financing through the capital markets was much less prevalent than in the US and the UK and consequently these markets remained relatively underdeveloped.

The OPEC I oil crisis in 1973 sowed the seeds of change. The economy is heavily reliant on imported oil as a source of energy and the rise in oil prices increased industrial costs and led to a deceleration of growth. Additionally, it contributed to a move from a surplus to a deficit on the balance of trade. The government responded by increasing expenditure and encouraging the central bank, the Bank of Japan henceforth refered to as the Bank, to relax monetary control by lending more generously to the major banks. The result was a growing budget deficit and a rapid rise in inflation whilst growth remained sluggish by the standards of previous post war decades. Following the OPEC II oil price rise in 1979, in common with US and European authorities, the government has attempted to reduce the budget deficit and the Bank has made control of inflation and the money supply its primary objective. The government has, therefore, been converted to fiscal conservatism and the Bank to monetarism.

The increased government borrowing, made necessary by the accumulating government debt, was occurring at a time when the corporate sector's demand for funds from the banking system was declining because investment was being curtailed and corporate liquidity was increasing. The government's growing demand for funds, however, exceeded the slackening demand from the corporate sector and forced the authorities to explore more diversified sources of funding. This led to a deregulation of long term interest rates and internal pressure for reforming the capital markets.

The government's funding needs are likely to remain high in the forseeable future, despite efforts to cut the budget deficit. Taxes remain relatively low and proposals for an increase in indirect taxes has met with considerable opposition in 1987. Meanwhile the population is ageing rapidly, placing increased demands on the welfare system. Since older people save a larger proportion of their income, the savings ratio is likely to remain high, but, because of the increasing demands of the elderly on government expenditure, there is judged to be little scope for a substantial fiscal stimulus. The ageing population has had the effect of creating a rapid growth in the demand for pensions. Previously this market was small because people relied on state provisions and lump sum payments from major companies on retirement. With state provisions likely to be curtailed, a general increase in wealth of the household sector, and a move by the corporate sector toward pensions schemes in place of lump sum payments, pensions business has become one of the fastest growing areas in the financial sector.

In the early 1980s, the balance of trade again moved back into surplus and export led growth resumed. The yen, however, failed to appreciate and the dollar became overvalued. Japan's bilateral surplus with the US increased and the US balance of trade deficit increased rapidly. This generated an influential protectionist lobby in the US, Japan's major trading partner. The US administration, committed to free trade, urged Japan to encourage imports and officials from the US Treasury entered into talks with the Japanese monetary authorities in 1983. The US authorities were seeking a package of measures designed to encourage the international usage of the yen in international trade and as a reserve currency. It was hoped that measures could be introduced to increase the demand for the yen, relative to the dollar in particular, causing it to appreciate with the result that the Japanese trade surplus with the US would decline. It was also hoped that a freer outflow of yen, in the form of overseas lending and investment, would offset the tendency for the Japanese surplus to drain funds from the international markets. Whether or not the US authorities were far-sighted enough to see it, the outflow subsequently occurred and much of it was invested in the US Treasury bill and bond markets. This helped the US to fund its burgeoning budget deficit without having to raise interest rates to the levels that would otherwise have been required. Japanese savings, therefore, helped to supplement US savings, which are low by international and particularly Japanese standards. Higher US interest rates, which were already high in real terms, would have exacerbated the international debt problem, making it even harder of LDCs to fund their debt payments, discouraged US investment and growth, and added to the problems faced by various sectors of the US banking system.

Whilst the talks were in progress, the US authorities introduced the additional demands : that the financial system, and particularly interest rates, should be deregulated; and that foreign financial institutions should be given greater access to Japanese financial markets. As a result of the talks the Japanese Ministry of Finance (MoF) announced a package of measures in May 1984. The package[58] included measures designed to promote usage of the yen and promised some deregulation and an opening up of business to foreign institutions in the future. It demonstrated that the MoF negotiators had successfully fought off US pressure for a fundamental and far reaching reform. Instead a gradual approach to liberalisation was to be pursued, building on measures introduced since the late 1970s. These had included the removal of exchange controls in 1980. The effect of US pressure had been to increase the pace of liberalisation which was already in process. Since 1984 external pressure for liberalisation has come from the UK, and latterly the German and Swiss, authorities. Their approach has been to seek reciprocity of access for their domestic institutions to Japanese markets, in line with that afforded to Japanese institutions in their domestic markets.

The MoF has, in the 1980s, become generally more disposed to deregulation. This followed the appointment of a number of liberals to key positions in the various bureaus of the MoF. Whilst accepting that liberalisation is necessary, MoF officials, especially in the banking bureau, seemed unwilling to sanction their rapid introduction. There have been no significant bank failures since the war and the MoF aims to avoid promoting a series of failures akin to those associated with US interest rate deregulation. It wishes to proceed at a pace that will allow the smaller banking and securities institutions to adapt to the new conditions, either by merging with larger institutions or by forming more cohesive groupings. The smaller banking institutions would, as in the US, be particularly threatened by interest rate deregulation. It would increase competition for deposits and loans, driving deposit rates up and loan rates down and thereby squeezing margins. The larger banks are better placed to survive these trends because of their ability to diversify into other business, especially international and fee earning business. The pace of deregulation is also influenced by the desire of various institutions, which have well-organised lobby groups, to protect their traditional interests. The tax bureau of the MoF inhibited deregulation by opposing removal: of privileges from the postal savings system, which is an important contributor to government funding; and of withholding tax on foreign interest and dividend income, which was a prerequisite for the establishment of an offshore banking market. The Bank, has generally favoured the introduction of a Treasury bill market and short term interest rate deregulation, as advocated by foreign monetary authorities, because it would improve its ability to control the money supply through open market operations. It did, however, oppose the establishment of an offshore market, because it would increase foreign monetary flows and make monetary control more difficult. With so many conflicting interests amongst the authorities and the various pressure groups, it is not surprising that, given its consensus approach to decision making, the MoF adopted a relatively cautious line on liberalisation.

A consensus in favour of accelerating liberalisation does, however, seem to have been reached in 1985. Short term interest rates on large deposits were liberalised in 1985, and liberalisation of rates on small deposits is promised in the future. An offshore market was established in December 1986, with withholding taxes removed but corporation, local and turnover taxes remaining. The tax bureau seems to have been persuaded by the view that withholding tax revenues were largely illusory in the absence of significant foreign activity in the Japanese banking and securities markets and that their loss would be outweighed by increased tax revenue from corporation tax and other business generated by a thriving offshore centre. The Bank also seems to have accepted that, by modelling the market on US IBFs,[59] domestic and international monetary flows can be kept separate and monetary control will not be impaired. It has also become concerned about the implications of wider international usage of the yen on its ability to control the money supply and wishes to see the Euroyen business brought onshore, where it can be monitored more closely.

Following the Plaza agreement in September 1985,[60] the yen appreciated significantly against the dollar. By mid-1986 the adjustment was causing concern at the Bank, which felt that the appreciation had gone far enough to cure the trade imbalance and was beginning to damage the prospects of industry. Having reduced interest rates rapidly[61] it had little room to manoeuvre and was unwilling to prejudice monetary control by a significant further reduction although it finally acquiesced with a $\frac{1}{2}\%$ cut in early 1987. These developments are likely to encourage further internal pressure to reform the economic and financial systems. Export led growth will need to be replaced by internally generated growth, as the Maekawa Report[62] acknowledges. The government is, however, constrained in its fiscal policy by concern over the ageing population and widespread opposition to major tax reforms such as the introduction of a sales tax. Some way has to be found to stimulate the economy, whose growth is flagging significantly in the latter half of the 1980s. The US and European, especially the UK, economies experienced appreciable consumption led growth following financial liberalisation in the early 1980s. Consumers have been largely neglected by Japanese banks hitherto. With corporate demand for their lending on the wane, the banks have begun to court retail custom. The way forward might lie in liberalising the system in such a way that it would encourage consumer spending and housing demand and thereby generate internal growth, which would also increase the demand for imports and help reduce the trade surplus. With the latter objective in mind, the US administration has been encouraging the Japanese government to stimulate its economy. It responded with a fairly meagre reflationary package in Autumn 1986. Many feel that a fundamental tax reform is required to encourage consumption and reduce saving. Liberalisation of short term interest rates and other reforms designed to encourage competition for consumer lending business, and reduce its cost, could also have a role to play in the near future. The tax reform package under consideration in 1987 includes the introduction of a 20% withholding tax on interest from bank and postal savings deposits. Japan's tax allowances on savings, particularly those applied to the postal savings system, have been criticised by the US and European governments for discouraging consumption and their removal could help to stimulate consumption and reduce savings. Until further domestic liberalisation is introduced, however, the banks and securities houses are likely to continue to build up their overseas operations, attracted by more liberal regimes and higher profits.

ii) The Banking System

Japanese banks have tended to put growth before profits. The corporate sector, like those of other major economies, has experienced a build up of liquidity and a slowdown in investment in the 1980s and has increasingly resorted to direct financing, often through the Eurobond market where funding is often cheaper. It has thus become less reliant on banks for finance and corporate treasurers have become more active players on the financial markets, investing and lending their own funds. This trend was enhanced in Japan by the opening of a bankers acceptance market in June 1985 as part of the 1984 US-Japan agreement and will be further encouraged if a commercial paper (CP) market is introduced. Such markets were introduced in France and the UK in 1985. The US market has grown meteorically since 1980 and the Euro CP market was also thriving in the mid 1980s. CP markets allow the corporate sector to lend and borrow money without the intermediation of the the banking system. With an export oriented corporate sector which was increasingly raising its declining funding needs in the Euromarkets, the banks have actively developed their international business in the 1980s. Following the liberalisation of exchange controls in 1980, they established foreign exchange trading operations. They built up international yen securities trading capabilities after 1982, and more recently, they have concentrated on expanding lending to non Japanese corporate borrowers in world markets. As the Japanese trade surplus grew in the 1980s the financial sector was well placed to recycle it. The Gulf OPEC countries, in contrast, had used other countries' banks to recycle their surpluses. The Japanese banks have played a part in the recycling and so too have the securities houses, insurance companies and pension funds. Much of the financial outflow initially went into US Treasury bills but Japanese investors began to diversify into other securities, such as equities, in the latter half of the 1980s. In developing their international direct lending the banks have become net takers from, rather than placers with, the Eurocurrency market, which is effectively an interbank market. Their rate of growth has been very rapid. In 1979 the largest Japanese bank was tenth largest in the world. In 1985 there were five Japanese banks in the world's top ten and three in the top five, the largest of which was second only to Citicorp. In 1986, because of the effects of the depreciation of the dollar on asset values, the four largest Japanese banks became the largest in the world. Of Asia's top 25 banks, 22 were Japanese in 1985. Meanwhile the 'big four' securities houses have been making their mark in the Eurobond market. All four rank in the top 20 lead managers in the fixed interest market and they had been building up their business in the floating rate note market until it ran into difficulties at the end of 1986. The securities houses have been prospering from the corporate sector's move towards capital financing and the growing interest in securities markets shown by an increasingly wealthy and more financially aware public searching for a better return on their money than available from bank deposits. In 1985 the largest securities house became the most profitable financial institution in Japan, overtaking the major city banks.

In 1984 the biggest companies raised only about 15% of their external funding needs from banks; compared to an average of approximately 56% in the previous five years and 80% in the 1960s. Further, they paid back more loans than they took out, so that only the non manufacturing sectors were borrowing, and kept only 20% of their working capital in yen deposits, compared to an average of 30% in 1978-1983. They were investing more heavily in securities which earned market related interest. The securities houses faired better because equities and bonds each accounted for approximately 43% of the corporate sectors' external financing, yielding them healthy underwriting fees. The securities houses have, however, also been encouraged to look abroad for business because an increasing proportion of direct finance was being raised abroad. In 1983 overseas bond issues overtook domestic bond issues by the corporate sector and since then the domestic corporate bond market has looked increasingly moribund. Whilst barred from underwriting domestic equities and bonds, government bond issues excepted, by Article 65, the banks have been competing for the business in the Eurobond market, through their London based merchant banking subsidiaries, and building up experience in the hope that they will be allowed to participate more fully in domestic capital markets in the future. Meanwhile, also freed from domestic restrictions, the securities houses have been diversifying through their overseas operations and the largest, Nomura, in 1986, and second largest, Daiwa, in 1987, were granted deposit taking licences by the Bank of England. Despite domestic restrictions, the banks and securities houses have increasingly competed with each other by introducing new securities backed instruments offering money management facilities and market related interest rates. Unless Article 65 is revoked they are likely to continue to monitor with interest the attempts of US commercial and investment banks to find loopholes in the Glass-Steagall Act. If allowed to compete directly in the future the major banks and securities houses are likely to develop rapidly into universal banks akin to the German and Swiss ones and those evolving elsewhere in Europe, especially France and the UK.

The banking system consists of a number of groups of banks each with, hitherto, well defined business: the commercial banks; the long term credit banks; the trust banks; mutual and cooperative banks and credit and labour associations; and special, government backed, institutions. Other major financial institutions include the post office system, the insurance companies, and the securities houses.

The commercial banks include the city banks and the regional banks.[63] The twelve city banks are the dominant banking group. In the early 1980s they collected about 20% of the funds in the system. Their branches are mainly in the major cities and they, therefore, rely quite heavily on raising wholesale funds through the money markets. Their main business has traditionally been with major corporations; providing a variety of banking services and advice on corporate strategy. They commonly own shares in their clients and they are amongst the largest shareholders in Japan. They held 25% of company sector shares in 1984. They stand behind their corporate borrowers, willing to absorb losses and coordinate rescues. In return they have expected loyalty and retired bank officers frequently sit on the boards of large customers. Because of differences in their origin, which have influenced their client bases, the city banks can be further subdivided into three groups.

The origins of four of them lie in the banks which supported the enormous pre-war financial and industrial complexes (Zaibatsus). The Zaibatsus were broken up by the US occupying authorities after the war. These four city banks, however, remain heavily involved, as main banks, with the trading companies that have emerged out of the Zaibatsus since the war and include the second, third and fourth largest city banks . The second group are the five new city banks. Some of them were formed by a rapid series of mergers of local and mutual banks in the 1930s and 1940s and two of them emerged in 1969. They are more heavily involved in new industries and more retail oriented. Finally there are the two former government banks which were privatised under the occupying US authorities. In both cases their long term lending operations were incorporated into the Long Term Credit Bank of Japan. They are similar to the new city banks but place more emphasis on lending to smaller companies, consumers and primary industries. The largest of the former government banks, Dai-Ichi Kango, became, by some definitions, the largest bank in the world in 1986.

The city banks have become increasingly reliant on wholesale funding through the short term money markets. They have suffered from a reduction in corporate deposits and a declining share of retail deposits. This has been due to the rapid growth of the postal savings system, which has enjoyed interest rate and tax advantages, and a growing preference amongst savers for higher yielding long term deposits and securities. They have been further handicapped by restrictions on branching, which were introduced by the MoF in the 1960s because it felt that country was overbanked. They could not expand as rapidly as they wished into city suburbs, which were attracting migrants from rural areas, and smaller banks and the postal system benefited at their expense.

Their lending is typically short term, commonly three months, but rolled over repeatedly. Lending rates are set, by the Federation of Bankers Associations of Japan in conjunction with the Bank, at a fixed percentage above the Bank's discount rate. They are subject to greater window guidance from the Bank than other banks. This has caused them to lose business when credit squeezes have been imposed. They have been diversifying in response to market developments: providing export finance and then seeking international business; developing leasing and consultancy subsidiaries; and entering securities business, wherever permissible. They were, for example, permitted to participate in government bond underwriting by the 1981 reforms to banking law, which also made other alterations to the type of business banks could conduct. Like the other banking groups, the city and regional banks are subject to laws governing their own particular group.

The 63 regional banks are, together with the city and the foreign banks, governed by Japanese banking law. They are the second largest[64] group of private sector banks. They rely less heavily on the wholesale markets than the city banks, having a strong retail base, and they finance medium sized companies of all types. Like the city banks, they accept deposits with maturities up to three years and 75% of their deposits are time deposits. Because of their solid retail base they rarely need to borrow from the Bank and are, therefore, relatively free from 'window guidance'. They are important suppliers of funds to the short term money markets. The largest of them are similar in size to the city banks and have prospered by operating on the fringes of Tokyo where many industrial concerns are situated and the population is swelled by migrants from rural areas. The remainder are generally smaller and are situated elsewhere in the country. They have close relationships with local governments : acting as fiscal agents; providing a significant proportion of their finance; underwriting their bonds; and receiving approximately 13% of their deposits from them. They also act as local agents for the central government and are members of the government bond underwriting syndicate. Unlike the more prosperous regional banks located in and around major urban areas, the smaller ones face a shortage of good quality borrowers. They make securities investments but, lacking analytical management skills, tend not to invest in equities to the same extent as city banks. They are benefiting from growing consumer and home loan business. They have been developing their international business but have not been permitted to develop overseas networks at the rate desired.

Foreign banks are subject to the same laws as domestic banks and to Article 65. They have found competition for loan business tough and have tried to create new markets and provide services through their international networks. They often operate both banking branches and underwriting subsidiaries. A limited number were granted trust banking licences in 1985[65] and some of their subsidiaries became members of the Tokyo Stock Exchange in 1985.[66] They hope to benefit from the development of the offshore banking market in Tokyo in the near future.

In addition to the commercial banks, primarily involved in lending short and medium term to medium sized and large corporate concerns, there are a number of specialised banking institutions : the long term credit banks; the financial institutions for small businesses; and the financial institutions for Agriculture, Forestry and Fishery industries. These are also private sector institutions.

The long term credit banks specialise in providing five to seven year funds to industry. They are wholesale banks which are allowed to raise cheap funding by issuing debentures and re-lend funds at lucrative fixed rates. Because they are not aligned to the Zaibatsus in their post war manifestation, they have been able to lend to the best rated companies. With investment declining and corporations raising more funds from the capital markets, the demand for long term funds has declined. Their response has been to internationalise their business and establish branches overseas. The Industrial Bank of Japan (IBJ) was formed by the government in 1902 to supply long term funds to nascent capital intensive industries. It played a key role in post war reconstruction and was privatised in 1950 under the occupying US authorities. Latterly, in common with the other long term credit banks, it has been involved in economic development. The Long Term Credit Bank (LTCB) was created in 1952, when two government banks[67] were privatised under the US authorities. Their short and long term lending divisions were separated on privatisation, the former becoming commercial banks and the latter being merged into the LTCB. The Nippon Credit bank, so renamed in 1977, was formed in 1957 after the re-organisation of another government development bank. IBJ is the largest of the three and one of the most important banks in Japan. Its present and former staff are on the boards of many major companies and, following the Stock Exchange crisis in the 1960s, IBJ men were appointed as presidents of the four largest securities houses. Apart form debenture issues, it also raises funds by taking deposits from central and local governments and corporate loan clients. It does not take deposits from the public. Recently, it has expanded its short term lending and has come into more direct competition with the city banks, which have responded by extending their long term lending.

The interest rates on debentures are set, at levels below market rates, by the three long term credit banks and the trust banks, following consultations with the MoF and the Bank. As more financial instruments offering rates responsive to market conditions have become available, including certificates of deposits (CDs), gensaki investments,[68] and, increasingly, government bonds, the attractiveness of debentures has declined and funding costs have risen.

The long term credit banks channel funds to sectors judged by MITI[69] to be important and help to finance the Export-Import (EXIM) bank.[70] With demand for their long term lending declining they have developed research departments to help in the restructuring of traditional industries and to monitor the needs of high technology industries. They have also diversified into short term lending, although they face a ceiling on the proportion of this business in their balance sheets and can't use funds raised from debentures for such lending, home loans, and international business. In the latter connection the IBJ in particular is active in the Euromarkets. They are also involved in securities business, underwriting public sector bonds and working in conjunction with securities houses and other banks.

Trust banks can undertake both trust banking and commercial banking business, although they must keep them separate. They were established at the end of the nineteenth century to channel private wealth into industrial investment. In 1923 there were 488 trust banks. The seven remaining domestic trust banks were formed in the 1960s when the MoF ordered city banks and securities houses to separate off their trust business. The four largest are descendants of the pre-war Zaibatsus. They conduct their commercial banking operations in accordance with the same regulations as city banks. Their trust banking business is funded by trust accounts, which are similar to pass book accounts and they issue certificates similar to debentures. The interest rates on the latter are set in conjunction with the long term credit banks and they too have faced rising funding costs as higher yielding securities of similar terms to maturity have become available. They have also suffered from competition from higher yielding accounts, especially those offered by the postal savings system. Prior to 1971 their lending was restricted to sectors of industry favoured by the government. Since then they have broadened their range of corporate lending and increased lending: to small and medium sized business; to consumers, for house purchase and consumption; and to Serakin.[71] Their access to the foreign markets has been controlled by the MoF. They also provide trustee services, such as the safe keeping of listed securities and related agency services, to individuals and companies. They have a majority share in the management of pension funds. The latter is one of the fastest growing sectors of the financial markets because of the ageing population, as mentioned above. Their pension fund management policy has been conservative and, possibly to shake the business up, nine foreign banks were licensed to undertake trust banking business in 1985, following the agreement with the US monetary authorities in 1984.

Before discussing the other specialised banks, the Bank of Tokyo should be mentioned. It is a multinational hybrid bank. It is the bank with the largest overseas representation and earns the majority of its income from abroad. Its dominance in this field is fading as the major city banks and the IBJ develop their overseas business. It was created in 1880, half owned by the Emperor and half privately owned, and given the monopoly of the nascent foreign exchange business. It concentrated on short term trade financing as international trading links grew. After the war it was forced, by the occupying US authorities, to close its extensive overseas network and adopted its current name. The Emperor was forced to divest himself of commercial interests, including his stake in the Bank of Tokyo. It then sought private sector business and began expanding overseas again following the signing of the peace treaty in San Francisco in 1952. In 1954 it was given a monopoly over foreign exchange transactions and certain other privileges concerning trade credits and bills, but had restrictions imposed on its domestic operations. In the 1960s it enjoyed rapid growth as exports and imports increased rapidly and, to meet the growing demands on its funds, it was given permission to issue debentures in 1962. In the 1970s restrictions on its domestic operations were removed and other banks were allowed to develop business in the areas over which it had enjoyed a monopoly. It, therefore, became more like a city bank but continued to be allowed to issue debentures. It now takes deposits but is more reliant on wholesale and foreign funds and has fewer domestic branches than the city banks.

The remainder of the specialised banking institutions, like the regional banks, are more local or regional in orientation. They are the most important lenders to small and medium sized businesses and to agricultural, forestry and fishing business. As well as the private institutions there are a number of government subsidy disbursing specialised institutions. Each of the private groups is regulated by its own law and most are also subject to the provisions of the banking law.

The 71 mutual loans and savings (Sogo) banks vary considerably in size. Those situated near large cities have been thriving and some are nearly as large as the smaller city banks. Many of those in the provinces are much smaller or grow only slowly. They are funded mainly through deposits and usually have surpluses which are invested in the money markets. They are important lenders to small businesses, particularly in the retail, wholesale and construction sectors. In the past they were subject to branching restrictions designed to restrict them to their prefectures and prevent them from gravitating towards cities. These restrictions have been lifted to encourage mergers between Sogos in different prefectures. They have found it more difficult than the, usually larger, regional banks to build good loan portfolios but are too big to develop the personal relationships that have allowed credit associations to prosper and they are being squeezed out. Consequently they form the weakest and most troubled sector of the financial system and they are trying to overcome their problem by cooperating with each other. It is felt that the weakest amongst them need to merge with stronger institutions but their management, in accordance with Japanese business culture, has opposed mergers, preferring instead to sell branches to city banks to raise funds.

At the end of 1980 there were 461 credit associations. As a group they have a sizeable branch network. They vary considerably in size and are similar to the US credit unions. Their capital derives from fees paid by their members, which include small firms. They take deposits from and lend primarily to members. They are closely associated with local communities and operate healthy localised businesses. They enjoy tax advantages and are allowed, by the Bank, to pay higher interest than their main competitors, the regional and Sogo banks. They are competing particularly successfully with the Sogo banks, who seek to lend to similar clients. They do, however, face a shortage of good loan business and consequently lend to the short term money markets and invest in the secondary bond market. Until the early 1980s they were barred from international business, despite their desire to help local firms to pursue international business. They had to pass the business on to regional and city banks. The National Federation of Credit Associations acts as their central institution.

The majority of the remainder of the specialised banking institutions are rural banking organisations. At the beginning of the century government financial institutions provided the bulk of funds for the agricultural sector. There were separate institutions supplying short and medium term funds, on the one hand, long term funds on the other. After the war the bank supplying long term funds was privatised and its long term funding operation was incorporated in the LTCB. Its former functions are now carried out by the Agricultural Forestry and Fishery Finance Corporation.[72] The short and medium term financing organisation was expanded after the war and renamed the Central Cooperative Bank for Agriculture and Forestry (Norin Chukin Bank). It has continued to play a major role in rural finance. Finance is channelled to the rural sector through a network of private co-operatives and their prefectorial and national associations and through the Norin Chukin Bank.

The agricultural, forestry and fishery sectors are declining but the institutions catering to their needs are flourishing. In an attempt to discourage migration to urban areas the government has tried to equalise rural and urban incomes by granting generous subsidies. The rural financial institutions distribute the subsidies and have surplus liquidity. They consequently invest heavily in the money and securities markets. There are three main groups of rural cooperatives, each subject to its separate legislation. The agricultural cooperatives are the largest group by far. They offer services to the farming community and function as general cooperative banks; offering financial services to members, taking deposits, and advancing loans. Interest rates on deposits are administered in accordance with the Interest Rate Adjustment Law and, like credit associations, they offer higher rates to depositors than banks. A law designed to promote mergers was passed in 1961 and their number has halved to leave 4490 operating at the end of 1980. At that time there were over 1750 fishery cooperatives and a much smaller number of forestry cooperatives. The former operate in a similar manner to agricultural cooperatives, whilst the latter were more restricted in their operations.

The agricultural cooperatives have combined to form a number of central organisations (Shinnaren) which represent them in each of the 47 prefectures. The Shinnaren accept deposits, discount bills for and extend loans to member cooperatives. They deposit half of their surplus with the Norin Chukin Bank and the rest is used to develop diversified portfolios of financial assets. The fishery and forestry cooperatives also have similar institutions. There are for example 35 credit federations of fishery cooperatives (Shingyaren).

The Norin Chukin bank is owned almost entirely by the rural cooperative banks and their national associations. It acts as a rural central bank and has a nationwide presence with 37 branches. Most of its deposits come from agricultural and fishery cooperative banks. It is allowed to issue debentures and to pay higher interest rates to members. It has recently suffered from competition for deposits from the postal savings system and the higher costs involved in debenture finance. Additionally, the Shinnaren and Shingyaren have invested an increasing proportion of their surplus in the securities and money markets to earn the higher yields now available there. With the rural cooperatives financially healthy, the Norin Chukin bank has only a minor lender of last resort role to play and, as lending opportunities have declined, it has begun to lend to customers only loosely associated with agricultural activities. It became an authorised foreign exchange bank in 1973 and set up an international department in 1979. The cooperative banks have engaged in trade financing and rapidly developed an overseas investment portfolio.

To cater for the large number of small and medium sized firms there are a number of urban financial organisations. Small firms are often family owned and in 1980 employed 80% of the work force. They accounted for 50% of production and 35% of exports. They have difficulty raising finance from major banks and have no opportunity to tap the equity market. A number of financial institutions, endowed with special subsidies and other advantages, service this sector along with the Sogo banks and credit associations described above.

Credit cooperatives supply approximately 6% of loans and are amongst the smallest financial institutions in Japan. There were 480 at the end of 1980. The larger institutions converted to credit associations in 1949 whilst those wishing to do business only with members and retain their autonomy kept their cooperative status. They are governed by separate legislation, which was amended in 1969 to change the eligibility of depositors and borrowers. Their main customers are local small and medium sized businesses. They are allowed to pay higher interest than the commercial banks and are funded by member depositors. Excess funds may be deposited with the National Federation of Credit Cooperatives, which acts as their central bank. It lends to them and invests their surplus in the money markets and on the bond market. A steady stream of mergers has been encouraged by the government.

The Central Cooperative Bank for Commerce and Industry (Shoko Chukin Bank) was established in 1936 to provide low cost finance to small businesses. It is 68.7% government owned and the government adds to its capital each year. The remainder of the shares are held by affiliated credit cooperatives, trade associations and small businesses. It is regulated by its own law and has 93 branches and 360 credit cooperatives act as agencies for it. It is closely monitored by MITI and the MoF and senior management appointments are made by the government. It is funded mainly by debenture issues and restricted largely to lending to affiliated organisations. Loans are subsidised and, as many of its clients have engaged in international trade and investment, it has developed an international department to service their needs.

Also playing a role in urban finance are the Labour Credit Associations, which are organised to provide funds for workers. There is now one in each of the 47 prefectures and they operate under separate legislation. Membership includes labour unions, consumer cooperatives, civil service associations, other workers associations and individuals. They accept deposits from members and their close relatives and the government and are allowed to pay higher interest than commercial banks. They can lend only to members and must not support political activity. Recently they have become more involved in extending housing loans. They have a national organisation, the Federation of Labour Credit Cooperatives, which acts as their central bank. The system runs a surplus and invests in other financial institutions and securities.

Lying outside the banking system, and, therefore, not subject to the Bank's reserve requirements or influence, but competing directly with it, is the postal savings system (PSS), which is managed by the Postal Savings Bureau of the Ministry of Post and Telecommunications (PSB). The PSS is the world's largest deposit taker, attracting over 25% of all deposits with Japanese financial institutions. It does not adhere to the fixed interest rate structure organised by the MoF and the Bank and sets rates slightly above the commercial banks. The PSB makes no effective check on income tax evaders, whereas other deposit taking institutions abide by rigorous identification and claims procedures for customers seeking tax exemption on deposits up to Y3m. Consequently, customers evade tax by holding multiple accounts to qualify several times over for the tax exemptions for small savers. The banks, exposed to competition through its 23,000 branches, have not surprisingly complained about its favoured status. It lends its funds to the Trust Fund Bureau (TFB) of the MoF and receives interest below the yield on bond issues.

Alongside the commercial, cooperative and mutual banks there are a number of government financial institutions which play a key role in providing finance to sectors of the economy that are risky or unprofitable. They are used to rescue and restructure older industries and to sponsor the development of key new industries. They receive government loans and funds from the budget and issue bonds and debentures to raise supplementary funds. There are 123 semi-independent government bodies. The Japanese Development Bank (JDB) is government owned and used to implement long term economic policy. It is the prime example of the alliance between government and big business and was founded in 1951 to fund reconstruction by providing and guaranteeing loans. It supported basic industry initially but as the economy has prospered it has concentrated increasingly on new industries. The TFB provided 74% of its funds in 1980 and it borrows overseas, especially on the Euromarkets. It participates in syndicated loans, providing 30% of funds for government approved projects. The other participants in the loans are private banks, contributing 30% of the funds and the beneficiary corporation, providing 40% from internal funds. Interest rates vary in accordance to the priority of the project. Half of its board consists of former officers of the Bank, MoF, MITI and other ministries and the remainder are from the bank. Despite extending subsidised loans it operates at a profit.

There are ten public finance corporations which are used to finance small and medium sized business in specific sectors in accordance with government policy. The size of subsidy in the loans varies. The Housing Loan Finance Corporation and the Agriculture, Forestry and Fishery Finance Corporation are fairly heavily subsidised. The Housing Loan Corporation is the largest and most popular. It finances the construction and repair of dwellings and supporting infrastructure. These institutions are partially funded by the TFB and place a heavy financial burden on the government which has led the MoF to propose their rationalisation.

The EXIM Bank extends subsidised loans to encourage the growth of exports, imports and foreign investment. It is a government agency which receives ample funding at cheap rates and it operates at a profit. It supplies credits issued by the export insurance programme of the MITI and uninsured credits and loans. Like the JDB it operates relatively independently, but its top staff include retired Bank, MoF and MITI officials.

The fastest growing group of financial institutions are the securities houses, which are similar in some respects to US investment banks. They are barred from commercial banking business. They have benefited from the switch by corporations from indirect to direct financing which has given them lucrative brokerage, dealing and underwriting business and internationalisation has allowed them to develop new underwriting business at home and abroad. They have become the most profitable financial institutions in Japan and the trends that helped them to prosper in the 1970s have been accentuated in the 1980s. The process of securitisation has accelerated, more foreign institutions are investing in Japan, Japanese investors are buying more foreign assets and the Tokyo Stock Exchange has enjoyed a sustained boom period. The major liberalising reforms have also been to their advantage and they have been allowed to enter into banking business overseas. Unless Article 65 is repealed it seems likely that they will overtake the city banks as the dominant financial force by 1990.

Before the second world war the Zaibatsus owned most of the outstanding shares in the country's industrial companies. Consequently few shares were traded and there wasn't enough business to support a viable securities industry. Securities firms were small and dealt mostly in bonds. After the war the Zaibatsus were broken up and the Emperor and the government were forced to sell their shareholdings in major institutions, such as the IBJ and the BoT. The securities industry began to grow as shares became an investment alternative to the wider population. The industry received government aid through the establishment of securities finances companies backed with funding from the Bank. The securities companies established large retail networks and gathered institutional clients. Prior to the war, underwriting of public share issues had been dominated by the Zaibatsu banks. After the war share underwriting became the monopoly of the securities houses. The fall in stock market prices in the early 1960s forced a number of small and medium sized houses to the brink of bankruptcy and one of the 'big four' had to be bailed out with concessionary loans from the Bank. The government, in response to the crisis, imposed new restrictions and introduced a licensing system. Securities houses must now get separate licences for broking, dealing on their own account, underwriting and the distribution of and qualification for each is subject to strict capital requirements. This has encouraged a series of mergers. Their major growth period started in the mid 1970s, as economic activity picked up, activity increased in the securities markets and inward foreign investment was liberalised.

There are three different types of securities houses. The 'big four' are dominant but there are another ten smaller integrated houses and 214 medium and small houses. The 'big four' account for over 50% of secondary trading in the stock market, 80% of trading in over the counter (OTC) bonds, 80% of the primary market in new stock and bond issues, and 80% of international stock market business. They have nationwide branch networks, with approximately 100 branches each, and have made record earnings since the foreign investment boom began in 1979. Nomura is by far the largest and has a strong overseas representation. It received a deposit taking licence in the UK in 1986. The middle ten are much more reliant on brokerage and dealing for their income, though they have underwriting and distribution licences. They have less extensive branch networks and many are satellites of the 'big four' but they also maintain close relationships with one or more of the big banks. Several were formed as a result of mergers following the problems of the early 1960s. Overseas firms, including Deutsche bank and NatWest subsidiaries, were granted securities licences in 1985 and 1986 respectively and further licences have subsequently been granted so that competition intensifying and as a result more mergers are expected. The smaller houses are not large enough to qualify for underwriting licences. Most concentrate on broking and dealing and the larger ones do some distribution. Many are satellites of the larger houses and the MoF is encouraging mergers. The larger houses have been diversifying into banking and trustee business as far as they are allowed and have set up consultancy divisions. Many banks and overseas institutions have also set up consultancy and advisory firms, hoping eventually to gain entry into the securities market. These activities have since been regulated by the Investment Advisory Law passed in October 1986 which introduced a licensing system[73]

Investment trusts, which are closely involved with securities houses, are also important players in the securities markets, along with banks, life assurance companies and pension funds. Investment trusts channel private savings into securities. They were modelled on UK institutions and introduced in 1937. They virtually disappeared after the war, during the period of rapid inflation. They re-emerged in 1951, under seperate legislation, with the role of channelling small savings into equities and bonds. The major securities houses set up their own investment trusts and ran them in conjunction with their brokerage activities, but in 1959 the MoF ordered them to be separated off as independent companies. They have become increasingly popular as savers have sought higher returns than those availible from bank and PSS accounts as interest rates have fallen to historically low levels in the mid 1980s. Other key players in the securities markets are the securities finance houses. They monopolise all stock financing on the Tokyo Stock Exchange. The largest by far is the Japanese Securities Finance Company (JSFC). It dominates bond financing and is the major source of working capital for small and medium sized securities houses. It is a de facto central bank for the secuirites industry, acting as lender of last resort. Its role has declined as the securities houses, especially the 'big four', have prospered. Latterly banks have also extended finance to securities houses. The JSFC has benefited from the growth of the government bond market and has been allowed access to cheap loans from the Bank, to encourage bond sales. It can, therefore, offer cheap finance for bond purchases to the securities houses.

After the US, Japan has the second largest insurance market and it is possibly the most profitable. The market has grown rapidly since the war. Insurance companies are the biggest institutional investors and rank just behind the banks as the biggest shareholders, owning approximately 25% of shares listed on the Tokyo Stock Exchange. They also underwrite and subscribe to public bond issues and are rapidly developing as the foremost industrial investors. Each major industrial group has its own life and non life insurance companies.

The modern trading companies are descendants of pre-war Zaibatsus. They act as main banks to many small and medium sized manufacturers, although they face increasing competition from the commercial banks in this area. They are heavily involved in financing overseas operations and trade for small and medium sized companies, which gain multinational representation through them. They have responded to competition from banks by offering cheaper rates. Their dependence on banks is being reduced by their increased liquidity and by tapping domestic and overseas securities markets. They raise funds on the Eurobond markets and overseas commercial paper markets and will clearly be major players in the domestic commercial paper market, scheduled to open in 1987. Their profitability has been declining and they are heavily involved in overseas investment.

The payments' system is well developed and coordinated as a result of considerable cooperation amongst the various banking groups. There are marked differences in the payments media used by the household and business sectors. The Bank has been the sole note issuer since 1885 and is responsible for the distribution and quality of notes in circulation and for the development of an efficient money transmission system. Coins are minted by the government. The household sector makes little use of cheques for retail payments, preferring cash and credit cards, which have been successfully promoted since the 1960s. For regular bill, wage, pension and dividend payments use is also made of pre-authorised direct debit and credit systems. The banks, having been unsuccessful in their efforts to promote cheque usage in the 1960s, have developed large networks of cash dispensers and ATMs. They are widely used and in the early 1980s Japan had the highest number of ATMs per head of the population in the world. The business sector makes extensive use of cheques, bills, and promissory notes. Consequently cheques are the most important, by value, in cashless payments, followed by credit cards, postal cheques and postal giros. Direct credits and debits account for over half of the volume of cashless transactions but a relatively small proportion of the value.

All 86 domestic licensed banks[74] have offices in Tokyo and are members of the Tokyo Bankers Association which runs the Zengin System, in conjunction with the NTT,[75] on behalf of the Federation of Bankers Associations (FBA). The Zengin System is a nationwide system of funds transfer in which nearly all private financial institutions participate. The city and regional banks are the most highly computerised and handle the largest share of cashless payments. There are 179 clearing houses, operated by the 72 banking associations which belong to the FBA , which clear, on a local basis, cheques, bills and other paper instruments. The Bank has 34 offices, through which it distributes cash, but plays no direct role in cheque clearing, providing only central settlement facilities. In regions where the Bank has no branch banks select a 'representative bank'. The Bank is soon to introduce an online settlement system to replace its telex system. The post office has its own online telecommunications system for financial and money transfers and has been expanding its range of payments services. As a result of the growing competition between banking groups since the early 1970s, virtually all private banks offer some payments services. They have, however, cooperated to establish interbank networks such as the clearing houses and the Zengin System, from which only the trust banks are excluded. The postal system is the private system's greatest rival; although finance companies, retailers, insurance companies and securities houses are beginning to offer payments services via credit cards and accounts which are close substitutes for traditional bank deposits. Technological advances have added impetus to this process.

The banks also share cash dispenser and ATM networks. There are two types of interbank networks : one based reciprocal access to ATMs and one operated by the Nippon Cash Services Company (NCS). Four networks were launched in 1980, each of which is run by different categories of banks. Cardholders use the dispensers of their own bank free and pay a small fee for use of other cooperating banks' machines. The NCS system, launched in 1975, is a network jointly owned by 54 banks. A small charge for the services was introduced in 1984. Terminals in the latter network are placed, for general convenience, in supermarkets, department stores, hotels and railway stations, for example. Those in the other networks tend predominantly to be attached to bank premises. The post office also has an extensive ATM network.

The retail payments system has largely bypassed cheques and operates mainly with cash, credit cards, and electronic payments. The Zengin system's size and complexity is unparalleled in the world and the Tokyo Clearing House is an automated system processing magnetic tapes submitted by large corporations containing instructions for credit and debit payments concerning their customers, clients, and employees. At the retail end the banks have invested heavily in automated counter terminals. Paradoxically, EFTPOS[76] is not well developed, although experiments are planned by a number of large retailers. Further, there is no high value same day clearing service available to the corporate sector, which relies heavily on cheques. The Bank is studying a new data communications system, like the US Fedwire,[77] between itself and the financial institutions and government departments. It hopes to introduce an interbank EFT system in place of the interbank cheque system, which relies on cheques drawn on the Bank's accounts. A number of banks are conducting home banking trials and office banking terminals have already been installed. In the future the operating hours of ATMs are likely to be extended. Under banking law ATMs are treated as branches and are only allowed to open for slightly longer than normal banking hours. This restriction has been imposed primarily to protect smaller banks and allow them to negotiate participations in shared networks. The favourable treatment of the postal savings system and its rapid development of MTSs has attracted criticism from the banks. The integration of its system with that of the banks might prove to be a problem in the future, if it is ever deemed to be desirable.

iii) Regulation and Supervision

Through its seven bureaux and a minister's secretariat, the Ministry of Finance (MoF) undertakes many of the functions associated with the following US institutions: the Treasury Department, the Internal Revenue Service, the Securities and Exchange Commission, state banking commissions and the Federal Reserve System and other federal banking supervisors. It regulates and influences the activities of most financial institutions. The International Finance Bureau is responsible for financial inter-relationships with the rest of the world and deals with foreign banks in the first instance. The Securities Bureau supervises the securities industry and issues licences to its participants. The Banking Bureau supervises and licenses most banking institutions and oversees the EXIM bank and the Japanese Development Bank. It also influences the policies of the Bank of Japan, oversees the Deposit Insurance Organisation, formulates the annual savings promotion plan and supervises the insurance industry. It has an important influence over changes in the financial system. The other bureaux are responsible for the tax system, administering central government borrowing, drawing up the national budget and customs and tariffs. The minister's secretariat is responsible for achieving a consensus amongst the bureaux, which enjoy a fair amount of autonomy and often have conflicting interests.

Working in conjunction with the MoF is the Bank. As central bank it is sole issuer of bank notes, lender of last resort to the commercial banks, the government's banker, and arbiter over monetary policy. It conducts monetary policy with a view to maintaining the internal and external value of the yen. It, therefore, tries to control inflation and intervenes on the foreign exchange markets. It is also required to conduct monetary policy in a way that will encourage orderly growth. This exposes it to potential conflict with government objectives.

A central bank, modelled on the Bank of England, was established in 1885 and by 1889 it had become the sole bank of issue. The Bank's current public sector status is the result of the 1942 Bank of Japan law, which gave it sweeping powers to stimulate the economy. The law was amended under US occupation, in 1949, to give it greater independence from the government in line with that enjoyed by the Federal Reserve System. Subsequent attempts by the MoF to gain more control over the Bank have failed. The Governor and Assistant Governor of the Bank are appointed by the cabinet for a five year term. The Governor is usually a retired MoF official. Seven executive directors are appointed, on the recommendation of the government, for four years by the MoF. These nine officials form the Executive Board which administers the bank's sixteen departments, two internal offices, 33 branches and twelve local offices. The Policy Board is an additional policy making body. It has seven members and meets twice weekly: to peg discount rates, set reserve deposit ratios and maximum deposit interest rate ceilings for banks, and determine availability of credit to the private sector. Its members are the Governor and one representative from each of the following : city banks; regional banks; industry; agriculture; the MoF; and the Economic Planning Agency. Representatives from the latter two organisations are non voting members. The Policy Board makes decisions based on recommendations from the Bank's departments.

The government owns the majority share in the Bank, the remaining 45% being held by private investors. It is the largest and most profitable bank in Japan. Its independence is prejudiced to a certain extent because top appointments are made by the government and the MoF, which tends to view the Bank as one of its bureaux and to have a responsibility for implementing government policy. The Bank can influence the banking system through 'window guidance' and more general moral suasion but it carries no official backing in this respect; unlike the MoF whose ordinances and administrative guidance has explicit or implicit cabinet backing. The MoF, therefore, carries primary responsibility for the regulation and supervision of the financial system. The Bank has operated reasonably independently since World War Two and there was little friction with the government until the 1970s, when its influence wained. Previously, the Bank had, in periods of monetary restraint, been able to set quotas on loans granted by individual banks. These direct credit controls had no legal foundation but compliance was virtually assured because of the city banks' dependence on Bank loans and discounting facilities. Following the 1973 oil price increase, corporations borrowed less from banks which in turn became less reliant on the Bank and the effectiveness of window guidance diminished. The growth of the postal savings system, which does not fall within the Bank's jurisdiction, also began to erode its control of the money supply. In 1976 it reviewed its monetary control methods in the light of its failure to control the inflation after 1973. It had been encouraged by the MoF to expand the money supply to stimulate growth, which had declined after the oil price shock, and the rate of inflation had increased. Following the review, it adopted inflation control as its primary objective. After the 1979 oil price shock it decided to control the rate of growth of the money aggregate M2 in order to control inflation. Towards this end it raised the discount rate from the record low of 3.5% to 9% in eleven months. Whilst not officially setting target growth rates for M2, it started to set quarterly projections for it. These have turned out to be remarkably accurate. Additionally, following the review, it set about decontrolling the money market interest rates over which it had control and pressing for the liberalisation of other short term interest rates. It hopes that their liberalisation will increase the effectiveness of open market operations (OMOs), which it intends to use as the main instrument of monetary control now that the effectiveness of window guidance has diminished. Liberalisation of short term interest rates on small deposits is, however, a complex issue which will be discussed below.[78]

The deposit protection fund was established in 1971. It is small and offers only limited protection to individual depositors. It would be exhausted by a significant failure and the depositors would not be fully reimbursed. Prior to interest rate decontrol it will have to be beefed up, if it is to act as a safety net and to prevent undue reliance on the Bank as lender of last resort, unless the MoF can successfully encourage struggling banks to merge with stronger ones.

Prudential restrictions on banks influence their scope of business and impose limits on exposure and reserve deposit requirements. Additionally, interest rates on loans are influenced by the Bank and the Policy Board, which sets the discount rate. Other deposit rates are related to the discount rate by fixed margins agreed by various groups of banks in conjunction with the Bank and the MoF. There are also restrictions on underwriting broking and dealing activities. Article 65 bars banks from such activities in the equity markets , although banks are allowed to hold equity portfolios and they can engage in such activities in the government and municipal bond markets. Only a limited number of banks are authorised to issue debentures and there are restrictions on the extent to which banks can engage in foreign exchange and international business. These latter restrictions have been liberalised significantly since the mid 1970s and exchange controls were removed in 1980. The MoF sets capital and reserve requirements, receives regular reports from banks and is empowered to seek additional information. The capital requirements were very stiff and virtually disregarded. They were revised in 1986 and set at more realistic levels. The banks were given five years to comply and allowed to use hidden reserves to bolster their ratios. Additionally, a risk asset ratio has been adopted and account has been taken of off-balance sheet risks, in line with the recommendations of the Cooke Committee.[79] Despite these changes, the banks are widely regarded by their international competitors as enjoying liberal capital requirements which give them a competitive advantage. Banks and other financial institutions are required to hold non interest bearing deposits with the Bank, which determines the reserve ratios. Concerning exposure, loans to a single borrower are not allowed to exceed 20% of a bank's capital stock and reserves.

The setting of the discount rate, which is charged for discounting commercial bills, is a powerful instrument of monetary control because many interest rates have a fixed relation to it. In 1981 a new lending facility, modelled on the Bundesbank's special Lombard rate, was introduced. It is a standby measure used to force up interest rates temporarily, to stem capital outflow in times of emergency for example. It can be used to break the link between the central bank lending rate and other rates and increases the Bank's independence from the MoF. In the 1960s it become apparent that 'window guidance', which relied on encouraging banks, especially city banks, to adopt an overloan policy and to rely on the Bank for cheap funds, was distortionary. When credit was being squeezed it often resulted in business being diverted from city banks to other banks and it encouraged corporate dependency on bank funding, or high gearing. It also inhibited the development of consumer services.

A new scheme for monetary controls was introduced in 1962. It aimed to rely more heavily on OMOs but its impact was limited by the underdeveloped state of the money markets. The Bank tried to develop new markets and instruments but was constrained by the cautious attitude of the MoF. A bill discount market was, however, introduced in 1972 and certificates of deposit (CDs) were introduced in 1979. There is also a call market and a gensaki market, which is operated by the securities houses and beyond the control of the Bank. The latter was introduced in the 1950s but really only took off in the 1970s. Its participants trade in bonds with repurchase agreements. The Bank undertakes OMOs in the bill discount market, buying and selling commercial and Bank of Japan bills; the call market, which it uses only to influence overnight rates; and the short term government bond market, where the Bank purchases the whole issue of sixty day bills and sells them to drain liquidity as required. It also purchases medium and long term bonds when it wishes to supply money to banks without extending loans. Its activities in the bond market in the 1970s helped stimulate the primary market and encouraged a switch from indirect to direct financing by the corporate sector. It does not intervene in either the gensaki or the yen CD markets, which are among the few that reflect the influence market forces without government or Bank interference. Reserve deposit requirements were introduced in 1959. Since then they have been applied to a wider range of institutions and accounts as a result of various revisions to the 1957 law that allowed them to be imposed. They are generally kept low on domestic yen accounts. They are not used as a key instrument of monetary control and have little prudential merit in view of the large hidden reserves held by banks. High requirements would anyway run contrary to the Bank's loan policy. They have been manipulated on non resident yen accounts to influence exchange rates. Apart from wishing to see short term rates deregulated the Bank also favours the introduction of a Treasury bill market, because it believes that it would increase the leverage of its OMOs.

iv) Deregulation

Despite the liberalisation that had occured in the 1970s, the financial system entered the 1980s in a highly regulated state. Exchange controls were significantly relaxed in 1980 and long term interest rates had been virtually deregulated in order to allow the government to fund its growing budget deficit and service its accumulating national debt. Restrictions on domestic and overseas branches and international operations involving domestic and foreign currencies had also been relaxed. Nevertheless the yen's importance as an international currency did not reflect Japan's position as an important industrial power and a major trading nation. The dollar remained the overwhelmingly dominant reserve and trading currency. Restrictions on short term interest rates still prevailed and Article 65 of the Securities and Transactions Law, which separates commercial banking and equity underwriting business, remained in force. Banks and securities houses had nevertheless begun to encroach on each others traditional territory. The banks had been allowed to become increasingly involved in government bond underwriting as the governments funding needs had grown and the securities houses had begun to offer accounts resembling interest bearing deposit accounts. The aim of Article 65 was to ensure that the equities market provided a source of equipment funds whilst the banks provided operational funds. The corporate sector, however, became heavily reliant on banks for most of its funding after the war and, consequently, more highly geared than the corporate sectors in the US and most European countries. The capital markets remained relatively underdeveloped. The banking system served industry well and contributed to the successful post war reconstruction of the economy and its rapid growth in the 1960s.

Because it is so reliant on imported oil as an energy source, the 1973 oil price shock hit Japan particularly badly and caused an abrupt deceleration of growth. Since then the economy has shown signs of maturing but has continued to rely on export led growth. In common with most other industrial countries, Japan's corporate sector reduced its investment and its liquidity subsequently increased. It also turned increasingly to direct, rather than indirect funding. The sector has, therefore, become less reliant on banks and the low interest rates provided through the regulated interest rate system have become less crucial as corporations have been increasingly able to raise cheaper funds on domestic and international securities markets.

The basic rationale for the regulated system, the channelling of cheap funds to industry, has, therefore, been undermined. As the demand for their funds from large corporate clients has dwindled the banks have begun to take a greater interest in lending to small and medium sized firms. The need for a special section of the banking system to provide for such firms has also, therefore, declined. The increasingly wealthy consumer sector has also begun to be seen as an attractive outlet for bank funds. Largely neglected by the banks, consumers had turned, in the latter half of the 1970s, to the Serakin; which are loan companies which charged higher interest than banks were permitted to, and the Shimpan, which are instalment credit institutions. The banks and other financial institutions lent heavily to the Serakin and made a handsome return. Because of the unsavoury debt collecting operations run by the smaller Serakin, they were regulated[80] in the 1980s and restrictions on lending by other financial institutions to them were imposed. It now seems likely that, belatedly, the banks will develop their retail banking services and expand their personal and home loan portfolios.

During the 1980s there has been further deregulation but its pace has been inhibited: by conflicting interests within the MoF and between some MoF bureaux and the Bank; and by opposition from groups of banks and the securities houses which have tried to protect their vested interests. The banking bureau wishes to avoid a spate of bank failures and has no intention of allowing a replication of the US experience. Short term interest rate deregulation seems to have been a key cause of the rise in US bank and 'thrift' failures. Because it had increased competition for both loans and deposits, interest rates on the former were competed down whilst those on the latter have been bid up. Margins have, therefore, narrowed, threatening the weak. The MoF, consequently, seems to be saving short term interest rate deregulation till last , preferring to proceed on other fronts first. Meanwhile the Bank would like to see short term rates deregulated, in order to improve its ability to control the money supply using OMOs. The tax and budget bureaux have tried to protect the position of the PSS, which provides a useful source of funds. Interest rate deregulation and a clamp down on tax avoidance would, however, eliminate most of the PSS's competitive advantage. The banks feel that this would be fair and that the postal savings system should perhaps be privatised. The tax reform package under consideration in 1987 will, if passed, remove the tax exempt status of the PSS. In return the PSS is to be allowed to sell government bonds over the counter, extend loans to customers using bonds as collateral and manage part of the funds collected, rather than transfer them all to the TFB as in the past.

There have also been external pressures for deregulation. Initially the US monetary authorities entered into discussions with the MoF with a view to internationalising the yen. It was hoped that this would cause the yen to appreciate against the dollar and help to cure the growing trade imbalance between the countries. The measures agreed in May 1984 provided for more dealing in the yen outside Japan and gave greater access to the Japanese markets to foreigners. The MoF did not accede to US pressure for the establishment of a Treasury bill market, fearing that it would undermine short term interest control, which it also refused to set a deregulation date for. It did, however, state that it would allow a bankers acceptance market[81] to be introduced and that foreigners would be granted trust banking licences. It also agreed to look into foreign membership of the Tokyo Stock Exchange, over which it had no jurisdiction concerning membership. Subsequently[82] nine foreign banks were granted trust banking licences and six foreign brokers have been allowed to purchase[83] seats on the Tokyo Stock Exchange. Continued foreign pressure for liberalisation has come mainly from the UK and German authorities. They are seeking reciprocity of access for their domestic institutions, in line with that enjoyed by Japanese institutions in their markets. This has exposed Japan to pressure to liberalise Article 65. Little pressure has come from the US, which has a similar legislation.[84] With Germany's long history of universal banking and the liberalisation of the Stock Exchange in the UK,[85] no such restrictions apply in these countries and Japanese banks and securities houses, in principle, have the opportunity to enter business abroad not open to them at home. As a result of these negotiations, UK and German bank subsidiaries were granted securities licences in the mid 1980s and Nomura and Daiwa Securities were granted deposit taking licences in London. The Bundesbank has, however, refused to allow Japanese banks to lead manage German government bond issues until German banks are accorded similar privileges in Japan.

Throughout the 1980s Japanese overseas investment, a counterpart to the growing trade surplus, has increased and it has accelerated since the 1984 agreement with the US authorities. Japan has become the largest creditor nation in the world as a result and the US has been transformed from the major international creditor to the major international debtor. In 1986 Japanese banks overtook US banks as the largest holders of foreign assets. They have played a major role in overseas investment and were particularly attracted to US Treasury bills in the mid 1980s. The latter have remained attractive, despite the depreciation of the dollar in 1986, because of their liquidity. The remorseless growth of the major Japanese banks has elicited calls from other international banks for the creation of a 'level playing field'. The Japanese banks, it is felt, have enjoyed a competitive advantage because of small capital ratios they are allowed to operate with. They have plenty of room for further expansion because overseas assets account for only 25% of their total assets, compared to 50% in the case of many other major international banks, and the domestic economy has become relatively undemanding, as growth has ground to a halt in the latter half of the 1980s, whilst the savings ratio remains high and the supply of funds is consequently plentiful. The Japanese authorities are likely to come under pressure from the US and UK authorities, following their January

1987 agreement to impose common capital adequacy requirements, to participate in similar agreements to further the prospects of creating a 'level playing field' for international banks.

In 1986 it was announced that international yen denominated business would be further encouraged by the establishment of an offshore banking market in Tokyo comprising of international banking operations modelled on the US IBFs. This approach is designed to isolate the domestic money supply from international influences, thus overcoming the concern of the Bank about an offshore centre's implications for its monetary control. The tax bureau has also agreed to the removal of withholding tax in the offshore market, hoping to be more than compensated by other revenues generated through corporation and other taxes. It is likely that the market, opened in December 1986, will attract a considerable amount of Euroyen business to Japan, in the way that IBFs have brought Eurodollar business back to New York, and that the centre will soon begin to rival Singapore and Hong Kong. In December 1986 181 banks opened Japanese Offshore Market (JOM) accounts and transfered $55bn to them, which was more than expected. Subsequent growth was disappointing, however, and in January 1987 outstanding assets stood at $93bn. This compares with $750bn in London, the largest centre, $260bn in New York's IBFs and, more relevantly, from a regional perspective, around $150bn in both Hong Kong and Singapore.It is believed that further liberalisation will be necessary to make the JOM thrive. One possibility is the removal of local taxes to make them more like New York's IBFs. Stamp duty is another problem but its removal would require legislation and the tax reform package under consideration in 1987 was already bogged down. The MoF seemed to be happy to oversee a quiet opening which will allow it to monitor market developments prior to further liberalisation.

With respect to short term interest rate deregulation, rates on large deposits have been deregulated as a result of the advent of government bond investment funds, money market certificates,[86] lower denomination CDs,[87] and international investment securities. In July 1985 the MoF announced that deregulation of short term interest rates on large deposits would be completed by 1987 but no time scale was announced for the deregulation of short term rates on small deposits.

Deregulation is being pursued, as far as possible, at an orderly pace in order to allow both large and small institutions to prepare themselves for a more competitive environment. Caution is obviously required to protect smaller institutions but the interests of large banks and brokers are also being protected. Towards this end joint domestic ventures between large Japanese securities houses and overseas banks have, for example, been prohibited. In August 1986, however, Sumitomo, the third largest city bank, formed an association with Goldman Sachs, the US New York investment bank. Under Japanese law, banks cannot have more than a 5% stake in a securities house. To get round this Sumitomo has taken a non-voting stake in Goldman Sachs, which has already been admitted to the Tokyo Stock Exchange, and has the right to top it up in the future. Further deals of this sort would undermine Article 65. In January 1987, however, the MoF granted a banking licence to the London based subsidiary of Merril Lynch, the leading US investment bank. Having already granted securities licences to the securities subsidiaries of US and European banks in 1985 and 1986, this development is likely to increase pressure from domestic banks and securities houses for the repeal of Article 65. Banks are keen to engage in domestic corporate securities business, because of the trend towards securitisation, whilst securities houses want to engage in banking and especially foreign exchange business, which would complement the growth in 'swap' backed securities business. The MoF's willingness to grant trust banking licences to foreign banks seems to have derived from its desire to improve the efficiency of pensions' provision.

Similar considerations are likely to condition the pace of future deregulation, although pressure from overseas, and the growing momentum caused by already sanctioned changes, might lead to a faster pace of deregulation than the MoF desires. The government seems to be responsive to overseas pressure and intervened in the discussions between the MoF and the US authorities in 1984 to force a more rapid conclusion of the agreement than might otherwise have occurred. External pressure could increase as a result of a decision to include services in the round of Gatt negotiations launched in 1986.

The MoF faces internal pressure for more rapid deregulation from the city banks, the Bank, the securities houses and the Financial System Research Council, an influential government advisory committee. In July 1985 it recommended sweeping reforms including : interest rate deregulation; merger and acquisition promotion; and competition to replace the 'convoy' policy.[88] It also advocated further consideration of homogenisation of the banking system, by removing restrictions on long and short term lending banks in particular. In order to safeguard the system it called for : increased disclosure; and an improvement in the deposit insurance scheme to increase its cover, from Y3m to Y10m per customer, by raising premiums. The deregulation of short term interest rates on small deposits would lead to a fall in loan rates and a rise in deposit rates, although the latter would probably be smaller than in the US because of Japan's higher savings ratio, and margins would be squeezed. The possibility of failures would arise, although they would be much fewer than in the US because there are only about 1000 banks in Japan compared with about 14,500 in the US. Greater disclosure, easier mergers and acquisitions and improved deposit insurance would be necessary for prudential reasons.

The granting of trust banking and securities licences to foreign banks has naturally led to lobbying from city banks, which wish to be given similar freedom to diversify. They have been gaining experience in securities underwriting and dealing overseas through the Eurobond market and they have also set up investment advisory and management subsidiaries at home and established tokkin funds.[89] They hope to convince the MoF of their competence in securities business and to be granted securities and trust banking licences, giving them access to pensions fund market.

As a result of a series of scandals, the investment management business has been regulated by the Investment Advisory Law passed in October 1986 and the first licences were issued in November 1986. The aim of the regulations is to protect investors from unscrupulous investment advisors. Minimum capital requirements have been laid down and foreign investment companies are allowed to apply for licences provided that their parents are adequately capitalised. It is expected that it will pave the way for Tokyo to become a major international fund management centre rivalling London and New York and, perhaps most importantly, Hong Kong and Singapore. Previously only trust banks were allowed to manage funds, other than tokkins, for others but the absence of specific legislation allowed unqualified people into the business. In related action the MoF announced in February 1987 that it would introduce new rules for tokkin funds to prevent abuses. Life assurance companies, in particular, had been using them to conceal poor investment decisions and securities houses had set up quasi tokkin funds, which illegally offered a guaranteed rate of return, implicitly paying interest on deposits, which they are not allowed to do under Article 65. Meanwhile securities houses have been allowed to issue quasi deposit accounts since 1984. These accounts are linked to bond yields and remittance networks are organised through regional banks. They have also been allowed to make loans with bonds as collateral. The banks retaliated by issuing money market certificates to attract corporate clients. The brokers and securities houses want to overtrump and offer money management accounts.[90] The securities houses are also using post offices to remit securities dividends, effectively increasing their branching, and setting up deals with supermarkets to establish ATM networks and to install stock information screens with a view to selling stocks through retail outlets.

In September 1985 two new financial instruments were approved by the MoF. Banks were permitted to grant loans against the collateral of approved securities, along the lines of Swiss and German banks. The securities are to be held with the securities houses. Trust banks were allowed to offer money trusts in compensation for the decision to allow foreign banks to enter into trust business. The latter liberalisation was delayed by the regional banking lobby group which feared that it would cause a flight of funds from deposit accounts.

The distinction between LTCBs and city banks has been diminishing. Now that short term rates on large deposits are market related the LTCBs are able to compete on short term loans. Meanwhile the city banks have been finding loopholes in the legislation and have been issuing long term securities and increasing their volume of long term loans. They are still seeking permission to issue debentures and hope to be allowed to do so if foreign banks are permitted to issue bonds. The twelve major city banks[91] want to be put on an equal footing with the securities houses, especially in view of the possibility that the latters' overseas banking subsidiaries might be allowed to open offices in Japan, and they have consequently supported the latter development. They believe that if they are granted securities licences, as many of their foreign competitors might be, there would be a healthy increase in competition in the securities market, which is dominated by the 'big four' securities houses. Their profits, which have been hit by the decline in their traditional corporate business, would be boosted and they would be able to compete more effectively with European universal banks.

The introduction of a commercial paper (CP) market, which is to be permitted in 1987, will increase competition between the securities houses and the major banks, as it has done in the US. In Japan, the banks have claimed the right to participate in CP dealing because they specialise in short term lending and have already experienced a loss of corporate banking business. The securities houses , however, claimed that the issuance of CP is securities business and that the banks should not be granted a monopoly over short term finance. The Commercial Banks Association[92] came out against the CP market in July 1986. They claimed that its introduction would upset the financial order and disturb the close relationships between banks and the corporate sector. Their major worry, however, was probably a loss of corporate business to the securities houses who, along with 78% of corporations, are in favour of the introduction of a CP market. The 'big four' securities houses submitted draft rules to the MoF in 1986 which proposed that both banks and securities houses be allowed to underwrite and sell CP. Y10m denominations were suggested along with pricing on a discount basis to avoid withholding tax. In 1987 the MoF decided to allow both banks and securities houses to underwrite CP issues. CP is to be categorised in the same way as commercial bills and not as a security. The MoF invited revised plans from both banks and securities houses and wanted a quick response. International non resident companies will be permitted to issue Euroyen CP in April 1987 and one year later so too will Japanese companies. Since February 1983 overseas branches of Japanese banks have been allowed to deal in foreign CP and in April 1987 banks and securities houses will be able to underwrite Euroyen CPs. Many industrial companies have already issued CP overseas and believe that a domestic market would reduce funding cost and increase their flexibility. Such companies have increasingly active treasury departments.

The MoF had previously thought it appropriate to develop the Treasury bill and bankers' acceptance markets to maturity before introducing a CP market. The bankers' acceptance (BA) market has fallen short of targets since its introduction in June 1985 and a Treasury bill market is yet to be introduced because of the fear that the short term interest rate fixing arrangements would be undermined. By 1987 the BA market was moribund. It is regarded to be overregulated and stamp duty has ensured that its main users, exporters and importers seeking trade finance, find loans cheaper and easier to arrange. In March 1987 the MoF decided to relax its controls over the market to provide a stimulus to it. The US, UK and German authorities feel that a Treasury bill market is needed to provide a secure and liquid yen investment. It is also felt that an active interbank market should be encouraged in order to increase liquidity. The Association of Foreign Banks also called, in May 1986, for the introduction of a Treasury bill market and other deregulatory measures including : deregulation of interest rates; greater access to discount facilities; removal of collateral requirements on foreign banks to free the interbank yen market; full liberalisation of the Euroyen market; and greater securitisation.

The banks' case for being allowed to diversify into securities and long term credit is being supported by the adverse effects of deregulation on their profits. In May 1986 they reported on a consolidated basis for the first time and their combined profits had declined by 1 %. Their margins had been squeezed by a decline in lending rates and a rise in the cost of wholesale funds as a result of the deregulation of short term rates on large deposits. Their results also showed that they were making headway in their overseas operations.

In common with banks overseas, the Japanese banks have been under pressure to raise capital. In 1985 the big five made new share issues at market rates, rather than through allotments. In order to protect the weakest banks, the MoF had previously encouraged banks to manage their stock prices to ensure that differentials between them were small. This was achieved via allotments to existing shareholders. By the mid 1980s, however, the major banks needed to raise capital to fund their overseas expansion and modernise their branch networks and this led to the breakdown of the 'convoy' system. Despite poor profits, the shares in the big banks have been booming in the mid 1980s because deregulation is expected to strengthen their position.

In April 1986 a risk asset ratio (RAR) was introduced to provide tighter supervision of overseas operations and off balance sheet risks. It is to be applied to international assets whilst traditional equity ratios, including hidden reserves, are to be applied to domestic assets. The introduction of the RAR and capital backing for off balance sheet items can be seen as a response to international developments in supervisory coordination but many overseas banks feel that capital ratios remain low by international standards and further pressures to conform are likely following the US/UK accord in January 1987, discussed earlier and in section 2.2 and chapter 1. In 1986 the authorities also encouraged the banks to make larger international loan loss provisions, in order to bring them in line with European levels. It was proposed that the tax free portion of provisions should be increased to 5%, from the prevailing 1%, of their exposure. This was vetoed by the tax bureau. The authorities' concern over the Japanese banking system's exposure of $60bn increased in 1986 as the prospects of a number of the debtor nations deteriorated. The Bank of Tokyo and SumitomoBank, the third largest city bank were particularly heavily exposed. In 1987 the MoF approved a plan, formulated by 28 banks, to set up a company in the Cayman Islands tax haven to buy loans to third world debtor countries at a discount and then securitise and resell them. Discounts are expected to be as high as 60% and banks will be allowed to deduct capital losses from taxable income. They will also be allowed to use the proceeds to boost their capital. Future negotiations with debtor countries will be simplified because the loans will be concentrated in one place, to the extent that they remain unsold. The process is expected to start modestly and could have significant implications for banks in other countries because, by establishing discounts, it might lead their auditors to require them to reduce the the value of their loans to market levels.

Other initiatives have been taken which will allow banks to boost their capital to international levels. These include granting them permission to to put a market value on hidden reserves, particularly equity holdings, and to include them as part of their capital. At a time when the stock exchange has been booming, this is particularly attractive. The stock market conditions have also allowed them to make rights issues to raise capital especially as bank shares have been doing well. The MoF is also believed to be considering the possibility of allowing city banks to issue debentures. Previously this privilege has been largely reserved for LTCBs and such a development will be opposed strongly by them. The greater the pressure to conform to international capital adequacy standards, however, the more likely this liberalisation is to occur. Additionally, legislation was passed in 1986 requiring banks to reduce their holdings in individual non bank companies to a maximum of 5%. Consequently many banks will have to sell off some of their equity holdings and they will be able to use the proceeds to boost their capital in order to achieve the new ratio requirements introduced in May 1986.

In 1986 additional measures to encourage the capital outflow were also introduced as fears arose that the dollar's decline would discourage the outflow to the US by making investment in dollar denominated assets less attractive. Trust bank rules were eased to allow them to handle foreign currency trusts, for example. In November 1985, pension funds were allowed to substantially increase the proportion of overseas assets in their portfolios in an effort to increase the outflow of capital and stem the yen's appreciation. The business of servicing the outflow of capital is highly profitable and has so far accrued largely to the securities houses.

The 'big four' securities houses are likely to continue to dominate the Stock Exchange in the foreseeable future, despite the entry of foreign institutions, unless the major city banks are also allowed to participate . In the absence of city bank entry, fixed commissions are likely to remain since their removal would allow the 'big four' to squeeze out their smaller competitors.

In 1987 further measures were introduced and under consideration to stimulate the money and bond markets. The MoF was looking into ways of increasing their liquidity and bank competition for funds by easing minimum deposit restrictions and extending the maturity of money market certificates, which are the only instruments through which banks can raise funds by setting rates independent of government influence. It was also considering easing deposit requirements on larger bank deposits and CDs. An announcement was expected in Spring 1987. The underwriting procedure for domestic corporate bond issues was also under review. The aim is to revitalise the market to lure bond issues back to Tokyo, from the Euroyen bond market, and end the spectacle of Japanese companies issuing yen denominated bonds, which were mainly purchased by Japanese investors, in the Euromarket. Towards this end, rules on Samurai, yen denominated, and Shogun, dollar denominated, bond issues by foreign corporate borrowers were eased in November 1986.

The Euroyen bond market has been booming as Japanese companies, attracted by lower costs and currency risks, have been raising funds in Europe, where both banks, through London based merchant banking subsidiaries, and securities houses have been acting as traders and underwriters. In the mid 1970s the banks agreed not to lead manage Euroyen bond issues but in February 1987 Fuji Bank's UK merchant bank subsidiary led an issue for a UK company. It claimed that the agreement only applied to issues for Japanese companies but some securities houses were unhappy with this development. The banks had previously confined themselves to participating in underwriting syndicates, rather than leading them. The secondary market in Euroyen bonds has been increasingly attracted to Tokyo since October 1986 when an 'over the counter' secondary market, dominated by the 'big four' securities houses, suddenly emerged. By February 1987 it was twice as large as the Samurai bonds market. Previously Euroyen bond trading had attracted interest primarily from US and European investors and had been based in London. Tokyo now also rivals London as the major Eurocurrency trading centre.

To stimulate the Euroyen market and promote the further internationalisation of the yen, in February 1987 the MoF reduced the minimum permitted maturity of these bonds, from five to four years, and allowed non residents to issue them. This was strongly opposed by the city banks, which saw it as a further threat to their medium term corporate lending business, and the LTCBs, which were concerned about its potentially adverse influence on their costs of raising funds through debentures. A revitalisation of the domestic corporate bond market would have similar effects. The MoF is, however, believed to be considering reducing the minimum maturity to three years and the Securities and Exchange Commission, an influential MoF advisory body, also recommended, in 1986, that four year corporate bonds should be allowed. Its proposals are still under consideration.

In March 1987 reforms were also announced concerning government bond allocations. Medium term bonds are auctioned to a syndicate of securities houses and banks with an account at the Bank. The MoF proposes to allow foreign banks without such accounts to participate in the auction. This might open the way to reciprocal access of Japanese institution to the German government bond syndicate, from which they have been barred, see section 3.3. The syndicate of banks and securities houses which purchases and distributes long term bonds is also under pressure to increase its meagre allocation to foreign institutions. Foreign commercial and investment banks are campaigning for the introduction of an auction system for long term bonds. The market lacks the liquidity of the UK and US markets, despite its unprecedented expansion since 1985. It is the second largest government bond market after the US Treasury bond market. As older long term bonds are approaching maturity in increasing numbers a de facto short term bond market has been created and this has increased the attractiveness of the market to foreign investors. It is felt that, particularly in the absence of a Treasury biil market, the government should build on this by issuing more short term bonds.

Having ruled on the CP market the MoF next has to consider a dispute between banks and securities houses concerning the establishment of a futures market. The Federation of Bankers' Associations revealed a plan for a futures trading in currencies, interest rates, stocks and bonds in February 1987. The securities houses have been pushing for a stock index futures market, from which banks would be barred by Article 65, although they might have to consider letting them participate in a government bond futures market because they are members of the underwriting syndicates. The Securities and Exchange Commission is to set up a special committee and report.

There has, therefore, been significant deregulation in the 1980s. Its pace has accelerated since the 1984 agreement between the US Treasury and the MoF and seems to have gathered a momentum of its own. Conflicting interests between domestic institutions and departments of the MoF are likely to inhibit further substantial progress but a countervailing force is the more widespread pursuit of reciprocity by international supervisory authorities. The 1986 UK Financial Services Act, for example, contains a reciprocity clause allowing the Department of Trade and Industry to disqualify, from investment, insurance and banking institutions from countries not allowing equivalent access to UK financial institutions. The Secretary of State has announced that these powers will be used should the Japanese authorities not grant access to UK institutions on a par with that enjoyed by Japanese institutions in post 'big bang' London.

Despite this deregulation, including the abolition of general exchange rate controls in 1980, various specific restrictions on international capital flows remain and the yen is still infrequently used in international trade transactions, although its usage in international banking has increased and so too has its role as a reserve currency. Short term interest rates on small deposits remain regulated. In 1985 short term rates on deposits exceeding Y1m were deregulated and in 1986 this was first extended to deposits of Y500m and then Y300m, and there are plans to reduce the limit to Y100m, which is approximately £½m and therefore still high. Demarcations between various types of banks and securities houses, which are becoming increasingly anachronistic in the light of world wide developments, remain. Stock Exchange membership is still restricted and commissions remain fixed rather than negotiable. Few foreign institutions have been granted membership and banks are still barred. Nevertheless the pace of deregulation has been faster than expected by most analysts.

1) Canada also had legislation separating commercial banking from corporate sector securities business until 1987, when liberalising legislation, allowing banks to participate in Stock Exchange activities, came into effect.

2) In both Germany and Japan, however, there are moves to reduce bank participations in non-financial companies. Legislation has been passed in Japan requiring banks to reduce such participations to 5% over a period of time but no legislation has yet been proposed in Germany.

3) By the Labour Party for example, see Labour Party Financial Institutions Study Group (1982).

4) See section 2.2iv for further discussion.

5) Since they have not allowed any bank failures since the Second World War.

6) Savings and loan associations, credit unions and mutual savings banks.

7) In August 1982 Mexico declared a temporary moratorium interest payments on its debt to commercial banks and heralded the onset of the Latin American debt problem, see Lever and Hulme (1985) for further discussion.

8) Continental Illinois, then the eighth largest money centre bank, had been the subject of rumours concerning its liquidity in the light of its bad debt exposures, especially in the energy sector, and had to be rescued by the authorities. See below for further discussion.

9) See Mayer et al (1981) pp 48–51.

10) Including Switzerland and Germany.

11) DIDMC Act, see below for further discussion.

12) Banks with loans to the energy sector that amount to more than 25% of their capital.

13) In December 1985 Saudi Arabia persuaded OPEC to to expand production to try to win back some of the market share it had lost to non-OPEC producers.

14) Banks with loans to the farming sector that amount to more than 25% of their capital.

15) See sections 2.2iii and iv for further discussion.

16) See Dale (1984) for further discussion.

17) See section 2.2iii for further discussion of the role of the Federal Reserve Board (FRB).

18) Such as NOW accounts, see also section 2.2iv.

19) See also section 2.2iv.

20) See also section 2.2iv.

21) See also sections 2.2iii and iv.

22) See also section 2.2iii.

23) See also sections 2.2iii and iv.

24) See section 2.2ii.

25) See section 2.2ii.

26) First Boston, through a subsidiary jointly owned with Credit Suisse, was the top lead manager for Euroband market issues in 1986.

27) Created by the need to recycle the OPEC surplus.

28) See section 2.2iv.

29) They were generally set slightly higher to encourage flows of funds into 'thrifts' at a time when they could not compete with the commercial banks by offering a similar range of services.

30) See section 2.2iv.

31) See Heaton and Dunham (1985) for further discussion.

32) Discussed in section 2.2iv.

33) These were particularly attractive to private sector depositors seeking both liquidity and a high return at a time when interest rates on savings deposits were regulated.

34) See Luckett (1984,Chapter 6) or an equivalent textbook for details.

35) Which was $100,000 in the mid 1980s.

36) See below and section 2.2iv.

37) See Heaton and Dunham (1985) and Dunham (1985) for further discussion.

38) See Terrill and Mills (1983) and Chrystal (1984).

39) For further discussion of the role of the Federal Reserve Banks see Balles (1984).

40) Normally 14 years.

41) See Mayer et al (1981) for a brief review of the debate.

42) See below and section 2.2iv for further discussion.

43) Namely, Massachusetts, Ohio and Maryland.

44) The FRS, the OCC, the FDIC and the FHLBB.

45) See Federal Reserve Bulletin (1984).

46) See Committee on Banking Regulations and Supervisory Practices (1986)

47) Deposits greater than $100,000.

48) All deposits were guaranteed by the FDIC, backed by the FRB, in order to prevent a further drain on Continental Illinois liquidity and to contain potential knock-on effects which might have threatened the stability of the wider banking system.

49) See Maisel (1981).

50) Which had attempted to maintain the Bretton Woods system of fixed but adjustable exchange rates following the US government's decision to devalue the dollar and suspend its convertibility into gold, see Grubel (1984) for further discussion.

51) See Simpson and Parkinson (1984) for details on the deregulation of deposits.

52) In October 1986, for example, it led a $4bn asset backed floating rate note issue on the Eurobond market which rivaled the issue earlier in the year by the UK government, which had been managed by its Euromarket affiliate Credit Suisse-First Boston, as the largest FRN issue to date. The deal took 20 of its employees six months to put together and marked a significant evolution in securitisation. It contained three main innovations, see the Financial Times 30 October 1986 p33. The issue was backed by over 360,000 vehicle loans extended by the General Motors Acceptance Corporation. They were bundled together into three tranches of notes of varying maturities. Vehicle loans were the logical next step, in the extension of asset backed business, after mortgages. First Boston had been a pioneer in the use of mortgages as collateral for US securities market issues ten years earlier. Later in 1986 there were a number of collateralised mortgage obligation (CMO) backed FRN issues on the Euroband market. The FRN market, however, ran into difficulties at the turn of the year.

53) See Syron (1984) and Dunham and Syron (1984).

54) Which had reached 329.

55) After California.

56) See Wallich (1984).

57) Insider dealing occurs when individuals working for a financial institution use information gleaned from its clients, by departments handling sensitive and supposedly confidential information, to trade in securities at a profit.

58) Discussed in section iv below.

59) See section 2.1ii.

60) At which representatives of the five major industrial countries agreed to undertake coordinated intervention in the foreign exchange markets in order to reduce the value of the dollar.

61) To 3.5%.

62) The Maekawa Report was commissioned by the Prime Minister, Mr Nakasone, and published in April 1986. Mr Maekawa, the chairman of the commission, was previously governor of the Bank.

63) Sometimes called local banks but so too are the sogo mutuals. In this book they will be called regional banks and the mutual banks will be called sogo banks.

64) In terms of market share rather than number.

65) See section iv below.

66) See section iv below.

67) Kangyo and Hokkaido.

68) The gensaki market is operated by the securities houses, discussed below. It is a secondary market for bonds with repurchase agreements with maturities ranging from one to 364 days, although the one and two month maturities are the most popular. It opened in the 1950s and has grown rapidly since the early 1970s.

69) Ministry of International Trade and Industry.

70) Discussed further in section ii below.

71) See section ii below.

72) See section ii below.

73) See section iv.

74) There are 13 city banks, including the Bank of Tokyo, 63 regional banks, 3 long term credit banks, and 7 trust banks.

75) Nippon Telegraph and Telephone, a public company.

76) Electronic Funds Transfer at Point of Sale (EFTPOS).

77) See section 2.1ii.

78) In section iv.

79) The Committee on Banking Regulations and Supervisory Practices that meets at the Bank for International Settlements in Basle and is chaired by Mr W.P.Cooke of the Bank of England. Through it central banks coordinate supervisory practices.

80) Following their rapid growth in the early 1980s, regulation was imposed in 1983. The top four Serakin are as large as Sogo banks and have ATM networks as extensive as some of the city banks. They are likely to remain in business and seem to be favoured by the MoF. From 1983 Serakin have been licensed and a maximum interest rate of 73% has been imposed. This is to be brought down to 40% in 1988. They had previously charged around 110%. Banks have been prohibited from lending to the smaller and less reputable Serakin.

81) It began operating in January 1985.

82) In January 1985.

83) The admission fee is high.

84) The Glass-Steagall Act.

85) With effect from 27 October 1986.

86) All financial institutions were allowed to deal in money market certificates in 1985. The minimum denomination was set at Y 50m.

87) Certificates of deposit were first introduced in 1979. Denominations were high but they were reduced from Y300m to Y100m in 1985 and the minimum maturity was reduced from three months to one month.

88) The MoF's 'convoy' policy aimed to protect the smaller and weaker banks by regulating the banking system in such a way that it moved at a pace they could keep up with.

89) Tokkin are specified money trusts. In the mid 1980s they became perhaps the most powerful force on the Tokyo Stock Exchange. Their popularity increased following a change in the tax code in 1980 which allowed banks and non financial companies to segregate, for fiscal purposes, equities held in specified trusts. In October 1984 insurance companies were permitted to invest up to 3% of their total assets in tokkins and to pay any resulting capital gains to policy holders as dividends. Thenceforth tokkins boomed. Commercial banks were allowd to act as investment advisers and gained experience in fund management through them. They can also appoint investment advisers for their own tokkins and this has allowed them to to sell shares in client companies anonymously. Previously fund management had been the preserve of the trust banks and investment advice had been supplied by brokers and securities houses. By building up a track record in tokkin management and investment advice the banks hope

to persuade the MoF give them power to offer a full fund management service. Consequently, Japanese banks have become increasingly active players in the stock markets in the mid 1980s. In the early 1980s tokkin money was almost entirely invested in bonds but by the mid 1980s the proportion invested in equities had grown considerably and was contributing to the boom on the Tokyo Stock Exchange.

90) Modelled on those introduced by US investment banks. They combine money market mutual funds, which invest in money market instruments and offer a higher return than generally available from bank savings accounts, with services such as cheque books and credit cards allowing easy withdrawals from the funds.

91) The major city based banks excluding the Bank of Tokyo.

92) Which represents the twelve city banks excluding the Bank of Tokyo.

3

European Banking Systems

3.1 Introduction

In this chapter the banking systems of France, Switzerland and the Federal Republic of Germany, henceforth called simply Germany, will be outlined. Whilst the banking systems in other Western European countries also have interesting features, these systems are chosen because of the relative importance of their major banks in the international banking system. As in previous chapters, the approach will be to concentrate on the dynamic developments of the systems rather than institutional details. France and Germany are members of the European Communities, and have, therefore, been subject to directives aimed at harmonising the banking and financial laws and regulatory and supervisory practices within Europe, whilst Switzerland is not a member. Another contrast between the systems is the relative size of their economies and indigenous populations. Germany and France have the largest economies in continental Western Europe and, therefore, have strong domestic demands for banking services. Switzerland, in contrast, has a small economy and has concentrated on attracting international banking business.

Germany has a universal banking system in which the major banking groups offer commercial banking services to both the retail and corporate sectors as well as services associated historically with merchant banks in the UK, banques d'affaires in France, investment banks in the US and securities houses in Japan. The Swiss banks also offer a broad range of services and have long been major participants in the Eurobond markets. In contrast, France, like the UK, has historically had a system in which groups of banks and other financial institutions have specialised in the provision of well defined groups of financial services. This began to change following the reforms of the banking system in the 1960s. Since then the various banking groups have begun to offer broader arrays of services and there has been a move towards universal banking. A further distinguishing feature of the French system has been the degree of state involvement. The three major commercial banks were nationalised in 1945 and most of the rest of the non-mutually organised banking system was nationalised in 1982. Even prior to the latter nationalisations, which are scheduled to be reversed by 1992, state influence was extensive because of the existence of a number of specialist, state controlled or backed, credit institutions.

The regulatory and supervisory system in France is also more strict than in Germany or Switzerland, or the UK for that matter. French governments have, since the war, generally been *dirigiste* and have imposed quantitative and qualitative controls on bank lending as well as providing subsidies for lending to certain sectors, notably agriculture. Deregulation is now proceeding apace in France, probably more rapidly than elsewhere in Western Europe, including the UK. The French system has not yet become the most liberalised, however, because it started from a highly regimented state. The German, Swiss and UK systems have long been much more liberal and it is notable that the German authorities talk not of deregulation but of further liberalisation. A catalyst for more rapid deregulation, or further liberalisation, in Germany, France and Switzerland has been the changes in the UK system caused by the build up to the 'big bang' in October 1986. One aim of the latter was to establish London as the major financial centre in the European time zone by putting it in a position to capture a major share of the emerging globally traded share market. The French and German authorities have responded to the threat that London might attract business away from Frankfurt and Paris. The Dutch authorities have also introduced deregulatory measures to bolster Amsterdam's position as a financial centre and elsewhere in Europe, notably Scandinavia, liberalisation has been permitted to help domestic banks to compete in the evolving international money and capital markets.

3.2 The French Banking System

i) Introduction

Banks are the main deposit taking institutions in France and they dominate the financial system, collecting the majority of funds made available by the non-financial sector. Insurance companies and other investing institutions play a relatively minor role compared to countries such as the UK and the US. This may be due to the existence of a relatively generous state pension scheme, which reduces the incentive for private pension provision. State pensions are funded from social contributions on a pay as you go basis. Hence, large pension funds requiring investment do not exist on the same scale as they do in countries such as the UK and the US, where private pension provision is more important. Additionally, the household sector has shown a strong preference for liquidity in the past. This may change if inflation[1] is maintained at low levels for a sustained period and attempts to encourage wider share ownership[2] prove successful. The initial indications are that liquidity preference has started to decline. The privatisations of St. Gobian, a non-bank firm, and the Paribas investment banking group, in late 1986 and early 1987 respectively, were heavily oversubscribed and there was considerable interest from small investors. Lower inflation reduces the attractiveness of traditional inflation hedges, such as property and other physical assets like gold, and increases the attractiveness of financial assets. Although still offering positive real interest rates, bank deposits have become less attractive in relation to securities as an investment because of the high yields on the latter and the opportunities to realise capital gains on the booming stock markets of the mid 1980s.

In the provision of finance, long term credit institutions, which raise the majority of their funds from other financial intermediaries, have played a more central role; making a significant but declining contribution relative to banks. The securities market is underdeveloped relative to the rest of the financial system, especially when compared to the US and the UK. Measures have, however, recently been introduced[3] to encourage its development. The bond market has been an important source of finance for the government, the nationalised sector, and the special credit institutions.[4] The secondary market in bonds has, however, been relatively inactive. One motivation for the liberalisation of the financial system[5] was to make the funding demands of the socialist government, especially following its extensive nationalisation programme, easier to meet. The equity market has been of limited importance as a primary source of funds for private industry; which has relied heavily on long term finance from banks and special credit institutions. Following the large number of company failures, during the recession in the early 1980s, there was a growing realisation by the government that it was important for companies to be better capitalised and less reliant on bank finance. The banks too realised that improved capitalisation of their corporate customers would reduce the risks involved in lending to them; which have forced them to make extensive and expensive bad debt provisions. Thus the banks have encouraged corporate clients to improve their capital ratios. The socialist government, and the conservative government that preceded it, introduced a series of measures to encourage private share ownership. The conservative government that succeeded the socialist one in the Spring of 1986 is likely to continue with the policy both for ideological reasons and in order to fulfil its massive privatisation programme. In line with most major stockmarkets around the world, the Paris Bourse enjoyed a sustained rise in the mid 1980s and, most encouragingly, the secondary market came alive.

The financial system is heavily regimented and has a high degree of state involvement. The restrictions on the system have been imposed for both prudential and allocative purposes. The high degree of public control and involvement was deemed necessary for the post war reconstruction of the economy but it has continued subsequently in conjunction with indicative planning exercises and the *dirigisme* that has typified postwar socialist and conservative administrations alike. The newly elected conservative government committed itself to breaking this mould by pursuing more market orientated policies. Direct control has been exercised through : ownership of financial institutions, significantly extended by the socialist government in 1982;[6] appointments of the top management of public and semi-public institutions; and by delineation of the permissible activities undertaken by public and semi-public institutions. State owned institutions have, however, traditionally been given a large amount of operational autonomy.

Reforms introduced in the mid-1960s[7] freed deposit taking and investment banks from a number of restrictions and led to a reduced role for specialised credit institutions. Banks were encouraged to extend their involvement in medium and long term lending and to diversify their activities in the direction of universal banking. The reforms also removed branching restrictions and deregulated some lending rates.[8] Interest paid on retail deposits continued to be set by the monetary authorities and charges for money transmission related retail services continued to be prohibited. Following the reforms, there was a series of mergers and re-organisations which had the effect of increasing concentration and modernising banking technology. Several investment banks acquired the status of deposit banks,[9] and other investment banks were absorbed by deposit banks. Additionally, competition from the mutual sector[10] intensified in the fields of retail banking and small business finance, particularly at the regional level.

Having been permitted to accept savings deposits in the late 1950s,[11] commercial banks increased their role in the provision of retail banking services, including housing finance. The savings banks were not allowed to lend freely to the personal and corporate sectors but they developed their range of peripheral services to include : mutual fund management; insurance broking; and financial advice and trust business. The agricultural credit banks in particular began to offer a full range of financial services to residents of rural France and benefited from the ability to cross-sell services to customers with whom they came into contact in their capacity as distributors of state subsidised agricultural credits. The reforms also stimulated interest in international banking. Many banks established overseas branches either individually or in conjunction with other banks. Given that French banks were already well represented abroad, as a result of France's colonial past, the result has been that the overseas presence of French banks is roughly equivalent to that of the UK banks and bettered only by US banks.

The reforms of the 1960s generated rapid change in the banking system which have continued to be encouraged in the subsequent two decades by the changing demands of the more prosperous and financially mature society. In the early 1980s, however, there was a feeling both within and outside France, that change had not gone far enough. France was regarded as being over-banked with overmanned networks. The large banks had extensive branch networks and competed by offering new products and incentives and through advertising; price competition being restricted, especially in the retail sector. Many of the commercial banks complained that they suffered from unfair competition from the special credit institutions, which enjoyed fiscal and other privileges. Restrictive credit controls prevailed and profitability, measured in terms of return to capital, was low in comparison with other major international banks. Also, the capitalisation of the major commercial banks was low by international standards. Their international credit ratings, however, remained high by virtue of the implicit state backing afforded by their nationalised status. Finally, the socialist government, elected in 1981, felt that the banking system could play a greater role in stimulating industrial and commercial development. It consequently nationalised a further 36 banks, in addition to the 'big 3' commercial banks nationalised in 1945, the Paribas and Suez financial holding companies, a couple of major insurance companies, and a number of industrial corporations. The aim was to nationalise the banking system, and to use it as a vehicle for promoting industrial growth, both through directing its lending more effectively and utilising its profits to finance the government.

In the event this initiative proved disappointing in almost every respect. After the 1982 Mexican crisis bank supervisors around the world encouraged banks to increase their capital ratios. It was clear that French banks would have to do the same if they were to maintain their international credit ratings. Further, attempts to modernise by introducing new technology were causing a drain on their capital whilst their profitability was being impaired by their obligations towards newly nationalised industries and the need to make provisions against losses amongst private sector corporate clients as a result of the recession. The socialist government, therefore, gave the banks a virtually free rein, from 1983 onward, to rebuild their capital positions and increase profitability and provisions. With the state unable to inject capital, because of other pressing uses for its revenue, the banks turned to the securities markets. The three major commercial banks had lived without equity since the war but in 1984 and 1985 they were given permission to tap the private equity market by issuing non-voting shares.[12]

Pressures for change continued to build during the early 1980s as a result of : the globalisation of banking markets; securitisation; technological innovation; deregulation in other financial centres, especially London; moves toward further European monetary integration; and the enhanced financial awareness of French society. In response to these pressures the government has accelerated the rate of deregulation.[13] Further, the newly elected conservative government's five year privatisation programme will require major changes to the system. Increased capitalisation and improved efficiency, brought about by a reduction in overmanning and the introduction of new technologies to improve productivity, will be required to ensure successful privatisations. To achieve this some mergers may be required to rationalise the system and increased concentration in the banking sector is likely to result.

ii) The Banking System

There are a number of distinct banking groups between which there is a strong element of, hitherto largely non price, competition. Regardless of type of ownership, because of the constraints placed upon them, they have tended to put growth before profits. Segmentation of the retail banking sector has not been a feature — unlike the UK, where, historically, segments of the financial markets have been dominated by particular groups of institutions.[14] Most banks have been moving towards the establishment of universal banking operations, especially since the reforms of the 1960s.

In the decade following the reforms there was a vigorous expansion of branch networks by the three major banks nationalised in 1945 and by the Crédit Agricole and savings bank groups, accompanied by aggressive campaigns to attract accounts. There was also a rapid spread of the banking habit[15] as a result of successful marketing efforts aimed at converting manual workers from cash payment to monthly direct transfers to bank accounts.

Although the choice between banks was considerable the range of services offered was limited by restrictions on the introduction of new products and pricing policies, especially in the retail sector. Consumer loans were severely restricted by credit controls and housing finance was also regulated. Payment of interest on cheque accounts was prohibited and interest rates on savings and small time deposits were fixed by the authorities. The competitive energies were therefore diverted into the development of a range of peripheral services, including : mutual funds; insurance broking; and trust business. These have not attracted extensive public interest and the inability to cross-sell attractive savings deposits, personal loan finance, and other related services restricted the return from branching and the spread of the banking habit.

Banks were defined[16] as enterprises or institutions whose customary business is to receive funds, in the form of deposits or otherwise, from the public which they employ for discount, credit or financial transactions.

The system has a wide variety of banking institutions, which have been developed under various laws and statutes over the last 150 years.[17] The number of public institutions was increased dramatically in 1982, but prior to that there were public, private and semi-public institutions. The four major commercial banks, two of which were subsequently merged to leave three, and the central bank, the Bank of

France, were nationalised in 1945. The 1945 legislation also created a new regulatory and supervisory framework. The reforms of the mid 1960s left the basic structure unchanged but led to a shifting of the balance, and a blurring of the distinctions, between the major banking groups. The 1982 nationalisation programme was due to be followed by a series of proposals designed to reform the system by rationalising the regulatory and supervisory framework and reducing the number of independent branch networks. The socialist government introduced a new banking law in 1984 which rationalised the regulatory framework for credit institutions but did not set in motion any major restructuring of the banking system itself. More restructuring is likely to result from the five year privatisation proposed by the conservative government, elected in March 1986, than from the period of extended nationalisation. Even the three major commercial banks, nationalised in 1945, are to be privatised. There has, however, been some rationalisation within the nationalised sector which, prior to the privatisation of the Paribas group, contained two investment banking oriented financial holding companies, Paribas and Suez, and four commercial banking oriented holding companies — the 'big three' banks nationalised in 1945, the CIC group, which consists of a chain of regional banks including CIC Paris and Credit Commercial de France (CCF). The bank holding companies to be privatised after Paribas consisted of 42 banks. The major banking groups are large by European standards and following privatisation are likely to be amongst the largest private sector banking groups in Europe.

The private sector banking system existing prior to 1982 evolved largely during the last century[18] and during this period, particularly following each of the world wars, there was a parallel development of special credit institutions. The latter have played an important role in the financial system and were created to fill gaps left by the private sector in order to serve the national interest.

Commercial banks have historically concentrated on short term financing through direct advances and the discounting commercial bills, which are confusingly called commercial paper in France, and their operations reflected the national preference for liquid assets. The special credit institutions were created to compensate for their inadequate provision of medium and long term loans for industrial development. The need for such institutions was particularly apparent during the industrial reconstruction periods following the two world wars. These institutions either make medium or long term loans to the private and public sectors or make available state guarantees or refinancing facilities to commercial banks, in order to encourage lending by them.

Prior to 1966, banking law had categorised banks into short, medium and long term institutions. This maturity division was abolished in 1966, along with branching constraints, by liberalising legislation.[19] The latter also led to increased competition between the various banking groups which resulted in some reorganisation of the banking system, involving mergers and acquisitions and the formation of holding companies and increased concentration.

Banks were required to register with the CNC[20] in one of three main categories: deposit banks (banques de dépôts); investment banks (banques d'affaires); or medium and long term credit banks (banque de crédit long et moyen terme). The deposits banks formed the largest group and were dominated by the three banks formed following the 1945 nationalisations: Banque Nationale de Paris (BNP); Crédit Lyonnais (CL); and Société Générale (SG). Although nationalised, they have operated, subject to general banking restrictions, on a commercial basis. A large proportion of the banks in this category are more or less under the direct control of six major banking groups. Deposit banks offer a wide range of banking services and, since 1966, have been permitted to purchase limited holdings in nonbank companies.

The traditional role of investment banks, such as Paribas and IndoSuez, is to invest in and manage existing industrial and commercial holdings and to participate in the development of new companies by introducing them to the capital markets. Prior to 1966 they were only allowed to take time deposits but subsequently they have been granted the same freedom as deposit banks. They are not, however, allowed to finance nonbank holdings with short term deposits. Although no banks in this category were nationalised in 1945, they were already heavily supervised. Representatives nominated by the Ministry of Finance were appointed to all investment banks. They were entitled to attend board meetings and had the power of veto. If it was exercised, the bank was permitted to appeal to the CNC. Following the 1982 nationalisations, this arrangement became unnecessary but it still prevails for foreign controlled banks in this category.

Due to the inadequacy of their branch networks, investment banks were ill equipped to exploit their freedom, granted in 1966, to take deposits. To adapt themselves to the new system, many of them reorganised : entrusting equity participations to specialised subsidiaries; and transforming banking departments into companies with the status of deposit banks. They then established branch networks through mergers and acquisitions involving already established deposit banks. Because of their relatively restricted branch networks, however, a large proportion of their liabilities consist of funds borrowed from deposit banks and other deposit taking institutions.

The medium and long term credit banks were not directly affected by the 1966 reforms, being mostly subsidiaries of the major banks. Their principal role is to receive term deposits and grant credits for periods in excess of two years. Their resources are derived mainly from their parents or from borrowing on the money markets, through the discounting of bills or promissory notes for example. They are subject to the same limits on industrial and commercial holdings as deposit banks. They have established their own specialised credit institutions, such as leasing companies, some of which have the status of finance companies.

Finance companies (établissements financiers) must register with the CNC and are subject to most of the regulations relating to banks. The majority are subsidiaries of large banking or insurance groups. They are entitled to take sight or time deposits and resources not generated internally are raised from the money markets. They operate mainly in specific areas of instalment credit such as : hire purchase; equipment leasing; real-estate leasing; factoring; and mortgage finance. They are prohibited from securities administration.

The mutual and cooperative banks also play a significant role in the banking system. Until 1984 they were not required to register with the CNC. The larger institutions[21] resemble the large deposit banks in the scope of their operations. They have enjoyed fiscal and other privileges relative to the registered banks and have grown rapidly since the 1960s, widening their array of services and attracting a substantial proportion of total deposits. The agricultural credit banks are mutual associations with a membership composed of individuals and companies resident in rural areas and engaged in agricultural activities. There are two categories of banks in this sector; those affiliated to Crédit Agricole (CNCA)[22] and those unaffiliated. These banks dominate the mutual and cooperative group. The affiliated banks consist of approximately 3,000 local associations which are grouped into about 90 regional banks under the control of the CNCA which is a public body and acts as the supervisory body, the clearing house, and a medium and long term credit institution. It receives subsidies and grants from the state allowing it to lend at low interest to its members. Three registered banks enable the group to offer a wider range of services. The local banks traditionally grant short, medium, and long term loans for working capital, purchases of plant and machinery and projects in the agricultural sector. These loans may be discounted with the regional banks, which may in turn discount them with the CNCA. Resources are raised through deposit taking and bonds issued by the CNCA. Non-affiliated banks have their own federation. They do not enjoy all the advantages of the affiliated group and are less developed but nevertheless have grown in importance since the 1960s. Their central body is a registered bank.

The agricultural credit banks have about 5,000 branches, take 15% of all deposits and grant 13% of credits. They have grown faster than the general banking sector, enjoying fiscal privileges and benefiting from being able to provide subsidised credits which have helped them to cross-sell other banking services. Since 1981 they have been subject to the same corporation tax as registered banks and, in compensation, they were allowed to finance housing and other household needs and to conduct business with small and medium sized companies operating outside the agricultural sector. They are, therefore, likely to become local and regional banks with a more varied clientele in the future.

Crédit Mutuel (CNCM)[23] is a group of over 3,000 local associations organised, like Crédit Agricole, on a mutual basis. These banks have not, however, specialised in a particular industrial sector. CNCM has a network of twenty regional federations and it adopts an administrative coordinating role for the system. The banking activities are carried out by about twenty regional banks, two of which are registered banks, and the CCCM[24] provides banking services to the group as a whole. The associations have no coordinating public body but are subject to state controls over their activities. They issue savings books, which confer credit or tax advantages on depositors similar to those of savings banks and are regarded by the banking community as having an unfair advantage in attracting depositors.

The popular credit banks were also created on a mutual basis. Many were cooperatives formed by individuals in the provinces, who pooled resources for mutual benefit. They now consist of about 40 regional banks attached to the CCBP,[25] which administers the groups' funds. The whole grouping was supervised, until 1984, by the CSBP.[26] The banks lend primarily to small and medium sized companies, sole traders, and professionals. Crédit Hotelier[27] is affiliated to the group.

The CCCC[28] is the central organisation of the cooperative banks. It was formed in 1938 and acts as the central agency, supervisory body, until 1984, and medium and long term credit institutions for the savings and credit institutions, consumer and non-agricultural producer cooperatives, maritime credit banks, which specialise in lending to the fishing industry, and other non profit making associations. It administers the groups' funds, together with a registered deposit bank,[29] and provides banking services to the group.

There are also a number of public sector deposit takers. These include the ordinary savings banks,[30] the national savings bank,[31] the Caisse des Dépôts and Consignations (CDC), and the Treasury and PTT Financial Services.[32] The ordinary savings banks were created mainly by local authorities and now have an extensive network. Most of the funds collected are channelled into the CDC, a state agency described below. They have been extending their range of services and are likely to continue to do so. They offer cheque accounts and make loans to local authorities and to the personal sector, primarily in connection with housing. They have fiscal advantages and the commercial banks are unhappy about the extent to which they have been allowed to diversify whilst retaining these privileges. They compete directly with the national savings bank, which provides services through the post office branch network and is a department of Post and Telecommunications Administration.[33] Traditionally savings banks issue passbooks to depositors in which deposits and withdrawals are registered. They also sell savings schemes and medium term savings certificates issued by central, local and provincial government authorities.

The Caisse des Dépôts centrals (CDC) is an autonomous state agency which was created in 1816 to perform the role of public trustee. It is controlled by a supervisory committee appointed by parliament. It draws most of its resources from the centralisation of savings bank deposits and consequently it is one of the largest financial institutions. It also accepts deposits from solicitors, the social security department, mutual provident associations and consignations[34] and administers various pension and insurance schemes. Consequently, it has a substantial holding of securities and it manages several investment companies, whose shares are sold through savings banks or to institutional investors. It plays an important role in the capital and the mortgage market, where it grants loans to local authorities and associations, which administer low rent housing. It makes loans to public and semi-public enterprises and to state controlled specialised credit institutions. Finally, it is an important lender to the money market, due to its command over liquid resources, and it subscribes to bond issues by public and semi-public institutions, which form a major part of its securities holdings.

The postal and telecommunications services (PTT) collects savings through the national savings bank network and deposits them with the CDC. Additionally it provides the economy in general and public administrations and banks with two modes of payment : postal transfers, for collection and payment and post office current (cheque) accounts, which function in the same way as bank current accounts. Net receipts drawn from these services are paid to the Treasury; which itself has an important role as a financial intermediary.

The Treasury is the executive agent for the administration of the budget and uses the Bank of France as its banker. The public sector departments, local authorities and special credit institutions, also deposit funds with the Treasury. It offers savings certificates to the public and issues Treasury bills to financial institutions. It approves loans granted to the public and private sectors, in accordance with state development plans. Through the social and economic development fund (FDES)[35] it grants medium and long term loans, primarily to public enterprises. It also makes short term loans to local and regional authorities.

The special credit institutions principally provide medium and long term financing to the public and private sectors. They are official and semi-official specialised banking institutions with a special legal status. They provide long term finance using public funds raised through bond issues and they guarantee or refinance medium term credits advanced by commercial banks.

Crédit National (CN) is an industrial development bank. It is under state control and was founded in 1919 to channel government subsidies to the victims of the war and to attract additional financial resources. It is the main long term credit institution, supplying investment funds to private industrial and commercial firms and public enterprises. Loans are made directly through the FDES, through which the state also finances loans. They are mainly financed by issues of bonds and medium term securities to banks and other financial institutions. CN also refinances equipment loans made by banks. Following the second world war banks were encouraged to finance purchases of plant and equipment. They traditionally specialised in short term credit business. Because of the short term nature of their liabilities, which were predominantly current account deposits, they could not engage in long and medium term lending to a great degree without developing significantly mismatched positions. The Bank of France, therefore, offered refinancing facilities to underwrite the commercial banks liquidity. To avoid the risk of over reliance on the Bank of France, it seemed sensible to create public and semi-public institutions with sufficient liquid resources to cover some of the refinancing requirements. Because of its past experience in refinancing, CN was encouraged to involve itself in the financing of industrial investment, acting as a rediscounting institution for medium term finance in its own right and in conjunction with the Bank of France.

Crédit Foncier de France (CFF) is a mortgage loan bank. The membership of its governing council must receive the Finance Minister's approval and its governor and his two deputies are appointed by the government. The Comptoir des entrepreneurs, the contractors' bank, is organised similarly and is closely related to CFF, with which it effectively forms a two tier institutional system. These institutions play a similar role in housing finance to that played by CN in industrial and commercial lending. They decide, in conjunction with the Bank of France, on medium term credit financing. CFF also distributes public assistance to house building, takes part in local authority financing and is responsible for the mortgage market[36] created by the government in 1966. CFF is financed mainly by bond and medium term securities issues.

Crédit Hôtelier[37] (CH) was created at the same time as CN. It was placed under the authority of the Chambre Syndicat des Banques Populaires in 1945 and consequently has special relationships with the popular credit banks. Its resources are drawn largely from the issue of state guaranteed securities.

The regional development associations (SDRs)[38] were created in 1955 in connection with a decree establishing the basis for rational development policy. They were to provide regional firms with decentralised financing institutions. Sixteen of them cover the whole of France in combination. They are under the control of the Ministry of Finance and their shareholders include special credit institutions, large banks, private sector companies and individuals. They provide and facilitate finance on favourable terms to companies investing in their specific regions. Their capital is employed in participations as well as long term finance and they issue securities on behalf of firms which would be unable to raise such finance individually. Security is granted by the state.

The state controlled foreign trade bank (BFCE)[39] specialises in import and export financing. It operates jointly with COFACE,[40] which is the foreign trade insurance company. Within their own spheres of competence, like CN and CFF, they take decisions jointly with the Bank of France regarding the advisability of granting access to rediscounting facilities. The BFCE also grants export and import credits directly to business. It is authorised to issue bonds and to take deposits on the same basis as registered banks.

The state projects financing banks (CNME)[41] is an autonomous public institution which was created in 1936 and placed under the Finance Ministry's control. Its main function is to guarantee credit through endorsement. It traditionally supports public sector firms, guaranteeing long medium and short term credits extended to them. It also helps SDRs obtain credit for investment projects. It reinforces other special credit institutions, sharing risks or making their loans eligible for refinancing at the Bank of France. It helps to implement state investment policy and, together with CN and CH, takes part in the review and distribution of FDES loans in support of industrial reorganisation and development.

The industrial development corporation (IDI)[42] was founded in 1970 to provide financial backing to enterprises temporarily short of capital in sectors deemed to be of national importance and to assist generally in the reorganisation and restructuring of industry. It is required to act jointly with other financial institutes and mainly concerns itself with medium sized businesses. It can grant fixed period loans, buy bonds or take up shareholdings.

Finally, the CEPME[43] was created in 1980 as part of a programme to encourage the flow of medium and long term finance to small and medium sized enterprises. It has the status of a registered medium and long term bank.

In conjunction with the 1966 banking reforms a series of reforms were introduced to modernise methods of short term financing by modifying the money markets. The commercial bill of exchange was the traditional short term instrument. The discounting of such bills, with 90 of less days to maturity, was one of the primary functions of the Bank of France. A new form of promissory note was introduced in 1966 to provide a less costly and more controllable method of rediscounting. It did not have the anticipated success and a further new instrument, the LCR,[44] was introduced in 1973. It was similar in concept to the bill of exchange but adapted to modern electronic data processing systems. Commercial bills, however, remained widely used.

The money market allows the institutions authorised to operate in it[45] to adjust their balance sheets in the light of daily cash surpluses or shortages. The main suppliers of funds are the CDC, the Bank of France, and other institutions under public control. Long and medium term credit banks and finance companies are generally borrowers and banks lend or borrow according to the structure of their balance sheets. The Bank of France undertakes open market operations, dealing in first class bills and notes only, through the market. Interbank transactions generally take the form of sale or purchase of bills, with agreements to repurchase or resell.

The capital market has been criticised for not meeting the requirements of industry. Until the 1980s, when further initiatives were taken by the government to reform it,[46] it remained a narrow market by international standards, in spite of previous government attempts to develop it. It was heavily dominated by public enterprises and special credit institutions. The secondary market revolves around seven bourses of which the Paris Bourse is by far the most important. In the early 1980s there were about 10 stock brokers, who were mandatory agents for all transactions.

In common with banking systems in other countries, the French one incurred rising costs in connection with paper funds transfer services. Because of restrictions on bank charges they could not recover the costs of providing such services. The problem was compounded by restrictions on interest paid on savings accounts. There was thus a great incentive to adopt cheque truncation methods and to develop electronic payments methods in order to reduce costs.

The cheque is the dominant means of non cash payment accounting for 80% of non cash payments, compared with 60% in the UK, in the mid 1980s and the cost of paper funds transfers has risen in line with the rapid growth in the volume of transactions. Approximately 4.5bn cheques are written a year, compared with 2.5 in the UK. The Bank oversees the payments system and organises provincial clearing offices, computer clearing centres and regional cheque record exchange centres. A working party on the means of payment was established in 1979. It included representatives of all interested parties : the banks; mutual and cooperative networks; public authorities; and public sector financial agencies. Its discussions led to a consensus in various areas, including the establishment of a future national network for automated interbank exchanges.

The paper based system has been fragmented with little reciprocity between individual banks or the rival networks of the commercial banks, mutuals and savings banks. Through the working party and under the leadership of the Bank, cooperation in the development of a more efficient paper clearing arrangements and of an electronic payments system has been encouraged. The banking industry set up a number of full scale trials of the various payments scenarios, involving both magnetic stripe and memory, 'smart', or 'chip' cards and off and on line authorisation and payments systems. They aim to develop a unified nationwide EFTPOS[47] system, to avoid an uncontrolled proliferation of systems. The trials, launched in 1982 and 1983, involved virtually all the banking institutions. The Council of Ministers decided in 1984 that the memory card should be adopted and the Visa or Mastercard affiliated banking groups have agreed to cooperate and share common equipment such as ATMs and POS terminals. 17m smart cards are expected to be distributed between 1987 and the end of the decade. This is behind the original schedule but the banks are still keen to develop a nationwide EFTPOS system. They see it as a means of improving payments security and reducing fraud as well as stopping the escalation of paper funds transfer costs. Home and office banking links are also widely available to telephone subscribers.

iii) Regulation and Supervision

The central bank, the Bank of France, was established in 1800 by Napoleon as a private bank with state participation and was nationalised in 1945. It participates in the formulation and implementation of monetary policy and intermediates between the banks and the Ministry of Finance,[48] which has overall supervisory responsibility for the banking and financial system. The Bank's headquarters are in Paris and it has an extensive[49] branch network in the provinces. It communicates instructions to banks either directly, in consultation with the AFB,[50] or through the CCB[51] or the CNC.[52]

The Bank of France is the only bank authorised to issue notes and it distributes notes and coin. It is banker to the government and the banks. Its primary duties are to regulate money in circulation and credit supply, to protect the value of the franc, and to ensure effective domestic and foreign settlements. In pursuit of these responsibilities it has had recourse to discount rate policy, open market operations, quantitative and qualitative credit controls,[53] foreign exchange regulations[54] and cash deposit and minimum reserve requirements.

An extensive system of exchange controls have been imposed to conserve foreign currency resources and protect the franc against speculative currency movements. The Bank of France administers the controls under powers delegated by the Ministry of Finance. These controls are being progressively released (see section iv).

The Ministry of Finance plays a central role in the formation and application of monetary and fiscal policies and takes part in the decision making process at the CNC and the CCB. It also participates in the direction and control of credit institutions with special legal status and regulates and supervises the activities of institutional investors. Although the Ministry of Finance is ultimately responsible for the regulation and supervision of banks, its powers are largely delegated to the Bank of France, the CCB and the CNC.

The CNC was established by the 1945 Banking Act. It has the function of advising on and examining the stance of monetary and credit policy and it scrutinises the conditions of operation of the banking and financial system. Its chairman is the Minister of Finance and its vice chairman the governor of the Bank. Other members of the council include representatives from participants in the economy and the financial system, including the banks and the AFB. It functions through sub-committees drawn from the membership of the CNC. The banking regulations committee lays down general rules applicable to credit institutions concerning standards of security, interest rates and network establishment, for example. The committee on credit institutions is responsible for all decisions, authorisations or exceptions of an individual character. The committees are autonomous but work closely with the CNC which in turn works closely with departments at the Bank, which provides administrative support for the CNC.

The CCB was established by the 1941 banking laws and maintained by the 1945 legislation. It was composed of a small number of regular members,[55] including the governor of the Bank and the Finance Minister. The governor chairs the commission, which has at its disposal a secretariat and staff seconded by the Bank. Since 1984 it has been known simply as the CB, the Banking Commission, and it has the task of ensuring that credit institutions comply with banking regulations. It scrutinises their operations and monitors their financial structure, using compulsory returns, the required content of which it determines. The Bank is responsible for organising and carrying out on-the-spot checks on the CB's behalf. Its punitive measures can range from warnings to suspensions. It also deals with appeals against individual decisions made by the CNC, especially concerning registration.

New legislation, in January 1984, provided the banking system with a uniform legal framework. All institutions undertaking banking operations[56] as their customary business became known as credit institutions. These include the registered banks, the mutual banks and municipal credit banks, the finance companies and the special financial institutions. All credit institutions subsequently came under the authority of the CNC and its two special committees and the CB. Previously the CNC and the CBC had been primarily responsible for registered banks and financial establishments.

The AFB was established by the 1941 legislation to replace the managers' unions that had previously existed. All banks operating in France, including foreign banks, are required to join. One of its main functions is to ensure adherence to the decisions of the CNC. It receives instructions and information directly from the regulatory bodies and transmits it to the banks. In addition it represents banks in meetings with the regulatory bodies and acts as the banks' representative in collective bargaining with the unions. It studies requests from foreign banks wishing to establish branches and its opinion is requested by the CNC, which makes the final decision. Perhaps because of its origins, the AFB has been accused of organising a cartel amongst domestic banks and encouraging corporatism. The banks' response to tariffication, discussed in section iv, brought forth such accusations from consumer groups.

Banks are subject to capital requirements, liquidity ratios and medium and long term lending limits. Minimum capital requirements must be met prior to authorisation. These vary according to the size and type of bank. Liquidity ratios apply to all credit institutions under the 1984 act. Ratios relate to francs, foreign currencies and all currencies combined. Banks are required to restrict non-rediscountable medium and long term credits to pre-set coefficients of their capital and their savings accounts or time deposits. In addition to the minimum capital requirements, there are also solvency ratios, relating capital assets to total risks, which are calculated using weights measuring the risk attached to various liabilities. The banks have generally been encouraged to increase their capital ratios, which are low by international comparison, towards levels prevailing abroad. Under the conservative government, elected in March 1986, a new prudential ratio is to be introduced to ensure that banks have adequate long term funding to cover their long term loans. This is to be phased in gradually and transitional measures are to be applied. Additionally a new prudential liquidity ratio is to be set and the treatment of financial instruments subject to interest rate risk is under review.

In connection with monetary policy, the banks are required to hold non-interest bearing reserves with the Bank. These were initially set as a percentage of customer deposits in 1967. Under the 'Encadrement du Credit' system, introduced in the 1970s, reserve requirements were also set as a percentage of loans. Supplementary reserves were applied at punitive progressive ratios to that fraction of loans exceeding the progression permitted by the encadrement system. During the 1970s the encadrement became the principle instrument of credit control. The principle behind the system was similar to that underlying the UK's Supplementary Special Deposit Scheme, or 'corset', which also operated in the 1970s. Banks exceeding pre-set credit or loan growth guidelines were to be penalised by calls on their liquidity, reducing their potential earnings on current deposits and restricting their potential for further credit expansion. Quantitative and qualitative credit control is also exercised by control of access to refinancing by the Bank and the specialised credit institutions.

In 1984 the socialist government announced that the twelve year old encadrement system would be phased out. It is to be replaced by a system operating on reserve ratios and greater use will be made of open market operations. The newly elected conservative government completed the phasing out of the encadrement system at the end of 1986. Whilst lending limits have been removed, monetary targets have been retained and the Bank aims to manipulate interest rates, using open market operations in the money markets, to hit the targets. To facilitate this, banks will be required to hold new mandatory non-interest bearing deposits with the bank in proportion to their deposits. These are higher than the previous requirements, which were set in relation to loans, and are designed to ensure that the banking sector normally needs to borrow from the Bank. This will give the Bank greater influence over interest rates. The banks have baulked at the size of the mandatory requirements but, like the new prudential measures, they are to be phased in and there will be transitional measures.

iv) Deregulation

The reform of the French banking system has been on the agenda for some time. The conservative government, in 1978, commissioned a study by the Inspector General M. Mayoux[57] to examine the structure of the banking system in order to determine charges required, to encourage greater involvement in financial activities at the regional level and the greater regional investment of funds collected from the regions. The report, published in 1979, concluded that : there was excessive centralisation, with the credit function too heavily concentrated in Paris; there was overbanking, due to the multiplicity of networks collecting deposits and granting credits and unfair competition, due to the privileged position of certain institutions and networks; small and medium sized business facing financing problems; and there was an excessive variety of credit instruments and a lack of information on credit conditions. Proposals included the following: the three national banks should be broken up into regional institutions; the fiscal and monopolistic advantages enjoyed by some networks and institutions should be eliminated; the encadrement system should be abolished because of its distortionary effect of inhibiting the more dynamic banks and protecting the weaker; freer competition on interest and commission rates should be permitted.

The election of a socialist government in 1981 preempted legislation on the report by the conservative government. The socialist government nationalised 36 additional banks, as well as the Paribas and Suez financial holding groups in 1982. It also introduced legislation, in 1984, harmonising the regulation of credit institutions and proposed to implement some of the Mayoux report's proposals, including the phasing out of special privileges; the reduction of centralisation; the simplification of credit instruments; and the revision of monetary policy by phasing out the encadrement system. It appointed new chairmen to the banks who were required to reform their management structures. Many banks were encouraged to increase their support of smaller and medium sized businesses.

Initially many of the banks were drawn into supporting ailing companies, financing nationalised industries and exports and helping to finance the budget deficit. The change was not as stark as might appear, however, because banks had become used to qualitative and quantitative credit guidance under previous administrations. The banks did not become mere appendages to the government. They retained substantial autonomy and a wholesale revolution in the banking system did not occur. Pressure to bail out ailing companies and to support nationalised industries began to dissipate in 1983 as the government instead encouraged banks to improve their profitability and provisioning against bad or doubtful debts. This was in line with decisions taken by supervisory authorities in other industrial countries to encourage banks to increase their capital ratios and their provisioning in the light of the Mexican debt crisis and other developments in international banking. The profitability and capital backing of French banks was already low by international standards and it was necessary to take action to maintain their international status, despite the increased state backing afforded by the nationalisations. Increased involvement with ailing companies would clearly have reduced profitability and required further provisioning.

The banks, being nationalised, could not raise equity capital and the government, with many competing demands on its resources, could not inject capital. Instead the banks were allowed to retain a larger portion of their earnings to build up provisions and to raise capital from the Bourse, after 1984, by issuing non-voting loan stock.[58] By encouraging banks to retain earnings to build up provisions the government forewent tax revenues and dividends from which they had hoped to benefit. The net result of these efforts has been to raise the major French banks' combined capital and provisions to levels equivalent to those of US money centre banks and slightly below those of the major German banks. If provisions are ignored, however, capitalisation remains weak by international standards.

The conservative government, elected in March 1986, is likely to preside over a period of more dramatic change for the banking system than its predecessors. It proposes to denationalise 65 companies, including seven major banking groups and three major insurance groups, over a five year period. The privatised banks will be expected to compete more actively in the domestic market following the government's retreat from *derigisme*. Their strong corporatist spirit may militate against this and competition will probably be stimulated initially by the exposure of the French banking system to competition from foreign banks as the deregulation and globalisation of the international financial system proceeds apace.

In preparation for privatisation many banks will have to continue to bolster their capital positions by issuing non-voting shares up to the permitted limit of 25% of their capital and many of them have begun to diversify. Within the nationalised sector the traditional barriers between different parts of the financial sector have begun to be eroded. The two major state owned insurance companies have, for example, taken important stakes in banking groups. Additionally the major commercial banks have been rapidly developing merchant and investment banking activities and are to be allowed to deal on the Bourse alongside the traditional specialist brokers. Some of the smaller nationalised banks have had to be bailed out or merged with other banks. Further reorganisation is likely to be required to make privatisation of some of the weaker banks an attractive proposition and additional mergers and absorptions are likely to be necessary.

A further measure designed to improve the banks' financial position has been the granting of permission, in 1986, to introduce service charges for cheque accounts, a process known as 'tariffication'.This should allow them to recoup some of the costs of collecting retail deposits at a time when falling interest rates have reduced the endowment effect emanating from non interest bearing cheque accounts. The introduction of charges would also help to speed up the establishment of a nationwide EFTPOS system, by demonstrating the cost reducing potential of EFTPOS to the consumers, and to discourage further growth in cheque usage. The introduction of bank charges was postponed from the beginning of 1987 to April 1 1987 following a consumer outcry. Consumer groups accused the commercial banks of operating a cartel because of the marked similarity of their charging systems. In January 1987 the banks were asked by the Finance Minister to postpone the introduction of charges. This leaves banks in a difficult position. They continue to be incumbered with high cost branch networks and cannot discourage a further growth in cheque usage. They need to reduce their costs and raise revenue from the provision of monetary transmission services in order to be able to improve the other services they offer and boost profit levels, which have been squeezed by falling interest rates. They may now have to offer inducements, such as cheaper loans to customers with high balances. The banks cannot afford to alienate their retail customers at a time when they are losing the business of some of their major corporate customers, who have been bypassing the banking system and borrowing directly from the markets by issuing short term securities and commercial paper. Consumer loans and asset management are among their most profitable lines of business but to reap maximum benefits costs must somehow be reduced.

In accordance with French custom, the new government appointed new chairmen to the nationalised banks in 1986. The first three companies to be privatised were announced in September 1986. These included Paribas and a major insurance company. The denationalisation programme will, of necessity, be executed gradually, since the equity to be sold will amount to approximately a third of the Bourse's capitalisation and will have to be preceded by further issues of non-voting shares if the banks are to achieve adequate capitalisation. It could, ironically, prove to be a highly profitable exercise in state capitalism, since the Paribas and Suez groups were, in 1986, worth four times their nationalisation value and the terms of nationalisation were regarded as generous at the time. The success of the initial privatisations, including that of Paribas, however, indicated that fears that the equity markets would be unable to digest the new issues were unfounded. The programme is instead likely to be stepped up. CCF had been chosen to follow Paribas as the second bank in the programme and the success of the Paribas flotation prompted the government to select Société Generale, the smallest of the 'big three' commercial banks and the fourth largest of all the banks, as next for privatisation in the second half of 1987. It was chosen ahead of its great rival Crédit Lyonnais, the second largest commercial bank, and the Suez group which contains Paribas's major investment banking rival, IndoSuez. It is believed that the privatisation of the four insurance companies, the three largest of which were nationalised in 1945, will prove more problematic.

The privatisation programme, apart from contributing to government revenue, thereby permitting a reduction in the public sector borrowing requirement, and facilitating promised tax cuts, will allow the government to pursue its policy of encouraging wider share ownership. For it to succeed the right conditions had to be created on the Bourses. The groundwork in this area had already been laid by the two previous governments, which introduced a series of complementary measures to encourage equity holding in France. The programme will itself increase liquidity by reducing the public sector borrowing requirement and consequently state funding through the capital markets and by promoting wider participation in the equity markets. It will also provide the banks with opportunities to earn fee income and to gain experience in the capital markets.

In addition to the Paris Bourse, which is by far the largest, there are six regional exchanges but even the Paris Bourse is small compared to the exchanges in New York, London and Tokyo and it is smaller than the Frankfurt exchange. Following the oil price rise in 1973, companies became even more dependent on the banking system and the Finance Ministers, M. Barre, M. Monorey and M. Delors, of previous governments who tried to reverse this tendency. In July 1978 the Manorey Law was passed. Before its effects could be judged a socialist government was elected. The socialist government wished to regenerate industrial activity. To do this savings had to be encouraged and directed towards the corporate sector. The 1982 Dautresme Report concluded that financial reform was necessary to achieve this goal. The report inspired the Delors Law, enacted in January 1983.

The Delors and Monorey laws shared the common aim of encouraging equity and stable long term finance of the corporate sector, to strengthen industry and remove the inflationary bias caused by dependence on bank lending. The aim was to redirect savings from short to long term financial assets by increasing the role of the capital market relative to financial intermediaries. Both laws introduced tax incentives and disincentives, to influence savings and borrowing, whilst attempting to make the institutional framework more receptive to new financial products. The Delors law was a more fundamental reform than the Monorey law, which offered households tax inducements to purchase stocks in French companies. Its aims were to reduce reliance on bank credit and encourage wider share ownership. The Monorey law tried to direct savings towards long term assets, by raising taxes on earnings from short term assets such as Treasury bills and savings accounts and engineering a rise in long term interest rates. It also introduced subordinated loans, which are long term credits, which could be regarded as capital stock and shares without voting rights.

The Delors law maintained the main provisions of the Monorey law, increased tax incentives, and further encouraged the issue of shares without voting rights. Both laws, therefore, provided a legal framework for an array of new financial instruments, previously prohibited or not available, aimed at reducing the dependency of firms on banks. They gave impetus to the development, in 1983, of an unlisted securities market, or Second Marché, on the Paris Bourse, and to the development of venture capital operations which were judged to be critical for the development of small and medium sized firms. The laws have had the effect of increasing household investment in long term financial assets and widening share ownership, despite a fall in the household savings ratio, experienced in common with other major industrial countries. Under the socialists there was a rise in bond issues by the state and public sector institutions and there was a revival in the share market, in line with developments on the major stock exchanges around the world but perhaps more striking than on most of them. The conservative government, elected in March 1986, has a policy of further extending share ownership and can be expected to stimulate further interest in the equity market in order to fulfil its massive privatisation programme, which will itself stimulate interest.

The Second Marché proved to be a successful innovation and may help in the revitalisation of the Bourse in the future as the more successful participants in the Second Marché seek listings on it.

Other major developments in the financial markets have included the establishment of a financial futures market (Matif) which opened in February 1986 and the introduction of certificates of deposit (CDs) and commercial paper, under socialist Finance Minister, M. Beregovoy, who continued to encourage the breakdown of barriers between sectors of the financial markets. In December 1984 it was announced that CDs would be permitted in order to bring the markets in line with international ones and rejuvenate the financial and money markets. They were introduced in 1985. This followed initiatives with a similar motive, such as the granting of permission to issue zero and ECU bonds in 1984. Then in 1985 permission was given to issue commercial paper (CP), called billets de trésorerie to distinguish them from trade bills which were already called papier commercial. The first paper was issued in early 1986, five months ahead of the opening of the sterling commercial paper market in London. The market grew explosively, causing concern, at the Bank and the Finance Ministry, about its implications for monetary control and its possible effect of draining liquidity from the banking system and funds from he bonds market. Matif flourished in its first year, by 1987 new contracts had been introduced alongside the initial government bond futures contract and others were under consideration. Matif has also launched a drive for new, and especially foreign, membership and is seeking links with international futures exchanges overseas. In 1986 the Eurofranc bond market reopened as well.

In September 1985, a new mortgage agency[59] was established, modelled on the US Federal National Mortgage Association (Fannie Mae). It issues bonds to back housing loans made by the big banks and it is hoped that it will revitalise the mortgage market and cut the cost of housing finance. It was established by the major banks participating in construction and housing credit. The bonds are issued with state guarantees.

The new government has continued to attempt to harmonise the bond, mortgage and money markets and to create a full range of financial instruments. It has also continued with the policy of piecemeal removal of exchange controls, promising their complete removal in the near future in order to remove the remaining handicap to Paris's ambition to become a major international financial centre. The new Finance Minister, Edouard Balladur, announced four separate batches of exchange control liberalisations between March 1986 and the end of that year and claimed to have removed 90% of the controls. The previous government had joined West Germany in suppressing its withholding tax on non-resident bond purchases. These measures will open the financial system to further foreign competition.

The new financial instruments and procedures have gained rapid acceptance amongst the larger banks, which were eager to extend the range of services they could offer and to bolster their fee income by acting as lead managers and advisors. Further opportunities will be provided by the privatisation programme. In 1986 fee earning business still only accounted for about 10% of the earnings of the major banks, compared with 30% in the major foreign banks. As mentioned above, disintermedition is causing commercial banks to loose business with large corporate clients and they have found that they were too reliant on corporate loan income. They have responded by reorganising themselves by regrouping their activities to form: personal banking, including unit trusts and mutual and money market funds; corporate or merchant banking; capital market or securities divisions; and, in some cases, specialist financing, including leasing, divisions. The aim aim of this last group is to concentrate on small and medium sized companies which do not have direct access to the securities markets, on the retail sector and on developing fee earning capabilities.

The government is also to continue to remove discriminatory privileges enjoyed by the special credit institutions and networks, such as Crédit Agricole, and to allow banks to extend their range of services and to give them more freedom in setting interest rates and making charges. There were around 50 varieties of subsidised credit until 1984, when the subsidies started to be removed. Competition should, therefore, increase and the role of some of the special credit institutions will be called into question by the phasing out of subsidised credits, which accounted for 50% of total lending in 1985.

Since 1984 the pace of deregulation in the Paris markets has exceeded that in Frankfurt and Zurich. All three centres have had to respond to the challenge of worldwide deregulation, especially that taking place in London. France, however, started from a much more regimented position than Switzerland or Germany and there is some way to go before Paris can catch up with the other major European and world financial centres. Nevertheless in three years access to the financial markets has been opened up, a full range of financial instruments has been created and competition between banks has been encouraged. The sustained 'bull market' has helped to broaden the markets. The government aims to move progressively and at a slower pace than the UK authorities in order to monitor developments in London. Its ultimate aim is to prepare for the opening up of the European financial services sector, which is scheduled for 1992.

The decision to encourage the introduction of a wide range of financial instruments was taken in response to the need to fund the growing PSBR in the early 1980s. This made revitalisation of Treasury financing essential but the process went much further. The new instruments have opened up a full range of maturities to a wide range of investors. In February 1987 the conditions on CD and CP issues were further relaxed, allowing issues of smaller denominations and maturities ranging from 10 days to 7 years. In December 1986 the Finance Ministry named 12 primary dealers for the Treasury bond and bill markets. They included: the major commercial and investment banks; Crédit Agricole and the Caisse des Dépôts, the state controlled financial institutions; and two consortiums, which grouped together stockbrokers and other banking institutions. The dealers will be expected to quote continuous two way prices and are expected to add to the liquidity of the market. The cartel restricting the lead management of bonds issued by the government and state institutions to the 'big three' banks was removed in 1985 and primary bond commission rates were liberalised in the winter of 1984. Spreads have declined since the reforms began under Pierre Beregovoy and the market is now much more like the UK gilts and the US Treasury bond markets. Securities in the Treasury markets are becoming the benchmarks for CDs and CP.

Deregulation, and reform of the Paris Bourse in particular, has come to be seen as a necessity for ensuring the survival of Paris as an international financial centre. After the reform of the government debt market, the next priority is to reform the equity market. There has been an absence of market makers willing and able to take positions and quote continuous two way prices. New and more highly capitalised jobbing ventures are expected to emerge by 1989. Attempts have been made to discourage the migration of equities business to better equipped, lower cost, financial centres. Action has been taken to reduce brokers' commissions. Brokers and banks have been permitted to form associations, and banks are to be able to undertake jobbing functions, acting as principals in the market. In future it is expected that, as in London, the brokers' privileged position will be removed and that banks will be allowed to function as brokers. Computerised trading has also been rapidly developed and was introduced in 1986.

3.3 The German Banking System

i) Introduction

The West German banking system provides the premier example of a universal banking system in which the major banking groups offer banking services associated with commercial, investment, and merchant banks in other countries. The most important segregation in the financial system has been between banking and insurance business, but even this began to break down in the mid 1980s.

The banks have operated within a fairly liberal environment for some time. Exchange controls were removed long ago and interest rate regulation was abolished in 1967. In the mid 1980s the talk has been of further liberalisation, rather than deregulation. Another distinguishing feature of the system is the high degree of independence of its central bank, the Deutsche Bundesbank. The Bundesbank has been critical of the pace at which financial innovation has proceeded in the early 1980s and the major German banks have also proceeded with caution. Nevertheless, it has had to respond to the deregulation occurring abroad in order to protect its major financial centre, Frankfurt, against competition from other financial centres, especially London. The extent to which the Bundesbank has permitted further liberalisations has depended on its view of their influence on its effectiveness in pursuit of monetary policy. It is responsible for protecting the value of the Deutschemark (D Mark) and, therefore, for controlling inflation and developing exchange rate policy. During the 1970s it took the view that an expanded role of the D Mark as a foreign reserve currency would impair its ability to control the domestic money supply. In the first half of the 1980s it adopted a more permissive stance towards the expansion of the D Mark's foreign currency role, in the belief that it could to some extent sterilise the influence of foreign currency transactions on domestic money supply growth. In 1984 it took a step actively to attract foreign capital inflows. Whilst the dollar continued to appreciate against the D Mark the Bundesbank became concerned about the possibility that capital outflows would accelerate, especially following the removal of withholding tax[60] by the US authorities. The German authorities responded by removing the coupon tax on interest payments to foreign holders of D Mark bonds. Further liberalising measures were introduced in 1985[61] to stimulate foreign interest in the German financial markets. In 1986 the D Mark appreciated considerably against the dollar and some of the other major currencies, particularly sterling, leading to substantial capital and money inflows and it remains to be seen whether this will inhibit further liberalising moves or whether the pressure to promote Frankfurt vis à vis London and other financial centres prevails.

As in France, there has been a strong preference for liquidity and banks have been the dominant financial institutions. The equity market consists of eight regional bourses, of which the Frankfurt Bourse is by far the largest. Because of the commercial sector's dependence on the banks for finance, the equity market is relatively underdeveloped. The bond market has been dominated by the banks and is effectively an interbank market. Again like France, a generous state pension scheme, funded on a pay as you go basis, has meant that the role of insurance and pension funds in institutional investment has been a minor one compared with the UK or the US. The equity market has nevertheless enjoyed a four year period of rising prices and secondary and new issue activity has increased. This was stimulated by foreign investment seeking currency gains as a result of an expected appreciation of the D Mark against the dollar and other currencies. The hope has subsequently been realised and it is feared that foreign interest will wane unless the equity market is rationalised.[62] An encouraging feature of the stock market boom has, however, been the interest shown by German residents in shareholding. The government can be expected to encourage this trend, perhaps by introducing tax incentives and by pursuing its privatisation programme. The programme is, however, much smaller than the UK and the French ones. It is recognised that the corporate sector had become over-reliant on bank finance and was undercapitalised. This forced the German banks to increase their bad debt provisioning during the recession of the early 1980s, when there was a record incidence of bankruptcies, and the banks have since encouraged their corporate clients to increase their capital backing.

The German banking system is highly competitive. There are competing commercial, cooperative and savings bank networks all offering universal banking services. The country is generally regarded as overbanked because of the overlap in these networks. Competition is likely to increase further as a result of an influx of foreign banks attracted by the liberalising measures introduced in the mid 1980s, the extension of the Bundespost's banking business and the threat from the largest insurance company, the Allianz, to extend its financial services. It has already bought a stake in an important Bavarian bank. In November 1986 the fifth largest insurance company bid for the fifth biggest non-state bank. If successful it will achieve the most significant inroad into banking so far made by an insurance company. Meanwhile the banks have been entering into insurance business . In 1984 Deutsche Bank began offering a savings scheme with life assurance attached.

In the past the major commercial banks have concentrated on their corporate clients, largely ignoring the retail sector. The latter was the domain of the cooperative and savings bank, which also provided services to local businesses and authorities. The increase in the wealth of the retail sector has changed this and the banks branch networks have expanded rapidly. In the mid 1960s there were 25,000 branches but by 1980 there were 40,000 and the commercial banks had become active competitors in the retail sector. There is a considerable amount of state (Länder) autonomy in Germany and this has encouraged the development of a number of regional banks, mainly publicly owned Länder banks, and accounts for the relative independence of the eight bourses.

As a member of the EEC, like France, German banking law has been adapted to take account of various EC directives.[63]

ii) The Banking System

After the recession of the early 1980s the profits of the major banks recovered rapidly. Apart from the more favourable conditions provided by the economic recovery, falling interest rates have proved beneficial by reducing funding costs faster than lending revenues.[64] In 1984/5 their profits were boosted by the dollar's strength and they have also been boosted by the sustained stock market boom in the mid 1980s. Additionally they have benefited from a reduction in their mismatching. In the late 1970s they had lent long when short term costs were rising rapidly. The banks have, since the 1982 Mexican crisis, been encouraged to bolster their reserves. This was also implicitly required by provisions in the 1984 banking legislation.[65] With the stockmarket booming, they have found this more easy to achieve than expected. Even though the commercial banks' exposure to country, and especially

Latin American, debt is less than that of many of their foreign rivals they have also made generous provisions against bad and doubtful debts. These can be on lent to low risk customers, adding to profits. Further, they are believed to carry sizeable hidden reserves. The major banks are, therefore, in a strong position to compete in the developing global banking markets. Their interest margins have, however, been falling. Competition in the retail sector continues to intensify, largely due to domestic developments, as various institutions compete for savings and credit business.

The influx of foreign banks will add to competition in the domestic and Euro Deutschemark (D Mark) markets. The foreign banks also hope to pick up corporate business, particularly from medium sized export orientated companies. Large and medium sized banks, however, usually have one main banker or 'house bank', which is the main supplier of short term finance. Salomon Brothers, the major US securities house, however, sees opportunities in the Euro-D Mark market, where it hopes to to be in the forefront of innovations. It also intends to engage in corporate finance and mergers and acquisitions business. There has not been much of the latter in Germany hitherto, however. Foreign bank interest in the capital markets is likely to increase further if the government fulfils its January 1987 election pledge to remove turnover tax or 'stamp duty'. The foreign banks' strategy is, therefore, to offer peripheral services at competitive prices and other services not available from the house bank, such as currency dealing in many cases. The growth in fee earning generated by securitisation and attempts by banks to offer a broader range of services to the corporate sector, has been a major contributor to the profits growth. Here too competition, especially from foreign banks,[66] is likely to continue to increase. The banks have also made record profits from securities dealing, in the booming bourses and Eurobonds markets, and exchange dealing on their own accounts.

Since the 1950s concentration in the banking system has increased as a result of a series of mergers and the number of operating banks has been reduced to a third of the level of that time. There are now three major commercial banks in Germany[67] and these compete with the cooperative and savings bank networks, which are coordinated through regional and central institutions and can consequently also offer the range of services associated with the commercial universal banks. There remain a significant number of independent and private banks which often specialise in various banking services, however. In all there are about 5,000 banks with almost 45,000 offices. There is roughly one office per 1,400 residents and one office of the big banks per 20,000 residents. In the UK there was one branch per 2,737 residents, if building society and post office branches are ignored, and in the US and Japan the number of bank offices per person were 6,568 and 6,900 respectively, again excluding other savings institutions in the mid 1980s.

Because of the range of their activities it is probably preferable to call the commercial banks credit banks. They grant long medium and short term credits, or loans. They issue bonds and act as underwriters in the capital markets. They buy and sell securities on the stock exchanges and they engage in foreign currency transactions. In both cases they deal on their own behalf and on the behalf of their customers. They also engage in trust business and instalment financing and provide other services, including monetary transmission , to the retail and corporate sectors. Additionally, they hold participations in companies and are represented on the boards of many large corporations. This has become a contentious issue in the mid 1980s even though it is a feature of the German banking system that has been admired because it ensures that banks take a long term interest in their corporate clients. In the UK in particular banks have been criticised for not providing enough medium and long term finance to industry whilst the institutional investors have been criticised for basing their investment decisions on short rather than long term prospects. In December 1986 the Academic Advisory Council (AAC), an influential body which advises the Economics Ministry, issued a report which criticised universal banking because it creates conflicts of interest. In the UK banks have not hitherto held equity stakes in the non bank corporate sector, although there is no law against it, as there is in the US. The AAC believes that conflicts of interest arise because banks hold stocks and lend to the same company and this gives them an information advantage when dealing on the stock exchange and dampens competition. The AAC therefore concurs with the German monopolies commission's view that bank stakes in non banks should be limited to 5% of each company's total equity. The major banks have responded to past criticisms, especially by the monopolies commission, by reducing the number of stakes they hold in excess of 25%, which must be reported to the commission. In the UK it is believed that stakes of 15% can give a controlling interest and the banks are believed to have increased the number of such stakes that they hold. The AAC believes that banks should conform to normal cartel rules and the monopolies commission may well reduce the 25% reporting requirement. Their influence is not limited shareholding. They are empowered to exercise proxy votes and they are represented on supervisory boards in the manufacturing, trading and retail sectors. They also dominate stockmarket management committees and new issue business on the eight bourses. Deutsche Bank takes a particularly large share of new issue business. The independent brokers want their cartel-like domination of the bourses broken. The savings banks also support divestment by the commercial banks. The larger banks are expected to reduce their equity holdings and increase investment in alternative securities at home and abroad.

At the end of 1985 there were 236 credit banks in Germany, including 63 branches of foreign banks. The credit banks include the 'big three' banks and their Berlin affiliates, the regional banks and other credit institutions, foreign bank branches, and private banks. A major cause of the fall in the number of banks has been the increased market share of the major banks, achieved through mergers and competitive pressure which has forced many small private and cooperative banks to cease operation. The number of private and commercial banks has decreased by 66% since 1957, whilst the number of consumer loan corporations has declined by only 50%. The number of commercial banks has declined by 33% whilst the number of savings banks has declined by only approximately 25%.

The 'big three' banks, in the private commercial category, accounted for just under 10% of the total bank business volume at the end of 1984. This is small compared to other major European countries. In France the 'big four' had about 20% of banking business. In Switzerland the 'big three' had about 45% and in the UK the 'big four' had over 50%. Before the first world war the share of the big private sector banks was about 80%. Their share had declined to around 20% by the 1950s, largely due to the increased importance of savings and cooperative banks. Of the big three Deutsche Bank is by far the largest and most profitable. In 1986 its profits were four times those of its nearest rival. According to the Financial Times top 500, published in November 1986, Deutsche Bank is, after the Union

Bank of Swizerland (UBS), the second largest in Europe. It was the ninth largest company in Europe whilst UBS was the seventh largest. The other two major Swiss banks were the third and fourth largest banks. Dresdner was seventh largest, after NatWest and Barclays of the UK, and was the [forty-ninth] largest company. Commerzbank was ninth in the banking league, after Lloyds bank of the UK, and the fifty-sixth largest company. Midland bank of the UK was tenth largest. Dresdner is the second largest German bank and Commerzbank the fifth largest. The banking league table excluded the large French and Italian public sector banks. The 'big three' engage in securities dealing and foreign trade finance, as well as credit business and deposit taking. Housing finance and leasing business has become increasingly important and so too have their activities in the Euro markets. They have around 3,000 bank offices spread throughout Germany, giving them access to both retail and corporate business. In connection with the latter, they play a significant role in mergers and acquisitions. Their share ownership is widely spread and they hold substantial shareholdings in industrial and trading companies. Additionally they have acquired interests in other, particularly mortgage and specialised, banks. As well as opening overseas branches and subsidiaries, they have developed close relationships with international banks abroad through various international banking groups.[68]

The regional banks, as their name implies, originally confined their operations to specific regions and most still do not have branches nationwide.[69] They often also have offices abroad. Whilst the three largest are all stock corporations, regional banks may alternatively be partnerships or private limited liability companies. At the end of 1984 the 103 regional banks accounted for just over 10% of total business volume. Their market share was, therefore, larger than that of the 'big three'. Whilst conducting regular commercial banking business, some regional banks are also involved in special operations, such as mortgage loans and the issue of mortgage and municipal bonds to finance long term lending.

Private banks include amongst their number, which has decreased dramatically since the second world war, the oldest credit institutions in Germany. They are organised as general or limited partnerships. In 1970 there were about 170 registered private banks. By the end of 1984 76 remained. Their share of banking business is less than 1.5%. They normally specialise in one or more of the following : investment banking; export finance; money management; trust business; medium term financing for industry; and business relating to mergers and acquisition. In other words they usually seek niche business in areas associated with investment, merchant or trust banks overseas.

Foreign bank presence has been increasing. There were 15 foreign banks incorporated in Germany in 1957. By the end of 1984 there were 62 and the number has continued to grow since then due to the deregulatory measures introduced in 1985,[70] which allow them to participate more actively in the domestic bond and D Mark Eurobond markets. At the end of 1984 they maintained 112 offices, mainly in larger cities, and they had about a 2.5% share of the market. Their most important clients hitherto have been foreign subsidiaries of multinational corporations, for whom they have conducted import and export transactions. Like other banks, they are subject to German banking law, which also imposes requirements particular to them.

In combination, the private commercial banks had just over 22% of the total banking business volume at the end of 1984. This understates their overall importance in the financial sector because of their significant role in the securities business.

There are two groups of credit institutions covered by public law: the savings banks and their central institutions. These public banks account for about 38% of total banking business volume. There were 591 savings banks with over 17,500 offices and a 22% share of the market at the end of 1984. They were traditionally deposit takers and long term financiers of municipal investment and housing. They now offer most of the services associated with the universal banks of the private sector. They continue to concentrate on savings deposits, attracting 50% of the total. Their guarantors are cities, boroughs and district authorities. Their operations are confined to the area of their guarantors and there is consequently little competition from other savings banks. Foreign operations are of limited importance for most of them.

Their central institutions (Girozentralen) are owned by the savings banks and the state in which they operate, either individually or jointly. They act as bankers to savings bank associations, providing clearing services, holding their liquidity and providing them with funds and other services, such as those connected with foreign payments. Because they hold the savings banks' reserves, they are important participants in the money markets. By virtue of their ownership structure, they are usually the principal banks for the federal state (Länder) in which they operate and are commonly calledLändesbanken. The Girozentralen in turn have their own central giro institutions[71] which holds the liquidity of the 11 Girozentralen and acts as a clearing house for federal and international payment transactions. The 12 central giro institutions had 257 offices at the end of 1984, and accounted for 16% of total business volume. The three largest central institutions were ranked amongst the ten largest banks in Germany. The largest, WestdeutscheLändesbank, being the third largest. Apart from municipal lending and other state sector business, they have engaged increasingly in wholesale corporate and international business. They have a good standing in investment markets because of the status of their guarantors. They are also active mortgage lenders.

The credit cooperatives and their central institutions form the third large group of credit institutions. They offer a full range of financial services to all their clients, who no longer need to be members as they did in the past. At the end of 1971 the associations of urban (Volksbanken) and agricultural (Raiffeisen) cooperative banks formed a joint central association and further reorganisation with a tendency towards centralisation and concentration has occurred subsequently. The number of cooperative banks declined from 11,795 in 1957 to 3,707 in 1984, as a result of mergers and takeovers. The number of bank offices, however, increased up until 1981, reaching 19,732, but has declined marginally since then. They have the largest network of any banking group, with more offices even than the savings banks. Their main focus continues to be on collecting sight and savings deposits and extending short and medium term loans to members, but most offer a much wider range of services.

There are nine central cooperative banks, which act as clearing houses and offer other services to member banks, including a central institution[72] which is authorised to operate as a universal bank. The cooperative banks and their central institutions had 16% of banking business at the end of 1984. Many of the offices are consequently small and only about 2,300 are large enough to be required to report to the Bundesbank.

In addition to the private commercial, savings and cooperative banks, and their central institutions, there are a number of specialised and special credit institutions. The majority of these are mortgage banks, offering loans for housing and, industrial and agricultural investment. They also lend to municipal and other public authorities and European Communities' institutions. Funds are raised on the capital market by selling municipal and mortgage bonds. Most of the 25 private mortgage banks are owned, at least in part, by the 'big three' banks, regional banks, or insurance companies. The 12 public mortgage banks specialise in mortgage loans whilst the private banks also take loans and deposits and engage in a slightly wider range of financial activities. The private banks have nearly 9% of business volume whilst the public banks have just over 5%. Instalment credit institutions have just over 1% of business volume and constitute the smallest banking group. Their number declined from 194 in 1957 to 95 in 1984. Their heyday was in the period following the second world war in which consumer spending increased but overdrafts and consumer loans from the big banks were not widely available. They grant loans directly, through other credit institutions, and on the basis of bills of exchange. They deal primarily with the consumer sector, with whom direct loans are most popular, but also lend to the industrial sector, predominantly through commercial bills. They now face stiff competition from the universal banking groups.

Apart from the two specialised groups of banking institutions there are also some institutions with special functions. The Reconstruction Loan Corporation (Kfw),[73] was founded in 1948 as a public institution to provide medium and long term finance to aid German economic reconstruction. Since the 1960s it has operated largely as a development bank funded by the Federal Republic, bond issues, and the Euroean Recovery Programme (ERP) Special Fund. It is the largest government owned bank and the tenth largest German bank. The federal government has an 80% stake in it and state governments have a 20% stake. It is not allowed to offer ordinary banking services. Instead it lends via the bankers to its clients, which are primarily small and medium sized companies, and these banks are required to service the debt and assume liability for it. It plays an important role in regional and structural policy and it is the exclusive channel for concessionary loans made by the government to developing countries. Its role as a supplier of credits to exporters was increasing in the mid 1980s and in January 1987 it issued its first Eurobond to fund such activities.The export credit company[74] (AKA) was founded in 1952 by major banks involved in export financing. It grants medium and long term export financing for industrial goods. The industrial credit bank[75] (IKB) is jointly owned by the major banks and insurance companies. It supplies small and medium sized companies in the industrial, trade and services sectors with long term loans. It is funded by long term loans from public authorities and securities issues. Together with the other banks with special functions, these banks have a market share of nearly 7% and altogether there are 16 banks in this category.

The German postal administration, Deutsche Bundespost, has two postal savings offices and 13 postal giro offices. They take savings and interest free sight deposits. Deposits and withdrawals can be made through post office branches in most towns and villages and cashless payments services are offered. Their share of banking business is about 1.5% and they attract approximately 5.7% of savings deposits.

The various banking institutions and other related financial institutions[76] participate in one or more of the following markets : money, bond, equity, and foreign exchange.

Participants in the money markets are mainly the Bundesbank, the banks and some public bodies, although non banks are not excluded. The major instruments are Treasury bills and discount papers, prime acceptances, and latterly certificates of deposit. The Bundesbank issues Treasury bills and discount papers, sometimes called mobilisation and liquidity papers and engages in open market operations through their sale and repurchase. The bond market is the largest sector of the securities market and banks play an important part as both issuers and investors. They also participate actively in the equities market, holding portfolios, underwriting new issues, and dealing on behalf of clients. Additionally, they are the major dealers and intermediaries in the German foreign exchange markets. There are five currency exchanges in Germany but the Frankfurt one is most important. In 1984 it ranked fourth, behind London, New York and Zürich, as a major international centre for currency exchange, although Tokyo has since been gaining ground rapidly.

The payments' system varies considerably between the household and the corporate and public sectors. Approximately 95% of household transactions involve cash payments whilst enterprises and public authorities affect their payments almost exclusively on a cashless basis. Consequently most large payments are made on a cashless basis whilst the majority of small transactions involve cash. The rise in the total volume of cash and cashless payments since the late 1970s has encouraged the banking system to change over from expensive paper to electronic media for cashless payments and to introduce cash dispensing machines (ATMs).

The payments' system relies heavily on giro accounts, rather than cheque accounts, reflecting the historical importance of the postal system and the savings banks as providers of money transmission services based on credit transfers. In 1983 nearly 54 million giro accounts were held with banks and post offices and used to execute cash and cashless transactions. 8% were held with the post offices, the remainder were held with banks. There are four main payments circuits: the postal giro and systems operated by the commercial banks, the savings banks and the cooperative banks. The three largest commercial banks each have their own internal giro network whilst the savings and cooperative banks, in coordination with their central institutions, form uniform giro organisations. The Bundesbank provides interface links for the various systems through its regional computer centres and 203 branch offices, and plays a key role in the operation and evolution of the payments' system, in line with its responsibilites under the Bundesbank Act. It has consequently tried to encourage cooperation amongst the banks concerning developments affecting money transmission. In 1982 it set up the Payments' System Information Group to deal with developments in the field of payments and communications technology. It consists of representatives of the central associations of the banking groups, the Ministry of Post and Communication, and the Bundesbank, which chairs the Group. Additionally, the commercial banks have established a Common Payments' System Company, which is primarily concerned with developing the Eurocard and Eurocheque systems.

In 1983, 57% of cashless payments were effected using credit transfers, 11% by cheques, and 32% by direct debits. The dominance of credit transfers has been declining for several years in response to the changing needs of economic agents. Because of the dominance of the non-commercial banks in the retail sector, in the period following the war, and their preference for credit transfers, cheques have never been widely used. Since the Bundesbank introduced a cheque clearing system in the 1950s, their usage by the retail sector has increased significantly and this has been encouraged by the development of the Eurocheque system with cheques guaranteed by the Eurocard. Whilst the number of cheque payments has been increasing, their share in cashless payments has declined. This is because of a significant shift by the business sector from cheques to credit transfers and direct debits. Charges levied on Eurocards and cheque transactions have discouraged an even faster growth in the usage of the Eurocheque system, however, and so too has easier access to cash through ATMs.

Most households have clearing accounts, because it is the almost universal practice of employers to pay salaries and wages, using noncash transfers, into their employees accounts. 18 million of the 40 million bank customers have Eurocheque accounts, which also give them access to ATMs. The majority of ATMs so far installed are simple cash dispensers, but more complex machines, offering a wider range of services, are now being installed. The ATM networks are not as extensive yet as in some of the other major European countries. Credit cards play a relatively minor role, although their usage is increasing. In 1985 there were approximately 800,000 credit cards in circulation. Debit cards had yet to be circulated in 1985, although Eurocheque cards had been used in various EFTPOS pilot schemes in Munich in 1983. The banks have displayed a cautious approach to cashless shopping, whilst investing heavily in developing ATM networks and computerising internal operations. The Munich experiment was an offline[77] one and subsequent experimentation with an online[78] system has been made in W. Berlin. Progress has been slower than in France, where the authorities have successfully encouraged the coordinated development of a nationwide EFTPOS system. As in the UK, where there has been considerably more experimentation, progress has been inhibited by failure to agree on the appropriate system to use and to agree on an acceptable sharing of the costs with retailers, who have so far shown insufficient interest. No decision has yet been made, for example, over whether to persevere with the magnetic stripe card or to adopt the chip card, preferred in France. To further promote the Eurocheque, the commercial banks are trying to ensure compatability with overseas ATM networks.

A significant development has been the launch, in October 1985, by the savings banks of a new magnetic stripe card, the S-card. It will allow their customers access to their cash dispensing machines and may eventually be used for EFTPOS. There are no plans at present for it to be usable as a cheque card. Many savings bank customers were unable to get EC cards and did not want to, because of the charges. This barred them from using ATMs. The commercial banks claim that the introduction of the S-card violates an agreement, reached in the 1960s by banks, to cooperate in the development of payments systems. They fear that it will undermine the EC card system. The savings banks counter that their card will supplement, rather than replace, the EC card. The commercial and cooperative banks have harmonised the EC system and there are now over 30 million cards in Europe. Only half the 20 million savings bank customers, however, have EC cards. The savings banks also aim to launch their own EFTPOS experiments in the future.

iii) Regulation and Supervision

Banking supervision is exercised by the Federal Banking Supervisory Office in conjunction with the Bundesbank on the basis of the Banking Act, which was last revised in 1984. In 1957 the Deutsche Bundesbank Act was passed, introducing a unified central bank to replace the previously prevailing two tier system, modelled on the US Federal Reserve System, which was established after the second world war. The latter consisted of a legally independent Länd central banks,[79] in each of state[80] of the Western occupied zones, which acted as central banks in their territory. In 1948 the Bank Deutscher Länder was established in Frankfurt as a joint subsidiary of the Länd central banks, responsible for note issue, policy coordination, and central functions, such as exchange control. Its Board of Directors, which consisted of the presidents of the Länd central banks and the President of Bank Deutsche Länder. The Board was responsible for determining discount and minimum reserve policy, amongst other things. It laid down guidelines for open market operations and issued credit directives. A distinguishing feature of the system was its independence from German political bodies. It enjoyed a degree of independence which was possibly even greater than that of the FRS on which it was modelled.

The Bundesbank Act granted the Bundesbank continued independence, to a degree unrivalled by the other major central banks around the world. The Länd central banks adopted the status of the main offices, representing the Bundesbank in each of the states. As mentioned above, the Bundesbank also has a large number of smaller offices throughout the county.

Apart from its responsibilities as supervisor of the banking and payments systems, which involve it in note issue, currency distribution, and clearing, it also provides other services to the banking system and is the banker of the federal government. Its prescribed duties, under the Bundesbank Act, are: to regulate money in circulation and credit supply; to protect the value of the Deutsche-Mark (D Mark), and to ensure the settlement of domestic and foreign payments. Its primary task has been to safeguard the currency and in performing this role it has been granted independence from the federal government. This is designed to prevent a return to the hyperinflation experienced under the Weimer Republic in the 1930s. It has generally pursued a policy of tight monetary control, interpreting its brief to include both the prevention of inflation and the maintenance of the external value of the D Mark. In the latter connection, it also intervenes on international foreign exchanges. Whilst enjoying independence, it is also required to support the general economic policy of the government, to advise the government on monetary policy matters and to provide information on the government's request. In turn the government should invite the president of the Bundesbank to attend policy discussions to which monetary policy relate. Members of the government are entitled to take part in the deliberations of the Central Bank Council, which is the Bank's main policy making body, and may propose motions but not vote. They can also request deferral of decisions for up to two weeks. Federal and state governments exercise some influence over appointments to the Council and the Directorate of the Bundesbank. Once appointed members serve for at least two, and normally eight, years.

The Council is the supreme policy making body of the Bank. It is composed of the President and Vice President of the Bank, the presidents of the eleven Länd Central Banks, and the other members of the Directorate. The Directorate is composed of the President and Vice President of the Bundesbank and up to eight other members. In 1985 there were four, nominated by the federal government and appointed by the President of the Federal Republic. The Presidents of the Länd central banks are appointed by the Bundesrät,[81] and the other members of their Managing Boards are nominated by the Council and appointed by the Bank's president. The procedure is designed to prevent the government from gaining domination over monetary policy making through its appointees. The arrangements have proved successful and the Bank has pursued an independent policy with surprisingly little friction with the government, which has generally pursued a conservative budgetary policy to complement the Bank's monetary policy. The Bank operates at a profit and transfers the proceeds to the federal treasury.

The Council meets fortnightly to review monetary and credit policy and issues guidelines on the conduct of business and bank administration. The Directorate is responsible for banking services offered to the banks and the Federal government, foreign exchange transactions and interventions, and open market operations.

The Bank's major monetary policy instruments are minimum reserve requirements, open market operations, refinance facilities, and deposit requirements. It may also issue unofficial guidelines to which the banks are expected to adhere. Minimum reserve policy has, hitherto, been one of the more important instruments. The Bank is under pressure to relax or abolish the policy, in order to promote foreign interest in Frankfurt as a financial centre. Greater emphasis is consequently likely to be placed on open market operations in the future. The minimum reserve policy requires banks to deposit a percentage of all deposits, on which no interest is paid, with the Bank. It is designed to influence banks' liquidity and consequently their capacity to grant credit. The requirements vary between types of deposits and with size of credit institution. The reserve requirements prevailing in 1986 had been set in October 1982 and the instrument had, therefore, not been used actively since 1982 to manipulate liquidity. Its role had been rather to act as an automatic break on monetary expansion. Since 1982 open market policy have been used more extensively. The Bank sells Treasury bills and bonds of various maturities and buys specified short and long term securities on its own account in order to influence liquidity in the money and capital markets and interest rates. In January 1987, however, the Bundesbank was forced to cut the discount rate by $\frac{1}{2}\%$ in an effort to halt the appreciation of the D Mark against the dollar, which was attracting an inflow of money and causing monetary targets to be overshot. At the same time it moved to soak up excess liquidity, particularly the funds that had flowed in, ahead of the January 1987 realignment of currencies in the Exchange Rate Mechanism of the European Monetary System. It announced a 10% rise in the minimum reserve requirement and an 8% cut in the rediscount quotas discussed below. The Bundesbank thus made money both cheaper and scarcer and it announced that it hoped to return to the use of open market operations to control the growth of the money supply subsequently.

The refinancing policy is effected through the rediscount and Lombard policies, which are designed to influence interest rates and the money supply. The Bank sets a rediscount quota for each bank and buys rediscountable bills at the discount rate, which it sets, up to that quota. It can also grant loans to banks against specified securities at the Lombard rate, or occasionally the special Lombard rate, which are also set by the Bank. The Lombard rate is normally set one or two per cent points higher than the discount rate, and the penal special Lombard rate at yet higher levels. The Bank ensures that the banking system is permanently indebted to it and consequently seeking rediscount credit. The choice of spread between the Discount and Lombard rates is, therefore, also a policy instrument that can be employed in conjunction with variation of rediscount quotas.

The Banking Act of 1961 has been amended in 1971, 1976 and 1984. Changes in connection with the latter becoming effective from the beginning of 1985. The

Act provides for comprehensive authorisation and supervision of banking institutions and the amendments have been made to comply with EC directives and internal and external developments affecting the banking system. The Act designates banking activities requiring authorisation. These include : lending, deposit taking, discounting, securities dealing, investment banking business, trust business, guarantee business and money transfer and clearing business. Banks are required to have sufficient equity capital, reliable personnel with appropriate professional qualifications and at least two managers. Licences may be withdrawn at any time if the requirements are not fulfilled. The Act also established the Federal Banking Supervisory Office, which grants the banking licences. This authority is responsible for the regulatory and supervisory system. It is part of the Ministry of Finance and its offices are in Berlin. It deals with credit institutions' equity and liquidity requirements, and the range of their business activities. Its roles are to prevent unprudent activities, to ensure the safety of deposits and other assets held by credit institutions, and to prevent adverse effects on the economy as a whole. It cooperates and confers closely with the Bank about credit institutions. The authority receives regular reports from credit institutions, which must notify it of material changes concerning its management or business activities. It has additional powers to gain sufficient information, to allow it to react quickly if necessary, by issuing additional requests and conducting investigations. It may also intervene, in cases of inadequate capital or liquidity and other cases involving high risk, by temporarily prohibiting certain banking business, removing managers, appointing supervisors, and having courts appoint new managers.

The Supervisory Office lays down principles of capital adequacy. These were changed, with effect from 1985, as a result of the February 1984 amendments to the Banking Act. From January 1985 banks were required to limit their lending to a maximum of eighteen, rather than fifteen as previously, times their own capital, which includes equity and reserves. Further, the application of this rule was extended to all subsidiaries in which banks had a stake in excess of 40%. Previously it applied only to 100% owned subsidiaries. In addition banks were prohibited from lending more than 50% of their capital, previously 75%, to a single customer. Exposures of over 18% to individual customers have, as before, to be reported to the Bank, which in turn informs the Supervisory Office. The 1984 amendment also required reporting to be in the form of consolidated accounts, including domestic and foreign subsidiaries. A five year transition period was permitted, since the new rules required banks to boost their capital in order to maintain prevailing lending levels and allow growth. The new rules were judged by the banks to be stricter than those applied abroad. In the event, however, the buoyant stock markets have allowed banks to boost their capital fairly rapidly. The amendments to the Act were, at least in part, a response to the 1983 EC Directive[82] on consolidated accounting, but the legislation faced opposition from the banking lobby. Opposition crumbled following the 1983 SMH[83] bank affair in November 1983. SMH, a private bank, had, largely through its Luxembourg subsidiary, become overexposed to a building machinery manufacturer. It had lent eight times its capital and ran into difficulties when this manufacturing firm went bankrupt. It was rescued and supported by a group of commercial banks and sold to Lloyds Bank, of the UK, in 1984. The Act does not require a deposit protection scheme yet, despite the 1977 EC banking directive[84] which prompted other EC member countries, including the UK in 1979, to introduce such schemes. The private commercial banks, however, voluntarily established their own scheme in 1976 to pre-empt legislation. The Cooperative and Savings banks have their own arrangements, organised through their central associations. Before being admitted into the deposit protection funds banks have to fulfil certain requirements, such as submitting to audit by the fund's auditors as well as their own auditors, as is required by law. It was in fact the fund's auditors which discovered the irregularities at the SMH bank. Although called a fund, there are no substantial reserves accumulated. The banks instead make commitments, presumably out of hidden reserves, to support each other and practically all deposits are supposedly covered, rather than just a percentage of the value of individual deposits, as in the UK scheme. The scheme would be unlikely to provide adequate support in the event of the failure of a large bank, however. The presumption seems to be that the Bundesbank would then step in, as lender of last resort.

In 1984 the cooperative banks deposit protection scheme was called into operation. The Hammer bank was rescued using the contingency fund contingency fund overseen by the association of urban and agricultural cooperative banks and no depositor lost money. The bank was subsequently slimmed down and merged with another local cooperative bank. The bank had run up a number of doubtful loans and its problems are believed to be indicative of a number of cooperative banks. A reform of the statute governing cooperative banks had been in preparation for nearly two years. The new rules, introduced in 1985, strengthened the supervisory power of the association, giving it powers to seek further information from cooperative banks and to act on the information by barring recalcitrant banks from access to the guarantee support system.

The Banking Act also restricts the extent to which, at the close of a day's business, banks can hold open positions in foreign currencies and precious metals. These rules were imposed in response to the Herstatt bank's collapse, in 1973, as a result of foreign currency exposure. Principal II of the Act aims to ensure that banks do not develop unduly mismatched positions, by ensuring that long term loans and investments are financed by sufficient long term funds. Principal III requires sound funding of illiquid assets. Banks not obeying the principles of the Act can have their refinancing quotas decreased and in severe cases the stronger sanctions, referred to above, can be invoked.

Finally, a new rule, to take effect in June 1986, has been introduced which requires banks to cover themselves against off balance sheet risks. The rule is tougher than the banks had hoped for and aims to ensure that banks underwriting of Nifs[85] have adequate capital backing. The Supervisory Office decided that 50% of a bank's obligations under Nifs should be counted as loans for the purpose of calculating capital to lending ratios. Previously no capital backing had been required. The action was taken following BIS and Basle Committee reports[86] on financial innovation and off balance sheet risks in 1986. Central banks had been concerned about these developments and the Bundesbank had been particularly vociferous in urging the banks to proceed into these new banking activities with caution. The banks had suggested that 25% of their Nif obligations should require capital backing and that in any event the rule applied should not be harsher than that imposed by supervisory authorities overseas. The Bank of England had introduced a 50% of loan capital backing requirement, but the Japanese and US central banks opted for a 25% requirement. The Bundesbank and the Supervisory Office had been monitoring closely the build up of bank involvement in securitisation, especially through foreign subsidiaries, and may subsequently issue rules covering other new financial instruments involving banks in contingent liabilities. It is also likely to respond the joint US and UK proposals on capital adequacy and backing for various assets, including off balance sheet items, announced in January 1987. They proposed to reduce the required backing for Nifs in the Uk to the 25% level prevailing in the US.

iv) Deregulation

The Supervisory Office and the Bundesbank have adopted a cautious attitude to Euromarket developments, especially in London, but have nevertheless introduced deregulatory measures, or further liberalisation as they prefer to call it. Whilst wishing to avoid introducing unsettling influences into the banking system they have also wished to maintain the appeal of Frankfurt as a financial centre and to prevent loss of business to other centres, particularly London. Their concern in the latter connection was heightened by the decision, announced in 1985, by Deutsche Bank, the largest commercial bank, to move its non D Mark bond business from Frankfurt to London.

In 1984 the coupon tax on interest payments to foreign holders of D Mark bonds was abolished in response to the removal of withholding tax by the US authorities earlier in the year. Then in 1985 foreign banks incorporated in Germany were permitted to lead manage D Mark bond issues, provided similar privileges were granted to German banks in the country of origin of the foreign banks. The reciprocity requirement barred Japanese banks until discussions in process between the German and Japanese supervisory authorities reached a satisfactory conclusion. In 1985, the authorities also permitted new instruments, particularly floating rate notes, currency swaps and zero coupon bonds, to be issued and traded in Germany. Finally, at the end of 1985, the Bundesbank announced that it would permit the issue of D Mark certificates of deposit (CDs) in 1986.

The liberalisation concerning lead management and Euro-market instruments immediately attracted foreign bank interest. The major Swiss banks were particularly quick to establish a German presence to take advantage of such further liberalisation and Salomon Brothers, the major US investment bank, was attracted in 1986 and received a licence in November of that year. It is felt by some experts that liberalisation will have to proceed even further to maintain Frankfurt's position vis a vis London and other major European and international financial centres. A number of restrictions relating to the bond dealing procedure remain an irritant to foreign banks. ECU[87] accounts, but not ECU bonds, are barred because of the implicit index linking they provide. Index linking is not permitted in Germany. The Bundesbank has, however, declared that, following further evidence of European monetary integration, it will permit residents to hold ECU accounts. It is looking for further reductions in exchange controls by France and Italy and adherence by the latter to the normal 2%, rather than the concessionary 6%, currency band[88] within the Exchange Rate Mechanism (ERM) of the European Monetary System. Previously it has also stated that further evidence of policy and inflation convergence amongst EC member countries and UK participation in the ERM were also prerequisites, but it has latterly dropped mention of these requirements.

Minimum reserve requirements are to be applied to CDs and are expected to inhibit the development of the CD market. The existence of minimum reserve requirements has already led to a migration of Eurobond business to subsidiaries in London and Luxembourg, where no such rules apply. When CDs were introduced the minimum reserve requirements were reduced but domestic and foreign banks are hoping that they will eventually be abolished, or at least lifted for Euromarket business centred on Frankfurt, which would then become an offshore centre more able to compete with London. The Bank fears that abolition of the minimum reserve requirement would impair its ability to control the money supply and seems to be justified by the events in late 1986 and early 1987, discussed above, which prompted it to raise the minimum reserve requirements to soak up liquidity. Some financial experts believe that it should be possible, however, to insulate domestic markets from international financial transactions or to sterilise the effects of international money flows on the money supply. The Bank's room for manoeuvre was restricted by the fact that monetary growth had been exceeding policy targets significantly in 1986 and that the D Mark had appreciated considerably against the dollar since the end of 1985, attracting considerable inflows of foreign currency. The conditions prevailing in 1984 and 1985, when the dollar was appreciating against the D Mark and the money supply was under control, which had proved so conducive to further liberalisation, no longer prevailed. At that time liberalisation posed little threat to monetary control and the measures, by attracting foreign funds, were also consistent with the Bank's commitment to maintaining the external value of the D Mark. Continued depreciation of the dollar and excessive monetary growth are, therefore, likely to put a brake on liberalisation as long as they prevail, given the Bank's responsibilities concerning the internal and external values of the D Mark.

Another area where reform could be considered is the equity market. Here too there is a risk of loss of business to the major centres and especially London, following the 'big bang'. By 1986 the market had enjoyed a three year boom. New issue activity had increased significantly but secondary trading had not increased markedly. Foreign interest had been considerable, largely because the D Mark was judged to be undervalued and investments carried the prospects of future currency gains, which were realised in 1986. Foreign interest may, therefore, wane when D Mark exchange rate with the dollar eventually stabilises. There have, however, been clear signs of renewed domestic interest in shares too. This has been a response to the boom conditions, tax changes, and the fall in inflation, encouraging a move away from traditional hedges such as property (the price of which fell for a while in the mid 1980s) gold and works of art and into financial assets. To make further progress, some feel that further tax incentives will be required, to encourage wider share ownership, in line with those introduced in France and the UK in the 1980s. The government's privatisation programme, although meagre by French and UK standards, may also help. Additionally the market will need to be reformed in order to make the dealing system more efficient and to comply with the EC's investor protection and securities dealing requirements. There are plans to improve the coordination of the eight bourses but progress has been inhibited by jealously guarded regional autonomy. In mid 1986 the Federation of German Stock Exchanges was formed to coordinate more closely the activities of the bourses in order to meet the international challenge. Its executive vice chairman is a former Bundesbank official and one of its first initiatives was to introduce aggregate joint bond and equity turnover statistics from January 1987. These showed the combined turnover to be much closer to that of the London exchange than expected. Frankfurt has 50% of turnover, Dusseldorf has 30%, and Munich close to 10%. Integration, therefore, depends primarily on these three exchanges. Frankfurt was, in 1987, the home of the Bundesbank and 373 banks, 255 of which were foreign. Its claim to be an international financial centre cannot therefore be disputed and any centralisation of the bourses activities would involve gravitation towards Frankfurt. Munich, however, guards its independence jealously and independent brokers fear that centralisation will lead to increased domination of bourse activities by the major banks, especially Deutsche Bank. The government is to encourage the establishment of an equivalent of the UK USM[89] and the French Second Marché to further regenerate the stock markets and provide equity finance for medium sized firms. Such firms have not approached the Bourses because of high fees and exhaustive regulations. Legislation under consideration in 1986 aims to tackle those problems. An over the counter market already exists and some experts fear that there will be little room for an unlisted market, with stricter regulations, as well.

The Bundesbank has been pressing the federal government to abolish 'stamp duty'. This levy has inhibited secondary activity on the Bourses and, because it also applies to FRNs and other new financial instruments, has encouraged the migration of secondary market business in the new financial instruments to London. In the UK the 'stamp duty' has been halved twice since 1983. It is, consequently, much lower than in Germany and may be abolished altogether if the government submits to pressure from the London Stock Exchange, which wishes to establish an international equity market in London. The German government, re-elected in January 1987, made an election pledge to eliminate 'stamp duty', or turnover tax, but made no commitment about when this would happen. Reduction or elimination of 'stamp duty', therefore, looks likely to be the next step in the process of further liberalisation designed to maintain the attractiveness of Germany, and particularly of Frankfurt, as an international financial centre. As in France the authorities approach is expected to be be more cautious than that of the UK authorities, as they attempt to learn from developments in London, but they will also face continued pressure for reform as long as London has a deregulatory lead.

3.4 The Swiss Banking System

i) Introduction

Switzerland is a confederation of states comprising 26 cantons and half cantons which have autonomy within the limits of the federal constitution. They are autonomous except in matters of state such as defence, communications and some aspects of the economy. Regional autonomy is jealously guarded and the country is multilingual with German, French and Italian speaking areas. A stable or conservative political climate prevails, the country having been governed by a coalition of the four major parties since 1959. The coalition dominates both the National Council and the States Council, which represents the cantons. The two houses of the Federal Assembly elect the seven ministers of the Federal Council, which is the executive body and governs by consensus. Referendums are, however, frequently held on matters of major importance, but substantial majorities are required to affect change. In 1984 a Banking Motion, which would have led to far reaching changes in the banking system, was emphatically rejected in a referendum. In 1986 the electorate rejected a government proposal to join the United Nations in favour of retaining the country's traditional neutral status.

Contrary to many perceptions, Switzerland is an important industrial country. It is not dominated by its agricultural, tourist and financial services sectors. Its economy is of a similar size to that of Sweden but its industrial sector is larger. The service sector is, relatively, a smaller employer than that in Sweden or the UK, which also has a smaller industrial sector, as a proportion of Gross National Product (GNP), than Switzerland. In the mid 1980s the industrial sector was reasonably healthy, having recovered from the recession of the early 1980s following some reconstruction aided by the banking sector. The banks, especially the big ones and the cantonal institutions, are considered to have a duty to support the Swiss economy when necessary. In the decade from 1976 they have provided considerable support to ailing companies and in 1986 they continued to build up bad-debt provisions against their exposure to domestic industry. Some major sectors, such as watch making, remained troubled but the process of de-industrialised was not as evident as in some other major economies. The non financial services sector is also well developed. With an indigenous population smaller than that of London, industrial growth is necessarily export oriented. Because of the country's dependence on imported raw materials and energy sources, it generally has a deficit on the trade account. This was reduced somewhat in the first half of the 1980s by falling commodity, and particularly oil prices. The trade deficit is traditionally more than offset by a surplus on the invisibles account resulting from high services and investments income, the major contributor to which is the financial sector, particularly the banking and insurance sectors. As a result a current account surplus normally prevails and this is offset by a net outflow of capital.

The net outflow of capital is sustained by the high savings ratio in Switzerland. The country has one of the highest per capita GNPs in the world and consequently, despite having a lower ratio to GNP than Japan, has the highest per capita savings level in the world. The domestic economy is unable to absorb these savings and Switzerland has a historical reputation as a major capital exporting nation. The domestically generated pool of loanable funds is swelled by funds attracted from overseas. This enables Switzerland to act as a sort of entrepôt port for international capital. In Switzerland this is described as a 'turntable' operation involving the attraction of foreign funds by the banking system and relending them abroad. Swizerland began to attract large quantities of foreign funds in the 1920s and 1930s when it stood out as a haven of political stability within an unstable Europe. Its multilingual society and neutral status added to its attraction which was further enhanced by the 1934 Banking Law which gave legal underpinnings to bank secrecy. These attributes have allowed it to develop fiduciary or trust business which is supplementary to what is regarded as standard banking business. The secrecy provisions have attracted international criticism because they make it difficult for foreign governments to pursue investigations into tax evasion and criminal activities and to trace flight capital. They remained intact following the referendum on the Banking Motion but are still a cause for concern. [90] They continue to be important in attracting private funds but the banking system is becoming increasingly involved in developing business with institutional clients for whom the advantages of secrecy are less apparent, given their reporting and disclosure requirements.

In order to function as a major international capital centre Switzerland must also attract borrowers to its securities markets, otherwise its banks would either have to lend or invest abroad the vast majority of all the funds they attract. Borrowers are attracted by low interest and inflation rates and a relatively stable currency as well as the high placement power of the major Swiss banks. [91] The low interest rates in particular ensure that funds can be raised cheaply. In contrast, its money markets are relatively underdeveloped. This is attributable partly to the tax system, [92] which discourages its development, and partly to the fact that all sectors of the banking system are normally in surplus, because of high savings, a plentiful supply of fiduciary business and relatively restricted domestic lending opportunities. A demand for short term funds by banks does not, therefore, normally exist. They are primarily concerned with finding profitable outlets for such funds. Inter-bank transactions that prove necessary are usually undertaken on the Eurocurrency markets. In addition to being a major international capital market centre, accounting for approximately 10% of all international securities issues, Swizerland is also a major international foreign exchange and gold and precious metal trading centre.

The description of Switzerland as a single financial centre is a matter of convenience but somewhat misleading. The country has a number of cities which serve as financial centres. By far the most important, and in order of merit, are Zurich, Geneva and Basle, but Lugano, which is growing in importance, St. Gallen and a number of other cities also transact an appreciable amount of domestic and international business. Historically, [93] Geneva was the dominant centre but Zurich is now by far the most important. As a whole, Switzerland's growth as a financial centre has been slower than London's in the 1980s, although it continues to attract foreign banks and Zurich overtook Frankfurt as a foreign exchange centre in 1985. Its share of the gold market has been declining relative to London's since exchange controls were lifted in the UK in 1979.

Its future prospects as a financial centre have been questioned as deregulation has proceeded apace overseas, especially in London, and reduced the comparative advantage of its relatively liberal financial system and overseas banking systems have adopted universal banking. Although not heavily regulated, it suffers from a disadvantageous tax regime relative to London. [94] This is believed to account for the loss of gold business and the minor importance of Eurobond trading in Switzerland relative to London. The capital market is almost entirely Swiss franc (Sfr) denominated, although there has been a rapid growth in currency swap backed issues since 1985. Currently only institutions domiciled in Switzerland can issue Sfr securities. There is pressure[95] to allow the development of a Sfr Euromarket in which issues could be made abroad by domestic and overseas banks. The fear is that, unless the tax regime is brought into line with the UK's, business will be rapidly lost to London which already attracts a significant proportion of secondary trading business in Sfr securities.

Whatever the future holds for Switzerland as a financial centre, the major Swiss banks are well placed to compete in the global markets. They already have branches, representative offices, or subsidiaries in all the important international financial centres and hold predominant positions in the Euromarkets. They are universal or full service banks, combining the functions of commercial, merchant and investment banks or securities houses abroad. They have a sound retail deposit base by virtue of their nationwide branching and the high domestic savings levels. The combination of the latter and their ability to attract deposits and fiduciary business from abroad gives them high placement power. They engage in underwriting, stockbroking, lead and investment management and commercial banking business and have achieved a fairly even balance between their commercial banking securities and portfolio management functions. Their earnings are approximately evenly divided between fee and interest income and their balance sheets show an almost equal proportion of domestic and foreign assets. They are, therefore, well placed to take advantage of the current trends toward globalisation and securitisation.

Although already represented in the most important international financial centres, the major banks are able to move rapidly, because of their high capitalisation, to take advantage of new opportunities. This was demonstrated in 1985 when, following the further liberalisation in the German securities markets, [96] they established themselves in Frankfurt. [97] As well as their high placement capacity, their ability to attract business in the Eurobond and domestic Sfr securities market is attributable to their high, by international standards, capital ratios. These ratios are further supplemented by hidden reserves which are believed to be substantial. They have also made extensive provisions against domestic and international bad debts whilst their exposure to the debtor nations which have rescheduled is much lower than many other, especially UK and US, banks which have made less substantial provisions. Their general lack of exposure is in turn attributable to their well established reputation for sound and conservative management which adds to their ability to attract international business. Their own securities issues consequently attract top ratings.

With deregulation proceeding apace internationally, new universal or full service banking groups are being formed by UK banks and by US and Japanese banks and securities houses which are moving as far and as fast as they can in overseas financial centres despite restrictions imposed by domestic banking laws. [98] Thus new competition, in addition to that from the well established German and the newer French universal banks, is emerging from highly capitalised institutions which themselves have substantial worldwide placing power. The Japanese institutions, by virtue of Japan's huge savings surplus, are proving to be particularly awesome competitors in the Euromarkets and have established themselves in Switzerland. US institutions are also well represented in Switzerland and are proving to be highly innovative and thereby winning an increasing share of the domestic new issues markets. Life will, therefore, become more difficult for the major Swiss banks in the emerging global markets and in the domestic foreign bond market. They will, however, be competing from a position of high repute and capitalisation and perhaps have better balance sheets and a sounder mix of off and on balance sheet business than many of their established and emerging competitors.

It is important for them to have good international prospects because domestic opportunities are restricted. The country is generally regarded as overbanked, [99] extensive branching having occurred since the first world war. The banks themselves see few benefits from further domestic branching. Although industry was relatively healthy and the economy was growing at a respectable rate by European standards in the mid 1980s, it was unlikely that a substantial increase in domestic corporate business would be generated. Retail lending opportunities were also likely to remain restricted because of the high per capita income, the propensity to save and because of substantial competition in the domestic retail banking sector. Although the major banks have been successful in winning business from smaller domestic banks in the last decade, the major opportunities would appear to lie abroad. They are, therefore, likely to continue their current trends of building up foreign assets, fee earning and off balance sheet business and seeking quality business. They have made it clear that they are interested in winning wholesale banking and securities business abroad and do not intend to get involved in foreign retail markets.

ii) *The Banking System*

Swiss companies engaged in banking and finance can be classified as banks, finance companies or commercial companies depending on the nature of their business activity, their method of doing business and the judgement of the Federal Banking Commission (FBC) concerning whether they are fully or partially covered by the Federal Banking Law (FBL) or exempt from it. There is no formal legal definition of a bank but a bank is generally regarded as an organisation engaged in providing financial services funded by customer deposits or the proceeds of capital market issues. Most institutions that solicit deposits are classified as banks. Finance companies generally have a smaller range of assets and concentrate on corporate finance and participation in public securities issues. They do not normally deal with private domestic retail customers although many do manage fiduciary funds, which are not included in their balance sheets and must be reported separately. Companies organised under Swiss law can engage in the business of finance without being subject to the FBL provided that they do not solicit deposits from the public and do not engage in interest differential business. [1] They can, however, raise funds through bond issues. Switzerland also has a well established insurance sector of high international repute. Zurich Insurance and the Swiss Reinsurance group were both in the top 60 of the Financial Times Top 500[2] (FT 500) European Companies in 1986, for example.

The major banks in Switzerland are large universal banks. The 'big three' were among the top four banks in the FT 500 in 1986. The Union Bank of Switzerland (UBS) was the largest European bank, the German Deutsche Bank was second largest and the Swiss Bank Corporation (SBC) and Crédit Suisse (CS) were third and fourth largest. They were all in the top 25 companies and ahead of Barclays and NatWest, the largest UK banks, which made the top 30 and are the sixth and fifth largest banks. UBS's capitalisation was more than twice that of NatWest, the highest ranking UK bank, and more than three times that of Dresdner, the second ranking German bank. This illustrates the market valuation placed by investors on Swiss banks, which are far from being Europe's largest in terms of balance sheet size or profitability. It should also be stressed that the list omits the French and Italian state owned banks which are among Europe's largest. Following the proposed privatisations of banks in France and Italy, their position could be rivalled in the future. In the mid 1980s UBS overtook Nestlé in the FT 500 to become the most highly capitalised company in Switzerland.

The 'big three' are, therefore, large by general European corporate standards and are rivalled in the private sector top ten banks only by the major German and UK banks. Their character differs from the German and the evolving Japanese universal banks in that they have much smaller direct participations in non financial companies and a greater emphasis on underwriting. Their participations are limited by the capital requirements to which they are subject [3] and have been acquired largely as a result of their involvement in the restructuring of ailing companies in Switzerland. They are, however, more heavily involved in capital markets than the major French, German, Japanese, US and UK commercial banks. This is because the capital markets are relatively underdeveloped in France and Germany and because of the restrictions on bank involvement in securities business, and securities house participation in banking business, in Japan and the US. The UK clearing banks also have a lot of ground to make up because their involvement in securities markets was limited prior to the 'big bang'. [4] Other UK institutions with more experience in securities' underwriting and trading and portfolio management tend to lack the capitalisation to make a significant impact on the global markets.

The major Swiss banks' full service status is the result of permissive legislation designed to assure investor and depositor protection. In the light of the financial problems experienced in the 1920s and 1930s the US authorities felt it prudent to separate banking and securities business and US banking legislation reflects this. [5] This view continued to prevail after the second world war and the occupying US authorities imposed a similar separation of securities and banking business on the Japanese financial system. [6] The Swiss authorities took the contrasting view that prudence would be better served by allowing banks to develop as they saw fit and saw no reason to restrict their efforts to diversify. Diversification is after all a well known method of spreading risks and reducing them in total by reducing the proportion of exposure to certain types of risk and allowing risks from various sources to offset each other.

Industrialisation encouraged a major change in the structure of the Swiss banking system, which had its origins in the opportunity to service north-south trade flows passing through Switzerland. [7] As in Germany, a capital market did not exist to provide industrial finance and banks filled the void. CS was established in the mid nineteenth century and UBS and SBC were formed, following mergers of other banks, towards the end of that century. The Cantonal and other major banks were also established in the nineteenth century but the 'big three' have held a dominant position throughout the twentieth century. The Cantonal and regional banks, like the 'big five' (grossbanken) commercial banks, are full service banks. The 'big five' are the 'big three' plus Bank Leu and Volksbank, which have fewer foreign assets than the 'big three'. The Cantonal and regional banks have an even smaller proportion of foreign assets in their balance sheets. Nevertheless, 40% of the assets of the banking system as a whole are foreign.

Not all of the banks are universal though. Specialisation is particularly evident amongst the private banks, which count amongst their declining number the oldest Swiss banking institutions, and the bank-like finance companies. There is a symbiosis between full service and specialist banks, many of which are subsidiaries of grossbanken and regional banks, and the system as a whole works effectively.

The Occupational Pensions Act of 1985 made it mandatory for most Swiss Companies to provide staff pension schemes. This is expected to have a significant impact on flows of funds. Personal liquid assets and retail deposits are expected to decline. The beneficiaries will be the life assurance companies and, to the extent that they can attract pension fund management business from companies, the banks and other financial institutions. More money will, however, be tied into investments and less will be available for loans. The general decline in the supply of liquid funds could encourage the development of an interbank market and provide a role for the money markets in the future, especially if financial taxes are reduced. Another trend is towards greater domestic concentration in the banking sector as a result of the increasing dominance by the grossbanken of the domestic market, and their ability, by virtue of their substantial capitalisation and hidden reserves, to make acquisitions. Apart from acquisitions and the establishment of subsidiaries, the scope for domestic expansion is limited by the fact that the country already had one bank branch per 1276 people in 1982, more than Germany, which had one per 1374 and was also regarded as overbanked. The retail sector has an exceptionally high mortgage indebtedness [8] and high income levels, so opportunities in this area are relatively limited. As noted above, the major banks had their origins in corporate finance. As industry became more export oriented they developed international operations and trade and foreign exchange departments to service its needs. They also responded to corporate preferences for equity finance rather than loans by developing their capital market services. They were, therefore, well prepared for the current corporate appetite for securities finance and the internationalisation and confluence of the banking and capital markets.

Having given an overview, the banking system will next be briefly outlined. The largest group of banks are the five grossbanken, all of which are universal or full service banks. The 'big three' are much larger than the other two. The Zurich based UBS is larger than the Basle based SBC which is in turn larger than the Zurich based CS. Bank Leu is also Zurich based. These four are all joint stock companies. The Volksbank, based in Bern, is a cooperative bank. The grossbanken dominate the capital markets in which the private banks and some of the finance companies, especially the foreign owned ones, and specialised broking firms also participate. They are also well represented, especially by the 'big three', in the major financial centres, in order to service their domestic corporate clients and to take advantage of the opportunities in the Euromarkets provided by deregulation abroad. CS, for example, formed a partnership with the US bank First Boston (FB). The London based CSFB bank headed the Eurobond issue leagued with UBS and SBC not far behind. In the run up to the 'big bang' in London, both UBS and CS bought into London stockbrokers, which they were allowed to take full control of in March 1986. SBC has adopted the alternative strategy of building up its merchant bank in London to take advantage of post 'big bang' opportunities in the Stock Exchange equities, gilts and options markets.

Following the decision by the Bundesbank to allow the introduction of various financial innovations and to permit foreign banks to lead manage German bond issues in 1985, [9] CS purchased and subsequently merged two local German banks and SBC decided to set up a fully fledged Frankfurt subsidiary in 1986. UBS meanwhile obtained a Frankfurt Stock Exchange listing. Apart from the opportunities provided by the German liberalisations, the major Swiss banks also see an opportunity to win a share of the fast growing corporate business provided by medium sized, often family owned, companies which form the backbone of German industry. They are well placed, compared with other foreign banks, in this field because they face no language barrier and have contacts with many companies which also trade in Switzerland. The only surprise is that they have not moved sooner. About a dozen German banks, including their 'big three' commercial banks, have established themselves in Switzerland, in most cases in the 1980s, to take advantage of the secrecy laws to win funds from the Middle Eastern depositors. The 'big three' have been granted trust banking licences in Japan [10] and are amongst the first foreign banks to be granted securities trading licences there. The trust licences will be useful given their experience in fiduciary business and they are expected to use them to place securities with pension funds and other Japanese institutions, adding to their already massive placement power. They hope that by demonstrating their placement power they will also be able to win underwriting business in Japan. The 'big three' Swiss banks are also represented in New York, Hong Kong, and other major centres.

The grossbanken account for about half of the bank balance sheet business in Switzerland and also dominate the securities market and fiduciary business. About 50% of their assets are foreign and their fiduciary business is about a fifth of the value of their balance sheet assets. Despite their large and rising share of domestic business, the 'big three' had only about 11% of domestic bank branches. They also have over 30 branches, over 60 representative offices, and over 30 banking subsidiaries in major and secondary financial centres abroad. The domestic activities of the grossbanken are clearly centred in Zurich, which is the largest urban conurbation and contains the major stock exchange, regardless of the location of their head offices. Zurich is also the insurance sectors' centre. They are also well represented in Geneva and Basle and the other major financial centres such as Lugano, Lausanne and St. Gallen. Bank Leu is, however, represented outside Zurich only by subsidiaries because it is confined to Canton of Zurich.

Their business includes commercial and investment banking, trust management, underwriting and stockbroking. They also engage extensively in foreign exchange business, in which their involvement initially grew out of the opportunity to service Swiss industry's needs. They have subsequently become major players in the global markets and use the Eurocurrency markets as an interbank market in the absence of well developed domestic money markets. The role of the domestic foreign exchange market is enhanced by the way in which the central bank, the Swiss National Bank (SNB), conducts its monetary and currency policy. [11] Zurich is also a major gold or precious metal trading centre. The Zurich 'Gold Pool' is dominated by the 'big three' banks but has been losing ground to London in the 1980s. London has managed to retain its central role in 24 hour gold trading system revolving around New York, Tokyo, Zurich, Hong Kong and Sydney. After 1979, when exchange controls were lifted, London's five bullion houses had been joined by six other houses by the mid 1980s, including UBS and CS, and SBC was expected to join the market in the near future.

The 'big three's' dominance of the domestic securities new issue market began to be eroded in the 1980s following a shift in preference toward swap based issues led by foreign bank, especially US, subsidiaries. In 1985 Sfr bond issues accounted for nearly 9% of all issues and the leading banks had over 50% of the business. Their loss of share was, however, offset by a surge of new issues, particularly on behalf of Japanese and US companies attracted by the low interest rates, and, in the latter case, by the appreciation of the Sfr against the dollar. They responded to this competitive pressure by reducing brokerage fees on large transactions with effect from January 1986. Foreign banks, through subsidiaries, branches and finance companies, have also been grossing an increasing share of the fiduciary business. Fiduciary accounts are placed in Swiss based institutions, usually by overseas residents, or on their behalf, at the risk of the customers. They are not included in the bank balance sheets. Because the business comes from abroad it is not clear whether the foreign controlled institutions are winning business from the major Swiss banks or bringing in new business. It is generally believed, however, that they tend to bring in business from their established clients which would not have been secured by Swiss banks.

They are very active in the Eurobond market and in the mid 1980s it was estimated that between a third and a quarter of all newly issued Eurobonds were acquired for portfolios managed by Swiss banks. Their permanent participations in Swiss enterprises are minor and have usually been acquired by force of circumstance in connection with ailing companies. They have also proved extremely conservative in their provision of venture capital. International loans are usually associated with the export orientation and multinational nature of Swiss corporations. They have maintained a high asset quality, although details are clouded by lack of public disclosure. Their total exposure to rescheduling countries, including South Africa, is a much smaller proportion of their net worth than many of their international competitors. They have made extensive provisions in this connection, well in excess of the 20% of exposure requirement of the authorities. The provisions are in fact about 30% of their exposure and have been encouraged by the fact that they are exempt from taxation. It is estimated [12] that, allowing for provisions and hidden reserves, their exposure is about 25% to 40% of actual equity and only 5% of assets. They have tended to take a pessimistic view of the outcome of the third world debt crisis, and so has the Federal Banking Commission (FBC). In 1986 the banks continued to build up provisions and the FBC indicated that it might further increase minimum provision requirements in the future. The smaller banks have sold off their Latin American loans altogether and the larger banks have given the Baker Plan [13] a cold reception. Their concern over South Africa where they are relatively heavily exposed, was demonstrated by the fact that Dr Fritz Leutweiler, the former president of the Swiss National Bank (SNB), was chosen in 1985 to mediate between the South African government and the group of international banks to which the country was indebted.

Domestically the major banks operate a pricing cartel [14] to which other domestic and foreign banks tend to conform, although the latter do not participate to any great extent in the domestic market. They have a rough balance between commercial and investment banking and interest, fee and trading income, as well as between domestic and foreign assets. The proportion of their commission income could decline following their decision to reduce stock exchange commissions on large transactions although they should receive some compensation from the rise in commissions on small transactions. They have historically been strong generators of fee income, especially from fiduciary business, and enjoyed robust income from non interest bearing business in the mid 1980s. In 1984 income from loan transactions ranked third as a source of income, behind income from bills of exchange and money market paper. The contribution of net interest from credit transactions was 22% in 1984. It had been 35% in 1974. Commission earnings were 33% in 1984, compared to 27% in 1974. Income from securities holdings had risen to about 18% from about 11%. Bills and money market instruments contributed nearly 15% compared to about 8.5%. Foreign exchange and precious metal trading contributed 9% compared to nearly 14.5% in 1974. The 'big three' were therefore well balanced and truly universal banks by the mid 1980s. The major trends were rising proportions of fee and commission based income and foreign assets. They were strongly capitalised by international standards and had substantial hidden reserves and provisions. Their exposure to bad debts was relatively small, their networks were cheaply run, and their reputation for sound and conservative management was intact. This in turn made them attractive to investors [15] and allowed them to win quality business and top ratings [16] for the securities they issued.

The 20 cantonal banks are the second largest group. They are publicly owned and each canton and half canton has at least one bank. They were created by cantonal decree and in most cases the canton is fully responsible for their liabilities. Some of them, which were created by cantonal decree prior to 1883, have 'assimilate' status, in which case the canton is not responsible for their liabilities but does elect the bank council. They are restricted to branching within their domestic canton and subject to cantonal legislation. As a group they have over 1,300 branches and a fifth of the aggregate balance sheet of the banking sector. They grant loans and credits to local retail sector clients, commercial and agricultural businesses and cantonal authorities and are funded through deposit collection, medium term debenture issues and mortgage funds. In 1984 they attracted 36% of all savings accounts. They don't traditionally invest in stocks or shares on their own account and, in contrast to private sector banks, have not pursued profit as a primary objective. About 50% of their assets are mortgages or mortgage backed loans and they accounted for just under 40% of the total mortgage lending business in 1983. Half of their liabilities are savings and deposit accounts. They are major borrowers on the domestic bonds market along with institutional investors and stockbrokers. They have been losing ground in the savings market to the grossbanken and have found mortgage business less profitable as mortgage funding costs have risen.

Because of the relatively low profitability of their traditional business and the relatively low returns on their savings book accounts, they have been diversifying to seek more profitable business and meet the needs of their customers. Despite a falling market share they were doing well in the mid 1980s and recording rising interest earnings and commission income. They cooperate to offer a full range of banking services and are trying to develop a better balance between fee and commission income and on and off balance sheet business. With a view to expanding their off balance sheet business, which is generally more profitable than their traditional business, as a group they bought a majority stake in the Omnibank group in 1985 and renamed it Swiss Cantonbank (International). It has offices in London, Frankfurt, New York and Hong Kong and specialises in off balance sheet business, such as foreign exchange and securities trading and letters of credit activities, to which the restrictions in their statutes relating to overseas business do not apply. Most have foreign assets well within statutory limits anyway and, therefore, have room for further expansion in this direction.

They are members of the Association of Swiss Cantonal Banks and cooperate in a number of areas. They operate a joint underwriting syndicate for public bonds, a central mortgage bond institution, two investment trusts and a number of subsidiaries handling pension fund accounts and generally collaborate to improve the range of services they can offer as a group. There is an emerging trend for them to convert into public companies. In 1984 some of them issued participation certificates, which are non-voting shares, thus achieving some independence and making a step toward privatisation. The cantonal banks of Zug and Jura and the two Vaud cantonal banks are joint stock companies. As privatisation spreads they will clearly become more profit oriented.

The foreign banks are the the third largest banking group. They maintained about 30 branches and over 10 representative offices in the mid 1980s. Many foreign institutions have chosen to establish finance companies rather than branches or representative offices. More than a third of the bank like finance companies, of which there are over 70, are foreign owned and most are situated in Zurich. In the decade to mid 1985 the number of banks represented, in one way or another, had grown from 120 to 200, making Switzerland one of the world's largest financial centres. Some of the finance companies belonged to foreign, especially Japanese, securities houses or brokers, rather than banks. The Japanese presence is explained by the fact that Japanese corporations are heavy borrowers on the Swiss capital market.

The foreign banks engage mainly in fiduciary business, corporate business and trade-related finance, which is mainly transacted with multinationals and exporters, and merchant and private banking. They find it difficult to win domestic Swiss banking business because of the standardised interest rates and charges administered by the Swiss Banking Association (SBA). Mortgage lending rates are one of the few rates that are not completely controlled and mortgages and mortgage secured lending accounts for about two-thirds of local currency loans. The rates are, however, sensitive to political pressures and kept fairly low. Foreign banks began to lead manage Sfr securities issues in 1985 when the US owned institutions made a significant impact with swap backed issues.

The majority of the foreign units are controlled by institutions from OECD [17] countries, although some are also owned by institutions based in OPEC, [18] Eastern Europe and Less Developed Countries. Since 1969 legislation has required special licensing for foreign banks and a principle of reciprocity applies. [19] The foreign banks are represented by the Association of Foreign Banks, which includes foreign controlled finance companies in its membership. Through representative offices foreign banks cannot undertake business in Switzerland but can promote the business of the sponsoring bank by maintaining a presence. They are subject to Swiss banking law and must abide by its secrecy provisions and can use the label Swiss bank. As a group the foreign institutions hold over 20% of the reserves of the banking system. If fiduciary business is included their share is larger than the cantonals. They have a very high proportion of foreign business, which accounts for over 70% of their assets. Their growth has been rapid in the decade to the mid 1980s.

Finance companies are broadly divisible into two types: bank-like finance companies and industrial and commercial finance companies. The latter are usually Swiss companies which limit their activities to financing groups of companies. If they do not take deposits but raise only bond finance then they are not subject to banking law but to the Federal Code of Obligations covering the corporate sector. Those taking deposits are subject to banking law. The bank-like finance companies undertake a wider range of business, including corporate finance and participation in the syndication, management, and underwriting of bond and share issues. Their assets, a large proportion of which are foreign, grew by 60% between 1979 and 1983 and have since continued to grow rapidly. Only four of them solicited deposits in 1984 and these were subject to all the articles of the banking law. Those not taking deposits are subject only to Articles 7 and 8 which relate to accounting and reporting requirements and make it obligatory to seek permission to make large scale capital exports. Because of their ability to engage in virtually all banking and securities business without being subject to the full rigours of the banking law they are attractive to foreign institutions. They are effectively offshore banking facilities, but they do not enjoy a favourable taxation status.

The foreign owned finance companies do not normally take deposits and their operations are usually financed by their parents and refinanced on the Euromarkets. They do, however, advance credits and participate in bond issues and the SNB has become concerned about the risk associated with some of their activities. It wants five conditions attached to their licensing: minimum capital ratios; organisational rules; conduct guarantees; reciprocity; and regular auditing control. It hoped to have such provisions included in a revised Banking Act but would probably be satisfied if they were imposed by decree. The FBC has doubts about the need to regulate the finance companies more strictly and the Swiss Bankers Association (SBA) does, however, want the finance companies to be required to adhere to capital ratios similar to those applied under banking law and their licensing to be subject to the reciprocity requirement applied to foreign banks. The foreign owned finance companies compete to some extent with the commercial and the private banks but seem to bring in mainly new business.

The next largest group of banks are the regional banks and savings institutions. There are approximately 220 of them and they concentrate on providing retail banking services. They collect small savings and grant loans, mortgages and domestic credit. They were previously divided into mortgage, local and savings banks. Most are members of the Association of Swiss Regional and Savings Banks. They tend to have a limited geographical spread of branches and to concentrate on long term deposits and mortgages. They are sometimes classified as mortgage banks if mortgage loans account for more than 60% of their assets. Savings banks are distinguished by having a high proportion of savings accounts as liabilities. Many of them are effectively both savings and mortgage banks. In 1983 they had over 1,000 branches and an 8.5% share of the aggregate bank balance sheet. Foreign assets counted for only 1.4% of their total assets. They take a variety of organisational forms, including : private banks, cooperatives, foundations, municipal banks, mutual societies and communal institutions. They are not growing rapidly and their share of the banking market has declined from 20% just after the first world war. In 1981 they established the Clearing Centre of Savings and Regional Banks.

The grossbanken, cantonal banks, foreign banks and regional and savings banks accounted for about 90% of the aggregate banking balance sheet in the mid 1980s. The remaining 10% was divided between the Raiffeisen banks, the private banks, the finance companies subject to bank law and other specialised banking institutions.

The Raiffeisen banks or loan associations and the credit unions are normally grouped together for statistical purposes. The Raiffeisen banks are cooperative savings and loan associations, based on a system developed by Friedrich Wilhelm Raiffeisen. They aim to collect funds from local communities and lend them on fair terms to members of the same community. There are two associations representing this group. By far the largest is the Association of Swiss Loan Societies (ASLSs), to which the Raiffeisen banks belong. It has over 1200 member cooperatives which gather community funds and lend on a secured mortgage basis, primarily to member farmers and small businesses. They are financed through savings deposits and the issue of medium term notes. The ASLS maintains a central institution in St. Gallen, which is also organised as a cooperative. The much smaller number of mutual loan associations are represented by the Federation of Mutual Credit banks.

In 1985 there were 24 private banks. They are the oldest type of bank, originally performing roles akin to UK merchant banks. Their number has declined from 180 at the beginning of the century and about 50 at the beginning of the 1960s. They are represented by the Swiss Private Bankers Association and undertake most forms of banking business, although they mainly engage in portfolio management and do not normally advertise publicly for deposits, dealing instead with private customers. Although they have declined in number and faced competition from a growing number of finance companies their volume of business has been rising. They have recently benefitted from the return of the artisan, requiring tailored services, and the general worldwide trend towards the provision of tailored private banking services to wealthy individuals. Although private investment fund management makes up the bulk of their business, they are increasingly winning business from institutional investors. To attract such business they are having to invest in information technology and to provide research facilities. They are traditionally organised as partnerships or limited companies with heavily concentrated equity holdings. The partnerships in particular have been finding it difficult to raise sufficient capital internally and there is a tendency for private banks to convert themselves into limited liability companies. Many of them are diversifying into foreign exchange and precious metals trading, seeking fee earning business, and developing international links or establishing overseas offices to exploit opportunities in the US and Euromarkets.

Finally, there are a number of specialised types of banking institution, including 24 trade banks and 41 institutions specialising in stock exchange and securities transactions and asset administration. They are all organised as corporations. Switzerland is also the home of the Bank for International Settlements, which is situated in Basle and provides banking services to the central banks which own it.[89]

The SNB became the sole bank of issue since 1907, following the National Bank Act of 1905 which also requires it to circulate and maintain the quality of notes and coin and to contribute to the development of an efficient payments' system. Currency is circulated through its two head offices and eight branches to banks and post offices. Current account facilities are available to the general public from grossbanken, savings and regional banks, Cantonal banks and cooperative banks. Private banks also offer current accounts to selected clients. Besides the 4,900 or so banks offices there are also nearly 4,000 post offices which provide a giro transfer service. The Postal Administration is strictly regulated and post offices are not allowed to open savings accounts or grant overdraft facilities in connection with giro accounts. In 1983 there were 1.5m bank current accounts and 1m post office giro accounts. Cashless payments are effected mainly through giro credit transfer; which accounted for 99% of their total value and 88% of their volume in 1983. The remaining volume was accounted for by bank cheques (10.6%), credit card transactions (0.6%) and direct debits (0.8%). Of the giro transfers, 60% were postal, 39% bank and 10% was accounted for by the SNB's own giro, which is used for interbank transfers and government transactions. The proportion of paperless electronic payments remained low because no general agreement had been reached on the development of an electronic payments' system. One problem is that it will require high usage to cover fixed costs in such a small country. The retail sector dominates cash payments and credit cards are not as widely used as in other major industrial countries, although their usage is spreading rapidly in the 1980s.

The giro system was dominated by the Postal Administration until the 1950s when the banks reached a consensus and established their own rival system with settlement accounts held centrally with the SNB. The SNB has encouraged coordination to achieve a uniformity of payments instruments and a coordinating body, on which both the banks and the Postal Administrations are represented, has been created with the aim of improving the payments system. A feasibility study was commissioned in 1983 to examine the conditions under which EFTPOS could be introduced. The retail trade is also represented on the working party. Coordination is particularly important amongst banks, most of which affect payments. They have established a central body (Telekurs AG), in which banks are proportionally represented. In the last decade all innovations, such as cashless salary payments, cash dispensing (Bancomat) and Eurocheques, have been introduced on a coordinated basis. Innovations consequently tend to be widespread and have gained rapid acceptance.

Switzerland has a low velocity of circulation so that there is a high ratio of cash in circulation to GNP by the standards of major industrial countries. Cash is the dominant means of payment by private households which use cash for nearly all transactions with retailers and pay many bills in cash through post offices. There are two networks of cash dispensers : Bancomat, which had 273 machines in 1983, and Postomat, which had 104. Additionally there were 250 machines installed in local and regional bank networks. An attempt was made to integrate the networks in the mid 1980s.

With regard to cashless payments, the accounts offered by the Postal Administration through post offices have been highly regulated. They pay no interest and there are no charges for giro transfers. They do not accept third party cheques and cannot extend overdrafts. No initial deposit is required to use the service and despite their seeming competitive disadvantage their attraction seems to be their convenience by virtue of the widespread location of post offices. There has been a rapid growth in postal cheque accounts which provide for the direct crediting of wages and salaries as this itself has been rapidly and widely accepted. Over 10% of the population have post office cheque accounts and, as a major distributor of cash, the postal system provides an interface between cash and cashless payments.

The banking system maintains a smaller number of clearing centres than the postal system and can take longer to effect payments. This disadvantage will disappear when an electronic payments' system is developed. There is a clearing centre for each major bank and group of banks. The SNB acts as clearing house for the clearing centres, all the centres maintaining accounts with it. Telekurs AG is responsible for an Automated Clearing House, which processes customer transfers automatically and also processes payments of wages and salaries. Its role will be increased as paperless transactions become more widespread. Telekurs AG is also responsible for overseeing the further development of the bank payments' system, in which the banks have capital holdings in proportion to their size, and for joint activities such as Bancomat, Eurocheques, and Eurocards. The SNB is also a member of Telekurs AG.

The main non cash payments' instruments are giro credits. Direct debits are comparatively insignificant. Cheque usage is being promoted by banks which favour the standardised Eurocheques, which can be processed automatically. Credit cards are of minor but increasing importance. Point of sale cards, usable in telephone booths and petrol stations, have also been distributed but are not widely used. ATM cards are much more widespread and are being standardised. Both the postal and the bank giros work with machine readable vouchers so that over 50% of cashless payments are now computer processed. All banks are entitled to participate. Most do but a few of them use others as agencies. There is no proper clearing of interbank transactions through the SNB, payments being handled individually without using offsetting credit and debit payments. An interbank clearing project is in process to rectify this deficiency. Plans were reaching an advanced stage in the mid 1980s for introducing EFTPOS and improving interbank payments. Credit cards, probably used in conjunction with EFTPOS, are expected to become widely and extensively used in the future. Secrecy provisions prevent banks from pooling information on customer credit risks and this may have reduced their speed of introduction. Electronic authorisation should reduce the risk of abuse of the credit card system and may provide banks with an opportunity to increase retail business in this area, which has proved profitable overseas.

The Swiss money market has not gained the depth and significance of money markets in other major financial centres. Well developed financial systems provide instruments to allow the short term lending and borrowing of excess liquidity. Such instruments do exist in Switzerland but for a number of reasons, [21] including the tax regime and the fact that most institutions are in surplus and, therefore, the demand for funds is small, they are not extensively used. The major banks instead tend to place their surpluses in the Euromoney markets and the cantonal and other smaller banks tend to place a large proportion of their surpluses with the larger banks. The major borrowers on the money market are the Swiss Treasury, which issues a small amount of Treasury bills, the cantons and the BIS. The money market will be discussed further in section iii in connection with the SNBs monetary policy.

It is the capital market which gives Switzerland its pre-eminent position in the international financial system. It can be split into five sections. The public domestic capital market contains all bond and share issues for domestic borrowers. It is dominated by the grossbanken and private bankers which form a syndicate. The next two sections which involve domestic and international private placements for which there is a limited secondary market are of less importance. The last two sections cover foreign issues in Swiss francs and the Eurocapital market. The former covers all bond issues for foreign borrowers in the Swiss capital market. These issues are made by a syndicate of grossbanken and private banks, but foreign institutions have been breaking into the market in the 1980s forcing the syndicates to trim their commissions. The Eurocapital market covers nonSfr issues and is dominated by the 'big three' banks. Its role as a Eurobond market centre is limited by the tax system.

On the investment side, the domestic capital market is dominated by the big institutional investors, especially the insurance companies, and pension funds. These tend to buy new issues and hold them to maturity, thereby reducing the volume of secondary trading. The secondary market for long term securities of all kinds is provided through the stock exchanges, the over the counter (OTC) market, and prebourse trading. Prebourse trading takes place in the Zurich bourse prior to its opening for normal business. It is an unlisted securities market. The important OTC trading takes place through telephone links. The use of the organised exchanges is not compulsory and many of the securities traded on the OTC market are often listed on the exchanges. Trading is, however, traditionally done through the stock exchanges, of which there are seven. Access to the exchanges is not confined to brokers. Instead, all kinds of financial institutions can engage in trading providing they receive authorisation from the supervisory authority of the exchange concerned. They are not governed by federal law and cantons have passed their own regulations. The stock exchanges of Berne, Lausanne, Neuchatel and St. Gallen are private institutions and trading is in local or regional securities. The major stock exchanges, in order of importance, are in Zurich, Basle and Geneva and are under cantonal supervision. Zurich is by far the largest. All listed shares, bonds, and investment certificates are traded on these major exchanges which have adopted a programme modernisation. In 1986 the Geneva exchange, Switzerland's oldest, moved to new purpose built premises and so did the Basle exchange. The Zurich exchange is overloaded and expects to move to its new building in 1991. The other two exchanges, having moved, have the capacity to admit new members and may take some of the pressure off Zurich in the interim. The three main exchanges have cooperated to develop an electronic information and reporting system and are to introduce a computer assisted trading system (CATS) for bonds and over the counter stocks in 1987. The spur to modernisation has come from foreign investors, particularly the large institutions, to which the Swiss banks look for profitable fund management business. The grossbanken, which hold a dominant position on stock exchange management committees, have therefore been willing and able to invest in modernisation to maintain the international competitiveness of the exchanges. The leading Swiss banks and bourses also set up a joint committee in January 1987 to operate the country's first futures and options exchange, due to open a year later. It is to be called Soffex, the Swiss Options and Futures Exchange.

The capital markets enjoyed an upsurge in business in the 1980s as foreign, especially Japanese and US borrowers, were attracted to the market by low interest rates which ensured that costs of raising capital were below those prevailing in the Eurobond market. This provided banks with healthy profits from their securites underwriting, broking and trading activities and opportunities to boost their capital bases in 1985/6. By the end of 1985 their aggregate capital was 122% of the minimum capital requirement, which is one of the stiffest in the world. The rapid growth of the OTC market encouraged the exchanges to modernise themselves following the establishment of a Tripartite Bourse Commission in 1983 and led to the reduction of commission fees by the syndicates. In 1986 the SNB abolished the Sfr 200m ceiling on bond issues, which was designed to regulate capital exports, thereby removing one of the remaining restrictions on the market. Also in 1986 Euromarket innovations such as zero bonds were brought into the markets and the practice of backing international bond issues by swap facilities became almost universal. These facilities allowed borrowers to exchange their Sfr proceeds for other currencies, which in turn led to an increase in foreign borrowers to the market, and they have yet to win mandates for major Swiss corporations. The dominance of the Sfr securities market by the major Swiss banks is maintained by the SNB's ban on the issue of Sfr obligations abroad. A Sfr Eurobond market has, therefore, not been allowed to develop. This forces issuers to pay tax and increases the cost of isssuing Sfr denominated bonds. The SNB has hitherto sought to control the Sfr bond market because of its importance to its method of monetary control. It is, however, coming under pressure to relax its ban on issues of Sfr securities abroad. [22]

The attractions of Switzerland as an international capital market are well documented[23] and have been briefly outlined above. Its future has been called into question by the growing competition, particularly from the European centres, especially London and perhaps Frankfurt, following the deregulation of the D Mark bond market, as deregulation proceeds apace. It clearly cannot count on maintaining an advantageous interest rate differential and if this disappears it will be disadvantaged by the relatively high financial taxes which prevail. It has already lost much of its Euromarket business to London and could likewise lose a significant proportion of its Sfr business if the ban on issues abroad is lifted, unless it reduces these taxes. The taxes in question were a withholding tax of 35%, applicable to all interest income excluding interest on foreign bond issues and fiduciary deposits, and a 'stamp duty' of 0.15% for resident borrowers and 0.30% for non resident borrowers. The withholding tax on bank deposits, dividends and bonds for non residents is reduced for residents of countries with which Switzerland has a tax treaty and waived altogether on a mutual basis with countries not imposing such taxes, such as the UK and Germany. The exemption of fiduciary accounts from the withholding tax applicable to domestic bank accounts clearly adds to the attraction afforded by their discreet character and ensures a healthy supply of such deposits despite the fact that they are more risky to depositors than traditional bank deposits. It is the 'stamp duty' that has done the most damage. It applies to sales of all securities and is independent of maturity and has, therefore, tended to inhibit the development of the money market. The UK 'stamp duty' was halved twice between 1980 and 1985 and may well be abolished altogether. The lower 'stamp duty' in Luxembourg and London has encouraged a shift of transactions to the foreign branches and subsidiaries of Swiss banks in those centres.

The government will, therefore, have to weigh the benefits of 'stamp duty', as a substantial, secure but possibly declining source of tax revenue, against the possibility that its reduction or elimination would promote the country's ability to attract international financial business in the face of competition from abroad and increase tax revenue from other sources. The future prospects of Switzerland as a financial centre will be discussed further in section iv. The domestic capital market should, however, be stimulated by the obligation on companies to provide pension schemes for employees. If, additionally, institutional investors come under pressure to improve the performance of pension schemes, as institutional investors abroad have done, they are likely to trade more actively on the secondary markets than in the past, when they tended to concentrate on secure investments held to maturity.

iii) Regulation and Supervision

The banking community is regulated by the Federal Banking Commission (FBC) which is located in Berne and consists of seven to nine members elected by the Federal Council. It is responsible for supervising the banking system and investment trusts and is independent of the central bank, the Swiss National Bank (SNB). It has the power to grant and withdraw licences, to issue decisions necessary to enforce banking law, and to prescribe the content and format of audit reports, which it can request to receive. It frequently issues instructions, through circular letters, to banks with respect to specific banking law regulations and reporting requirements.

Its semi-annual Bulletin publishes its major decisions and the outcomes of appeals to the Swiss Federal Court against its decisions, thereby providing an up to date report on the administration of Swiss bank legislation. In response to the growth in the market and the increasingly complex issues facing the banking system, the FBC enlarged its permanent secretariat substantially in the 1980s. The secretariat deals with day to day administrative work and includes legal and audit departments.

The SNB is a limited company whose issued capital is held by the cantons (59%) and private shareholders (41%). It has registered offices in Zurich and Berne and is organised into three departments, two of which are in Zurich. The Berne department is primarily concerned with bank rate issues and the administration of liquid reserves and gold. One of the Zurich departments is concerned with giro clearing, foreign exchange transactions and discounting. The other department is concerned with banking statistics, central banking problems and questions relating to banking law. The management of the SNB or Bank is headed by an Executive Board consisting of three members, a president and two vice presidents, elected by the Federal Council. The Bank Council is responsible for broad supervision of the bank and has 40 members, 25 of which are elected by the government, including its president and vice president. The remainder are appointed by the general assembly of shareholders. Despite the government's power to make appointments to the Executive Board and the Bank Council, the SNB has demonstrated an ability to maintain considerable independence. The SNB issues directives concerning, amongst other things, the maintenance of reserve requirements, expansion of credit facilities, acceptance of foreign source deposits, export of capital and foreign exchange transactions. As mentioned above, it plays a role in the functioning and development of the payments' system, it is the sole issuer of bank notes, and it is responsible for distributing and maintaining the quality of currency. It is also the agent responsible for implementing those parts of the government's monetary policy that relate to banks. Monetary policy and control will be discussed further below. It is trying to divest itself of supervisory roles, such as acting as guarantor and umpire for the Convention de Diligence discussed below, which do not relate to its statutory function of conducting monetary policy.

The Swiss Bankers' Association (SBA), with offices in Basle, is the most influential of the numerous banking associations. It has established rules and scales of charges which its members are obliged to follow. It promotes the interests of its 450 or so members and cooperates closely with the authorities in the development of new banking legislation. It is active in the development of a code of ethics for the Swiss banking community, often called the Swiss Banking Convention. Most foreign banks, although having their own association, have joined the SBA and most non member banks adopt its scale of recommended charges and conventions. Some US banks have not joined in for fear of domestic anti-trust action.

The major provisions governing the regulation and supervision of banks are contained in the Bank Law which was passed in 1934 and amended in 1971. Its main objective is to protect the interests of creditors and Article 23 of the law defines the task of the FBC. The amendments of 1971 were introduced through an Implementing Ordinance in 1972. The most important regulations deal with liquidity requirements, equity requirements, lending limits and reporting requirements. The law also provides for the licensing of auditors by the FBC. After the Banking Motion it was in the process of revision, which involved a lengthy consultative process.

The final draft bill was expected to be sent to Parliament in 1986 or 1987 and the revised law was unlikely to be enacted before 1988. In the event, however, a decision was taken in late 1986 not to amend the Bank Law after all. Instead the banks are required to make their own self regulatory arrangements or to negotiate rules with the FBC whose supervisory role is to become more important and the SNB, in matters relating to monetary policy. The SBA, the FBC and representatives of lawyers and trustees are negotiating a new system for policing fund management and deposit taking activities. The stock exchange admissions' board is also under review following complaints, especially from foreign banks, that the nine member board, set up in the 1930s under an agreement with the SNB, is too heavily influenced by the bond issuing syndicate run by the big banks and is too conservative in its judgement of securities suitable for bourse listings. The ordinance on foreign banks was revised in 1984 and sets forth regulations regarding the establishment and operations of branches of foreign banks.

The National Bank Law (NBL) was passed in 1953 and amended in 1978 to give the SNB more complete central banking powers. It establishes the SNB and its organisational structure and defines its relationship with the federal government and the scope of its functions. Its activities are also governed by Section V of the Bank Law. Institutions not deemed by the FBC to be subject to banking legislation must abide by the Code of Obligations which contains the general provisions concerning Swiss commercial law.

In 1982 Swiss and foreign banks belonging to the SBA signed an agreement with the SNB called the Convention de Diligence (CdD). Its purpose was to codify ethical rules which were already applied by Swiss banks. In regard to the secrecy issue, to be discussed below, the most important requirement was that banks should clearly establish the identity of potential customers prior to accepting funds from them. Further, banks cannot accept funds that they have reason to believe were acquired in a manner that would constitute a criminal act in Switzerland. The CdD established a Review Board to investigate alleged infringements and breaches of the convention are punishable by fines.

The controversial secrecy regulations are covered by Article 47 of the Bank Law, which prohibits information about customers to be divulged to third parties, without the customer's approval. It does not apply in criminal cases, as defined by Swiss rather than foreign law, bankruptcy or debt collection procedure, where relevant disclosures are mandatory. Disclosure of information to foreign authorities or governmental agencies is not normally permitted unless an international treaty provides for it. Numbered accounts offer extra secrecy because the knowledge of the identity of the code number is restricted within the bank. Although not subject to Article 47 of the Bank Law, finance companies must abide by the Code of Obligations, Article 398 of which implies a duty to keep customer affairs confidential.

The accounting principles allow the creation of hidden reserves and fiduciary accounts are not included in bank accounts and must be reported separately. Accounts are prepared and presented to both the FBC and the SNB. Whilst accounts presented to the authorities must be on a consolidated basis and include details of hidden reserves and loan loss provisions, published accounts need (and invariably do) not.

The capital adequacy requirements have been couched in terms of risk adjusted capital ratios for a number of years, a practice that is now becoming more widespread, as noted in previous sections. Liabilities are weighted according to their risk and capital requirements are set in the light of the aggregate risk. Capital includes equity and subordinated debt up to 10% of the capital required. In 1985 it was estimated [24] that the major banks had disclosed capital/asset ratios of between 5.8 and 6.4, which was higher than most of their international peers and would have been much higher on a fully disclosed basis with hidden reserves included. Contingent liabilities are included in the capital requirements and note issuance facilities (nifs) and revolving underwriting facilities (rufs) were included in 1986 with weightings of half that applied on consumer loans, as in Germany and the UK prior to the January 1987 agreement between the US and UK authorities discussed in chapter 1 and section 2.1.

The statutory liquidity requirement is conventionally low because of the by international standards, low loan/deposit ratios and the existence of a complex formula requiring short term liabilities to be matched by increasing liquid assets. There are no legal lending limits but banks are required to report any transactions that would cause borrowers' debt to reach 40% of net worth, on a consolidated basis, for secured loans or 20% for unsecured loans to the SBC. The banks are required to make minimum provisions of 20% against loans to 'problem countries'. Most have provisions nearer to 30%. Capital and provisioning requirements have been overfulfilled as a rule, in part because they are not liable to taxation. Because fiduciary deposits are made at the risk of the customer no capital requirements are imposed since they are effectively regarded as riskless off balance sheet business.

The secrecy provisions have generated much debate within the country and attracted considerable international criticism. The CdD initially came into being in 1977 when the Chiasso branch of CS was found to be actively soliciting overseas deposits without worrying about their origin. A problem with the CdD is that the identity of true owners cannot be discovered when funds are handled by lawyers or fiduciary agents which are bound by the Code of Obligations and cannot, therefore, disclose their clients' names. They are, however, supposed to declare that the transactions they are initiating do not abuse Swiss bank secrecy. A lot depends on their integrity and some are believed actively to tout for business. Accounts handled by lawyers are called Form B accounts.

In May 1984 the electorate rejected a Banking Motion, put forward by the Social Democratic Party and the Trade Union movement, which aimed to counter systematic abuses involving Swiss banks such as the 1977 Chiasso scandal, which involved the misappropriation of clients' funds by local branch managers. The Motion aimed to retain secrecy but to weaken it by requiring banks to supply information more readily to assist investigations into criminal activities by domestic and foreign authorities. It also sought to increase the amount of information disclosed to the public, limit the influence of banks on outside companies and to introduce a deposit insurance scheme. Although rejected, the Banking Motion and the Chiasso affair which generated it have brought about changes in the regulatory system. Within three months of the Chiasso affair the CdD was agreed by the SBA and the SNB. The SBA responded to the Banking Motion by establishing a mutual agreement to assist ailing member banks. No insurance fund was established. The proposals for the revision of the Banking Act included a requirement to establish a fund but the SBA continues to oppose it. In 1982 the SBA also came to an agreement with the Securities and Exchange Commission [25] (SEC) of the US, called the Memorandum of Understanding, which requires US clients to sign a waiver empowering their identities to be disclosed in insider dealing enquiries. At the time insider dealing was not a criminal offence under Swiss law and so the banks were under no obligation to supply information. A law making insider trading a criminal offence is expected to be enacted in 1987. The memorandum is now superfluous because banks have asked all clients to absolve them from secrecy requirements in cases of insider trading.

The key proposal of the Banking Motion related to relaxation of secrecy in cases of evasion of foreign tax legislation and foreign exchange controls. Such evasions are not criminal offences in Switzerland and, regardless of the status of the offence in other countries, they are not obliged to relax secrecy. This has caused friction with the US, French and Italian authorities which suspect Swiss bank accounts are being used by tax and foreign exchange control evaders. In July 1985 Switzerland, backed by Austria and Luxembourg which also have relatively tight secrecy regulations, managed to block OECD proposals for the relaxation of bank secrecy rules to help counter international tax evasion. The proposals were tabled by the US and backed by the UK and the Scandinavian countries. They aimed to reduce the distinction between tax fraud, which is counted as a crime in Switzerland, and tax evasion, which is not. Switzerland confirmed its willingness to cooperate in criminal cases. Nevertheless many politicians have become aware that flagrant abuse of secrecy can give Switzerland's financial centres a bad name. The country has a vested interest in maintaining an open international system and must maintain its own standards. It must not be seen to be giving active support to international flight capital or money that is being 'laundered'. They, therefore, feel that banks need either to make tighter checks or to prevent the inflow of 'dirty' money from abroad. The banks became fearful of a change in government attitude when it required them to freeze the assets of Mr Ferdinand Marcos, the deposed president of the Philippines, in 1985. The concern was heightened when the SNB announced in 1985 that it did not wish to renew the CdD, originally agreed in 1977 for 5 years and continued for another 5 years in 1982, in 1987 when it expired. Instead it wished to make the obligations legally binding and have them enshrined in banking law. The SBA not surprisingly opposed this, arguing that it would be inconsistent with Swiss law. The FBC feels it is unnecessary because it can enforce the agreement by seeking management changes in cases where it is flouted. With the reform of the Bank Law now abandoned and the SNB refusing to renew the CdD, the ball is in the FBC's court. Additionally, the Ministry of Justice published a report in February 1987 recommending that 'money laundering' be made a criminal offence with stiff penalties. It believes legislation is required to protect the reputation of Switzerland as a financial centre. The SBA reacted cautiously to the proposals but legislation is expected in the early 1990s.

Whilst the plans for full scale revision of the Bank Law were dropped following the defeat of the Banking Motion, a number of partial revisions were under consideration. One issue on which the SNB and the Finance Ministry, to which the FBC is affiliated, agree is the need for greater control over the proliferation of bank-like finance companies. They require no authorisation, although they have to report to the SNB and are subject to its regulations on capital exports. The SBA would like an authorisation procedure to be applied to finance companies; enforcing the principle of reciprocity and subjecting them to capital requirements comparable to banks, rather than those imposed through the Code of Obligations. The FBC would also like stricter reporting requirements to be imposed upon them and the SNB is concerned about their refinancing activities on the interbank market.

As central bank the SNB is lender of last resort and consequently offers discounting facilities. It implements monetary policy on behalf of the government and enjoys considerable independence in its pursuit of monetary stability and low inflation. Monetary policy is an important policy measure because tax changes are subject to referendum and the use of fiscal policy is consequently restricted. The SNB, therefore, has a significant impact on economic policy. Inflation has been kept low without a rise in unemployment on the scale experienced elsewhere in Europe. In the 1980s it has avoided interest rate and exchange rate intervention, confining its activities on the exchange markets to smoothing operations. It pursues annually set money growth targets by controlling the monetary base, in the light of projected changes in the demand for money. Base control is affected by buying and selling dollar swaps held by commercial banks. The SNB is the only central bank in the industrialised world to rely on the monetary base as a target variable and its policy has proved remarkably successful. [26]

In 1978 the Sfr appreciated against the dollar and the D Mark and exporters and some government ministers exerted pressure on the SNB to bring down the exchange rate. The SNB abandoned monetary targeting and complied. The resulting rise in inflation has made the SNB unwilling to repeat the episode, which it regards as an error in central bank policy, and it returned to monetary targeting in 1980. The episode did, however, illustrate the limits of its independence. The government and the Bank are required to consult each other and to coordinate government and central bank policy. The government usually manages to present a balanced budget so the major potential conflict is over the exchange rate. The government has the power to sack the bank governors but, given the high standing of the Bank, would be unlikely to do so. The Bank's main supervisory interests relate to ensuring its ability to achieve monetary control. In this connection it no longer fears the internationalisation of the Sfr and the creation of a Euromarket in Sfr securities.

Although foreign exchange market operations, particularly the purchase and sale of foreign currencies from and to Swiss banks, are the principal tool of monetary policy, other instruments are available. The SNB has become more active in the market for domestic securities, although the scope of open market operations on the money markets remain limited by the size of the market and the absence of a plentiful supply of Treasury bills because of the government's balanced budget policy. Reserve requirements have been varied in the past in preference to using open market operations. The Bank can also try to affect monetary policy through refinancing instruments such as discount and Lombard facilities but these are rarely effective because the banks normally have excess liquidity. [27]

iv) Deregulation

There are few further opportunities for liberalisation in Switzerland, which has long been converted to the principles of free trade and competition. 1985 saw the introduction of financial innovations such as perpetual floating rate notes and zero bonds, to the Swiss capital markets as foreign competition, especially from the US institutions, began to influence the traditionally conservative market. It also saw the first foreign bank lead manage a Sfr bond issue and a rapid spread in swap backed issues. In response to growing competition, brokerage fees on large deals were reduced and the stock exchanges announced plans to introduce options and futures contracts.

Exchange controls were completely lifted in 1979 and the remaining restrictions on capital exports, which resulted from a limit set by the SNB on the size of individual Sfr securities issues and a requirement to apply to the SNB for a time of issue, were lifted in 1986. The limit had already been raised in 1984 to Sf200m. Bank and securities companies are still required to seek permission from the SNB prior to exporting capital, however. In May 1986 the SNB also removed the last restrictions on medium term note issues by virtually abolishing the distinctions between note and public bond issues. One important restriction remains. Institutions not domiciled in Switzerland are not permitted to syndicate Sfr securities issues. There is consequently no Sfr Eurobond market.

As a major capital market centre, Switzerland already has a smaller share of the Eurobond market than would be expected. This is attributed to its disadvantageous financial tax regime. Stamp duty was raised in 1984 and turnover tax was extended to physical gold transactions. 'Stamp duty' at 0.3% remains relatively low by international standards. The 'stamp duty' in the UK having been reduced from 2% to only 0.5% in the 1980s, for example. The difference is that it applies to all transactions in securities regardless of maturity and covers all offshore deals booked in Switzerland. Swiss bankers consequently prefer to transact Eurobond business in London or Luxembourg, where no such tax applies. The 'stamp duty' has also inhibited the development of the money market, completely discouraging foreign interest. Further, the turnover tax on gold has led to a decline of Zurich relative to London as a gold trading centre. The tax regime may also inhibit Switzerland's development as a major centre for futures and options contracts. In 1986, however, there were three small tax concessions. The Federal Council reduced the duty charged on Eurobond subscriptions made through Swiss banks to 0.15%, from 0.3%. It abolished the 35% withholding tax on interest paid on interbank credits. Previously, only deposits whose term was one year or less were tax exempt. Finally, it lifted the 6.2% value added tax on sales of bullion and gold coins. The latter tax had been lucrative when it was introduced in 1980 but was generating little revenue by the mid 1980s and inhibiting gold trading in Switzerland.

Recent attempts to vitalise the money markets, by issuing short term government securities, have proved unsuccessful. Despite the benefits of stability, secrecy and low interest rates, it is feared that if the restrictions prohibiting the development of a Euro Sfr bond market were lifted much of the international bond market business would be lost to London. The authorities are, therefore, unlikely to sanction such a liberalisation until the tax regime is brought into line with the UK's. The SNB has come under pressure to act following the Bundesbank's decision in 1985 to allow foreign banks based in Germany to lead manage D Mark bond issues, which will add to the attraction of Frankfurt as a financial centre, and as a result of the growing appetite for dual currency bonds. These are bonds paid in one currency and redeemed in another. Foreign banks have requested permission to make dual currency issues including the Sfr. The SNB has so far judged such issues to be covered by its restriction of lead management of Sfr issues to banks domiciled in Switzerland. It is known to be considering the option of allowing Sfr and dual currency issues to be underwritten by banks outside Switzerland as long as the Swiss banks participate in the syndicate. Action awaits a tax change, however, otherwise Sfr bond issuing business might be transferred to London. The SNB's control over the market is declining as financial innovations cloud the distinction between primary issues and secondary trading. The SNB's approval only needs to be sought for the former. It does not want to be saddled with outmoded rules and would rather do away with them, requiring more information about trading and new issues in return. It is uneasy about its restriction on dual currency issues because it requires it to rely on the cooperation of other central banks to enforce its syndication rules.

'Stamp duty', or turnover tax, is imposed at 0.1% on all money market paper transactions up to a maturity of three months, and at 0.15% on longer term securities transactions, double rates applying to foreigners. The 35% withholding tax can only be reclaimed by nationals of countries with reciprocal taxation agreements with Switzerland, of which there are only five. The finance ministry is unwilling to give up these stable and significant sources of revenue without compensation. It is unable to raise corporation tax because of a decision taken in the mid 1980s to leave these unchanged. Unless other sources of revenue can be found, the case for tax liberalisation must rest on the general benefits to be derived, and taxes generated by, having thriving financial centres in Switzerland. In June 1985 a group of state senators proposed a motion calling for the abolition of 'stamp duty' on short term instruments, a removal of duty on Swiss Eurobond issues, and a reduction of the duty foreigners were liable to pay. In September 1985 less far reaching proposals were accepted by the lower house. These fiscal changes will take some time to be introduced and won't be voted upon until 1987 and therefore won't take effect until 1988 at the earliest. The Finance Ministry remains opposed to the changes, accepting only that the abolition of 'stamp duty' on short term investments would be beneficial because it would actually increase net fiscal income. It is hoped that the proposed abolition or reduction of 'stamp duty' will stimulate the money markets, and help the capital market recover Eurobond business lost to London. The SNB has supported the banks in their lobbying for a more liberal financial tax regime because it will allow it to liberalise its restriction on overseas Sfr issues and generally promote Switzerland as a financial centre at a time when its advantages are being eroded by deregulation in other international centres, particularly London.

Apart from the potential deregulatory changes of liberalising international Sfr securities issues and reducing financial taxes, re-regulatory developments are also being debated. Despite the outcome of the referendum on the Banking Motion, the SNB was pressing for a revision of the law relating to bank secrecy, the regulation of finance companies; and the establishment of a deposit protection scheme. Now that reform of the Bank Law has been abandoned, it will have to lobby the Federal Council and the FBC for reforms.

With regard to secrecy, the SNB would like a more formal agreement on banking practices to replace the informal agreement due to expire in 1987. In order to assuage foreign criticism it would like some concessions to be made by banks in cases involving tax avoidance and insider dealing, even though these do not currently violate criminal law. Legislation on insider dealing is, as mentioned above, expected in 1987 but legislation making tax avoidance a criminal offence is not expected in the near future. With public opinion seemingly moving in favour of such legislation it is, however, expected within a decade. The secrecy provisions also seem to have inhibited the development of the credit card market because banks are unwilling to establish a multibank information system. Such developments are seen by many banks abroad as the key to monitoring the quality of their lending. Whilst the banks responded to the Banking Motion by announcing a mutual support system for ailing banks, the SNB would still like an investor protection fund to be established to put the arrangements on a more formal footing. Finally, it would like finance companies to be subject to most of the banking law relating to banks. These effectively form an offshore banking sector in Switzerland and with tighter regulation their attractiveness to overseas institutions might be reduced. In order to compensate a reduction in financial taxes would again seem to be required.

Because of the consensus approach to politics, changes in the Bank Law have proved impossible to achieve, especially in the light of the rejection of the Banking Motion. The banks have proved to be a significant lobby group in opposing legislative reform and they have been campaigning hard to for a reduction in financial taxes. It seems likely that they will succeed but at the cost of losing the advantage of having Sfr securities business confined to their own back yard. They have already felt the competitive pressure from the finance companies and foreign banks in the domestic capital market and their dominance of the market has been declining. They will of course be happy to see the finance companies exposed to a similar degree of regulation and supervision and put on a more equal footing. In this connection they have also been campaigning for a stricter appliance of reciprocity conditions to finance companies; especially in relation to Japanese institutions which have been gaining access to the Swiss securities market and have built up their share of bond market business in the latter half of the 1980s. The Swiss banks meanwhile have not been granted such a widespread access to Japanese securities business. They took matters into their own hands by delaying the granting of Swiss bourse trading licences to Japanese institutions and thereby restricted their freedom to lead manage bond issues.

Despite the declining importance of secrecy in a world where an increasing proportion of securities business is transacted with institutional clients, the banks are also lobbying hard to maintain the present arrangements. Additionally, they feel that, given their combined capitalisation and hidden reserves, the creation of an investor protection fund is unnecessary. A compromise could perhaps be reached whereby formal commitments to mutual assistance amongst banks could be elicited as part of the licensing procedure and the creation of a fund could be avoided. Banks could instead be required to earmark a proportion of their hidden reserves, which are disclosed to the authorities, for investor protection purposes. This might indirectly encourage the establishment of a fund anyway, because principles of insurance would imply that the protection that a pooled fund would give could be bought with a smaller contribution than the amount of earmarked reserves that a bank would be required to hold.

It seems likely that before the end of the decade a consensus will be reached, with a little prompting from deregulatory developments abroad. As a result the financial liberalisation will be completed and the tax regime will be liberalised. In the meantime the FBC can be expected to pursue reciprocity more actively than in the past. This tendency was demonstrated in March 1986 when it imposed a temporary ban on the licensing of Japanese institutions whilst it reviewed the question of reciprocity with Japan. Since then the Swiss and Japanese authorities have, at least temporarily, resolved their differences. In late 1986 and early 1987 Swiss institutions were involved in dealings with: Dennis Levine, who was subsequently prosecuted in the US for insider dealing; the Guinness company , which had asked Bank Leu to purchase Guinness's shares on its behalf to boost their value and help it win a takeover bid; and the 'Irangate' scandal, involving the supply of arms by the US to Iran and the channelling of funds to the Nicaraguan 'Contras'. Further, the government agreed to order banks to disclose information relating to the Philippines government's investigation into the missing $1bn, allegedly misappropriated by the deposed president Marcos. The authorities seemingly want to be seen to be cooperating, in the light of international criticism, in order to shore up Switzerland's reputation as a financial centre. The banks are, however, concerned that the Marcos affair may have reduced confidence in the secrecy provisions. These events are, therefore, doubly damaging. Banks have stressed that the secrecy provisions remain intact. The FBC has, however, caused a stir by calling for the abolition of Form B accounts, which provide the double protection of lawyer and bank secrecy. Banks and lawyers are opposed to this proposal, fearing a loss of custom, but their abolition would assuage foreign criticism and frighten off the most suspect clients. The FBC also took a tough line on Bank Leu, even though it had not broken Swiss law. It used Article 3 of the Bank Law, which requires banks to conduct themselves in a 'proper fashion', to justify its investigation into Bank Leu's role in the Guinness affair. The FBC felt that, as an international bank, it should have been aware of the possibility that it was breaking UK law.

It is difficult to gauge how much business has been lost as a result of association of Swiss banks with the scandals and the question mark raised by the Marcos affair over the sanctity of secrecy. The banks have claimed that they have not lost deposits but that they have found it more difficult to win new business. Small account holders are now being attracted to European offshore centres, such as Luxemburg and the Channel Islands, instead.

It is clearly in both the banks' and the government's interests to guarantee the good name of Swiss banking. Further accommodation of the efforts of authorities in other countries, whose investigations have been inhibited by the secrecy provisions, is therefore to be expected. Swiss banks are, consequently, likely to become more willing to cooperate and compromise in cases of blatant wrongdoing, whether they involve illegal acts in Switzerland or not. They could make this clear by renegotiating the CdD with the FBC and coming to an agreement over the Form B accounts. They face a choice similar to that of other financial centres, especially the offshore ones between reforming regulations and risking losing business of doubtful repute, and doing nothing and losing reputable business.

1) Which fell significantly in the mid 1980s.
2) See section iv.
3) See section iv.
4) See section ii.
5) Discussed in section iv.
6) See sections ii and iv.

7) See Peat Marwick (1982) for further discussion.

8) The major exception being those relating to special credit institutions, which also received state subsidies.

9) After separating their investment and banking activities and transferring their non-banking subsidiaries to financial holding companies.

10) See section ii.

11) See Peat Marwick (1982).

12) Société Générale led the way in 1984 by issuing Certificats d' investissement (CIs), which are non voting preference shares. Since then CIs and Titres Participatifs (TPs), which are non voting loan stocks, have been issued by a number of banks to bolster their capital. The Finance Ministry gave the banks permission to raise capital in this way but required CIs and TPs to be limited to 25% of total capital.

13) See section iv.

14) As noted in Chapter 1, this segmentation has been eroded since 1970.

15) Over 90% of all households had bank accounts in 1980.

16) By the 1941 banking law, see Welch (1981).

17) See Kindleberger (1984).18) See Kindleberger (1984).

19) See Welch (1981) and Peat Marwick (1982),

20) Counseil National du Crédit.

21) Including, Crédit Agricole, Crédit Mutuel, Crédit Populaire, and Crédit Coopératif.

22) Caisse Nationale de Crédit Agricole.

23) Confédération Nationale du Crédit Mutuel.

24) Caisse Centrale de Crédit Mutuel.

25) Caisse Centrale des Banques Populaires.

26) Chambre Syndicale des Banques Populaires.

27) Caisse Centrale de Crédit Hôtelier, Industriel et Commercial, see below.

28) Caisse Centrale de Crédit Coopératif.

29) Banques Français du Crédit Coopératif.

30) Banques d'Epargne

31) Caisse Nationale d'Epargne

32) The financial services division of the postal and telecommunications corporation.

33) Which oversees the provision of postal and telecommunications services.

34) Which are securities which are mortgaged or the subject of dispute.

35) Fonds de Développement Economique et Social.

36) Marché Hypothécaire.

37) See note 27.

38) Sociétiés de Développement Régional.

39) Banque Française du Commerce Extérieur.

40) Compagnie Française d'Assurance pour le Commerce Extérieur.

41) Caisse Nationale des Marchés de l'État.

42) Institut de Développement Industriel.

43) Crédit d'Équipement des Petites et Moyennes Enterprises (CEPME).

44) Lettre de Change-Relève.

45) Banks, finance companies, special credit institutions, stock-brokers and institutional investors (mainly insurance companies and investment companies).

46) Discussed in section iv.

47) Electronic funds transfer at point of sale.

48) More formally, the Ministry of the Economy, Finance and the Budget.

49) It has 232 branches.

50) The Association Française des Banques.

51) Commission de Contróle des Banques.

52) Conseil Nationale de Crédit.
53) See also section iv.
54) See also section iv.
55) Other members included the director of the highest administrative court (the Conseil d'Etat) and two bank representatives, nominated by the AFB and bank staff respectively.
56) i.e. accepting funds from the public, engaging in lending operations and the provision of money transmission services.
57) The former general manager of Crédit Agricole and general administrator of Société Générale.
58) See note 12.
59) Caisse des Refinancement Hypothécaire.
60) Which is a tax on the interest or coupon earnings of overseas investors in domestic securities. The US initiative was taken to attract overseas investment to help fund the growing US budget deficit.
61) See section iv.
62) See section iv.
63) See Commission of the European Communities (1977, 1983a, 1983b, 1985, 1986) and European Economic Community (1973).
64) As a result of the large proportion of fixed rate loans outstanding.
65) See section iii.
66) The 'big three' Swiss banks set up operations in the mid 1980s for example and there is also a growing US, UK and French banking presence.
67) Deutsche Bank, Dresdner Bank, and Commerzbank.
68) Such as Europartner, Ebic and Abecor.
69) The Bank für Gemeinwirtschaft does, however, have branches throughout Germany. Its share capital is held by trades unions and consumer cooperatives.
70) See also section i and iv.
71) Deutsche Girozentrale-Deutsche Kommunalbank.
72) Deutsche Gennanschaftsbank.
73) Kreditanstalt für Wiederaufbeau (Kfw).
74) Ausfuhrkredit-Gessellschaft mbh (AKA).
75) Industriekredit bank AG-Deutsche Industriebank (IKB).
76) Such as investment companies, collective securities deposit institutions, credit guarantee associations and leasing institutions.
77) Offline systems do not provide for the immediate execution of payments. Instead requests for payment are presented in a batch at the end of the day.
78) Online systems provide for the immediate execution of payments.
79) Länd zentralbanken.
80) Länder.
81) The lower house of the government consisting of representatives from the regions or the districts.
82) See Commission of the European Communities (1983a).
83) Schroeder Munchmeyer Hengst.
84) See Commission of the European Communities (1977).
85) Note issuance facilities (Nifs) involve the continuous sale of short term paper to Euromarket investors. The offers are underwritten by banks or backed by credit lines which can be drawn if issues fail to sell at their specified prices.
86) See Bank for International Settlements (1986a) and Committee on Banking Regulations and Supervisory Practices (1986).
87) i.e. bank accounts denominated in European Currency Units, see Bank for International Settlements (1985,1986b) for further discussion of ECU accounts.
88) The currency bands define the range in which the currencies are allowed to fluctuate in relation to their central rates. These are set in terms of ECUs, which are a

weighted basket of the currencies of the countries participating in the European Monetary System.

89) Unlisted Securities Market.

90) See subsequent sections of this chapter.

91) The attributes of Switzerland as a financial centre will be discussed further in sections ii and iv.

92) See sections ii and iv.

93) See Faith (1982).

94) See sections ii and iv.

95) See section iv.

96) See section 3.3iv.

97) See section 3.3ii.

98) See chapter 2.

99) See section ii.

1) i.e. business from which profit is derived from the differential between lending and borrowing rates.

2) Based on market capitalisation.

3) See section iii.

4) See chapter 1.

5) See section 2.2iii.

6) See section 2.3iii.

7) See Faith (1982) on the history of Swiss banking.

8) Nearly all lending is on a variable rate basis.

9) See section 3.3iv.

10) See section 2.3iv.

11) See section iii.

12) See Salomon Brothers (1986).

13) The Baker Plan was announced in 1986 at the annual meeting of the International Monetary Fund and the World Bank. It aimed to encourage growth oriented adjustment amongst fifteen major debtor nations based on additional lending by the IMF, the multilateral development agencies and the commercial banks.

14) See section iii.

15) See Salomon Brothers (1986).

16) From the US credit rating agencies; Standard and Poor's and Moody's. Most other major banks have been downgraded from the AAA status enjoyed by the Swiss banks since the 1982 Mexican debt crisis.

17) Organisation for Economic Cooperation and Development.

18) Organisation of Petroleum Exporting Countries.

19) See section iii.

20) See Hirsch (1969) on the origins of the BIS and the annual report of the BIS for an account of its current functions.

21) See Corti (1983).

22) See section iv.

23) See Corti (1983) and International Monetary Fund (1986).

24) See Salomon Brothers (1986).

25) See section 2.2.

26) See Kohi and Rich (1985) for a discussion of the application of monetary base control in Switzerland and the conditions necessary for its success.

27) See Corti (1983) for further discussion.

4

Socialist and Islamic Banking

4.1 Introduction

Islam has been described as a continent of the mind embracing about a sixth of mankind. In many North African, Asian and Middle Eastern countries the majority of the population is Muslim and there are substantial Muslim communities in numerous countries. They are guided by the teachings of the Koran which they believe was dictated to prophet Muhammad, who lived from AD570 to AD632, by the Archangel Gabriel. In the centuries following Muhammad's death, the Islamic empire spread rapidly through Asia, North Africa and into Europe. Its northward expansion suffered a reverse in Europe in AD732 after which pessimism and contraction set in. In the post second world war period almost forty Muslim and semi Muslim countries achieved independence and embarked on various Western influenced development strategies ranging from socialism to market oriented industrialisation. The development strategies generally neglected the agricultural sector and caused a decline in the rural sector and a gravitation towards cities where jobs often could not be found. People increasingly sought refuge in religion and economists and government authorities began to look to the Koran for inspiration.

The formation of OPEC and its success in raising oil prices in the 1970s gave new confidence and impetus to the Middle Eastern Muslim states and spawned a resurgence of fundamentalist ideas. The oil price collapse in the 1980s has again damaged the confidence of many of the Islamic states and reduced their economic independence from the rest of the world. The Islamic revolution went furthest in Iran, which has demonstrated expansionist tendencies, and the Middle Eastern region remains relatively unstable. Future developments are, therefore, difficult to predict.

Despite the differing interpretations of the Koran by various Muslim sects the general principles of egalitarianism and democracy are widely accepted. It is only in the Shi'ite dominated country of Iran that a clerical hierarchy has been established. Islam's strengths have lain in its simplicity, clarity and adaptability. The Koran lays down rules for spiritual, economic and political guidance. Trade, finance and investment have, however, been heavily influenced by North American and European practices and Islamic economists have agreed that these three areas of activity should be brought in line with the Koran's teachings in order to create a conducive environment within which commerce and industry will thrive. In this chapter the major concern is with the implications of the Koran for the financial system.

159

The Koran explicitly deals with economic and legal issues such as contract, the distribution of property on inheritance, hoarding, usury, and the utilisation of financial resources. There is some debate over whether the Koran bans 'riba', which describes all kinds of interest, or 'al-riba', the usury rate of interest, in line with the teachings of most religions, including Christianity and Judaism. Fundamentalists and many Islamic economists have argued that the Koran is quite specific about barring 'riba' and that there was no intention to confine the ban to 'al-riba'. Most Muslim countries do, however, currently permit interest payments. Many Islamic ecnomists hold the practice of charging interest responsible for bad economic policies and lack of development. They concede the advantages of a money economy over a barter economy but believe that money should function primarily as a medium of exchange. They argue that the payment of interest encourages hoarding because it introduces a speculative motive for holding money. Variations in hoarding levels in turn can cause inflation and generate a business cycle. Some go so far as to argue that money should be subject to a carrying cost to discourage hoarding as well as recommending the abolition of interest. The informal 2% per annum 'zakat' donation to charity, recommended by the Koran, is effectively a wealth tax and is expected to ensure that money serves primarily as a medium of exchange. Interest is viewed as counterproductive, frustrating investment, causing business cycles and instability; and imposing hardship on certain members of the community.

From a conservative Muslim's viewpoint 'riba' incorporates all kinds of interest and lenders should be prohibited from accepting from a borrower any gifts or small favours unless it has been customary for the two parties to exchange gifts. Apart from the economist's rationalisation of the ban on interest, it is more widely opposed because it is viewed as a socially unjust practice. Interest charged on loans for the purchase of consumption goods amount to taking advantage of the borrower's inferior economic position and are, therefore, morally reprehensible. Further, the charging of interests on loans used for productive purposes is also regarded as unfair. It is not viewed as an equitable form of transaction because the amount of profit that may accrue from the economic activity funded is not known beforehand and there is no possibility of loss except in cases of default. The charging of a predetermined interest rate cannot, therefore, be morally justified. Generally, Islam frowns upon wealth not accrued by productive activities by those able to take part in such activities. Lending wealth simply to accrue more wealth is, therefore, reprehensible.

Islam does not, however, prohibit taking a return on capital if the provider of capital is prepared to share the risk of the investment with the borrower. Profit and loss sharing (PLS) schemes are consequently considered to be an acceptable alternative to interest in an Islamic economy. Lending in accordance with this principle is of course made in Western economies through equity participations, although limited liability is widespread. In the PLS system banks are established on the basis of share capital and accept current account deposits on normal no interest terms. They are also allowed to accept deposits into investment accounts. These accounts entitle their holders to an agreed share of the profits or losses accruing to the bank from the investment of the pool of funds collected through such accounts and are called Modaraba deposits. PLS is supposed to ensure that lenders take more interest in a bank's activities and that banks take more interest in the performance of their borrowers, by monitoring their activities and perhaps providing management services and advice. It is hoped that it will encourage investment and make the allocation of resources more efficient. The pursuit of profit is actively encouraged provided that it does not result from the exploitation of monopoly powers and priviliged positions.

A second permissible scheme for accumulating investment capital is called 'Musharakah'. In this case all of the participants contribute capital and a few of them manage the business. Such arrangements can be found in companies formed as partnerships with unlimited liability in the West. Cooperatives, mutual funds, and savings and loan associations organised in accordance with PLS would also be compatible with this arrangement.

The main function of an Islamic banking system, like Western systems, is to collect savings for productive use. Whilst it is easy to see how savings deposits can be used productively it is more difficult to see where current account deposits fit into the Islamic financial system. It is after all not the Islamic practice to use someone's money without ensuring that they share in the loss as well as the profit. By choosing to place money in a current account, however, the depositor has elected not to place money in an investment account and is not normally entitled to a return on the deposit. The depositor has elected not to take on any risk, probably placing the money with the bank for safety and to serve as a means of exchange. One way of resolving the problem would be to require banks to lend the money to the government or the central bank subject to an agreement that the money could be recalled at short notice. Then a method of remunerating the banks would have to be found to allow them to at least recover the costs of providing current account services. The latter could, however, be recovered through representative charges for services provided. This would provide a charge on holdings of medium of exchange balances but might encourage cash hoarding.

The Islamisation of banking, therefore, requires transforming essentially Western styled financial systems in accordance with the principle of Shiraket, which involves partnership and cooperation. A partnership between a supplier and a user of capital is called Modaraba and the principle of PLS should apply in place of fixed or variable interest rate charges. The distribution of profit shares between lenders and borrowers should be determined through a bargaining process. The PLS system can be applied fairly straightforwardly to term loans or participations funded by savings or investment deposits. Problems arise in applying the principle to current account deposits, which should only be used to meet short term financial needs, because short term loans and overdrafts to the commercial sector are used primarily as working capital which produces no easily identifiable profit. In providing such essential services banks incur costs and borrowers derive benefits, hence the bank is entitled to some remuneration in accordance with Islamic principles. The easiest solution would be for the banks to levy a service charge to firms. Alternatively, the borrowers could add a fixed mark up to the price of their products to raise the funds to service the loan, implicitly paying banks out of profits. The proliferation of bank charges could, however, be viewed as interest in another guise.

As mentioned above, there are also problems in applying the PLS principle to consumer lending, since the consumer sector makes no profit. Possible solutions include : government lending from funds collected through taxation; the formation of credit cooperatives or mutual funds by consumers; the offering of hire purchase or leasing arrangements by banks. In the latter case, the consumers could not technically be paying interest but would instead be buying the goods, from financial institutions, in instalments. The leasing solution would appear to be particularly appropriate for house and consumer durable finance.

Some of the potential problems involved in business finance could also be resolved by way of 'Ijara' or leasing. Islam permits the charging of rent on capital owned by the financier. Fixed leasing charges are, therefore, permissible. This would cover investment financing and the principle can also be applied to consumer durable purchases because hire purchase agreements are permissible through 'Ijara wa iqtina', which is basically a mark-up scheme. It also allows banks to purchase trade bills on a mark-down basis or in other words at a discount.

A further problem is that the PLS principle cannot be applied directly to loans to the government, because there is, at best, only a rough connection between uses and sources of funds. There are also the problems of non-excludability from use in the provision of public goods and of measuring the profitability of public services. Clearly a redefinition of the national accounts could relate uses to sources of revenue more directly and government investment projects, consumption and administrative expenditure could, perhaps, be separated. The problems that remained would still, however, be substantial. In order to raise funds to meet the public sector borrowing requirement, Karsten (1982) suggests that variable rate bonds could be offered. The return would vary with overall economic success. This could be measured by real GNP, or output per head, growth.

Western economists justify the charging of interest on a number of grounds. Firstly, it is argued that the lender is entitled to a share of the profit resulting from the productive use of capital. Secondly, people should be rewarded for saving because they are abstaining from current consumption which is usually assumed to yield a higher utility than future consumption. Thirdly, lenders should be rewarded for allowing someone else to borrow an asset which provides the service of liquidity. Finally, lenders are entitled to a premium because of the risk they take of non-repayment. [1] Because of the sacrifices made by savers and the potential profit to be made from investment a positive inducement must be paid to encourage saving and a charge made for the privilege of borrowing. Interest rates are then determined by the demand and supply of loanable funds. Islamic economists would argue that the supply and demand for loanable funds could be equated by replacing interest with the PLS principle and that a more efficient allocation of resources would thereby be achieved.

Socialist economists, adhering to Marxist or Marxian principles, regard interest as an element of surplus value accruing to finance capitalists. Like rent and profit it stems from the exploitation of labour. Marxist-Leninist regimes have typically maintained low interest rates, which are charged primarily to generate contributions to the costs of running banks and providing a payments mechanism. The interest rate levels and their differentials have not been used extensively as economic levers. Marxist objections to interest are the result of social, rather than religious, ethics. There does, however, seem to be a growing realisation that interest rate charges may be necessary, to achieve an efficient allocation of investable resources, to induce savings and reduce, or postpone, consumption. Interest rates may, therefore, be used more actively as a planning tool in the future. In order to achieve efficient allocation, the rate should be varied in accordance with the term and risk of the loan. In modern socialist societies, however, the interest rate levels do not depend on the supply and demand of loanable funds, they are purely planning devices and as such they are probably underutilised.

4.2 Socialist Banking Systems

i) Centralised Socialist Banking

The 'reforms' introduced by Kosygin in 1965 aimed to combine central planning and management of the national economy with incentives and sanctions. These reforms led to the introduction of interest rate charges and to the more extensive use of credit for investment funding.

In the USSR, the 'reforms' did not result in any fundamental changes in the organisation of the banking system. The role of credit has, however, become more important and so has the supervision of 'enterprises', with respect to management and the fulfilment of planned objectives, by banks. Increasingly the availability of credit has become linked to the efficiency of enterprises, as measured by their success in meeting targets set by the planning agency. As yet the rate of interest has not been used as an active policy instrument to direct credit to its most efficient uses.

The Soviet banking system has been described as a mono-bank system. Banks are the only authorised suppliers of credit. The main institutions of the monetary and credit ststem are: the Gosbank (state bank); the state savings institutions; the foreign trade bank; the investment bank; and the Lombards (pawn-brokers). The banking system is centralised and its activities are an integral part of the overall National Plan. It is used both to execute monetary policy and to supervise the economic life of the country. Its supervisory role has influenced its organisational structure.

The Gosbank is the bank of issue, the credit bank of the national economy, the central clearing agency and the regulatory agency concerned with money in circulation. Hence, all of the monetary transactions of the nation, whether involving currency or demand deposits, are made via the Gosbank. Consequently it has become the national accounting agency and is well positioned to supervise the economic and financial affairs of the USSR. Since 1963, the savings institutions have been managed by the Gosbank which also extends credit for foreign trade, settles foreign
accounts, and deals in gold and foreign currency.

The central management of the Gosbank is situated in Moscow and the Gosbank has offices in all of the Soviet republics, regions and areas or provinces. It also has subsidiaries and agencies or pay offices in all the districts, towns and population centres. It is managed by a board nominated by the Council of Ministers, of which its Chairman is a member. Its headquarters contain departments concerned with economic planning; money in circulation; finance and investment; credit for industry; foreign exchange and trade; cash issue; central bookkeeping; national accounts and the state budget. Given the inclusion of a treasury department, concerned with the state budget, it is effectively both central bank and ministry of finance. The Gosbank headquarters acts as banker to the central government, note issuer, and banker to the rest of the Gosbank system.

Although the savings banks were incorporated into the Gosbank in 1963, they operate in accordance with the 'autonomous profitability principle'. [2] Their main function is to accumulate the savings of the population and to deposit them with the state which then invests them. They also provide monetary transmission services, disburse state pensions, sell and purchase government bonds and organise lotteries. They offer a variety of accounts, including time deposits and cheque accounts.

The foreign trade bank has taken over most of the Gosbank's responsibilities for cash and credit transactions concerning foreign trade and tourism. The Gosbank effectively acts as correspondent to the foreign trade bank inside the USSR. The foreign trade bank also has correspondent relationships with banks outside the USSR and it has very close links with other banks within COMECON.

The main purpose of the investment bank is to supervise investment and related activities in conformity with party and government guidelines and directives. Consequently, it is closely involved in the planning of investments. It provides outright finance for investment and short and long term credits.

There are six Soviet foreign banks, including the Moscow Narodny Bank, in London, and the Banque Commercial pour l'Europe du Nord (the Eurobank). They are major foreign currency earners through their deposit liabilities and their dealings in Eurocurrency and interbank markets. They also operate as correspondents for the foreign trade bank and the Gosbank.

Other financial institutions include post offices and pawnbrokers. The post offices provide for telegraphic transfers of money between state enterprises and their business partners and consequently they are part of the monetary transactions mechanism.

As far as monetary circulation is concerned, the Gosbank is the most important financial institution. Total monetary payments in the USSR include total cash payments and total clearing settlements. Thus the exchange payments system can be divided into two parts : the currency circuit and the transfer payments circuit. The payments made between the state or enterprises and the consumers, and between pairs of consumers, dominate the cash circuit. Payments between the state and enterprises, as well as payments between enterprises, dominate the transfer circuit. The cash circuit serves in the control of consumer spending and the transfer circuit plays an important role in signalling departures from economic plans and, therefore, facilitates management by banks.

Because it is the predominant provider of short term credit, which enterprises need for working c funds, it can provide long term investment funds, through the Gosbank or the investment bank, in accordance with the National Plan.

The USSR does not attempt to control the money supply for anticyclical demand management purposes or to control inflation, and does not manipulate the interest rate to achieve such objectives either. The main reason for the existence of money in the USSR is that national planning cannot be undertaken solely in terms of quantities. A numeraire is clearly required, and money not only performs the function of a numeraire good but also avoids barter and thereby improves efficiency. It is more appropriate to regard monetary policy in the USSR as financial planning. The 1965 reforms made financial planning more flexible.

The overall direction and supervision of the banking system is exercised by the Ministry of Finance. The Gosbank is essentially an implementary agency in all phases of regional and national economic planning. Bank representatives do, however, participate in all major economic decisions, because the chairman of the Gosbank is one of the Council of Ministers and the Gosbank also has advisory roles.

The Gosbank also functions as the fiscal agency of the government. It distributes transfer payments and wages and collects taxes, which are debited directly from depository accounts or wage payments.

Apart from pawnbrokers, the savings bank offices provide the only retail banking facilities. There are no generalised deposit transfer facilities comparable to Western European giro or cheque clearing systems. Cheques can only be used to withdraw cash from an individual's own account. Additionally, in contrast to most savings bank systems in Eastern Europe, the Soviet savings bank do not make loans generally available to the public. Personal saving has been encouraged as a means of reducing excess consumer demand. Consequently, there are many saving schemes, including save as you earn arrangements. A large proportion of saving is, however, of a temporary nature with the objective of accumulating the sums of money necessary to make large purchases, such as consumer durables or holidays. Savings have increased rapidly from the 1960s.

Other Eastern European socialist countries have merged their investment and state banks in order to allow the banks to consider the overall, short term and long term, credit requirements of individual enterprises. The Soviet banking system has been frequently criticised for the lack of co-ordination between the Gosbank and the investment bank in its dealings with individual enterprises.

Interest rates have been rigid, reflecting the view that they have no significant regulatory or allocatory role in a socialist economy. Interest rates have been viewed as a service charge levied to contribute to the operating cost of the banking system. No attempt was made, prior to the 1965 reforms, to use interest rate differentials or levels, to influence the aggregate value and distribution of bank loans and the level of real investment, or to bring about an equilibrium in the demand and supply of loanable funds. The 'reforms' did not lead to a major revaluation of the use of interest rate charges to achieve such ends. Interest rates are uniform for all loans made for a similar purpose and any differentials in these rates reflect preferences concerning the targets of the planning authorities. Following the reforms, the differentiation of rates according to the purpose for which the funds are to be used has increased but these rates are not dependent upon the prospective economic effectiveness of the use of the funds. Hence rates depend on the planning priorities rather than upon bank officials' assessments of risk and profitability. Penalty rates are, however, charged to poor performers who need to apply for supplementary credit.

With respect to exchange control, the rouble is not a convertible currency and hence its exchange rate does not need to be managed. Foreign currency is, however, required to pay for imported goods. This can be earned through exports and derived through the deposit taking and dealings activities of the overseas banks and by borrowing in the Eurocurrency and bond markets, in which the overseas banks and the foreign trade bank also deal.

The Soviet monobanking model was 'adopted' in various forms by the Eastern European countries under the control of the USSR after the second world war. These countries previously had traditional Western style capitalist banking systems consisting of a central bank, commercial banks, and other deposit taking institutions. The traditional systems were reformed, following nationalisation, into monobank systems based on the Soviet model. Since then, however, the banking systems of the Eastern European countries have diverged from the Soviet model to varying degrees. [3] The German Democratic Republic (GDR) has, for example, developed a giro transfer system. Most of the countries have maintained the separation of the state and the savings banks systems, which were merged in the USSR in 1963. Many have, however, merged their investment and state banks since 1963. In many of these countries consumer credit is more readily available than in the USSR. Home financing arrangements also differ significantly amongst the Eastern European countries and between them and the USSR. The Yugoslavian banking system, which will be discussed separately below, has moved furthest from the monobank structure. Incidentally, China has also made a major break with the monobank system. In 1983 it formally separated the state bank's central banking functions from its commercial and investment banking functions.

Garvy (1975) reviews the post 1965 reform changes in East European banking. He notes that the reforms consisted mainly of : shifting investment financing from non-returnable grants to long term credits; simplifying the process of extending short term credit for working capital; and increasing the availability of consumer credit. He notes that Yogoslavia effected similar changes much earlier and moved much further towards a banking system geared to the needs of a 'socialist market' or decentralised socialist, as opposed to a centrally planned socialist, economy.

Garvy observes that more use has been made of the interest rate as a tool for credit control. In particular, differentiation between more and less 'profitable' production units has become a more important consideration in the granting of credit, and penalty rates have become stiffer and are reinforced more rigorously. He also notes that moves to separate central, from other, banking functions, to the extent that they have occurred, have been within the state bank systems. The GDR is an exception because its credit banks are directed and supervised by what is effectively a separate central bank. Also of note is the fact that the National Bank of Poland has refinanced loans, made by the agricultural and commercial bank in that country, making it the only state bank to engage significantly in rediscounting operations.

Pindak (1973) concluded that the post reform changes had in fact tended to increase centralisation and reinforce the monobank system in the East European countries. There had been hardly any decentralisation and the merging of the state and the investment banks had had the opposite effect. Further, despite the fact that East Germany had continued to maintain the separation of its state bank, to act as a central bank, from the bank for industry and commerce and had abolished its investment bank in 1986, the monopoly character of its banking system was not lost.

There were, however, signs of change in the second half of the 1980s. Hungary, which has been in the vanguard of economic reform, introduced a major reform to its banking system. With Mikhail Gorbachev in control in the USSR and favouring reform it seems likely that other Eastern European countries will introduce similar banking reforms if they prove successful in Hungary.

Hungary launched five new commercial banks. They are to compete with each other and be profit oriented. The aim is to make the allocation of financial resources more responsive to profit and to force agriculture and industry to become less reliant on state subsidies. The banks will compete, mainly in terms of service offered, in every sector of the economy. Interest rates will still be set by the National Bank of Hungary, which had previously combined commercial and central banking functions. It is to concentrate on central banking functions in the future and will direct and regulate the activities of the banks. The banks will be allowed to form consortia to share risks and will be able to create an interbank market to meet clients needs more fully. Initially Hungarian companies have been assigned to one of the five banks but after six months they will be expected to compete for business. Their starting positions are somewhat unequal, however. The Hungarian Credit Bank has been assigned most of the leading companies. They account for two thirds of the country's industrial output. The banks will also be subject to the supervision of the Ministry of Finance and the state will retain the majority shareholding. Hungarian companies will be allowed to become shareholders and this might have the effect of tying them to a single bank and reducing competition. Private citizens will not initially be allowed to buy shares but may be in the future. They are currently allowed to buy company bonds, which are popular because they offer a positive real yield. The new two tier system is designed to improve the efficiency of resource allocation by separating state disbursements from commercial loans. Also in January 1987 a new commercial bank, Unicbank, which was jointly owned by an affiliate of the IBRD, the IFC, two Western commercial banks, one German and one Austrian, and the Hungarian banks, which had the majority share was established. In 1986 Citibank of the US had established a bank, also in Budapest, in partnership with the Export Credit Bank of Hungary. Citibank is the major shareholder in this case. Citibank and Unicbank are permitted to deal in both Hungarian and Western currency. They are not licensed to advance loans to individuals but they can accept deposits from both cooperatives and state owned companies and extend medium and long term loans and finance trade.

Hungary also has an offshore bank, the Central European International Bank (CIB). The National Bank holds a 34% stake and the remainder is held by six European and Japanese banks. It deals in convertible currencies, lends to firms in both the east and the west, and provides export credits to Hungarian firms. The embryo bond market is unique in Eastern Europe. Since January 1983 enterprise and local governments have been permitted to issue bonds for sale to enterprises or the public, although in the latter case they must be government guaranteed.

In February 1987 Bulgaria announced that it too would be restructuring its banking system as part of a reform programme designed to improve efficiency. Like Hungary, it plans to introduce a two tier system comprising a central bank and a number of commercial banks. The banks will assume a greater role in the management of the economy by working more closely with companies and supervising them more strictly. The details of the plan were expected to be announced in the summer of 1987 and to provide for the creation of an economic bank, to finance large companies, a bank for agriculture and cooperatives and a bank for the development and production of consumer goods. The foreign trade bank and the bank for economic payments, which finances small and medium sized enterprises, are expected to be required to expand their activities and to start to vary the availability and cost of their credit in accordance to performance.

ii) Banking under Decentralised Socialism : A Case Study of Yugoslavia

The Yugoslavian banking system has developed to serve the needs of a decentralised socialist economy. [4] The goal of the Yugoslavian brand of socialism is to achieve a system of social ownership based on worker management of economic enterprises.

Such a system differs markedly from both Western mixed economies and centrally planned economies. Within the economy the role of the financial system is seen as that of stimulating saving and ensuring its efficient allocation. Investment by organisations of associated labour or 'socialist enterprises' exceeds accumulation but households are net savers, hence the financial system has the role of channelling savings from households into 'socialist enterprises'. There is also a significant pooling of resources by 'socialist enterprises' through banks.

Yugoslavia is a federation of six republics, each of which has lower territorial units, and two autonomous regions, making eight semi-autonomous regions in all. The three northern regions are the most prosperous and most heavily industrialised, the central regions have about average prosperity, and the southern regions are the least prosperous, being most heavily reliant on agriculture. Racial and linguistic variations are marked.

Yugoslavia has been courted by both the Western and Eastern blocs of countries but maintains a neutral status by not participating in Nato or the Warsaw Pact. It is a leading member of the non-aligned group of countries, a member of both the Bank for International Settlements (BIS) and the International Monetary Fund (IMF), and an associate member of the European Economic Community.

When the USSR relinquished control in 1952 the monobank system began to be decentralised. The government, however, maintained control over interest rates through the National Bank and kept these rates artificially low. Interest rates have, therefore, not been allowed to exercise the functions of influencing investment and savings flows and guiding funds towards efficient uses.

Since 1952 the banking system has evolved along three broad lines: organisational decentralisation; functional specialisation; and an increasing managerial role for socialist enterprises. A number of periods of development can be discerned. [5] The first period was one of organisational decentralisation and occupied the remainder of the 1950s. It included three major developments. The establishment of credit funds through obligatory contributions from 'socialist enterprises'. The disbursement of the funds was directed by the government. The separation of the central and non central banking functions of the National Bank of Yugoslavia (NBY). As a result, three specialised federal banks were created: the foreign trade bank; the agricultural bank; and the investment bank. Finally, three types of local bank were introduced: commercial banks associated with local governments; cooperative banks, whose primary function was to finance local agriculture; and savings banks, including post office savings banks (POSBs). At the end of the period most short term banking operations were still carried out by the NBY and the financing of investment was almost exclusively the responsibility of social investment funds with the specialised banks acting as conduits.

In the early 1960s the NBY ceased to extend credits to nonbanking sectors and transferred such operations to other banks. An attempt was made to simplify the system by fusing together the three types of local banks. In the latter half of the 1960s, fundamental organisational and functional changes were made with the aims of increasing the role of socialist enterprises in bank management; and achieving a more efficient allocation of resources. Commercial banks, i.e. local banks controlled by local governments, were replaced by 'business banks'. These were independent of local government influence and authorised to undertake a wide range of domestic and trade related international business nationwide. Three types of 'business bank' were initially introduced: commercial, investment and savings banks. They were soon integrated. In this period the social investment funds were abolished but special funds were established to aid less developed areas and an export credit insurance fund was established. The most important functional change was the transfer of investment financing to commercial banks. In 1970 there were 64 banks with 605 branches. Their share of total credits extended was 77%. The share of the social investment funds had fallen to 14% and the NBY's share was 9%.

Constitutional amendments in 1971 introduced significant changes to the central banking arrangements with the aim of giving the eight republics and provinces more influence. Eight regional National Banks (NBs) were created alongside the NBY with a view to creating an integrated central banking system. The system is managed by a Board of Governors consisting of the eight NB governors, who are appointed by their regional assemblies, and the NBY governor, who is appointed by the Federal Assembly. The eight NBs have supervisory responsibilities and help to implement monetary and foreign exchange policies. In the first half of the 1970s, government interference in the business policy of banks was reduced and the traditional separation of short term credit for use as working capital and long term investment lending has been eroded. Banks are, therefore, able to deal with all the financial needs of individual enterprises in an integrated manner. In 1975 the financial system involved the NBs, commercial banks, savings and loan associations, insurance institutions, and credit funds. There were 172 commercial banks, almost all of which belonged to one of the eighteen 'associated banks'. The five largest 'associated banks' accounted for 56% of aggregate banking assets and the ten largest for 78%. The 20 largest commercial banks were allowed to undertake foreign exchange transactions. Amongst the savings and loans institutions, the POSB was the largest. Cooperative banks and mutual savings banks, associated with socialist enterprises, also existed. Insurance institutions were of relatively minor importance. They commanded small funds which were required to be held with banks. The voluntary export credit fund and the fund for disadvantaged regions, funded by compulsory contributions, remained.

New legislation in 1976 and 1977 provided for a further change in structure to encourage the development of the 'socialist enterprise' system and reduce central bank intervention in financial intermediation whilst encouraging banks and 'socialist enterprises' to achieve the economic and social priorities laid down in the National Plan. The planning system has more in common with the indicative planning approach used in France, particularly in the 1950s and 1960s, than the central planning exercises of the Eastern European Countries. To achieve planning targets the banking system was to become more interdependent with 'socialist enterprises' and measures were introduced to assure the stability, liquidity and orderly performance of banks. Members of banks became the signatories to their self management agreements and banks were required to have a prescribed minimum level of resources. They take all the decisions and bear all the risks. The banks are run by an assembly made up of delegates of bank members. The new regulations provided for the following structure. The NBs would undertake all the functions commonly associated with central banks, including: currency issue; money supply control; exchange rate control; supervision; control of foreign indebtedness and channelling money from abroad into the country; and the provision of central banking services to central and regional governments.

The aims and targets of monetary and foreign exchange policy are laid down by the Federal Assembly and the NBY adopts the methods it deems necessary to achieve these goals with the cooperation of the other NBs. Credit ceilings have been the most frequently used policy instrument since interest rates have been rigid and kept low and there has been little scope for open market operations because monetary and capital markets remain underdeveloped. Additionally, deposits held with the NBs by banks have been frozen from time to time and moral suasion has been used. The measures have proved relatively ineffective and high inflation rates have been recorded since the mid 1970s. Foreign indebtedness also grew after the 1973 oil price rise and the country came under the influence of the IMF in 1980 and has had to reschedule its international public and commercial debts. The IMF encouraged Yugoslavia to raise its interest rates as a condition on further assistance and this requirement led to protracted negotiations between the IMF and the Yugoslavian government because it went against one of its fundamental policies.

The new structure provided for the remainder of the banking system to be organised as follows. Internal banks were to be founded by a self management agreement involving individual 'socialist enterprises' and complex socialist organisations, which are interconnected groups of 'socialist enterprises'. Their purpose is to provide basic banking services to the group and they have a restricted range of business. They are primarily responsible for pooling and allocating funds and cannot take sight deposits. Basic banks were also to be formed by self management agreements, which could involve groups of socialist enterprises and internal banks. They can carry out all credit and banking operations in Yugoslavia, if licensed to do so, and can make international payments and perform foreign exchange transactions. They vary considerably in size and range of business. They are the only institutions permitted to carry out all banking functions and some are commercial banks akin to universal banks, except that their securities business is severely restricted by the underdeveloped equity and bonds markets. Some of them are highly specialised, however, and their range of business is dependent on their articles of agreement. In 1983 only one bank had branches in all regions. Associated or united banks provide services to two or more basic banks. Their range of services is usually limited, in accordance with the mutual interest of the founding banks, in order to reap economies of scale. By the early 1980s the savings and loan organisations included: savings banks, mutually organised savings and loan associations and agricultural cooperatives. The savings banks are most important and include two types. The POSBs, managed by socialist enterprises which provide postal and telecommunications services, offer savings accounts and money transmission services, including account settlement and cash transmission. Their deposits are used to finance projects, as directed by regional, army, and telecommunications authorities, through basic and associated banks and the NBY. Other savings banks may be founded by socialist enterprises and groups of citizens. They offer savings and payments services and extend credits to households for consumption and house purchase and construction. They also extend credits through basic banks in pursuit of social planning targets relating to local communities. Finally there are various consortiums which are associations of banks facilitating interbank business cooperation.

All banking organisations must be members of the Association of Yugoslavian Banks (AYB), which is represented in the Yugoslavian Economic Chamber. The AYB aims to develop interbank cooperation and coordination with a view to implementing the Federal Social Plan and general economic policy. In particular it aims to improve banking techniques, provide professional and especially legal advice, conduct scientific research into banking, promote cooperation with federal agencies, including the NBY and the Social Accounting Agency,[6] and cooperate with foreign banks and international organisations, such as the IMF and the BIS. It performs no banking or credit operations.

The Social Accounting Agency (SAA) provides credit and debit clearing services to the banks. Yugoslavia operates a cheque system which has developed links with the Eurocheque system. [7] The SAA was created in 1961 when the NBY transferred its responsibility for direct accounting control to it. Its functions are: to keep records of transactions in order to scrutinise the use of resources; to ensure the accuracy of the data; to supervise the fulfilment of obligations to the community of users of social resources; to provide payments clearing services; and to carry out economic and financial auditing. It is, therefore, effectively the supervisory wing of the planning agency and it operates at the republic and provincial levels as well.

In June 1984 Yugoslavia came under renewed pressure from foreign bank creditors to strengthen and centralise its financial system. Yugoslvia's debt was split between international institutions, foreign governments and foreign commercial banks. It had become necessary to reschedule the debts falling due in 1985 and 1986 and the foreign banks were, therefore, able to exert pressure. As a result the NBY, hitherto one of the weakest central banks, was given powers to control foreign borrowing and to act as guarantor for new loans from abroad. Additionally, it was allowed to reach decisions by majority rather than consensus, which is the accepted practice in the country. This raised criticism from within the country because it implicitly weakened the powers of regional representatives at the NBY. In return for standby credit facilities the IMF continued to press its standard package requiring: the reduction of the budget deficit, and therefore the reliance of the government on the NBY for its funding; the removal of price controls; the raising of interest rates in line with inflation, and the devaluation of the dinar. The aim of the package was to reduce inflation, generate a balance of payments surplus to enable the country to service its debts, and achieve a market oriented structural reform of the economy. These policies, especially the latter, were broadly reinforced by the IBRD, [8] which was also lending to Yugoslavia. In 1984 approximately 45% of the country's foreign exchange earnings were being used to pay interest on accumulated debt and Yugoslavia was one of the most problematic debtors outside Latin America.

In the light of developments in Mexico and Venezuela, where multi year rescheduling agreements (MYRAs) were being negotiated in late 1984, Yugoslavia decided that it too would benefit from a MYRA. With the foreign governments refusing to take the lead through the Paris Club, [9] Yugoslavia was forced to come to an agreement with the IMF because the foreign commercial banks would not negotiate a MYRA without one. In March 1985 Parliament approved the IMF's credit terms, which included the relaxation of some of its price controls. A price freeze had been imposed in 1984 and many other prices were normally controlled. It also sanctioned some adjustment of the interest rate. The IMF backed down from its original requirement that interest rates should be raised in line with inflation, which would have implied rates of about 70%, and accepted a rise in interest rates to over 50%, leaving them negative in real terms. The dinar was also further devalued against the dollar. Later in 1985 a MYRA was concluded with the foreign banks and a rescheduling was agreed with the Paris Club. As a result, after six and a half years, supervision by the IMF was terminated in mid 1986 because the country ceased to be indebted to the IMF. Instead, in common with the MYRAs agreed in Latin America, the IMF was given a surveillance role throughout the term of the MYRA. The debt problem has by no means disappeared but it has at least been made more manageable and Yugoslavia has been freed from outside influence to a certain degree. Whilst under the IMF's influence the balance of payments deficit had been transformed into a surplus, largely because imports had been reduced as economic growth had ground to a virtual standstill. Real wages had also fallen in the first half of the 1980s but household income and consumption had been maintained by increased female participation in the labour force, the spread of the practice of taking second jobs and a run down of savings. Unemployment had, however, also risen. Inflation remained extremely high by European standards and in fact rose to 70% in 1985 and 80% in 1986, following the acceptance of the final IMF package.

In May 1986 the revolving [10] Prime Ministerial post passed to Mr Branko Mikulic from Milta Paninc. He promised a greater role for market forces but warned that, if necessary, he would not hesitate to impose price controls. He should have greater freedom in developing policy than his predecessor because his term started as the period of IMF supervision was ending. The general aim of policy will be to promote small businesses and encourage exports, productivity and savings through fiscal and credit incentives. Economic reforms are needed to make the planning system more efficient and to reduce regional divergence, which had increased in the first half of the 1980s. The problem of inflation remains and many politicians blamed the IMF's policies for its acceleration in the mid 1980s. Devaluation had raised import prices and the lifting of price controls, and the raising of interest rates were also clearly inflationary in the short term. The IMF's defence is usually that its policies, which aim to reduce restrictions on the operation of free markets and achieve budgetary and monetary control, will lead to a reduction in inflation and trade deficits in the long run. It is not clear that Yugoslavia intends to stick to such policies in the long run or whether they are equally applicable to both mixed economies and economies based on the principle of social ownership. Because adherence to an IMF package tends to reduce growth, at least in the short run, [11] heavily indebted countries find it increasingly difficult to service their debt. The Baker Plan [12] accepted the need for growth oriented adjustment and held out the hope that Yugoslavia would receive a more sympathetic treatment from its creditors in the future. Yugoslavia could perhaps apply to the IBRD for a structural adjustment loan but that institution would have to be sympathetic to the special needs of its atypical economy. With a MYRA still in force, Yugoslavia urgently needed to expand exports faster than imports, which it also had to allow to increase to facilitate economic growth and reduce domestic bottlenecks and therefore inflationary pressures.

In early 1987, however, it became clear that inflation was accelerating towards a triple digit figure and the trade balance was deteriorating. In February 1987 the OECD urged Yugoslavia to give top priority to fighting inflation. It was criticised for lax financial dicipline, insufficient monetary control and its high degree of market segmentation and the consequent lack of competition. In the same month, as part of its enhanced surveillance role, the IMF presented an unfavourable report on the country's economic adjustment and sought a greater say in the running of the economy. Towards the end of February Mr Mikulic called for further support from the creditors pointing out that Yugoslavia was one of the few countries that had fulfilled its obligations without new credit and that it now needed long and medium term loans to finance investment in new production facilities. To curb inflation, a retrospective wage freeze was also announced. Interest rates were also allowed to rise and the dinar was allowed to depreciate. The latter measures were a response to IMF advice but the banks may prove uncooperative in the next round of rescheduling discussions and unwilling to extend new loans unless Yugoslavia applies for a stand-by credit from the IMF and therefore comes under its supervisory influence again. The wage freeze proved to be extremely unpopular and caused a wave of strikes. As a consequence retrospective price controls were also introduced in March to reduce the impact of the wage controls on purchasing power. In March Mr Mikulic also appealed to the EEC to revive its flagging trade links and increase cooperation. 85% of Yugoslavia's trade deficit and 65% of its bilateral trade servicing obligations are with EEC members.

Outsiders have argued that the self management system is inherently inflationary because it allows workers to increase their own wages too rapidly, it discourages the profit motive to the achievement of efficiency and it leads to local and regional monopolies. Yugoslavians point to the fall in real wages in the first half of the 1980s as counter evidence but this may have been a necessity because company debt had risen — it does not disprove the general tendency. The federal structure, with jealously guarded regional autonomy, also reduces efficiency because many industries are duplicated in different regions and operate at well below their minimum efficient scales. Additionally it made it hard to apply the programmes agreed with the IMF.

Yugoslavia has less central government control than is typical in either Western mixed or Eastern European centrally planned economies. Economists in the East European communist bloc are equally critical of the country's loose federal organisation. Western commentators are particularly critical of the inadequate financial discipline in the country. The Federal government, they argue, lacks central financial disciplinary powers and banks act as financial filling stations to customers which are also often owners and seem unable to impose financial self discipline. Additionally they criticise the inadequate circulation of capital between banks and the consequent inefficiency in the allocation of resources. Because banks are controlled by socialist organisations, much of the money deposited is reused internally by these organisations, and it is supplemented by deposits from households in the locality. Economists' views of the efficiency of the financial system vary.

Mijovic (1982) argues that financial intermediation does not secure an efficient allocation of resources in Yugoslavia. He suggests a number of reforms that need to be made. Firstly, a more active and adequate interest rate policy is required to stimulate saving and more long term deposits and to ration demand for funds so that they are guided towards the most efficient users. Secondly, more inter-regional flows of funds are required to allow funds to find their most profitable outlets. The inadequate mobility of funds is the result of the territorial organisation of banks in the Federation, decentralisation, and worker control over the use of bank funds. Thirdly, a more efficient use of funds could be made if there was a pooling of funds between various complex socialist organisations. This implies that central money markets are required and the pooling of funds, to the extent that it led to a more efficient use of social capital, would serve the interests of both the community as a whole and the individual companies. Mijovic argues that banks should play a major role in the pooling of resources. Some progress has, however, been made towards the development of central money and capital markets. A small market in company debentures exists and there is a small market in shares run by sixty commercial banks.

In contrast, Goldsmith (1975) argues that a reasonably efficient system of financial intermediation existed in Yugoslavia, especially when compared with the systems of more centralised and directed Less Developed Countries of similar economic status. Periser (1982) discusses the difficulties involved in developing banking institutions consistent with the objectives of a democratic, decentralised, socialist market economy. He argues that, despite Marx's warnings, the power of banks exercised through credit relationships had been underestimated and misinterpreted and that Yugoslavia had become a 'bankocracy' by 1971. The process of development had produced a situation in which there was too much central control over the supply of money and credit and too much power concentrated in the hands of business banks. Such a system, he claims, is inconsistent with the ideals of worker control and self-management and democratisation of the banking system is necessary. To achieve this, more decentralisation is required to reduce the central bank's control over the supply of money and the regional banks' control over credit allocation. Further, company banks should be encouraged to provide the service back-up required to satisfy the needs of the member firms and, thereby, to serve the development of the self-management system.

If it is true, as many analysts believe, that the direct financing of the government's fiscal deficit by the NBY was the major cause of the inflation in the 1970s and 1980s, then continued efforts should be made to reduce the fiscal deficit, as required by IMF programmes. Alternatively, or additionally, financing through government bond issues will be required to allow stricter control of the growth of the money supply. The government has increasingly used bond financing but it could consider initiating a programme to help develop the domestic bond market [13] as means of state financing and encouraging inter-regional capital flows.

Further banking legislation was in preparation following the introduction of a bill on banking to Parliament in December 1986. It aims to make banks more independent so that they do not merely function as financial filling stations for 'socialist enterprises' and they are less subject to the influence of local and regional interests and politicians. It is hoped that freer financial flows across the country will result. Additionally, the bill proposes to introduce sanctions, such as the freezing of deposits belonging to corporate shareholders, against bank illiquidity. A bill on foreign exchange is also under consideration. This would force companies to sell their hard currency earnings to banks in order to create an active foreign exchange market.

4.3 Islamic Banking

i) Introduction

It has been argued that the development of a financial system based on the PLS principle would accelerate economic development by involving banks directly in investment planning and appraisal. Economies of scale could be reaped if banks adopted a number of management functions normally undertaken by companies. This extra involvement would add to the costs of banking operations but it might also result in an increased flow of profits, because of increased efficiency in the use of funds.

Karsten (1982) considers the consequences for savings and investment of a banking system, based on the PLS principle. In such a system, savers are turned into entrepreneurs because they are encouraged to participate directly in the financial success or failure of the investing business. Hence savers incur some of the risk burden normally undertaken as part of the service of financial intermediation in a fixed interest rate system, and become more like the shareholders in Western economies. The major risk in a fixed nominal interest rate system derives from the variability in the inflation rate. This risk is also faced by the Islamic saver. Given positive average risk aversion, one would expect there to be less saving, in the form of bank deposits, in a system based on the PLS principle, than in a fixed interest rate system. If the Islamic system were to operate side by side with the fixed interest rate system, however, then the effect might be to increase saving, because the menu of saving opportunities would be increased. Additionally, religious fundamentalists, who will not save with a traditional bank, might be more disposed to save with an Islamic bank. Further, Islamic banks might be able to offer higher average returns to offset the risk because their involvement in management and investment appraisal might lead to higher returns on investment funds. Because they monitor loans more carefully, Islamic banks may also require less collateral and this could benefit new enterprises and small businesses with unestablished credit worthiness.

The process of financial intermediation would be changed fundamentally if the process of transforming short term liabilities into long term advances was inhibited. The strict application of Islamic principles to financial intermediation would, arguably, have this effect. Further constraints would be imposed by linking particular loans to particular projects. The importance of such restrictions will depend on the freedom Islamic banks are given to decide how to use their various deposits. Additional features of the Islamic system are, Karsten argues, that interest rates are likely to be more flexible, especially upwards, and that banks are less likely to make windfall profits, as a result of the endowment effect, from rising interest rates. Karsten concludes that Islamic banks in Pakistan performed quite well in their first year and he also reviews the performance of other Islamic banks.

At the heart of an Islamic banking system there would be a central bank. In the times of the Islamic Empire there existed a central national finance house (Bait-al-Mal) which served as a state bank. The central Bait-al-Mal was situated in the capital of the empire and there was a regional Bait-al-Mal in each provincial capital. They were organs of the government and, in contrast to Western central banks, they did not have the right to issue currency. This was the responsibility of the state. Some modern Islamic economists argue that an Islamic central bank should issue currency and provide credit, in accordance with the PLS principle, to the member banks of the Islamic system. Monetary policy based on the manipulation of fixed interest rates could not be used and neither could open market operations and rediscounting involving fixed interest rate securities. Moral suasion supported by reserve asset ratios would appear to provide a basis for credit control which could be perhaps enhanced by open market operations in securities whose return accorded with Islamic principles.

The Dubia Islamic Bank, the world's first, [14] was licensed in 1975. Quoting from Islamic scripture, it has issued a pamphlet declaring that accepting bank interest is a crime thirty-three times worse than adultery. Prior to 1975, Gulf Arabs had few opportunities to avoid such a heinous crime short of hoarding or placing their savings in non interest bearing and, therefore, non earning accounts. Since 1975 dozens of Islamic banks have been established and they have attracted sizeable aggregate deposits and amassed impressive assets. They grew rapidly on the wave of the Islamic fundamentalist revival, which rejected Western values, and the growth in wealth following the oil price rise in 1973. Because of their rapid growth they were able to pay high returns on their deposits and consequently attracted investment funds as well as deposits made in accordance with religious principles, over which they have a virtual monopoly.

Their position changed dramatically as oil prices fell in the 1980s. This was a result of their closer dependence on the well being of the economy than traditional banks. Their dividends declined and they were faced with mounting bad debts. They are less able to protect themselves from recessions because, unlike traditional banks, they cannot rely on profits from maintaining, or even widening, interest rate margins and engaging in money market operations. As a result of the fall in dividends paid to their depositor-shareholders, the return they offered fell below the interest offered by traditional banks in the mid 1980s. As aggregate deposits and competition continued to grow in the early 1980s they found it more difficult to find high yielding investments. Matters became acute in the mid 1980s when the oil price collapsed and Gulf economies moved into recession. In response the Islamic banks have been considering the development of off balance sheet, forward currency and commodity and overseas banking business in order to boost profits. Such developments are viewed with considerable suspicion in religious circles.

Islamic banks are, strictly, only allowed to deal with each other and the interbank market is underdeveloped. Some Islamic banking officials are considering ways of remedying this. The relationships of the Islamic banks in the Gulf states is also a matter of debate. They are currently subject to minimal supervision when compared to ordinary commercial banks. Whilst officially encouraging their development, the monetary authorities are examining ways in which they should be supervised, in the interests of the consumers, and how they fit into the scheme of monetary controls.

The recession has also brought with it the problem of dealing with bad debtors. This is particularly acute for traditional commercial banks. In the Gulf states Western banking practices are being confronted with the principles of Islam, which forbid the receipt and payment of interest. In the 1970s, when economic growth was uninterrupted, the issue of bank interest was unimportant because borrowers' profits were so large that interest payments were a minor nuisance. The banks, eager to extend loans, commonly ignored the warnings of lawyers, especially in Saudi Arabia that interest charges were unenforceable and that the courts in Abu Dhabi would only accept interest charged on a simple, rather than compound interest, basis because compounding involves paying interest on interest. As the recession deepened and the number of defaults and liquidations increased the implications of the laws have become apparent. Banks are being forced into negotiations with debtors over the rate they are willing to pay on outstanding loans. Many Saudi Arabians refuse to pay any interest and some simply walk out on their debt commitments because they feel that banks are unwilling to take them to court. In Abu Dhabi a case was being heard in 1986 in which a bank customer was seeking a refund on the illegal compound interest that had been charged on his overdraft over the previous seventeen years. Many banks are considering withdrawing from the Gulf states, particularly Saudi Arabia and the Emirates, where the problems are most acute. Others are winding down operations, seeking quality clients, writing contracts under foreign law, and seeking collateral. In the latter case, however, there are problems under Islamic law. In some states, for example, land cannot be owned by foreigners. In Saudi Arabia the government reacted to the oil price collapse by delaying payments to local companies which consequently could not meet their loan servicing commitments. Many of these companies feel that banks did well in the good times and should be willing to make sacrifices, like everyone else, in the bad. The banks, however, believe that the rules of the game have been changed by people suddenly abiding by Islamic principles for convenience. Whatever the truth of the matter, it seems clear that the traditional, and especially the foreign, banks made insufficient concessions to local culture and can only survive profitably if they are more receptive to local advice and conditions in the future.

In Saudi Arabia and Abu Dhabi interest is forbidden altogether and the courts have, many feel, incorrectly regarded loan repayments, including interest, as repayments of principle. The Abu Dhabi case is, therefore, a key one and if the refund of interest were to be allowed new interest based lending could dry up. The commercial banks are seeking a government decree endorsing compound interest but the authorities are unlikely to comply given the sensitivity of the issue. In both states court orders have already reduced debts and in some cases interest receipts exceeding the amount of the original loan have had to be refunded. As a result, banks often prefer to settle out of court. Bankers in Abu Dhabi and Riyadh, the capital of Saudi Arabia, are considering drawing up black lists of bad debtors who refuse to repatriate known resources held overseas to meet their debts. Customers on the black list would be denied future credit by all banks.

Because of the potentially serious implications for future credit, and being unwilling to change the legal codes, the authorities have considered various actions. Saudi Arabia, for example, has tried to establish committees, overseen by the Commerce Ministry, through which disputes between banks and their clients can be resolved outside the courts. Alternatively, the Gulf states could establish special entities, funded by the state, to buy up all the bad debt on soft terms and renegotiate terms with the banks. Another, and probably cheaper, option would be for them to support their nationals, encourage the courts to rule against interest, and promote the spread of Islamic banking. The latter option would have been more realistic prior to the oil price fall in the 1980s and the decline in the Gulf states' share of the oil market. With many of the states facing financial difficulties it would be imprudent, at this juncture, for them to cut themselves off from outside sources of the funds for their development.

ii) Islamic banking in Pakistan

Pakistan and Iran are the only countries to attempt to implement comprehensive Islamic banking systems. Pakistan came into existence in 1947, when the British decolonised India, as a state for the Muslim people. It adopted a basically British banking system. The State Bank was the sole note issuer and undertook some central banking functions whilst the National Bank carried out government transactions and also took deposits. Commercial banks gradually developed and there was a significant foreign banking presence. There was some reorganisation in the 1970s. Some of the banks were amalgamated to form four banks which were nationalised in 1974.

In 1984 the Finance Minister announced that the country's gradual evolution as an Islamic society would include the Islamisation of the financial system. All of Pakistan's 22 nationalised and foreign owned banks and fourteen other financial institutions were required progressively to abandon the payment of interest on all new transactions, apart from international business, between January 1 and July 1 1985. Interest was to be replaced by remunerations based on PLS, service charges, mark-ups, and leasing. The country's seventeen foreign banks cooperated in the change after debating the precise details with the State Bank. The State Bank of Pakistan, along with the Pakistan Banking Council, monitors the banks' activities. Permission from the State Bank must be sought prior to opening new branches.

Following consultations, the foreign banks felt that they would be able to continue to charge commercial levels of interest under other names whilst possibly bearing more risk. The Islamisation programme had started in 1981 on a voluntary basis. By mid 1984 the five nationalised banks, including the National Bank, had taken 22% of their deposits in PLS non interest accounts. The State Bank ceased to fix interest rates. The banks had tended to offer uniform interest rates and not to compete vigorously. Under the new system, it was hoped that banks would be forced to compete by offering different profit sharing agreements.

The second stage of the three part adoption of Islamic banking was completed at the end of March 1985. Interest on all corporate accounts had been banned since January 1 1985 and at the end of the second stage the financing of individual customers and partnerships became interest free. The third, completed on July 1, required banks to stop accepting interest bearing deposits, returns instead being geared to the PLS principle. By March 1985 doubts were beginning to emerge about how Islamic the system really was and few businessmen believed that their relationship with their bankers had changed markedly. They felt that they were being charged interest in another name and there was little evidence of an Islamic partnership with their banks. This was partly because of the reticence of companies to disclose more information to banks than they were prepared to disclose to the tax inspector. Islamic fundamentalists were also highly critical, believing that interest had largely been replaced by service charges and mark-ups on the value of the goods rather than PLS. Banks were not forming Islamic partnerships and were not exposing themselves to the possibility of sharing losses. Bankers committed to the new system do not accept that it is essential for losses to be shared in an Islamic system. The Chairman of the Pakistan Banking Council, a government organisation representing and supervising the five nationalised banks, argued that the banks were instead required to make arrangements that would encourage prudent business practices and prudent banking. Having agreed a mark-up they could not charge penal rates on bad debts and consequently could not open themselves to unlimited liability either. Lax business practices should not be encouraged and the assets of their depositors should be protected.

In 1985, the State Bank issued a list of approved modes of corporate financing, the most important of which were: levying a service charge based on a bank's administrative costs; a mark-up on goods handled; and Musharika or PLS. Leasing, hire purchase, buying back through staged repayments, rent sharing on housing related to capital costs and a form of unit trust, known as Mudarba, were also permissible. Hire purchase was expected to be used to cover personal advances for the purchase of consumer durables. The State Bank has also issued guidelines on scales of mark-ups and service charges.

Initially most of the banks stuck to mark-ups and service charges, feeling unable to enter into PLS agreements because of their lack of expertise in vetting companies. The five nationlised banks have been offering Musharikas since 1982, but they had only negotiated about 100 such agreements by March 1985. The chairman of the Banking Council, however, believed that Musharikas would become a major form of finance by the end of the 1980s following the establishment, by the nationalised banks with the help of the IBRD, of industrial units to improve their industrial expertise. Two Mudarba unit trusts were launched in 1985 by industrial groups in 1985, one of them being heavily oversubscribed.

The foreign banks are expected to adopt a more cautious approach, taking deposits on a PLS basis, having deducted administrative costs, debt provisions, management fees and dividends due to equity holders, and lending on a mark-up or service charge basis. Depositors will therefore invest in an Islamic manner whilst enjoying security when the money is lent to bank customers. Although prudent, such an approach will clearly not please fundamentalists. Their experience in Pakistan will also equip them to offer Islamic banking services in the Gulf States and perhaps elsewhere. By February 1986 it became clear that the foreign banks were recording better results under Islamic banking than their local counterparts. The foreign banks have 52 branches, take 10% of all deposits and are generally regarded as better managed. Their overheads are, however, lower by virtue of their restricted branching and they enjoy more than 30% of the country's lucrative foreign trade business. Overheads are much higher for domestic banks because they are required, as a public service, to operate over 6,650 branches, a number of which are in remote villages generating small amounts of business. The nationalised banks have trouble recruiting quality staff and tend to be overstaffed with low productivity. They are also required to make some concessionary loans. In the six months following the full Islamisation of the banking system in July 1985 their deposits rose 135%. With such a rapid build up of deposits it was clearly likely that the profit rate would decline as profitable outlets, comparable to previous advances, would, at least in the short term, become harder to find.

By October 1986, eighteen months after the Islamisation of banking, there were few complaints about the system amongst bankers and businessmen in the commercial capital, Karachi. [15] The bankers felt that Islamisation had, ironically, liberalised some aspects of a previously tightly controlled system and had helped to boost bank profits. The banks had adapted to the new paperwork, computerisation and administration requirements, and businessmen detected little change in their dealings with the seventeen banks, whose combined deposits had continued to rise rapidly. A lot of the political impetus had evaporated since President Zia-ul-Haq (who had personally pushed the reforms) had handed over the day to day running of the country to the Prime Minister in January 1986. Politicians were judged not to be keen on Islamic banking but paid lip service to it as good Muslims. The fundamentalists remained critical but there was little political response to their claim that the system was at best cosmetic because it did not fully adopt PLS, on either loans or deposits, as required under Islamic partnership laws. The banks had in practice settled on a system of mark-ups, which critics say is interest under another name, for almost all lending and a modified form of PLS for deposits. The mark-up scheme, approved by the State Bank, allows banks to fix a rate of return, of between 10% and 20%, [16] for a fixed period loan. Contracts are usually signed for 120 on 100 but the banks aim to recoup only 114, similar to the 14% rate prevailing prior to Islamisation. The extra 6 on 100 is used as a buffer against bad debtors because banks cannot later do anything that would open them to accusations of usury, such as imposing penal charges or interest on interest. A special tribunal can be approached in an attempt to recoup bad debts but it has not so far been used. The system has allowed banks greater freedom in setting charges and improved profits.

The chairman of the Bank Council, which has overseen the change, had only recorded around 25 genuine Musharika loans in the eighteen months since full Islamisation. Most companies did not appear to want to share profits and banks seemed reluctant to risk sharing in the loss of businesses they could not control. The US banks could not enter into Musharikas anyway because of legal domestic constraints. Also, only a handful of Mudarbas had been recorded.

With regard to remunerating depositors under PLS, the banks can adjust what they pay according to costs. This affords extra protection to profits. The foreign banks have generally paid more than the nationalised banks and have increased their profits. Banks continue to guarantee the repayment of a deposit. The fundamentalists object to this. The general conclusion in banking circles was that after Islamisation banks could do more, particularly in the merchant banking field, then they could in the previous, strictly controlled, banking environment. Further, the system in operation was the best that one could expect given that the principles of commercial banking could not be unlearnt in a modern commercial environment where banks are not funding caravans going off into the desert and sharing profits and losses on their return. Nevertheless, the mark-up scheme allows the rates to be determined by the party that has control of the finance and does not involve partnership. The objectives and principles underlying the elimination of interest are, therefore, undermined. Further, Kahn (1986) points out that an Islamic banking system is expected to participate actively in achieving the goals of an Islamic economy and that this has much wider implications than simply operating interest free banking.

iii) The nature of Islamic banking

Kahn (1986) uses modern Western economic theory to analyse the main features of Islamic banking. Such systems require deposits, as well as loans and advances, to be based on equity participation. Kahn shows how an equity based banking system of the Islamic type would operate and examines its stability in the face of real economic shocks. He compares the results with a fractional reserve system, on which traditional Western commercial banking systems are based. Kahn's model attempts to incorporate constraints imposed by religion on financial transactions and to portray the types of Islamic banking systems that have operated in practice in various countries. The model has many similarities with standard models used to analyse bank behaviour at the aggregate level. Because Islamic banking is based on principles of equity participation it resembles proposals in the literature, especially in the US, for reforming the banking system to reduce its instability, which many economists regard as inherent. Kahn shows that, under certain assumptions, the Islamic system will be more stable and display less disruption to the payments' system than a traditional interest based system. This is because the equity based system precludes predetermined interest rates and does not guarantee the nominal value of deposits. Shocks to asset positions are, therefore, absorbed by changes in the values of shares (deposits) held by the public. The real value of assets and liabilities would remain equal at all times. In a traditional system, in which the nominal value of deposits are fixed, shocks can cause a divergence between real assets and real liabilities. It is not clear, a priori, how the disequilibrium would be corrected or how long the adjustment would take. Rigidity in the traditional system prevents instantaneous adjustment and can lead to instability.

Kahn concludes that the principle difference between Islamic and traditional banking systems is not that one charges interest whilst the other does not. It stems instead from the fact that an Islamic system treats deposits as shares and consequently does not guarantee their nominal value. In the traditional system deposits are guaranteed by the banks or the government, often through a deposit insurance scheme, which may or may not be state backed, and also through implicit or explicit central bank lender of last resort responsibilties. Kahn suggests that his paper implies that Islamic banks should operate two types of account. One would collect transactions balances and pay no interest. Such accounts should have a 100% reserve requirement to ensure that there is no possibility of using them as a basis for multiple credit creation. They would thus be rendered completely safe and would satisfy the preferences of risk averse individuals whilst preventing shocks to the system effecting the payments mechanism. The other type of account would be a PLS or equity account. Depositors in such accounts would be treated exactly like bank shareholders. The rate of return and the nominal value of the shares would not be guaranteed. No official reserve requirement would be necessary for such investment deposits but banks might maintain reserves for prudential reasons. The deposits would be akin to those in mutual funds or investment trusts. The authorities might, however, decide to impose equity to capital requirements in line with those applied to other public companies. Kahn observes that although some Islamic banks offer both current and PLS accounts there has been no basic change in the reserve requirements on the two types of account. A change along the lines suggested would, he feels, be advisable to maximise the safety benefits inherent in the system.

The advantage of equity based accounts is that they introduce an alternative source of finance in countries where equity markets, and capital markets in general, are usually underdeveloped. In non Islamic countries, especially the underdeveloped ones, they might, therefore, be usefully introduced as an alternative, rather than a replacement for, traditional accounts. Kahn's analysis shows that the abolition of interest does not ensure that a truly Islamic banking system, based on PLS and the implied principle of equity participation, will result. This has been the experience in Pakistan so far. The banks there have continued to protect the nominal value of deposits and, although the returns to depositors vary with profit, interest is charged on loans in another guise. The banks have not been willing to make equity like investments in the companies to which they lend, as would be required in an Islamic partnership agreement. To be fair to the banks, the companies have also proved reticent to enter into such arrangements. Until the borrowers and the banks do form Islamic partnerships as a matter of course, the banks will not be truly sharing the profits and losses of their customers and their depositors will not be participating in a truly Islamic banking system because they will be protected from sharing in losses. In its present form the Islamic banking system in Pakistan mixes Islamic and traditional commercial banking principles. It is perhaps not surprising that it has attracted a significant increase in deposits given Karsten's (1982) conclusion that if an Islamic banking system were to operate alongside a traditional one savings would be increased, largely because of the formers ability to attract deposits from devout Muslim savers. It has also led to an increase in bank profits, largely because an implicit interest charge of 14% has been maintained whilst returns paid on deposits can be varied as costs vary. Islamic banks in Muslim countries outside Pakistan have also operated fairly successfully and proved able to compete with traditional and commercial banks. It will be interesting to see how they fare in comparison with the commercial banks in the recessionary Gulf states of the mid 1980s. If the treatment of bad debtors by the commercial banks proves unacceptable to the authorities and the rulings of the courts intolerable to the commercial banks then the Islamic banks might gain a larger market share in the Gulf states and Islamic banking might be more actively encouraged by their governments in the future. The system is still really at an experimental stage and has yet to show how it will interact with the traditional systems, especially those abroad, whilst maintaining Islamic principles and that it can survive in a world dominated by traditional banking relationships. In a world in which securitisation is spreading rapidly, floating rates are common, and bonds are adopting some of the characteristics of equities, such an interaction is probably not impossible.

1) See Wilczynski (1978, chapter 3) for further discussion of the role of interest rates in socialist and Western banking systems.
2) See Kuschpeta (1978) for further discussion.
3) See Garvy (1975,1977) and Pindak (1973).
4) See Lydall (1984) and Prout (1985), for example, on the Yugoslav economy and market socialism.
5) See Association of Yugoslav Banks (1979), Mijovic (1982), Bankers Research Unit (1977) and Periser (1982) for further discussion.
6) Discussed below.
7) See chapter 3.
8) The International Bank for Reconstruction and Development or 'World Bank'.
9) Western creditor governments have developed procedures for negotiating with debtor nations and they coordinate their efforts as a group which meets in Paris.
10) President Tito required the one party federal government to adopt a revolving prime ministership to cope with national and regional conflicts of interest.
11) The IMF argues that the package increases growth in the long run and that growth has usually already slowed considerably before a country calls on it for assistance.
12) The Baker Plan, announced in October 1985, calls for growth oriented adjustment backed by increased financial support from commercial banks, governments and international

agencies. It applies to the fifteen most heavily indebted IMF member nations. Yugoslavia is the only European country amongst them.

13) See Bankers' Research Unit (1977) for further discussion of the nascent domestic bond market.

14) Although there were rural Islamic banking experiments in Pakistan in the late 1950s and other prototypes, in Egypt in the 1960s and 1970s, and elsewhere in the Gulf States in the 1970s, see Kahn (1983).

15) See Aftab (1986) for a discussion of the performance of domestic and foreign banks in the first year of Islamic banking in Pakistan.

16) Or 110 or 120 on 100 as they are cautiously described.

5

Banking in a Developing Country

5.1 Introduction

Nigeria is the largest country in black Africa. It has a population of about 100m and a well developed banking system. It is also a major trading nation and a classic one export commodity country, relying on oil for around 95% of its export revenues. As such it is representative of a number of lesser developed countries (LDCs) that rely heavily on one commodity and like them has suffered from the fall in commodity prices in the 1980s. Like Mexico, its problems are particularly acute because oil prices have fallen considerably — at first gradually during the first half of the 1980s, and then rapidly, in 1986, although prices rebounded somewhat following an OPEC agreement to restrict output at the end of 1986. Before the 1986 fall its debt problem had already become acute. It needs to reschedule its debts and raise further international finance urgently. The 1982 Mexican crisis has received extensive coverage[1] because the size of the country's debts far outweigh those of Nigeria,[2] and because of their potential impact on the international financial system. Nigeria's problems, on the other hand, are similar in nature to and indicative of the growing debt problems in other African countries and Africa is expected to become the major problem area once the Latin American debt problem has been stabilised.[3] Nigeria, in common with many Asian and African countries, has had to grapple with the problem of adapting to independence following colonial rule. The colonial power in this case was Britain and, like most ex colonial countries, the institutional infrastructure, including the financial system, has been considerably influenced by the previous colonial rulers. This accounts for the relatively well developed commercial banking sector in Nigeria which, until the indigenisation programme discussed below, was dominated by foreign banks. Because there is an extensive literature on the Nigerian financial system,[4] it is only necessary to give a brief outline of it in this chapter. The aims of this chapter are instead to review of relationship between a LDC debtor nation and the international banking system and to examine the role of a central bank in the development process of a LDC.

5.2 The Debt Crisis

Nigeria's international debt crisis is primarily the result of falling oil prices in the 1980s. Oil earnings had been halved by mid 1984, from $20bn in 1983. The civilian government, installed in 1979, had responded by cutting imports. This caused difficulties in all the major sectors, especially manufacturing and agriculture. Unlike the Latin American countries, which faced medium and long term debt problems, Nigeria's debts were predominantly short term ones resulting from trade arrears in connection with the escalation of its balance of payments difficulties since 1981. The Central Bank of Nigeria (CBN) had responded by slowing down its approvals of foreign exchange transfers, to conserve its foreign exchange reserves and keep disbursements in line with receipts.

By mid 1983 arrears on letters of credit totalled $2bn and the international banks agreed to a rescheduling in two deals, concluded in July and September, involving more than 60 banks. The reschedulings allowed the repayment of arrears over three years beginning on the first day of 1984. The agreement provided for the maintenance of existing credit lines and the opening of new ones, although few were in fact opened. It effectively converted some of the short term debt to medium term debt whilst the arrears continued to accumulate in the absence of new credit. The government then sought an agreement with uninsured creditors and overseas export credit agencies. Its attempts to reach agreements with the export credit agencies and to secure new finance from governments and international banks were frustrated by the absence of an agreement with the International Monetary Fund (IMF).

Talks with the IMF about an acceptable economic reform package began in April 1983 but at an early stage the government declared that it was unwilling to devalue the Naira or liberalise import restrictions. Such measures are normally included in an IMF approved programme along with fiscal and monetary austerity measures. Meanwhile the country's economic problems worsened. Import restrictions had inhibited industrial and agricultural growth and economic growth was slightly negative in the first half of the 1980s. Falling government revenues had increased the fiscal deficit and made it more reliant on the banking system for finance. Monetary control had consequently been lax and inflation rose from 11% to 33% between 1980 and 1984 and was still rising. The current account had moved from a surplus in 1980 to a deficit in 1981 which had grown in 1982. It was reduced slightly in 1983 as a result of import and foreign exchange controls. In the late 1970s, at the peak of oil production, Nigeria was amongst OPEC's largest producers. It was producing 2m barrels a day. Its OPEC quota was subsequently reduced to 1.3m barrels a day although, like many other OPEC countries, it has unofficially exceeded its quota and prices had been almost halved by mid 1986. Nigeria is reckoned to have oil reserves that will last 30 years and it also has substantial gas reserves. It became clear to outside observers that the country needed to diversify its exports and reduce the dependence of industry on imported raw materials and capital goods. Agricultural imports had risen in the boom years and Nigeria had become reliant on imported fertilisers and other materials. Export promotion and import substitution were required. Agriculture needed particular attention because past programmes had met with little success and the sector had been adversely affected by the drift of youthful labour to towns during the period of rapid urbanisation, associated with the flood of petrodollars, in the 1970s. Government sponsored infrastructural investment had stimulated the construction industry, as had the expansion of the banks, but it dried up in the 1980s causing a slump in production activity. The overvalued Naira inhibited the required adjustment, which would clearly have to be a medium to long term one. Short term prospects remained tied to the oil market about which there was little optimism from the producers' point of view.

A coup in December 1983 replaced the civilian government, accused of corruption and bad management, with a Supreme Military Council. Talks with the IMF were abandoned in December 1984 and the government pursued its own go it alone austerity programme based on cutting government expenditure and credit expansion. Little economic reform was considered and devaluation, which had proved to be the stumbling block with the IMF, was ruled out. In order to gain a supply of imports to keep the economy moving in the absence of adequate foreign exchange earnings, the government negotiated a number of counter-trade deals, effectively involving the the barter of oil for other goods. Although the trade balance had by then been turned into a surplus, there was a significant deficit on the invisible account because of debt servicing payments. In September 1984 a $500m counter-trade deal was concluded with a Brazilian trading company and in May 1985 two deals of a similar size were concluded with Italian and French companies and a further $20m deal was concluded with Austrian companies.

In August 1985 the second coup in 20 months occurred. The new regime first established an Armed Forces Ruling Council and then a National Council of Ministers, including civilians. It introduced a fifteen month Economic Emergency Period and aimed to continue with the austerity measures, which included foreign exchange restrictions, import controls, credit controls and curtailed government expenditure, whilst considering economic reforms. Under the previous regime, government expenditure had continued to grow but had fallen in real terms as inflation had risen to 40%. It proposed to review the counter-trade policy. The new President, General Babangida who had been the third ranking member of the Supreme Military Council in Major-General Bahari's regime, had criticised the counter-trade deals on the grounds that they were costly to the government and had been used by the government members for financial gain. He had also criticised the Bahari regime for using too much foreign exchange to repay international debts. Prior to re-opening negotiations with the IMF, Babangida's government initiated a nationwide debate on whether help should be sought from the IMF and the IBRD.[5] The focus of the debate soon turned to the devaluation issue. Substantial opposition to devaluation was voiced. In April 1985 the previous regime had reached an agreement with uninsured trade creditors providing for the rescheduling of outstanding trade arrears on the basis of six year promissory notes issued by the CBN. The new regime turned its attention to implementing this programme and to negotiating with the export credit agencies and international bank and government creditors, despite the absence of an IMF agreement.

The Babangida government introduced its first budget in January 1986. It paved the way for further austerity and a number of economic reforms. Despite the fact that the Naira was trading at 25% of its official value on the black market, the government remained opposed to devaluation. It did, however, cut state subsidies, especially to domestic petrol consumption, in accordance with previous IMF proposals. Apart from an anti-IMF sentiment amongst the public, devaluation was also opposed by those with a vested interest in making profits on goods imported at official exchange rates and sold with a huge mark-up on the black markets. The new budget also provided for a new import licensing scheme, the possibility of a two-tier exchange rate system, an export promotion scheme and an overhaul of agricultural policy.

The uninsured creditors remained frustrated by the long delays in the issue of promissory notes. Suspected of delaying tactics, the government declared a need to scrutinise the various claims carefully in the light of emerging evidence of frauds[6] involving import contracts with Nigeria. The UK's Export Credit Guarantee Department (ECGD) continued to refuse to reschedule insured trade arrears without an IMF agreement. Other export credit agencies had followed suit.

Nigeria's position deteriorated further when oil prices halved in early 1986. Imports had already been cut to the bone, from a peak of $21bn in 1981 to a forecast $7bn in 1986, and the fall in oil prices was expected to reduce its export revenue by more than 25%. Industry was judged to be operating at about 20% of its capacity because of import starvation and foreign exchange reserves were being rapidly exhausted. International banks had reduced their lending and both a debt rescheduling agreement and new finance were urgently needed. The foreign bank's exposure to Nigeria was the third largest in Africa, after S. Africa and Liberia. It had reached $9.5bn by mid 1985 and Nigeria was amongst the world's top 20 debtors. The government responded by freezing import licences in February 1986 and opened talks with the international banks in March 1986 over the rescheduling of the country's $7bn medium and long term debt. Total debts were estimated to be $12bn. The government had announced in January 1986 that debt service payments would be limited to 30% of export revenues but even this was likely to be difficult to achieve given the fall in the oil price and the limited scope for further import cuts. Talks with the IMF had been suspended in 1985 which, if concluded, could have secured a $2.5bn loan. The government creditors and the export credit agencies refused to negotiate in the absence of an IMF agreement. In March 1986 Nigeria took the further step of proposing a complete moratorium on repayments of principal on medium and long term debt to commercial banks for a 90 day period from April 1. Given the country's difficulties, the steering committee representing the 20 largest creditor banks recommended that the banks accede to the request. The government also declared its intention to reschedule its debts, with the London Club of commercial banks, the Paris Club of government creditors and export credit agencies, on mutually acceptable terms. By so doing it hoped to soften the impact of the moratorium and to prevent it from being regarded as an ultimatum. Government to government debt was excluded from the moratorium and all interest payments were to be met as due. The rescheduling of the debt to commercial banks could potentially reduce the country's annual debt servicing obligations significantly but service obligations would remain severe in the absence of an official debt rescheduling. In April 1986 it also sought a moratorium form the Paris Club. By August 1986 the counter-trading strategy was also in trouble because of the oil price slump which had made nonsense of the implied valued placed on oil in the agreements under negotiation. Of the $2m worth of deals involving raw materials, industrial goods and vehicle kits, only the Brazilian deal, the first to be agreed, had been concluded. The rest had been delayed or suspended pending renegotiation. Additionally oil production had been reduced, from 1.6m barrels a day to 1m, which was within its OPEC quota of 1.3m.

By October 1986 Nigeria's protracted attempts to manage its $6.5bn trade debt were close to collapse. The CBN informed creditors that it was unable to meet the first payment of principal on the promissory notes issued to cover arrears on uninsured trade debt because of the fall in oil export revenues from $11.9bn in

1985 to a forecast $6.5bn in 1986. The CBN's inability to raise what was judged to be a relatively small amount of foreign currency was indicative of the scale of the crisis. The CBN called a meeting of noteholders and proposed to renegotiate the period over which the principal would be repaid. Meanwhile trade arrears continued to accumulate. Later in the month there was, however, a breakthrough in the negotiations with the commercial banks. The Nigerian government had signed a letter of intent to undertake a programme of policies acceptable to the IMF in September 1986. This would have allowed it to draw SDR 650m from the IMF but it declared its intention not to draw on the money because of the hostility of public opinion to IMF imposed austerity policies. Under the outline rescheduling plan agreed in London the commercial bank creditors were asked to lend $320m. The plan involved the rescheduling of $1.5bn medium term debts falling due in 1986 and 1987 and a phased reduction of an estimated $2bn in arrears on short term letters of credit. The deal was seen as a breakthrough for Nigeria, in its attempts to restore order to its $20bn foreign debt problem, because the banks did not make the package conditional on Nigeria borrowing from the IMF. This had been the practice in negotiations with other debtors. Instead, the banks accepted the letter of intent and the drawing of a $430m loan from the IBRD, which had recently been agreed in connection with a programme designed to improve Nigeria's non-oil export potential, as sufficient conditions. The banks' concession was probably made to avoid jeopardising Nigeria's progress toward economic adjustment under the new government. In return Nigeria agreed to shorter term rescheduling of a smaller quantity of debt than it had originally aimed for. The deal stopped short of the sort of multi-year rescheduling agreements (MYRAs)[7] concluded by some of the Latin American countries since 1984. In separate negotiations Nigeria was close to concluding a $250m bridging loan agreement with a number of the central banks of leading industrial countries, including the Bank of England, and the US Treasury. The loan was to help finance the weekly foreign exchange auction and was seen in Nigeria as clear support by the Western governments for its economic recovery programme. It was drawn up in close consultation with the IMF and the IBRD. The loan was to bridge the period to December 1986, when the IBRD loan could be drawn.

The weekly foreign currency auction was launched in September 1986 as the centrepiece of, arguably, the most radical and far reaching reform programme in Africa. It resulted in a massive effective devaluation of the Naira. The package also included the virtual abolition of import licences and many price controls and subsidies. It was a response to the fall in oil prices which had caused export earnings to fall from $25bn in 1980 to an estimated $6.5bn in 1986. Imports of rice were banned and imports of wheat were to be banned in 1987. The six, state controlled, commodity boards were held partially responsible for low agricultural output and were to be wound up. A large privatisation programme was being considered and multi-year capital projects were being reassessed with the IBRD. Non oil exporters were allowed to retain 25% of their foreign exchange earnings as an incentive. The plan was endorsed by the IMF which declared Nigeria eligible for a $540bn stand-by loan. Following the successful conclusion of negotiations with the commercial and central banks for new loans, Nigeria hoped to be able to reschedule its remaining $7bn worth of medium and long term loans from the commercial banks and its debts to the Paris Club and export credit agencies.

An agreement with the commercial banks was finally concluded for the rescheduling of £3.5bn accompanied by a new loan of £320m in November 1986. An agreement with the Paris Club of creditor nations followed in December 1986. The next step was to seek a rescheduling of debt to the export credit agencies of the major industrial nations. The final and most contentious stage of Nigerias complex rescheduling negotiations will be to tackle the large and accumulating uninsured trade debt.

In January 1987 Nigeria missed an interest payment on the promissory notes issued against the reconciled debts. This will not only complicate negotiations concerning this debt but may also jeapordise the reschedulings already agreed with the commercial banks and the Paris Club and make an agreement with the export credit agencies less likely. In that month President Babangida announced that Nigeria would continue to limit repayments of external debt to 30% of export earnings. The CBN also indicated that the country's cash flow problem was so severe that it would seek to capitalise overdue interest payments. It seems likely that, under pressure from the IMF and the IBRD, which urgently need a success in Africa, and Britain, which has a vested interest in maintaining links with its most important black African trading partner, the various creditors will be persuaded to take a sympathetic line as long as Nigeria adheres to the programme agreed with the IMF. In addition to the $450m structural adjustment loan, the IBRD seems likely to provide $4.3bn to finance special projects between 1987 and 1990. In January 1987 oil prices had rebounded to $18 a barrel as a result of an OPEC agreement, in December 1986, to restrict output to achieve a target price of $18 a barrel. This should ease Nigeria's cash flow problem considerably. It was, however, so acute that Nigeria was forced to take the SDR650m loan offered by the IMF. The IMF approved the loan in February 1987 despite the fact that the banks had not achieved the critical mass of 90% normally required prior to an IMF disbursement. 330 banks were involved and commitments to the package had come in only slowly. By February the commitments amounted to between 80% and 90% of the $3.8bn rescheduling and the $320 new loan. The stragglers have been the banks with the smallest exposure and numerous banks are involved. The IMF's decision to disburse the loan can be interpreted as a signal of of its appproval of Nigeria's execution of the adjustment programme designed to encourage the remaining banks to participate. The missed interest payments on the uninsured trade credits may, however reinforce their reluctance to do so.

The reforms introduced in September are likely to be unpopular amongst a number of influential lobby groups and the new government will be hard pressed to retain power. In the past import licences secured an automatic foreign exchange allocation. With the Naira overvalued, licensees could make easy profits on the black markets. Now licences are granted as a formality and foreign exchange has to be bought at the auction at a much more realistic rate. Importers, a significant lobby group, will clearly be unhappy with this arrangement. The middle class will also be affected because they will no longer have cheap access to medical and educational facilities abroad, partly because travel will be more expensive. Civil servants have also been grumbling because of their loss of privileges and ability to grant patronage. The impact of austerity, and especially restrictions on agricultural imports, have been cushioned by good harvests in 1985 and 1986. A bad harvest in the next year or two would severely damage the government's popularity, which could already have been reduced considerably because the government was eventually forced to draw on the IMF stand-by loan. President Babangida had previously been able to convince Nigerians that, if they wanted to maintain their independence from the IMF, they had to accept tough measures. The political system is notoriously unstable and their was some rioting in early 1987.

The Nigerian government has also sought to revive the counter-trade deal signed with the Brazilian trading company in 1984. Because Brazil's trade position had deteriorated rapidly since mid 1986, a deal was likely to be mutually attractive. Brazil's exports to Nigeria, and vice versa, had slumped badly in 1986, following the decision by both parties to allow the agreement to lapse. Brazil had complained of corruption on the Nigerian side and Nigeria had complained that Brazil was supplying over-priced goods of poor quality. Nigeria also entered into negotiations with the Austrian company, with which it had a $200m counter-trade arrangement in 1985. These developments were judged to reflect short term expediency, the government being unlikely to resume substantial counter-trading in the longer term.

5.3 The Banking System

As a result of an indigenisation programme and the imposition of increasingly restrictive guidelines on banks' operations, the banking system has changed considerably since 1973. Nevertheless the banks have remained profitable, especially the 'big three', and the prospects were so good that many new banks had been established by the mid 1980s, when the debt crisis came to a head. About ten new banks were set up by state governments in 1981 and a couple of foreign banks participated in new banking ventures. During the 1970s and early 1980s many Nigerian organisations also sought project finance in the Eurocurrency markets.

Indigenisation was completed in 1980 following the outgoing military government's decision, in September 1979, that executive controls would have to be relinquished by expatriates and handed over to Nigerians. The indigenisation began in 1973, when the government ordered the Ministry of Finance (MoF) to take 40% stakes in the 'big three', foreign controlled, banks : the United Bank for Africa (UBA), the Union Bank, and the First Bank, as they became known. UBA is the largest, followed by First Bank. In 1976 the government declared that Nigerians should have a stake of at least 60% in most commercial and industrial companies, including banks. This usually meant that the MoF extended its share to over 50% because private and institutional share ownership was not widespread. Until 1980 management control was left with the minority shareholders. Standard Chartered maintained a 38% stake in First Bank, whilst Barclays Bank and the Banque Nationale de Paris maintained 20% and 25% stakes, respectively, in Union Bank and UBA. Few had expected the transfer to indigenous executive control to happen so quickly.

In the latter half of the 1970s the government had also imposed a number of controls on banks' activities: ceilings were placed on the overall growth of outstanding advances; lending and borrowing rates were specified; guidelines were set for sectoral lending; and banks were required to establish new branches in rural areas. 75% of loans were required to be advanced to preferred sectors, such as agriculture, manufacturing, housing and public utilities. Specific targets were set for each sector. Lending to non preferred sectors, such as imports, were not allowed to exceed 25% of all loans. Further, 70% of all loans had to be made to indigenous organisations. Fines can be imposed on banks not adhering to the guidelines. The rural banking programme will be discussed in the next section.

Surprisingly the foreign banks maintained their interest. Only Citibank, in 1976, pulled out and it was granted a new charter in the early 1980s. Initially new foreign bank interest was discouraged. The MoF declined to take a significant stake in Sociêtê Gênêrale's venture in 1977, for example. It was forced to find other local partners, which proved to be a lengthy process. The civilian government of the early 1980s, however, actively and openly encouraged foreign bank interest. Fears that indigenisation and lending controls would lead to nationalisation or reduced competition also dissipated under the civilian government. The domestic banks, although less profitable, thrived and the share of the 'big three' declined quite rapidly in the 1980s, to 50% of the banking market by 1986. Nevertheless the 'big three' also expanded rapidly and moved up the league table of the world's top 500 banks. The banks in general benefited from the rapid expansion of the money supply under the civilian government. Although the banking system had amassed considerable assets by 1980, large projects tended to be financed externally leading to a growth in international debt which, as noted in the previous section, proved difficult to service as oil revenue declined, especially in the mid 1980s.

The lending and interest rate controls have distorted capital market yields. This has led the Nigerian Stock Exchange to control the price of equities to avoid absurdly wide yield gaps. Companies consequently only resort to the equity markets when they cannot secure adequate bank finance and banks have no incentive to finance more risky ventures. Many feel that the controls should be relaxed now that bank management is firmly in Nigerian hands.

Although the commercial banks dominate the financial system there are a number of other banking institutions. The number of merchant banks has been increasing. They have been highly profitable and have managed to attract high quality staff from the commercial banks. They concentrate on providing wholesale banking services primarily to the corporate sector and the finance trade and the government. Their rapid growth coincided with rapid industrialisation and expanding foreign trade in the 1970s. Their future prospects are not as rosy, however, because of the recession in the mid 1980s and the restricted availability of foreign exchange. They were inhibited by the allocation system for foreign exchange but this was replaced in 1986 by an auction system which should benefit them.

There are also a number of specialised banks. The Federal Savings Bank, formerly known as the Post Office Savings Bank, is a government institution. It aims to mobilise savings generally and pays particular attention to underbanked rural areas. Interest paid on its deposits are not subject to income tax and deposit ceilings are imposed on personal accounts. It does not accept demand or time deposits or grant loans. The use of the bank's funds are regulated by law and it lends exclusively to the government. Its share of aggregate deposits has declined as commercial banks have grown.

The Nigerian Industrial Development Bank (NIDB) was established in 1964 following the reconstruction of the Investment Company of Nigeria Ltd. It provides both medium and long term finance and sometimes makes equity investments. It also provides technical and managerial assistance and has research and appraisal departments. It invests primarily in the indigenous manufacturing sector.

The Nigerian Agricultural Bank (NAB) commenced operations in 1973. Like the NIDB it received its initial funds from the government. It is empowered to raise funds from the public and aims to provide funds for the development, production, storage and marketing of agricultural produce. It deals with state governments, farmers' cooperatives and creditworthy individuals. To reduce reliance on imports and curb inflationary pressures agricultural development has been encouraged. Despite a series of programmes the sector remains underdeveloped and agricultural imports have increased.

The Nigerian Bank for Commerce and Industry (NBCI) was established in 1973. The Federal government and the CBN jointly provided its share capital, in proportions of 60% and 40% respectively. The CBN is permitted to sell up to 20% of its share to other financial institutions. The Bank's objectives are: to extend equity capital and long and medium term loans to indigenous commerce and industry; to provide merchant banking services; and to conduct other banking and commercial business. It can assist in identifying viable projects and in the preparation of feasibility studies and provide technical and managerial advice. It has provided finance for the acquisition of indigenous enterprises in connection with the indigenisation programme and complements the activities of the NIDB.

The Federal Mortgage Bank (FMB) was established in 1977 after the reconstitution of the Nigerian Building Society which followed the recommendations of a financial review panel. Its objectives are to provide loans to Nigerians to enable them to buy or build their own homes and to encourage the habit of saving. Mortgage loans are usually only advanced once individuals have acquired a certain level of savings and demonstrated an ability to manage their personal finances.

Nigeria also has a number of non bank financial intermediaries. The most important are insurance companies. Insurance was initially dominated by foreign, particularly British, firms. Indigenous companies are now more numerous than foreign ones but the foreign owned firms still dominate the business. The government has, however, bought equity shares of up to 49% in them. Their funds are mainly invested in stocks and shares. The government owned National Provident Fund collects resources from the private sector and invests most of them in government securities. Investment companies have been established by the government ministries responsible for agricultures, industry, housing and credit. They carry out a wide range of activities, including the provision of loans and equity finance, and are geared to promoting economic development. There are also some privately owned investment companies which provide hire purchase and leasing services and corporate investment finance. Finally, there are credit and cooperative societies organised on a mutual, non profit making, basis. They accept deposits from members and lending , which is usually made at low rates, is restricted to members.

No indigenous money market existed prior to the establishment of the CBN. There was some short term lending and borrowing based on commercial paper but this was essentially an extension of the London money market. It was used to bring funds to Nigeria to finance exports during the harvest season. The CBN issued the first Treasury bills in 1960. Issues were on a monthly basis until 1963, when weekly issues became the practice. Buyers must make applications through licensed banks or acceptance houses. The CBN underwrites the issues and provides rediscounting facilities. In 1963 a new money market instrument, the Treasury certificate, was introduced. Their maturity ranges from 12 to 24 months, compared to the three month Treasury bill maturity. The Treasury instruments dominate the market but there is also a commercial bill market. The banks and acceptance houses discount the commercial bills and the CBN provides rediscounting facilities. Finally, certificates of deposit were first issued, by merchant banks, in 1975. They can be held by commercial banks as liquid assets.

With regard to the capital market, the Lagos Stock Exchange was established in 1960. In 1977 its name was changed to the Nigerian Stock Exchange. Its development was the result of a CBN initiative. It launched the market by issuing a wide range of development stocks and government bonds.[8] The CBN underwrites such stock and sells some of its holdings to other institutions. The market was modelled on the London Stock Exchange. It separated the activities of jobbers and brokers. This practice was abandoned in London in October 1986. The money market arrangements also have similarities with the London Discount Market. Ojo (1976) is critical of developing institutions such as the stock market just for the sake of copying the financial structure of Western developed economies. He is particularly critical of the tendency to model the Nigerian markets on the London ones, which he felt might be historical anachronisms, rather than on the most modern and efficient institutions and markets elsewhere. In the event Ojo was correct about the London markets and reform might, therefore, be necessary in Nigeria as well. The question of whether Western style financial systems are appropriate for LDCs is a more fundamental one. Equity finance should clearly be available, as an alternative to bank finance, if a non-socialist economy is to be developed. But it is by no means clear that equity participation needs to be securitised and that a secondary market should exist. Islamic principles, discussed in chapter 4, could be applied, for example. Government finance need not rely on the issue of tradeable paper either. Whatever the merits of the case, the CBN saw the development of money and capital markets as part of its responsibility towards overseeing the development of the financial system and participating in the wider development of the economy.

The capital market was boosted by the indigenisation programme. In response to the Nigerian Enterprise Promotion Decree (1972), foreign firms issued shares for sale. In 1973 the Capital Issues Commission was established to regulate the price of shares and the timing of their issue. The government has also assisted in the development of the market by requiring insurance and pension funds to invest a proportion of their funds in local shares and government stocks.

The money and capital markets remain relatively new and underdeveloped. Share ownership is not widespread. The government had to take large stakes in many countries as a result of the indigenisation programme and the lack of domestic demand for shares. The other major shareholders are the insurance and pension funds.

Nigeria and other British West African colonies did not have their own currencies. Prior to independence, Nigeria's currency was managed by the West African Currency Board (WACB) which came into being in 1912. The WACB had an obligation to redeem the West African currency, in sterling, on demand and to issue West African notes and coins, on demand, against an equivalent amount of sterling. It was effectively a glorified money changer with little control over the amount of money it issued. The circulating currency was backed pound for pound by the sterling holdings of the WACB. Consequently a 100% sterling exchange standard existed. The amount of money in circulation depended on the levels and seasonal fluctuations in exports and imports.

Following independence, the government engaged the services of an adviser from the Bank of England concerning the establishment of a central bank in Nigeria. A previous adviser had not advocated[9] the establishment of a fully fledged, western style, central bank. He argued that such institutions were only required in well developed financial systems. The second adviser took a different view[10] and, following the 1958 Banking Ordinance, the CBN commenced operations in 1959. The original adviser seemed to have largely ignored the possibility that a central bank might adopt a role of actively developing financial institutions and markets, as the Bank of England, for example, has been doing even in the 1980s. He also, perhaps, underestimated the need of the new independent government for its own bank; to manage its accounts, arrange for its financing, and to execute its monetary policy.

The functions performed by the CBN since its inception have been: sole issuer of legal tender; banker and financial adviser to the federal government; promotion of monetary stability and a sound financial structure; and the maintenance of external reserves in order to safeguard the external value of the currency. It also provides banking services to state governments and government owned institutions. It can grant 'ways and means' advances to the government of up to 25% of the estimated government revenue. Treasury bills and certificates can be held in amounts up to 15% and 60% respectively, of the estimated revenue of all governments. The CBN is also authorised to lend to the government through long term securities, which it then holds. Such holdings must not exceed 75% of total demand liabilities. As adviser it seeks to ensure consistency between fiscal and monetary policy. It was assigned responsibility for managing the country's foreign exchange in 1969. In accordance with its responsibility of promoting a sound financial structure, it ensures that banks operate within the provisions of the banking laws. Control is exercised through the regular examination of the books of all banks by the CBN's Examination Department. The CBN is also empowered to prescribe liquidity or reserve ratios.

The CBN has responsibility for formulating and executing monetary policy. The main monetary instruments are the discount rate, reserve requirements, quantitative and qualitative credit control and moral suasion. Open market operations are not used extensively because of the relatively underdeveloped nature of the money and capital markets, which has also inhibited the use of variations in the liquidity ratio. Moral suasion and credit controls have been the most actively used instruments, although latterly the CBN has also set maximum lending and borrowing rates. The CBN also has responsibility for the custodianship and management of the country's gold and foreign exchange reserves. Previously foreign exchange had to be surrendered to the CBN which then supplied foreign exchange to the banks, as required. When foreign exchange became scarce in the 1980s, the CBN began using a quota system, based on past business volume, to allocate foreign exchange to banks. This tended to favour the larger banks and inhibited the growth of the merchant banks. In 1986 this arrangement was replaced with an auction system.[11]

In pursuance of its development role it has used qualitative credit controls, to direct credit to the industrial and agricultural sectors in particular and taken an active role in the development of the money and capital markets.[12] It has also overseen the rural banking experiment, discussed in the next section, and promoted the establishment of, and given continued assistance to, the government sponsored special financial institutions discussed above.[13]

The 1958 Banking Ordinance established the CBN as a corporate body that can sue and be sued. It is subject to government control in a number of ways. It is owned by the government, which supplies its capital and receives its net profit. The Head of State appoints the governor and deputy governor who, with five others members also appointed by the head of state, constitute its Board of Governors. The Banking Ordinance also provides for an Advisory Committee, made up of Federal and State Commissioners of Finance, which is required to make government opinion known to the CBN. Further, the CBN is expected to seek approval from the Federal Commissioner or the government on a variety of issues, such as the parity of the Naira, which, prior to the auction system, could not be changed without the approval of the Federal Executive council. Finally, in cases of disagreement with the MoF over monetary policy, the Commissioner for Finance is required to submit the views of the CBN and the MoF to the Executive Council which may then direct the CBN in its pursuance of monetary policy. The CBN, therefore, has to go through the MoF to gain approval for its policies and the Executive Council has ultimate responsibility for monetary policy. The CBN cannot, therefore, pursue a policy independent of government influence despite the fact that the Banking Ordinance makes it responsible for the formulation and execution of monetary policy.

There have been periods in which the interests of the government and the CBN have diverged and in these periods the CBN seems to have acquiesced by financing the government deficit,[14] e.g. during the Civil War of 1962-1970. There have also been lengthy periods in which democracy has collapsed and in these periods the validity of the statutory provisions for its independence have been questionable. The deficit financing by the CBN, in the civil war period, generated considerable inflation. The conflicts between the CBN and the Ministry of Finance were eased in the 1970s as the Government moved into surplus as a result of increasing oil revenues. In this period the balance of payments problems also abated. In the post 1974 period, however, the surplus liquidity in the economy also generated inflationary pressures. Following the oil price collapse in the early 1980s, the balance of payments and government financing problems re-emerged with a vengeance. The CBN and the banks again performed a deficit financing role and, with monetary policy lax, inflation increased to 30% by 1984. The military regimes installed in 1984 and 1986, however, imposed austerity programmes designed to reduce inflation and solve the country's foreign exchange problems.

The banking system has thrived, especially during the post 1973 oil boom period. It has grown both in terms of the number of banks and the volume of business. Despite the onset of the foreign exchange crisis, as the monetary expansion continued, it continued to grow in the first half of the 1980s and the 'big three' banks moved up the international league tables. Nigeria was clearly black Africa's most important financial market. In 1984, however, the banking system failed to escape the twin effects of recession and political upheaval but it remained in much better shape than most of industry and commerce. After a decade of uncoordinated expansion the banks had to make preparations to deal with bad debts, narrower margins and tighter credit ceilings. If they make adequate provisions and the austerity measures are maintained for a lengthy period then the banks are likely to emerge slimmer, fitter and more competitive. The military regime which installed itself in 1984 imposed two upheavals on the banking system. Banks were required to take over the entire system for allocating foreign exchange to the private sector, which had previously been administered by the CBN. They were also required to exchange old bank notes for new in an operation designed to catch out currency hoarders and black marketeers and drastically to reduce the cash in circulation. Purges of top management and staff were also ordered by the new regime, which remained the majority shareholder throughout the system.

The banks' most lucrative business, trade financing, has been badly curtailed by the foreign exchange crisis. They have been faced with a growing number of bankruptcies and, as oil reserves have declined, government borrowing has continued to grow. With growth slow and imports curtailed, the manufacturing and agricultural sectors have fared badly. The Babingida regime tried to tighten monetary policy and reduce the budget deficit by barring the nineteen state governments from further borrowing, but the Federal Government continued to have to borrow sizeable sums. The May 1986 budget raised minimum interest rates, but the rates remained well below inflation, which had reached 40%. The normal lending rates were raised for 6.5% - 8% to 8.5% - 10% and a maximum rate was set at 13%. Margins were consequently squeezed.

The IMF is expected to encourage the government to reduce its stake in the banking system. Because banks are required to be at least 60% owned by Nigerians and share ownership is not widespread, 50% or more of their equity is commonly owned by the government. The government has, however, shown little evidence of using its equity stake as a means of influencing banks. It seems happy to rely instead on the quantitative and qualitative credit controls administered by the CBN.

Despite the austerity programme, the banking sector continued to flourish in 1985, especially relative to other sectors, although the days of rapid expansion, which owed much to expansionist government monetary policy, were judged to be over. The money supply had doubled between 1979 and 1982 and grown by 12% in 1983. In 1984 the CBN had reduced the ceiling on credit growth from 25% to 12.5% and public sector borrowing from the banks had been severely curtailed. Private sector demand for credit continued to fall as the corporate sector raised its liquidity, by laying off workers and running down inventories, in response to government cuts in foreign exchange allocations. The increase in liquidity began to widen margins, which had been squeezed in 1984, because it reduced the cost of funds. The banks also found that their responsibility for allocating foreign exchange allowed them to cross-sell other services. Inflation remained rampant, well above the new 12.5% interest ceiling and the credit expansion ceiling was further reduced to 7%. The chosen method of dealing with debt to non insured trade creditors, the issuance of promissory notes, was also expected to benefit banks. Nigerian producers are required to put up Naira against the issue of notes and might consequently have to borrow from banks. The banks have also enjoyed increased business from contractors who have sought funding whilst they await for payment from state departments for projects completed but not yet paid for. Further opportunities may arise as the government attempts to reschedule the country's other debts. In the absence of rescheduling, however, the banks could face liquidity shortages. The 'big three' banks continued to dominate and grow but, because of the growth in the number of banks in the market, their share of all deposits had fallen from 65% in 1980 to 50% in 1985.

By 1986 inflation had been brought down and was officially recorded at 15%. The current account had registered a small surplus in 1984 and this had grown in

1985. With large debts outstanding, accumulating, and requiring servicing, foreign exchange remained in short supply. The banks' liquidity had grown to 68% in 1985, compared to the 25% statutory requirement. The rise in their liquidity was a result of low private sector credit demand and high government expenditure financed by short term securities issues which were held largely by banks. The corporate sector had generally raised liquidity and profits and curtailed investment plans because of its inability to obtain foreign exchange and secure an adequate supply of imports. Bad debts, for which provisioning was required, also continued to accumulate. The banks consequently retreated into short term lending via the Treasury bills tender. Their holdings of bills quadrupled in the 1981-5 period and 55% of their assets were in government securities, compared to 25% in 1980. In 1985 Union Bank established a bad debt recovery unit and doubtful debt provisions had reached 70% of pre-tax earnings. Despite growing provisions and a marginal fall in lending, pre-tax profits were up by 40%, largely due to the high interest rates paid on Treasury bills and other government securities. Naira deposits which were eventually to be exchanged for promissory notes, in respect of trade arrears owed by Nigerian firms to foreign firms, had also increased. When the notes are eventually issued[15] there should be a decline in liquidity. Profits remained assured as long as public sector demand for credit continued to grow. Government reliance on the banks could, however, be reduced by cuts in government expenditure and finance from abroad.[16]

The military coup in August 1985 replaced the previous military regime which had broken off negotiations with the IMF in December 1984 and had attempted to solve the problems alone through continued austerity and counter trading.[17] The Babingida regime initiated a public debate on devaluation and hoped to pave the way for a compromise deal with the IMF to unlock the door to rescheduling and provide access to new finance. Towards this end it introduced a number of measures in its first budget, in January 1986, to encourage economic reform alongside continued austerity. It remained unwilling to devalue the Naira formally and introduced a two-tier foreign exchange market instead. This provided for weekly auctions by the CBN, started in September 1986, of foreign exchange and lead to a massive effective devaluation of the Naira. The main bidders are the commercial and merchant banks, of which there were nearly 40. The auction determines the price for nearly all transactions except the servicing of the government's external debts. By the end of 1986 many felt that the auction had yet to set a realistic value for the currency and that it might boost inflation, which remained over 30%. The effective devaluation may increase oil revenues substantially because oil is priced in US dollars.

The public sector continued to dominate domestic bank lending in 1986 when it was taking 60% of domestic net credit. Its borrowing took off in the early 1980s as the civilian government faced falling oil revenues. From 1981 to 1983 it increased at an annual rate of 55%. The rate was slowed to 11% in 1984-6 by the military government which also reduced credit expansion from about 70% in 1981-3 to below 10%.

By mid 1985, 28 commercial and 11 merchant banks were operating through about 1250 offices. The indigenous commercial banks were the least profitable and the merchant banks the most profitable. Interest rates remained controlled by the CBN. Deposit and lending rates were generally in the 9 - 10% range, with a ceiling of 13 %. They remained negative and the gap between lending and borrowing rates had narrowed. 75 % of bank lending had to be directed to preferred sectors, manufacturing industry receiving 75 % of it and agriculture 12 %. The banks, however, rarely met their targets. Instead they lent excessively to the service sector, the government, and other, especially merchant, banks through the wholesale market.

5.4 The Rural Banking Scheme and the CBN's Development Role

In accordance with its development role, the CBN has overseen the extension of banks into rural areas. Central banks have often been seen as key players in the process of economic development of LDCs. Dorrance (1969), for example, has argued that their main contribution should be the maintenance of a sound monetary, credit and banking system. This entails encouraging the collection of savings and their efficient allocation and maintaining an environment conducive to foreign investment. The government should be discouraged from relying on the central bank or the banking system for financing. Additionally, foreign exchange reserves should be regarded as part of the country's infrastructure and maintained at levels sufficient to insure against international insolvency. He argues that domestic confidence in the currency will result from a sound monetary policy which should place prime importance on maintaining a stable exchange rate with international currencies. Inflation should, therefore, be controlled and devaluation avoided. Monetary policy is likely to be more important in LDCs, than fiscal or incomes policies, he feels. Also, because money and equity markets are likely to be underdeveloped, moral suasion and central bank directives are likely to be more effective than open market operations and can play a significant role in development programmes.

In the light of this assessment the CBN has correctly introduced credit directives, although lack of opportunities for profitable investment has reduced their impact and sanctions against banks have not been implemented as a consequence. The rural development programmes have not been particularly successful and it appears that more incentives, rather than financial directives, are required. The CBN has, however, been unable to prevent the government calling on it or the banks for finance, even though it has supported the development of money and capital markets to provide the possibility of at least some non bank financing of the government's budget deficit. In the face of a rapid decline in the country's external trade position in the 1980s, the CBN has also been forced to draw down considerably, to the point of virtual extinction, the country's foreign exchange reserves. International insolvency has resulted as a consequence.

Apart from encouraging the development of money and capital markets the CBN has also attempted to identify institutional gaps. One gap that seems to occur in both developed countries and the LDCs is in the provision of medium and long term finance to the business sector. Commercial banks tend to prefer short term lending. The CBN has, consequently, promoted the establishment government sponsored special financial institutions.[18] A means of encouraging commercial banks to extend more medium and long term finance is to offer refinancing facilities for medium and long term loans. Various institutions do this in France, for example. The CBN has, however, largely confined itself to the rediscounting of short term securities. Additionally, banks do not always promote thrift and it may be necessary to encourage the establishment of savings banks, perhaps through post offices. Towards this end the CBN instead chose to encourage bank branching into rural areas.

The CBN has also taken responsibility for the development of a clearing system in order to promote an efficient payments' system. It gave early attention to the development of an interbank clearing system and established the first clearing house in Lagos in 1961. Previously banks had operated reciprocal arrangements by holding clearing accounts with each other. Clearing houses were opened in a number of major centres subsequently and by 1977 there were nine of them, and more were expected to follow as the CBN opened additional branches in various locations as part of its branching programme.[19] The clearing houses handle cheques, drafts, warrants, debit notes and bankers' payments. Cheques are the dominant means of non cash payment and the volume and value processed by the clearing houses has grown progressively. All the expenses involved in providing clearing services have been borne by the CBN as a means of helping to promote the development of an efficient banking system.

Many economists[20] believe that central banks in LDCs should rely more heavily on reserve requirements than credit controls, allowing the markets a greater role in the efficient allocation of resources. Adherents to this perspective also advocate that central banks have refinancing roles and that they help development banks to raise funds, rather than lend to them or other economic agents directly. This is believed to be necessary to reduce inflationary pressures. They believe that, in their role as managers of government debt and banker to the government, central banks should also avoid inflationary government finance. This is easier said than done unless the constitution provides for an adequate degree of central bank independence.

The efficient development of the financial system requires both the mobilisation of savings and their efficient allocation. The rural banking scheme attempted to contribute to the former. Money and capital markets are seen as essential for efficient allocation and the CBN has also been active in this direction. Deposit insurance and adequate supervision can also encourage savings. Whilst performing a supervisory role, the CBN has not yet required the establishment of a deposit insurance fund but this could be helpful. More generally, it is important to avoid inflation and negative interest rates to ensure reasonable earnings from savings and discourage capital flight. The extent to which the central bank should be involved directly in development finance and credit direction is a matter of political debate and depends on the weights to be attached to planned and market based resource allocation in the development process. Even more fundamentally, a central bank could consider whether traditional commercial bank lending is the most effective way of allocating resources. It might judge that equity relationships are more beneficial that contractual interest rate relationships. The development of a capital market provides for equity finance as an alternative to traditional bank finance. Some countries, particularly Pakistan, have considered going further by reforming the banking system with a view to promoting equity participation based on lending.[21]

In 1977 the Federal Military Government accepted a number of the recommendations of its Committee on the Nigerian financial system. The Committee had advocated an extension of banking services to rural areas and the government mandated the CBN to implement its recommendations. It produced a two stage plan. The first stage was completed in June 1980 and the second phase began in July 1980. It was completed at the end of December 1983. The scheme was, therefore, implemented rather rapidly causing concern amongst banks which found that the rural branches did not generate sufficient business to cover their costs and trained manpower in the branches was usually under employed.

The first phase of the of the Rural Banking Scheme (RBS) required the eighteen banks, about half of which were owned by state governments, to open 200 branches between 1977 and June 1980. At least one bank branch was to be opened in each of the state government headquarter cities because even the urban areas were underbanked (see Umoh, 1984), as a result of concentration of financial activity in Lagos and a couple of other major cities. Banks already having rural branches were given smaller quotas than those without. Most banks achieved their quotas[22] and by the end of the first phase 188 branches had been opened, the number rising to 194 by the end of 1980. The first phase was, therefore, successful and most banks had complied despite operational difficulties. The banks that had not fulfilled their allocated quotas carried their uncompleted assignments into phase two.

The second phase commenced immediately after the ending of the first and the banks complained about the absence of a breathing space to allow evaluation because the most obvious locations had already been chosen. In phase two there were 266 branch allocations to the, by then, 20 banks. Quotas were again set in accordance with bank size and also took account of performance in stage one. Smaller banks received smaller quotas and the minimum allocation was five. The banks were expected to look further afield, beyond major towns and cities. The response was slow with only about a quarter of the assignment completed by the midway point. At the end of the period a further 181 branches had been opened and only three banks, none amongst the 'big three', had fulfilled their quotas.

The shortfall of about a third overall has been attributed to the difficulties banks encountered which included declining profitability — partly due to the worsening state of the economy, lack of patronage of rural branches, and the difficulties of finding sufficient adequately trained staff and persuading those available to work in rural areas. The CBN did not attempt to force compliance, preferring to maintain its relationship, which was built on trust and understanding, with the banks. It did attempt to use moral suasion, largely through the forum of the bankers' committee. It did not impose strict sanctions for failure to comply. It seems to have accepted that the second phase was overoptimistic. If the authorities were serious about bringing it to a successful conclusion, in the face of bank opposition, they could have introduced more incentives. The incentives actually offered included: a waiver on feasibility study requirements for rural branches; exclusion of rural branch credits from the calculation of a bank's total loans or advances which were subject to controls; a reasonable period of monopoly in a rural branch location; and more generous capital allowance for rural branch investments than normally allowable to industrial companies. Although many Nigerians thought these incentives to be too generous, the banks took the opposite view. Umoh (1984) felt that the government, which supposedly owns all the land, could have leased rural sites to banks for nominal fees and thereby reduced their costs considerably. It could have also helped to overcome staff opposition to rural postings by subsidising banks having to provide electricity generators, water pumps, and other infrastructural facilities. The lack of infrastructural back up increased the costs of establishing rural banks and in some cases, where banks provided their own facilities, there were external benefits. The second phase might also have been more successful had the CBN allowed a period of evaluation and involved the banks in its planning. The banks would then have been encouraged to set realistic goals and the authorities would have been able to assess the impact of past incentives and perhaps introduce new ones. The commercial banks would have become more involved in the development process and might not have regarded the scheme as yet another annoying official imposition.

The RBS had succeeded in increasing the number of bank branches to over 1,000 by the end of 1983. More widespread branching is not, however, synonymous with a significant spread of the banking habit or a marked increase in financial intermediation. The object of schemes like the RBS is to collect savings and ensure that they are efficiently allocated for investment and other uses. For the scheme to achieve such a goal the rural populace must use the branches. Here too the authorities should consider using both positive and negative sanctions and could also contribute by advertising rural banking services on government owned radio and television stations either free of charge or at a subsidised rate. One possibility, advocated by Umoh (1984), would be to encourage cheque usage and discourage cash payments, especially for larger transactions. This would require the opening of bank accounts and so too would a requirement on employers to pay wages and salaries by direct transfers to bank accounts.

Some Nigerians[23] feel that the RBS was misconceived. They feel that the CBN should have taken a more active role in the development of rural banking by establishing branches itself, as central banks or monetary authorities have done in some other LDCs. In countries such as Brazil rural credit outposts have been established to provide basic banking services. The frontier bank branches would be expected to provide services specifically designed to cater for the needs of the rural communities. They would first and foremost be savings banks and might ultimately be allowed to develop into cooperative or mutual banks. The branches opened under sufferance by the banks have been ill adapted to the needs of the rural communities and have inappropriately trained staff. The provision of payments transmission services and more widespread usage of cheques and other non cash payments methods are unlikely to be of primary importance. The main concern should be to encourage savings to enable the pooling of funds for use primarily in the development of rural infrastructure and local agriculture. Another alternative would be to offer savings bank services through an expanded post office network.

1) See Kraft (1984) and Lever and Huhne (1985), for example.

2) For details on Mexico's and Nigeria's debts see the Financial Times, 6 March 1987, page 4.

3) A special United Nations Session on Africa's problems was convened in June 1986, for example.

4) See for example Nwankwo (1980), Ojo(1976), Ojo and Adewunmi (1982), Okigbo (1982), Onoh (1982), Uzuogo (1981) or Central Bank of Nigeria (1979).

5) The International Bank for Reconstruction and Development or 'World Bank'.

6) In connection with the Johnson Matthey Bank affair, for example. In October 1984 the bank, which was recognised by the Bank of England under the 1979 UK Banking Act, had to be rescued because it had developed large exposures to a number of clients who were unable or unwilling to service their debts. Investigations into the affairs of the

bank's clients uncovered a series of frauds involving forged Nigerian trade documents.
7) See Gorman and Morales (1985) for a discussion of MYRAs.
8) See Central Bank of Nigeria (1979) for further discussion.
9) See Fisher (1953) and Central Bank of Nigeria (1979), which discusses his report.
10) See Loynes (1957) and Central Bank of Nigeria(1979), which discusses his report
which formed the basis of the 1958 Banking Ordinance.
11) See section 5.2.
12) See Central Bank of Nigeria (1979) for further discussion.
13) See Central Bank of Nigeria (1979) for further discussion.
14) See Central Bank of Nigeria (1979) for further discussion.
15) See section 5.2 on negotiation with uninsured creditors.
16) See section 5.2 on prospects for further overseas finance.
17) See section 5.2 for further discussion.
18) See section 5.3.
19) See Central Bank of Nigeria (1979).
20) See Brimmer (1972), Sayers (1957), or Dorrance (1969) for example.
21) See sections 4.1 and 4.3.
22) See Umoh (1984) for details.
23) See Ojo and Adewunmi (1982) and Osuntogun and Adewunmi (1983).

6

Offshore Banking

6.1 Introduction

The growing internationalisation of banking [1] since the 1960s encouraged the proliferation of offshore banking centres. This process accelerated after the 1973 oil price shock when added impetus was given to the growth of the Eurodollar market because of the need to recycle the surpluses of the OPEC countries. In the 1980s the emphasis had become one of globalisation; involving truly international banking and capital markets, which themselves began to merge, and 24-hour trading revolving around international financial centres. In this latter phase geographic positioning, particularly in terms of time zone, has become crucially important. It has become possible, for example, that 24-hour trading could revolve around a European centre, a North American centre and an Asian-Pacific centre. At present London, New York and Tokyo are the obvious candidates.

An offshore centre has been defined [2] as a place, which could be a country, an area, or a city, which has made a deliberate attempt to attract international banking business by reducing or eliminating restrictions upon operations as well as lowering taxes and/or other levies. International banking business here refers to non resident, foreign currency denominated, assets and liabilities. McCarthy (1979) identified twenty-one such centres including the Bahamas, the Cayman Islands, Bahrain, Hong Kong, Jersey, Luxembourg, Panama and Singapore. The distinction between major international financial centres, such as London, and offshore centres has always been arbitrary to some extent and has been further blurred by the international deregulation of the 1980s. London, for example, has offered similar advantages for Euromarket business, in terms of freedom from reserve requirements and other banking and securities regulations and a favourable tax regime, as those offered by Luxembourg. It has, consequently, become the main centre for Euromarket business. Through the 'big bang' the UK authorities have attempted to promote London as a major centre for international equity trading in the emerging global equity market. The new investor protection regulations to be introduced in the UK in 1987 [3] have been adapted in the light of lobbying from major international banks and securities houses to ensure that the new regulatory regime, which will apply to the previously unregulated London based Eurobond market, does not drive business offshore. In response to these efforts to promote London as the major international financial centre in the European time zone competitive liberalisation has been introduced in a number of other European centres. [4] Deregulation has also been permitted in

Japan and the US. [5] The US authorities sanctioned the opening of International Banking Facilities (IBFs), which are mainly based in New York, in 1981 [6] in an effort to win back some business from the Euromarkets and from offshore centres closer to home, particularly the Bahamas and the Cayman Islands. They have been markedly successful. Japan followed suit by opening similar offshore facilities, which are expected to be mainly based in Tokyo, in December 1986. [7] It is too early to judge the potential of the last, which retains many of the local restrictions and is still subject to a relatively unfavourable tax regime, but in 1986 London was the world's largest offshore market by far. It had outstandings of $750bn and was followed by New York's IBFs, which had $260bn. Tokyo's offshore facilities will have to compete with the well established centres in Hong Kong and Singapore and the other nascent centres in the area, such as Taiwan and Sydney. The future prospects of established centres such as Hong Kong and Singapore, threatened by Tokyo, and the Bahamas and Cayman Islands, threatened by the IBFs in New York, have, therefore, come under close scrutiny. In this chapter the banking systems of Hong Kong and Singapore will first be outlined and then their future prospects will be discussed.

Offshore centres may be classified as 'paper' or 'functional'. Paper centres, such as the Bahamas, act as locations of record with little or no banking activities being carried out. Functional centres are those in which deposit taking or final lending is actually carried out. The major functional centres have been caught up in the process of securitisation in which has led to a confluence of banking and capital markets in the 1980s. Thus, although traditionally called offshore banking centres they, are now more accurately called offshore financial centres. The functional centres serve as important links between the Eurocurrency and Eurodollar markets and other markets such as the Asian dollar and yen markets and help to channel funds from major financial centres to final borrowers. Paper centres are mainly used by international banks to minimise taxes and other levies and are sometimes called tax havens. Regardless of their type, most offshore centres do not require full compliance with local capital requirements, which must be held in the form of onshore assets. They also generally charge low licence fees, allow easy access, especially for large international banks, and provide for favourable fiscal treatment, such as exemption from withholding and turnover taxes and reduced corporate and other business taxes. Reserve requirements are rarely imposed. Many of them have advantageous geographical positions by virtue of their proximity to important loan outlets and deposit sources. Singapore is, for example, situated near the ASEAN countries. Hong Kong is also well situated in relation to the South-East Asian countries and China and Bahrain is an offshore base for petro-dollar transactions with the Gulf States. Their fortunes are to some extent tied to those of the regions they serve. Bahrain, for example, has not enjoyed such a rapid business growth in the 1980s as oil prices have fallen and some of the Gulf States have gone from surplus to deficit whilst others have had to draw down past surpluses to maintain growth.

The process of international deregulation is likely to be particularly damaging to paper centres. Functional centres generate profits for international banks through business opportunities usually available by virtue of geographic location. These profits do not depend solely on avoidance of taxes and levies elsewhere. Deregulation can, however, alter the relative attractiveness of centres serving similar areas. Because of their added attractions, functional centres can often impose profits taxes on offshore banks. Further, once established as a functional offshore centre, and having attracted a critical mass of banks, a centre's attractiveness to other banks may increase automatically. Take-off is probably achieved by the establishment of a sufficient number of banks because external economies are generated by the establishment of a financial infrastructure capable of serving additional banks at declining costs. The banks require accounting, legal, money broking, and communications services and will be attracted to centres where such services are known to be available. To establish the financial infrastructure from scratch is expensive and countries sponsoring new centres, especially mini-states, must weigh the costs against the potential benefits. The major benefit is likely to be derived from the expenditures of the banks and their staff which provide opportunities for local service industries, retailers, and producers of consumer goods. The benefit will probably be more closely related to the number of banks and the size of their staff than the volume of business routed through the centre, although this depends on the tax regime. Countries with smaller economies are likely to gain proportionately more from offshore centres. Apart from infrastructural costs, additional regulatory costs may be incurred. Some countries have also expressed concern that offshore flows of funds might impair domestic monetary control and swamp the domestic banking and financial system. In many centres, especially the smaller ones, international banks are prohibited from participating in onshore banking business. By establishing special facilities, Japan and the US have tried to ensure that domestic monetary control is unaffected. Only time will tell whether this is realistic. Increasingly freer money and capital flows seem likely to undermine the attempts of governments to control the growth money aggregates, which have anyway been distorted by the financial liberalisation and innovation [8] witnessed in the 1980s.

The imposition of charges and taxes on the international banks can enable the local authorities to appropriate some of the profits they make. This must be weighed against the loss of potential benefits from business diverted and banks discouraged from establishing. Their ability to impose levies and taxes depends on the magnitude of the benefit derived by the banks and competition from other centres. Paper centres have not generally been able to impose levies whilst many functional centres have done so. In the case of functional centres their ability to impose levies depends particularly on the competition from other centres serving a similar region.

Even where direct benefits are not substantial, indirect benefits may be derived, such as: improved access to international capital markets; a more efficient domestic financial system by virtue of exposure to competition from and the practices of the offshore banks; a cadre of locally trained staff; and an improved financial infrastructure. These factors may contribute to the faster growth of the domestic economy. Again such benefits accrue mainly to functional centres. On the negative side it may be difficult to prevent competition with the domestic banking system, the growth of which could be inhibited. The potential for tax avoidance and capital flight is also increased.

Paper centres are cheaper to establish than functional centres because the latter require a greater investment in financial infrastructure. They are also probably less beneficial and more sensitive to competition from other centres, as the establishment of IBFs in the US has demonstrated. The deregulation and improvement in international communications in the 1980s, which have made it easier to either do without paper or to route it through a smaller number of centres, is likely to cause a contraction rather than an increase in the number of such centres. There is also probably little scope for establishing new functional centres. The most obvious geographic locations have already been exploited and the established centres must cope with the fact the major financial centres in the emerging global markets, London, Tokyo and New York, all now offer offshore facilities. Further, the liberalisation and deregulation taking place worldwide is eroding the advantages of offshore centres and blurring the distinction between them and ordinary financial centres. This process has gone furthest in London, which is now the major centre in the existing and emerging global markets. It enjoys this position despite the fact that its host country has a smaller economy than many of the other major international centres, especially Tokyo and New York. Its position may be rivalled by the financial centres in the stronger European economies, such as Paris and, more likely, Frankfurt, in the future but until then the UK expects to enjoy the substantial benefit of the sizeable invisible earnings generated by London based international financial institutions.

6.2 Banking in Hong Kong

The banking system operates without a central bank and all domestic banks are privately owned. It consists of licensed banks and licensed and registered deposit taking companies (DTCs), which are merchant banks and finance companies. There are few specialist banks, such as industrial, mortgage or trust banks, or savings banks. Savings deposits are taken by licensed commercial banks only. At the heart of the system are two note issuing banks, the Hong Kong and Shanghai Banking Corporation (HKSBC) and the British owned Chartered Bank, which is part of the Standard Chartered Group. The Bank of China (BoC) and its twelve 'sister' banks have become increasingly influential in the mid 1980s and have emerged as a third major force in domestic banking. This followed the reorganisation of the Chinese banking system in 1983 which resulted in the separation of central banking functions, which were vested in the Peoples Bank of China, from commercial banking operation, which were vested in the BoC, and other industrial and development banking functions, which were vested in other banking institutions. The BoC and its 'sister' banks have long been present in China but their activity has increased considerably latterly and they were taking 20% of domestic deposits by 1986. Alongside these banks there are numerous foreign banks and DTCs, including most of the major international banks, and a number of small, often family owned, domestic and local S.E.Asian banks. In 1986 there were approximately 150 licensed banks and over 340 DTCs, as well as a number of foreign bank representative offices.

The licensed commercial banks have grown rapidly in terms of number, especially since the lifting of a moratorium on bank and DTC licences in 1981, largely due to the influx of foreign banks. The foreign banks were initially attracted by the active syndicated loan market but, with the trend international towards securitisation following the Mexican debt crisis in 1982, they have turned their attention increasingly to the capital markets. They are active in the interbank market and they engage in trust banking and safe deposit business, trade finance, and corporate lending. The BoC and its 'sister' banks initially specialised in financing trade between Hong Kong and China and China's substantial, especially property, investments in the colony but they have started to diversify their activities. The smaller local banks were mainly involved in property loans and stock market finance but have also begun to diversify. This trend had started prior to the property and stock market slump in 1984. Foreign acquisition of some of their equity and property interests and participation in their management has encouraged further diversification. They have remained a troubled sector, along with the smaller DTCs, in the post crisis period and as a result the colony is regarded as overbanked.

The HKSBC dominates the sector. It is amongst the top twenty international banks and the largest bank in Hong Kong. It owns 61% of Hang Seng Bank, which is the second largest bank in the territory.It is trying to develop itself into a global institution. In 1981 it bought a 51% stake in Marine Midland, which was the thirteenth largest US bank, for example. It feels that it is under-represented in Europe and has sought to remedy this deficiency by purchasing one or more European banks. Its attempt to buy the Royal Bank of Scotland in 1982 was, however, frustrated following a UK Monopolies Commission investigation. The deficiency remains for the present. HKSBC acts as a quasi-central bank and owns a British bank, the Mercantile bank, and the largest local bank, the Hang Seng Bank. Its wholly owned finance company also has a banking licence. Because of lack of disclosure it is not possible, from its global consolidate accounts, to determine the exact size of its local operations. Along with its subsidiaries, however, it is reckoned to control between 50% and 65% of the colony's assets and deposits.

The licensed banks have a cartel agreement which determines the maximum deposit rates, each group may offer on short term, one year or less, time deposits of less than HK$ 500,000. The Hong Kong Association of Banks (HKAB) is, however, under a statutory obligation to consult the government on these interest rates. The future of this arrangement was called into question when the HK$ was pegged to the US$ following the exchange rate crisis in 1983 and will be discussed further below. Lending rates are not fixed by the cartel.

Like licensed banks, the DTCs generally depend on their capital resources and deposits as their principal sources of funds and the foreign institutions raise little equity on the stock market. Debenture issues have been rare in the past, although note and bond finance has been increasing as the process of securitisation has gathered pace. They are excluded from the retail banking market and can only attract short term and time deposits on the wholesale market. They are not subject to the licensed banks interest rate agreement and can often offer more attractive rates. There are three main types of DTCs : merchant banks, finance companies owned by the licensed banks, and other finance companies. Some of the merchant banks are also subsidiaries of, or joint ventures between, licensed banks. The DTCs related to licensed banks tend to undertake complementary business. They do not compete directly with licensed banks, and are usually funded by them. The independent finance companies tend to have limited capital bases and capital resources and have caused the most concern to the regulators. In 1981 a new licensing system was introduced, over a two year period ending in mid 1983, in an effort to improve government control over credit creation and monetary growth. A three-tier regulatory system covering banks, licensed DTCs and registered DTCs was introduced. The licensed DTCs created in 1981 were allowed to take deposits of any maturity but only for sums in excess of HK$500,000, whereas the registered DTCs' deposit taking was restricted to sums of over HK$500,000 with maturities of three months or more. The limits have subsequently been adjusted.

The merchant banks are more specialised than the commercial banks. They engage primarily in underwriting, corporate advice, project finance, offshore currency loans, investment advice and long term fixed deposits. Finance companies owned by commercial banks are principally involved in hire purchase credit, mortgage loans, leasing, factoring and long term deposits. Other finance companies accept fixed deposits and mainly undertake hire purchase business or provide stock market and property finance. They generally confine themselves to local lending operations. The large merchant banks are active in arranging project finance for local companies and syndicating offshore currency loans for large scale projects both inside and outside the colony. Latterly their underwriting skills have been exploited as the process of securitisation has gathered pace. The emergence of DTCs is relatively recent. It gathered pace in the 1970s. The merchant banks dominate the sector.

Despite the absence of a central bank or any other government owned specialised banking institution there are a few official and semi official financial institutions engaged in lending activities. The Development Loan Fund is the most important. It is financed mainly by transfers from the government's fiscal revenue and through its own operations. The resources are used to finance social and economic development projects of a self liquidating nature, such as low cost public housing schemes. There is also a Lotteries Fund, which provides grants and loans to finance social welfare services, a Home Ownership Fund, established in 1977 to finance the construction of flats for sale to families within a specified income range, and the Hong Kong Building and Loan Agency Limited. The latter was founded in 1964 by the government in conjunction with the Commonwealth Development Corporation and four licensed banks. It aims to provide mortgage finance at reasonable rates to prospective home owners in middle income groups. Finally, the Hong Kong Credit Insurance Corporation was established in 1966 to provide exporters with protection of risk against non payment. Its capital is provided by the government, which underwrites its liabilities.

The government does not issue Treasury bills and specialised discount market and money market institutions, such as discount and accepting houses, [9] do not exist. This is attributed to the government's traditionally conservative fiscal policy and the absence of a central bank to rediscount eligible short term paper. Companies in Hong Kong did not issue promissory notes or other short term negotiable instruments until the mid 1980s when a commercial paper market emerged. Further, bills of exchange have generally been used to finance international trade, and they are not independently negotiable, except through the banks. Despite these limitations there is a fairly active interbank market in which the licensed banks, merchant banks, and larger DTCs participate. The lenders tend to be the major banks and the borrowers are normally foreign banks and DTCs which lack a substantial local deposit base. The business consists of overnight money, call money and short term money. Certificates of deposits were introduced in the mid 1980s. Lenders and borrowers transact business through the intermediation of authorised brokers.

There is an active foreign exchange market. Most licensed banks, merchant banks and large finance companies offer foreign exchange services. There are also a number of authorised foreign exchange dealers and money brokers. Swap facilities are well developed.

The bond market was dormant until the mid 1970s when a rare government bond issue was heavily over subscribed, largely due to the banks' interest in it. In the latter half of the 1980s bonds and convertible debentures were issued, in HK and US dollars, by first class local corporations such as the Mass Transit Railway Corporation. Some foreign bonds, such as European Investment Bank bonds, were also issued in this period but the market remained small until the post 1982 securitisation period. An active secondary market was also absent until 1983 because government bonds qualified as liquid assets under the Banking Ordinance and were, therefore, likely to be held by banks to maturity. Until 1985, when they were merged, there were four stock exchanges. The Hong Kong Stock Exchange had the longest history but the Far East Exchange had the largest turnover. The merger followed the 1981 Stock Exchange Unification Ordinance. All members of the four existing exchanges were invited to apply for membership of the new unified exchange company, the Stock Exchange of Hong Kong Ltd. Stockbrokers, dealers and investment advisors are required to register with the Securities Commission, which is responsible for ensuring compliance with the Securities Ordinance and the Protection of Investors (POI) Ordinance. The Securities Ordinance included regulations pertaining to registration and trading practices and provided for the establishment of a Stock Exchange Compensation Fund and the elimination of improper trading practices. The POI Ordinance aims to prohibit the use of fraudulent or reckless means to induce investors to buy or sell securities and regulates the issue of prospectuses. By 1981 it had become evident that the Securities Commission was not pursuing its supervisory role sufficiently rigorously. A series of bad practices and frauds had come to light. Sir Robert Fell, a high ranking official of the London Stock Exchange Council, was invited to take over as temporary Securities Commissioner to review the supervisory arrangements. He decided to stay to oversee the introduction of new arrangements, based on greater disclosure and more self-regulation, and the preparations for the merger. In December 1984 he moved over to the job of Banking Commissioner to oversee the reform of banking regulations discussed below.

Following extensive consultation with the securities industry, in March 1984 the Securities Commission recommended, to the Financial Secretary, the removal of the provisions forbidding the new exchange company to allow corporations, directors and employees of banks and DTCs, and practising solicitors and accountants, to become members. It also recommended that the formation of partnerships between members and non-members should be permitted. These proposals mirrored developments in London to some extent and were approved by the Executive Council in July 1984 with implementing legislation being passed in 1985.

Hong Kong has developed rapidly, particularly since 1970, as a financial centre for the Asian-Pacific region. The number of banking and near banking institutions grew rapidly as did the volume of offshore loans. It became the major centre for syndicating loans in the region and attracted sizeable overseas deposits. In addition there is a large congregation of nonbank financial institutions, including insurance companies, investment and brokerage houses, moneybrokers, unit trusts and mutual funds. As a consequence it is an important insurance centre. The stock exchange has long traded international shares for a long time and latterly the bond market has attracted sizeable international interest as the centre has adapted to changing trends in banking. It also has one of the four largest gold markets and a commodities exchange was opened in 1977. The government has not adopted a direct sponsoring role. It aims to provide the general framework and infrastructure only. Hong Kong's development has, therefore, relied on the spontaneous initiatives of the private sector.

This is in contrast with Singapore where the authorities have adopted a more active developmental role. Its attractions lie in its favourable geographic location, good financial infrastructure, including telecommunications, good air and sea links, low tax rates and simple tax structure, absence of exchange controls inhibiting flows of funds into and out of the centre, liberal policy towards the financial sector, strong economy, social and political stability and good urban facilities. Corporation tax and taxes on financial transactions and earning are low and the government has been able to raise the latter without a serious loss of business.

It has a substantial export oriented manufacturing sector which is currently diversifying. Textiles and plastics are being replaced by high-tech products. It exports world wide but its largest market is the US. It also has substantial entrepot trade because of its excellent shipping and air links and an increasing proportion of its re-exports are coming from China. The financial sector has been growing in importance but accounts for under 10% of GDP. Its favourable geographic location is a result of its traditionally strong links with S.E.Asia, its proximity to China, which is seen as a major market of the future and its ability to bridge the time gap between Japan and Europe.

The currency was pegged to the dollar in 1983. The government established an Exchange Fund (EF) in 1935 to back the bank note issue. Notes are issued by the HKSBC and Chartered Bank against their holdings of certificates of indebtedness, which are non interest bearing liabilities of the EF and are issued and redeemed as the amount of notes in circulation rises and falls. In 1976 the EF's role was expanded by the addition of the assets of the Coinage Security Fund, which held the backing for coins issued by the government and the bulk of the foreign currency assets previously held in the government's General Revenue Account (GRA). It was further expanded in 1978 when the government began to transfer the surplus HK$ balances of its GRA to the EF against the issue of interest bearing debt certificates, as had been done with the previous transfers. The bulk of the government's financial assets are now held in the EF which consists mainly of bank deposits in certain foreign currencies and the HK$ and various foreign currency denominated interest bearing instruments. The EF is managed by the Monetary Affairs Department under the direction of the Financial Secretary, who is advised by a committee comprising members of the banking community. The EF's statutory role is defined in the Exchange Fund Ordinance to be that of influencing the exchange value of the HK$.

Apart from a small fiduciary issue guaranteed by the government, notes are issued by the two note issuing banks against holdings of EF certificates of indebtedness. Prior to 1972, when the HK$ was pegged to sterling, certificates of indebtedness were issued and redeemed in sterling at a fixed exchange rate. A sterling currency board system was, therefore, in operation. During the floating exchange rate period, June 23 1972 to October 15 1983, issues and redemptions were made in HK$. Following the October 1983 exchange rate crisis the HK$ was pegged to the US$ [10] and since then certificates of indebtedness have been issued and redeemed against US dollars. The EF bears the cost of maintaining the note issue, apart from that relating to the fiduciary issue, and net profits of note issue accrue to it. The US$ linked exchange rate system restored stability to the exchange value of the HK$. It is, therefore, likely to be retained although the decline in the dollar, especially in 1986, has led to an effective devaluation of the HK$ with respect to other major currencies. This has boosted exports whilst not allowing full benefit to be derived on the import side because most commodities are traded in dollars. An adjustment of the peg may, therefore, be considered in the future especially as the US, its major trading partner, continues to run a sizeable trade deficit with the territory. Under the linked exchange rate system it has become more important to allow flexible responses in the interest rate to protect the exchange rate. With the dollar falling, interest rates have been allowed to fall and this has increased the attractiveness of Hong Kong as a capital raising centre. The cartel arrangement has not yet come under pressure, but to survive it will have to show itself to be sufficiently responsive to the exchange rate pressures which many feel will eventually bring about its demise or significantly reduce its effectiveness.

Banks and DTCs are covered by separate ordinances. Banking operations are governed by the Banking Ordinance (BO) of 1964 which was significantly amended in 1967. It vests responsibility for the general supervision of the banking system and for periodical investigations into the affairs of banks in the Commissioner of Banking, a full time civil servant appointed by the Government of Hong Kong. The Bank Advisory Committee advises the Governor on matters relating to the Banking Ordinance and banking in general. It consists of the Financial Secretary, who acts as chairman, the Secretary for Monetary Affairs, the Commissioner of Banking and four to twelve other members, usually bankers, appointed by the Governor. The BO defines banking business as either or both of the following: receiving funds from the general public, in the form of current, deposit and savings or other accounts repayable on demand, with maturities up to three months; paying or collecting cheques drawn by or paid in by customers. No banking business may be transacted in Hong Kong with companies not holding a valid licence issued by the Governor in Council. Licensed DTCs are excepted in that they may take short term deposits subject to the requirements of the DTC Ordinance. Applications for licences are made via the Commissioner who forwards the applications with his advice to the Governor. Applicants incorporated in Hong Kong must meet minimum paid up share capital requirements. Foreign banks must satisfy three main criteria : a minimum total asset requirement; acceptable reciprocity for Hong Kong banks; and incorporation in a country where the monetary authorities exercise effective prudential supervision and have no objection to the establishment of a branch in Hong Kong. Successful applicants are required to join the Hong Kong Association of Banks (HKAB) and permitted to operate only one branch in Hong Kong. The minimum asset requirement is reviewed annually. In practice, since 1981, indigenous applications for banking licences are only considered from locally owned DTCs which satisfy three main criteria : they must be limited companies incorporated in Hong Kong which are not subsidiaries of licensed banks and be able to meet a minimum paid up capital requirement; they must have been in the business of taking deposits from and granting loans to the public for 10 years and registered under the Companies Ordinance since it was enacted in 1976; and they must have deposits from the public, net of those from banks and other DTCs, and total assets of minimum prescribed levels. If successful they must become members of the HKAB. The size requirements are reviewed annually.

All licensed banks incorporated in Hong Kong must, in accordance with the Banking Ordinance, meet prescribed minimum capital and liquidity requirements. There are also restrictions designed to prevent overcommitment to single customers, overexposure to particular types of business and imprudent trading risks. An annual licence fee is payable. The establishment of branches or overseas representative offices requires the Commissioner's approval and there are additional annual fees for each local branch, overseas branch, and overseas representative office.

Annual financial statements have to be audited in compliance with the Companies Ordinance, which specifically exempts banks from a number of disclosure requirements. They nevertheless have to publish audited annual balance sheets. These arrangements were revised in 1986 and will be discussed further below. Banks incorporated outside Hong Kong can be exempted from auditing and publication of financial statements if the Commissioner is satisfied that the financial statements of the bank are audited in the country of incorporation. If such an exemption is granted to a foreign bank, it is only required to submit its full financial statements to the Commissioner and is, therefore, not required to publish audited financial statements of the Hong Kong branch separately.

All banks are required to submit regular returns to the Commissioner who has a duty to maintain secrecy. Monthly returns, which are also confidential, are also made under the Monetary Statistics Ordinance to the Secretary of Monetary Affairs.

Deposit taking by entities other than licensed banks is governed by the Deposit-taking Companies Ordinance, which was enacted in 1976 and significantly amended in 1981. The responsibility for the general supervision of DTCs is vested in the Commissioner of Deposit-taking Companies who is also the Commissioner of Banking. The Deposit-taking Companies Advisory Committee advises the Governor on matters relating to the DTC Ordinance and consists of the Financial Secretary, who acts as chairman, the Secretary for Monetary Affairs and the Commissioner of DTCs and four to ten others appointed by the Governor. Licensed banks are exempted from the provisions of the DTC Ordinance and so are deposits taken by insurance companies; registered dealers in securities; and employers, from employees. DTCs are divided into two categories: registered and licensed. Registered DTCs have much lower minimum deposits than licensed DTCs and short term deposits may be taken by licensed DTCs but not by registered DTCs. Applications to become licensed DTCs may only be made by adequately capitalised registered DTCs and are addressed to the Financial Secretary.

Liquidity requirements are imposed on all DTCs and they are subject to other restrictions, like the banks, designed to prevent over-exposure. There are annual fees for all DTCs and they are required to seek approval from the Commissioner prior to opening branches or representative offices, on which annual fees are payable.

DTCs must submit annual reports to the Commissioner and, if incorporated in Hong Kong, their financial statements must be audited in compliance with the provisions of the Companies Ordinance, which does not grant the exemption from disclosure requirements to DTCs that it does to banks. Companies incorporated outside Hong Kong may prepare financial statements in accordance with the law of the country of incorporation. Regular returns must be made to the Commissioner and monthly returns to the Secretary for Monetary Affairs, both of whom have a duty to maintain secrecy. These arrangements were also revised in 1986, see below.

The Commissioner is, therefore, the main supervisory authority. Other functions often associated with a central bank are undertaken by the two major commercial banks HKSBC and Chartered, although primarily by the former. Both these banks issue notes but the HKSBC issues the vast majority. The HKSBC also acts as banker to the government, runs the clearing house and acts as banker to the other banks. The clearing house of the HKAB sorts and clears the cheques drawn on the member banks and processes direct debits and credits and other transactions for them. The payments' system will be discussed further below. All licensed banks in Hong Kong are members of the HKAB. It determines the interest paid on deposits by member banks. DTCs are not bound by the agreement. The HKAB actively promotes the interests of licensed banks and played a part in the enactment of the DTC ordinance which seeks to regulate the activities of secondary banks.

Following the stock market and property market price falls in 1983 [11] a number of local, family owned, banks and DTCs have had difficulties. The first major casualty was the Hang Lung bank in September 1983. It had to be bailed out by the government, at considerable cost, using the Exchange Fund. A number of local DTCs subsequently collapsed. Criticism of the Banking and DTC Commissions mounted and confidence in the effectiveness of the supervision of the Territory's banking sector was undermined. At the end of 1984 Sir Robert Fell was appointed as Banking Commissioner to reform the supervisory mechanism in the light of a report published in April by a Bank of England team which had been invited to review the situation. The report found that the supervisors had become preoccupied with technical breaches of the Banking and DTC Ordinances and were paying insufficient attention to depositor protection. In 1985 new regulatory proposals were published and banks and DTCs were invited to comment. The licensed banks, through the HKAB, opposed many of the proposals, which included greater disclosure and the establishment of a deposit protection scheme. Their resistance was weakened considerably by crises at five other local banks in 1985, starting in mid 1985 with the government rescue of the Overseas Trust Bank (OTB) and its subsidiary, the Hong Kong Investment and Commercial bank. Later the San Hung Kai and Wing On banks had to be defended. To prevent a spread of the OTB crisis to other banks, the HKSBC and the BoC joined forces to guarantee the liquidity of the Ka Wah bank. This followed an invitation by the Ka Wah for a team of bankers to inspect its books in the wake of rumours about its liquidity. It transpired later that the government had also extended a credit line from the Exchange Fund.

The involvement of the BoC was a new departure and it was interpreted as a demonstration of China's commitment to Hong Kong as a financial centre. The government's reticence to announce its support, following the costly rescues of Hong Kong and OTB, showed that it was sensitive to growing unease about the use of the Exchange Fund to support the banking system. The failures of the banks and additional DTCs demonstrated that the territory was probably overbanked. Regulatory reform was required to protect depositors whilst allowing a thinning down of the domestic banking sector without frequent recourse to the Exchange Fund or risking crisis through knock on effects to other banks. Towards these ends greater disclosure seemed to be required, to avoid destabilising speculation, regulations on exposure needed to be tightened and a protection fund seemed to be required, to discourage depositors from withdrawing funds from troubled banks. In the absence of a central bank and a deposit protection fund, the government, through the Exchange Fund, and the major local banks had been forced to provide lender of last resort cover.

The problems amongst local banks and DTCs continued in 1986, despite a recovery of property and stock market prices. In March 1986 the Union Bank was bailed out and put under new management, confirming the weakness of small family owned banks not sheltered by big banks. It was the 26th largest of the 35 local banks and had twelve branches. Its troubles had resulted from problem overseas loans. The government again extended a line of credit from the Exchange Fund. By that time two of the previous problem banks, Wing On and Ka Wah, had been absorbed into larger companies. Wing On had been rescued by the Hang Seng bank and Ka Wah, which had also suffered from bad and doubtful debts, had been acquired by Citic, a Peking based company.

The problems did not end there, however, because the government assumed control of the Hang Nin Bank, a small family owned retail bank with four branches that had a frail liquidity position, in September 1986. It was much smaller than previously troubled banks and again the government extended a credit line from the Exchange Fund whilst the Chartered Bank agreed to manage it on the government's behalf so that it could continue to meet its obligations until alternative arrangements could be made. Most of its loans were advanced inside Hong Kong. There appeared to be no common cause of the failures. In some cases it was bad management. In others there was clear evidence of fraud and criminal activity. And some had suffered from bad and doubtful debts, especially abroad. The problems amongst the small family banks and local DTCs were, however, indicative of the weakness of such institutions which are faced with competition from larger banks, and institutions sponsored by them, at a time when local demand for their services had declined due to rising corporate liquidity and growing opportunities for fund raising through the capital markets rather than the banking system.

The controversy over the use of the Exchange Fund for local bank rescues erupted in April 1986 when it became known that the government had guaranteed the contingent liabilities of Ka Wah as part of the rescue agreement. Given past drawings and the knowledge that a number of other banks were on the problem list, there was growing public unease and demands for greater public consultation on the use of the secret fund. In 1986 the outgoing Financial Secretary, Sir John Bembridge, however, defended the use of the fund, which is equivalent to the national reserves of an independent country, for bank rescues. The money, he argued, had been used for public benefit; to protect depositors and maintain confidence in the territory's banks. Further, even under the worst possible outcome of all commitments being drawn, only the equivalent of the Fund's growth over the last three years would have been used up. He ruled out consultation on the grounds that it would prejudice secrecy, fuel speculation, and cause delays when rapid action was needed. In the absence of a central bank, his position was clearly the correct one but the existence of a deposit protection fund would have reduced the pressure to use the Exchange Fund for lender of last resort purposes. The new regulatory and supervisory apparatus discussed below should also help; by allowing the authorities to identify problem banks at an earlier stage and preventing problems arising through over exposure and bad management.

In April 1985 Sir Robert Fell,in an address to the Deposit Takers' Association, which had been formed in 1984 in response to government encouragement for the establishment of a representative body for the DTCs akin to the HKAB, called for wider discretion and more flexible regulatory powers as part of a major regulatory reform package. This was his first public announcement about the forthcoming revision of the regulations and followed two months of confidential consultations with bankers. He announced that the diverse activities of the territory's 140 banks and 350 DTCs made it essential for the Commission to impose separate capital adequacy and liquidity ratios for various types of business to replace the generally applicable set of requirements that prevailed at the time. He had apparently been considering requiring banks to reveal their hidden reserves but instead proposed that in future such reserves should be treated in a similar way to make trends in the reserves clearer. He announced that when the consultations with the banks were concluded and the written submissions invited from them had been received a Banking Ordinance, covering banks and DTCs, would be drafted over the summer with a view to placing them before the Legislative Council in Autumn 1985.

The government's hand was strengthened in June 1985, following its rescue of one of the territory's largest locally incorporated banks, the OTB. Sir John Bembridge pointed out that freedom and secrecy had their price and questioned whether the community was paying too high a price for maintaining these supposed advantages to Hong Kong as a financial centre. Because of the bank secrecy provisions, which were akin to those in Switzerland, [12] and the high degree of freedom to move funds into and out of the centre, Hong Kong had become a home for 'flight capital' placed by the rich overseas Chinese minorities of Indonesia, Malaysia, Thailand and the Philippines. Both Hang Lung and OTB had been recipients of such funds and both had links with rich families living elsewhere in S.E.Asia. The improvements in the bank examination system introduced by Sir Robert Fell enabled the Commission to identify OTB's problems at an early stage and to report to Sir John Bembridge, the Financial Secretary, when misappropriation of funds was discovered in May 1986. Consequently the government was ready to act in June 1986. This demonstrated that whilst some success had been achieved in bringing examination procedures to a level of thoroughness and toughness comparable to anywhere in the world action was needed to ensure that no more rotten apples could find their way into the banking barrel. The government was consequently able to push through some of its more controversial proposals for improved regulation and supervision more easily.

The Commission remained determined to introduce a deposit insurance scheme and its case was clearly strengthened by the OTB affair and public concern about the use of the Exchange Fund. The larger banks were strongly opposed to the establishment of a deposit insurance fund because they would have to provide a large proportion of its resources and would be the most unlikely to have to draw on it. In the absence of an insurance scheme, as subsequent events showed, the government would have to continue to use the Exchange Fund despite the fact that it had declared the rescue of Hang Lung to be a one off affair. It was clearly embarrassed by the OTB and subsequent affairs which had forced it to commit further fund resources. Repeated use of the Exchange Fund would encourage bad practices by allowing smaller banks to conduct business on the assumption that they would be bailed out. A classic lender of last resort problem, known as the Bagehot problem [13] would be created. At the time, to counter this possibility, the government ruled out a third rescue. It seemed to have honoured this commitment when Ka Wah was supported by the BoC and HKSBC instead. The government was also acutely aware that over-reaction and the imposition of extremely tight regulation and reduced secrecy might encourage business to move offshore. Its concerns in this direction were, however, eased by the knowledge that the Monetary Authority of Singapore and the Japanese authorities administer relatively strict regulatory and supervisory regimes.

The OTB's collapse weakened the resistance of the banking community to reforms concerning liquidity and capital adequacy, and greater disclosure and a closer contact between auditors and supervisors. The wider effects of the crisis would have been significantly reduced if the proposed reforms had been in place. The bigger banks were forced instead to fight a rearguard action against the proposed deposit insurance scheme. The OTB collapse caused a 'flight to quality' which benefited the bigger banks. The larger banks became less willing to extend interbank credit lines to small family owned banks whose soundness was called into question and whose profitability will be worse under stricter liquidity and capital requirements. Ka Wah's liquidity crisis can be seen in this light. Stricter supervision might also discourage 'flight capital' from Chinese families living overseas and weaken the smaller banks and DTCs further. Closer scrutiny of these institutions also revealed that they were relatively heavily exposed to the troubled electronics, textiles, and shipping sectors and made it more difficult for the government to find buyers for the Hang Lung bank, which had been nursed back to health. The supposed existence of substantial hidden reserves meant that the reasonable profit growth declared by the smaller banks were met with a doubtful response and did nothing to bring bank shares out of the doldrums. Overall loan demand remained low, although there was an increased demand for mortgages as interest rates fell.

In November 1985 outline proposals for reforming the regulatory system were submitted to the Executive Council. The proposed system would: require banks to disclose to the Banking Commission the identity of anonymous nominee shareholders; make DTCs the subject of the Banking Ordinance; and introduce new capital adequacy and liquidity requirements. The Banking Commissioner would have extended powers and there would be closer supervision and control of banks. Additionally, a representative of the Hong Kong Society of Accountants would have a seat on the Banking Advisory Committee as part of the attempt to achieve greater coordination between bank auditors and the supervisory authorities. The controversial issues, such as the establishment of a deposit insurance scheme and the ending of the three tier authorisation system, involving licensed banks and DTCs and registered DTCs, were sidestepped for the time being to enable the proposed reforms to be approved more speedily. Over the following Christmas holiday period the family controlled Wing On bank was rescued by the much larger Hang Seng Bank and, in January 1986, a large body of local bankers were attempting to keep the Low family's Ka Wah bank alive. Although the major international banks were unaffected, there was renewed concern that damage to the reputation of the territory's banking community might threaten its position as Asia's largest international banking centre. There was renewed pressure to bring the regulatory system into line with international practices. Ka Wah in particular had suffered from the 'flight to quality' because it was heavily reliant on interbank credit lines, as the substantial and unquantified support provided by HKSBC and BoC in July 1985 had indicated. Its problems confirmed the plight of the remaining thirteen family owned local banks and local DTCs. With demand remaining sluggish following the 1982 collapse of the property and stock markets, despite the subsequent recovery, and considerable competition for business, the colony was overbanked and a thinning down process had to be facilitated with as little pain as possible. By January 1986 only six of the thirteen family owned local banks were operating without the shelter of a 'big brother' and of the four not actively seeking shelter, one was large and professionally managed and three were too small or too liquid to worry about.

The long awaited Banking Bill emerged in March 1986. It contained the provisions that had been widely signalled as the government had sought public support for more radical proposals. The Bill was passed in July and became effective at the beginning of September. A particular target of the new rules was excessive exposure to single customers. Loans to one customer were limited to 25% of capital and reserves and loans exceeding 10% must be reported to the Banking Commission. To achieve better management control, it was required that there should be : disclosure of ownership of more than 10% of a bank; approval by Commission of all directors and company secretaries; approval for more than 50% control to be exercised over an institution; and approval for lending to the institution's holding company against the security of that company's shares. Regulation was extended to DTCs and a new capital requirement of 5% of risk assets, as defined by the Commission, is to be introduced over a two year period. The Commision has discretionary powers to adjust the rrequirement. The capital regulations parallelled initiatives in other major banking centres by adopting the risk-asset ratio approach. Off balance sheet risks, for example, were given a risk weighting of 50% of that applied to loans. Liquidity ratios were also established by the legislation. The tougher capital and liquidity requirements were expected to encourage the larger banks to raise more capital whilst forcing the voluntary closure of some of the smaller banks and a further decline in the number of DTCs.

It took only eight days for the new Banking Ordinance to prove its worth. The government had to take control of the Hang Nin Bank, the 29th largest of the 35 locally incorporated banks. Despite the fact that Hang Nin had already found a buyer, the Banking Commission acted pre-emptively to protect depositors by taking control and providing a credit line from the Exchange Fund. The Commission has been given considerable discretion in its pursuance of supervision. It intends to use it as off balance sheet risks proliferate. The securitisation process has caught on with the domestic corporate sector. It is increasingly forging links with the foreign banks which have the lead in this field.

The issue of the deposit insurance scheme remains shelved for a while but further drawings on the Exchange Fund to protect the local banks, which are finding competition, from both domestic and foreign banks interested in corporate business, tough and need to raise capital to boost their equity ratios and invest in new technology, may revive it. With capital requirements related to risk and regulations concerning exposure and disclosure in place, it would seem possible to introduce a scheme in which premiums were related to size. Under the new regulations the big banks would be less likely to have to provide funds, which would effectively be used to bail out small banks, and risk related premiums would be unnecessary in the light of risk related capital requirements. Because the provision of lender of last resort facilities can be seen as a public service and smaller banks are still more likely to draw on the fund than bigger ones, the big banks' opposition is understandable. Big banks have also opposed the establishment of deposit protection funds in Switzerland and Germany [14] and there have been complaints from the larger US banks about the way the US scheme is operated. [15] Similar problems were encountered in the UK when the Securities and Investments Board proposed the establishment of a central investor protection scheme rather than separate schemes administered by the self regulatory organisations. [16] The Securities Association, in particular, complained that it would be required to make a disproportionately large contribution to a fund which would be mainly drawn on by other SROs to protect the investors in institutions which they supervised. The solution seems relatively simple in the case of Hong Kong. If the government wants to reduce the use of the Exchange Fund for lender of last resort purposes, in order to protect the public interest, it could make loans to the insurance fund. This would reduce its reliance on the big banks for funding and promote the public good by enhancing depositor protection and underwriting the stability of Hong Kong as a financial centre. Alternatively, it could convert the Banking Commission into a quasi central bank by allowing it to open a discount window, along the lines of the Monetary Authority of Singapore, or vest further central banking powers in the HKSBC by allowing it to manage the protection fund and requiring it to act as a lender of last resort with access, if necessary, to the Exchange Fund.

The payments system in Hong Kong is well developed. In June 1985 a shopping system, called Easy Pay, was launched with 29 participating banks, nearly 40 retailers with 113 outlets and 278 terminals. The test period ended at the beginning of October when many more retailers were anxious to join in. It was the first single nationwide coordinated system shared by all the major banks of a country to be launched in the world. In 1982 HKSBC proposed the development of an automated interbank clearing scheme based on the New York CHIPS system. The HKAB agreed and a team was formed to develop a system called CHATS, Clearing House Automated Transfer System. In 1983 the central computer was purchased along with smaller computers for banks wishing to link into the system. By January 1984 the system was at the test stage and it went live in February 1984, five days before the Clearing House Automated Payments System (CHAPS) in London and without the teething problems experienced by the latter.

CHATS had 55 participating banks by the end of 1985 and accounted for 55% of interbank transfers in the territory. As more compatible computers are acquired its share of the total volume is expected to increase. The central computer had ample capacity for other uses and HKAB began to develop an EFTPOS system as well. It became apparent that for EFTPOS to be successful it would require wide usage. A limited company called EPSCO, [17] which any bank could join, was formed in August 1984 with 29 participating banks, including overseas banks. Any ATM card of the participating banks or any major credit card can be used in the resulting Easy Pay System which was up and running within a year of EPSCO's formation. The HKSBC was given a five year contract, by the consortium of banks, to oversee the establishment and development of Easy Pay and HKAB authorised it as the only EFTPOS system in Hong Kong, eliminating the possibility of overlapping competing systems which had inhibited the development of EFTPOS in other countries. The success of the scheme is attributed to Hong Kong's size and the fact that three successful ATM networks were already in operation so that many customers were used to plastic cards.

The launch of the system was backed by a strong marketing campaign to persuade the retailers that the system had substantial advantages for them. The fact that the service was marketed by a company rather than a group of banks probably eased negotiations with the retailers. Such negotiations have proved troublesome in attempts to introduce EFTPOS systems in other countries. Retailers pay a monthly rental for the telephone link into the system and charges proportional to the size of debit card transactions. No charges, other than the standard transmission fee

:harged by the card issuing companies, are made for credit card transactions and the terminals are provided free of charge. The non retail funds transfer system has also been automated.

In February 1984 an interbank giro system was established by adding EFT to the automated clearing house established eighteen months earlier. It was installed to reduce the number of cheques in circulation by allowing salary and credit and debit transactions to be made automatically. Whilst cheque clearing and retail banking are highly automated, wholesale and corporate banking automation still lags behind developments in Europe and the US.

6.3 Banking in Singapore

Like Hong Kong, Singapore's emergence as a major financial centre of South-East Asia is due to its strategic location and its traditional role as a centre for trade. This led to the establishment of financial institutions to handle short term trade related financial needs as the island developed as an entrepot centre for the region. After achieving independence in 1965 the new administration reformed the industrial and financial structure. A decisive factor in its development as a banking centre was the introduction of tax legislation in 1968 to enable Singapore to become the centre of the Asian currency market. From 1970 onwards, especially after the incorporation of the Monetary Authority of Singapore (MAS) in 1971, the government introduced additional fiscal incentives, relaxed and finally removed, in 1978, exchange controls and encouraged competition amongst financial institutions. The aim was to nurture the growth of financial sector. It also eased entry requirements to attract foreign banks and encourage the internationalisation of the banking sector.

The MAS, which acts as a quasi central bank was established by Act of Parliament in 1970 to act as banker to, and financial agent of, the government and to promote monetary stability and credit and exchange conditions conducive to the growth of the economy. The Ministry of Finance, which has ultimate authority over matters relating to banking, controls the banking sector through the MAS, which is a wholly government owned and controlled corporation. It commenced operations at the beginning of 1971 and performs all the activities normally associated with a central bank with the exception of currency issue, which remains the responsibility of the Board of Commissioners of Currency (BCC). The BCC issues and redeems notes and coin in exchange for other currencies and gold. It is required to maintain a 100% backing for the Singapore dollar in the form of external assets. The MAS, through its clearing system, acts as intermediary between the BCC and the banks in catering for the latter's currency needs. In May 1981 the Government of Singapore Investment Corporation was established to take over the management of the state's assets from the MAS and the BCC.

The policies of the MAS are governed by a Board of Directors chaired by the First Deputy Prime Minister, who is usually the Finance Minister. Day to day management is in the hands of Managing Director who is assisted by a Deputy and eight departmental managers. It licenses, or authorises, and supervises banks and other financial institutions including finance and insurance companies, merchant banks, discount houses, money brokers, gold dealers and leasing companies. It extended its authority to cover stockbrokers following the 1985 stock market crisis discussed further below. It also acts as banker and lender of last resort to approved financial institutions and provides clearing facilities, for cheques, remittances and inter bank settlements, through the Singapore Clearing House Ltd and the Banking Computer Services Ltd. It formulates and implements monetary and exchange rate policies. A floating exchange rate system has been adopted although the rate is loosely pegged to the currencies of the country's major trading partners by intervention operations. It plays an active development role, promoting the financial system and economic growth in general whilst maintaining the stability of the currency and control over inflation, which stood at -1.9% in June 1986.

There are over 120 licensed banks in Singapore. Three types of licence are issued : full, restricted and offshore banking licences. Most banks are permitted to operate Asian Currency Units (ACUs). Commercial banks granted licences before 1971 are allowed to carry out the full range of banking services approved under the Banking Act, irrespective of whether they are locally incorporated or foreign. Restricted licences were introduced in 1970 to protect the full licence banks from further competition for domestic deposits. By 1973 it was thought that there was a sufficient number of banks to serve the domestic economy and offshore licences were introduced to allow foreign banks to use Singapore as a base for international banking without increasing the competition for domestic business. In August 1983 there were 37 full service banks, of which 13 were domestic, 14 foreign banks with restricted licences and 70 with offshore licences. With the exception of 13 full service banks, all banks had ACUs. Only full service banks are allowed to operate branches and 171 of the 242 branches are operated by the 13 local banks. The local full service banks provide a broad range of retail banking services and the sector is dominated by the 'big four' banks: the Development Bank of Singapore (DBS); the Overseas Chinese Banking Corporation (OCBC); the Overseas Union Bank (OUB); and the United Overseas Bank (UOB). They have large local deposit bases and are very active in providing short term inter bank loans.

Restricted banks are not allowed to compete freely for deposits and rely on inter-bank funds to help to finance their local lending. The deposit taking and lending operations of offshore banks are even more restricted. The ACUs are predominantly active in inter-bank business. More than 70% of their assets and 75% of their liabilities are inter-bank. The Asian dollar market is largely a short term one with around 75% of liabilities and 60% of assets maturing within three months.

Merchant banks first appeared in the early 1970s and by August 1983 there were 50, of which 47 had ACU licences. Licences are not required but MAS approval must be sought. They are not allowed to take deposits or raise funds from the public. They are allowed to raise funds from most financial institutions, companies controlled by shareholders, and their own shareholders. Their ACUs are not subject to these restrictions. Many specialise in certain areas of business but collectively they provide loans, underwrite and float bond and stock issues, invest in securities, provide investment management and advisory services, manage unit trusts, arrange financial facilities for clients and deal in gold, money and foreign exchange markets. All but five are incorporated locally but only one is purely locally-owned, the majority being joint ventures with participation by leading domestic banks and foreign merchant banks or investment companies or consortia of foreign banks. Unlike commercial banks or finance companies they are not required to maintain minimum reserves. Many large foreign institutions maintain both merchant and offshore banks because the former permit them to issue securities and engage in short term financing from which the latter are excluded.

In 1983 there were 34 finance companies licensed by the MAS and all were incorporated locally. Sixteen were owned by banks, which established them to extend their activities to areas in which they were limited. They are permitted to accept time and savings deposits but are not allowed to provide cheque account facilities, operate ACUs, or deal in foreign exchange or gold. Like banks, they are free to quote their own interest rates. They usually concentrate on finance for housing, real estate, factoring, leasing, commercial loans, shipping loans and related activities.

The first international money broking firm was set up in 1971 and by 1983 there were eight, some with local share participation and all members of international broking groups with branches in the major financial centres. They are prepared to function only as agents for banks and are not allowed to trade on their own account or to deal with non-bank customers. They follow guidelines laid down by the MAS and arrange deals for banks. Their arrival greatly accelerated the development of foreign exchange business in Singapore and enabled large foreign currency option contracts to be introduced.

By 1983 four discount houses had been established. They were modelled on the London discount houses, [18] and act as intermediaries between the MAS and the banks. Their main business is to borrow short term from banks to invest in Treasury bills, commercial bills, short term government securities, and certificates of deposit. They underwrite the weekly Treasury bill issue and trade actively in the secondary markets in short term securities. Banks cannot discount Treasury bills with the MAS but must discount them with the discount houses instead. They are subject to MAS guidelines and have access to it, as lender of last resort, in difficult situations. Since the first one was established in 1972 discount houses have played an important role in widening the scope of the money market, which had previously been poorly developed.

The Post Office Savings Bank (POSB) was established, by government legislation in 1972, as an independent statutory corporation with the aim of mobilising domestic savings and encouraging personal savings habits. It had, however, been operating under various governments since 1877. Its deposits are guaranteed by the government and it pays tax exempt interest on deposits. It has over 110 branches equipped with online facilities, operates over 100 ATMs and has proved particularly successful since 1972. More than 50% of its funds are channelled to government institutions. It also provides housing loans through a wholly owned subsidiary, participates in the local money market and owns shares in private enterprises.

The insurance companies and the Central Provident Fund (CPF) are the most important of the other non-bank financial institutionals. The former play an important role as institutional investors and the CPF receives monthly contributions from employers and employees. It was established in 1955 to administer a compulsory pension scheme for employees. The CPF invests mainly in Singapore government securities and provides a substantial source of funds for the government. There are also a number of specialist leasing companies. The Export Credit Insurance Corporation of Singapore was established in 1975. Its ownership is shared between Singapore based banks and insurance companies and the government. The Economic Development Board was established in 1961 to promote industrial investments. It seeks out new investment opportunities and evaluates and helps to implement industrial projects. It has offices in many of the world's major cities. The Asean Financial Corporation was incorporated in 1981. It is a joint venture between the major domestic banks and financial institutions of the five ASEAN countries. It was established to mobilise and solicit both private and public resources to finance economic development in ASEAN. It holds an ACU licence and may float bonds and other debt instruments. It can also raise funds from commercial and non-commercial institutions and government agencies.

Singapore has emerged as centre of the Asian currency market, which is the most important financial market in Singapore. It is an international money and capital market in which all major convertible currencies, but mainly US dollars, are traded. Singapore's pre-eminence is attributed to its political and financial stability, its friendly relations with neighbouring countries and its convenient geographical location, which provides a link in the 24-hour foreign exchange trading clock, with London, Tokyo and New York. Like Hong Kong, it also has good telecommunications and travel links, a good financial infrastructure, well developed urban facilities, relatively low taxes, and it allows funds to flow freely into and out of the country. The market has expanded rapidly since its establishment in 1968. By 1987 there were 187 ACUs, 108 of which were operated by commercial banks, 47 by merchant banks, one by PICA, a private investment company, and one by the ASEAN Financial Corporation. Participants in the market cannot transact business in Singapore dollars. Interbank transactions feature prominently reflecting the use of Singapore as a funding base and for interest arbitrage. Loans to non bank customers count for just over 20% of total assets. The range of instruments in the market has increased since 1977, when the first Singapore floating rate US dollar denominated negotiable certificates of deposit (NCDs) were issued. Fixed rate NCDs are also issued but the former have been most successful. The parallel development of the foreign exchange market has supported activities in the Asian currency market.

The foreign exchange market has broadened in scope since the admission of international money brokers in the mid 1970s. The MAS requires local participation of at least 51% in joint ventures with foreign money brokers. The banks are active in arbitrage operations in both the spot and forward markets. The wider exchange rate fluctuations that followed the floating of the Singapore dollar in 1973 contributed to the expansion of the market. Its participants are banks, ACUs, merchant banks, international money brokers, companies, individuals, the MAS, and other government bodies. Market practices and developments are overseen by a committee of officials from the MAS, banks and money brokers.

Like Hong Kong, Singapore is a major Asian gold trading centre. It established a spot market in 1968 and a futures market in 1978. It also has a Stock Exchange which was established in its present form in 1973. [19] Until the market's collapse in 1985, [20] it operated as a self regulating body governed by its own rules. It had about 25 operating member companies and 109 individual stockbroking members. In 1983 nearly 300 shares were listed, including over 110 companies incorporated in Singapore. Most of the remainder were Malaysian companies, although some UK and Hong Kong companies were listed. Domestic and foreign bonds and units in domestic investment funds are also listed. In terms of turnover, the market held fourth place, behind Tokyo, Sydney and Hong Kong, in the Asian-Pacific area. It was, however, serving as an important regional market for the neighbouring countries, which had been growing particularly rapidly until the mid 1980s, and had acquired international recognition.

The most recently established market is the Singapore International Monetary Exchange (SIMEX). It was established in late 1984. It provides for 24 hour trading in futures and options and has links with the Chicago Mercantile Exchange. It proved successful and ran smoothly in its early days. By 1986 it was thriving and attracting strong Japanese participation. It provides a means of risk management, for Asian Currency and foreign exchange market traders, through a Eurodollar contract. Currency futures in all the major currencies have already been introduced and a currency options market is to open in 1987.

The Association of Banks in Singapore (ABS) provides guidelines to banks in their dealings with the public and amongst themselves and provides a forum for banks to discuss matters of mutual interest and to represent their views to the government and the MAS.

The Banking Act vests in the MAS the responsibility for supervising both local and foreign banks in Singapore and requires it to inspect the books, accounts and transactions of banks periodically. It is also empowered to investigate the affairs of banks suspected of carrying on business in a manner likely to be detrimental to the interests of depositors and creditors or having insufficient assets to meet their liabilities or contravening the provisions of the Act. Since April 1981 the supervisory function has become one of the responsibilities of the Banking and Financial Institutions department of the MAS. This was formed by merging the previously separate Banking and Financial Supervision Departments. The latter had previously specialised in supervising banks and other financial institutions.

Supervision is carried out using onsite inspections and analytical reviews of information which the MAS requires banks to submit. The MAS also relies to some extent on the work of internal and external auditors. External auditors are required to assess compliance with the Banking Act and other relevant legislation and to issue a supplementary report in this connection. They are also required by the MAS to assess: banks' accounting systems and internal control systems; the quality of banks' loans, advances and other assets; and any other weaknesses.

Both local and foreign banks are subject to the same system of supervision and are required to submit similar statistical and other returns. Merchant banks, by agreement, are also under the supervisory attention of the MAS. As a further protection, all foreign banks' head offices are required to give an undertaking to the MAS to provide financial support to their operations in Singapore, including the ACUs, in times of need. [21] The MAS imposes a gearing ratio requirement on merchant banks whose parents must also provide 'letters of comfort',

There is a banking secrecy provision in the Banking Act which prohibits the disclosure of information about the accounts of a customer except in certain specified circumstances. These include inspections or investigations carried out under the Act. Information divulged to the MAS should, however, be kept confidential by it. Aggregate information can be disclosed provided it does not prejudice secrecy. Numbered deposit accounts can be opened with the permission of the MAS. At the time of writing, none of the banks in Singapore was authorised to offer such facilities and there was no deposit insurance scheme.

The MAS has the reputation of being a strict and diligent supervisor. Consequently it has at times had a stormy relationship with foreign banks. Mutual disenchantment was particularly evident in 1983 and it was doing little to promote the island state's image as a financial centre. The foreign banks dominate the expanding fiancial sector, which grew by 50% between 1981 and 1986, when it contributed 25% of GDP. It has been one of the main contributors to the country's growth. The conflict arises from the MAS's desire to keep a tight control of its currency whilst eschewing exchange controls. In late 1982 the MAS fined several banks following a 'round-tripping' controversy and secured the recall of two foreign bank executives. The banks had booked Singapore dollar deposits into their Hong Kong branches which then relent the money back as capital. The MAS judged that this circumvented reserve requirements and violated regulations. The banks traced the change of attitude back to 1980 when there was a major changeover of senior MAS officials. The new officials were clearly determined to impose discipline and their approach contrasted sharply with that of the laissez-faire attitude of the monetary authorities at Hong Kong the time. The MAS made it clear that it did not want to see the Singapore dollar internationalised because a stable exchange rate was a key instrument of economic policy for a small open economy. It appears that the MAS felt that it could adopt a tougher stance without deterring entrants because of the innate attractiveness of Singapore as a financial centre. In 1983 tax incentives had anyway been introduced with the aim of attracting a greater volume of loan syndication and fund management business. This was traditionally the preserve of Hong Kong. The incentives proved successful and in 1984 the government's intention to promote Singapore as a financial centre was also demonstrated by its plans to establish SIMEX later in the year.

Also in 1984 there were two changes in banking legislation. Amendments to the Banking Act were passed in March and later in the year the powers of the MAS were altered. It was feared that these developments might impair Singapore's attraction as a major financial centre. The Banking Act amendments aimed to ensure that credit advances were spread over a large number of persons in diversified businesses by imposing new limits on bank lending to individual customers and on the number of large loans. Additionally, deposit liabilities of banks being wound up were ranked for the first time. The ranking gave preference to non bank customers, over banking customers, and to domestic depositors over Asian dollar market customers. This altered the status of certificates of deposit (CDs), whose holders previously ranked with depositors in the event of insolvency, and immediately caused a CD issue to be halted. It was feared that further issues of CDs could be curtailed and that Singapore's status as a major centre of the CD market in Asia could be threatened. The general thrust of the new clauses was in line with the MAS's traditional policy of individual, as opposed to institutional, investor protection. The amendments relating to the MAS formalised its supervisory procedures, especially with respect to consultations with financial institutions.

The island's foreign banking community was further shocked when the MAS revoked the licence of the merchant banking operation of a Hong Kong based bank in October 1984. This unprecedented action underlined how severely the MAS was prepared to punish any laxity it perceived. Confrontation with the merchant bank had escalated over the preceding two and a half years and the bank had already lost its offshore banking permit in 1982. The action was interpreted by some bankers as demonstrating the MAS's dislike of merchant bankers in general and banks from Hong Kong in particular.

In 1985 a five bank consortium introduced a cashless shopping system under the aegis of NETS (Network for Electronic Transfers Singapore) which was set up by the banks to manage the system. Like Hong Kong's Easy Pay system, the NETS system rapidly achieved widespread acceptance. As in Hong Kong, credit cards were not widely distributed but the public was used to using ATMs and made a large proportion of its transactions using cash rather than cheques. Consumers were therefore used to parting with their cash for goods and had not become accustomed to the credit floats available through credit cards. By the end of 1986 the Easy Pay system had 800 terminals in operation and the NETS system had 600, with another 400 on order. Singapore's system has perhaps been even more successful than Hong Kong's. Powerful government backing was given to the scheme which was seen as a method of reducing cash transactions and maximising retail productivity and as part of a national drive to improve the country's commercial competitiveness. Singapore's four leading banks, DBS, OUB, UOB, OCBC and the POSB formed a consortium which underwrote the initial investment and set up NETS to commercialise the project. During the six month pilot phase, NETS moved quickly to eliminate technical problems, such as the complaints from retailers that the original terminals were taking too long to effect transactions. More efficient terminals were installed as a consequence. These worked faster and integrated electronic cash registers with EFT. In Hong Kong there was some customer resistance in the first year of the system's operation. This was overcome in Singapore by a comprehensive marketing campaign directed at both retailers and customers. The Hong Kong campaign concentrated primarily on retailers, which in Singapore were offered charge-free one year contracts. However, even in Singapore, only 13% of the total population are using cash cards regularly and major retailers claimed that NETS accounted for no more than 3% of sales. The older generations continue to use cash. The young have proved to be the most enthusiastic users of EFTPOS. The experience of Hong Kong and Singapore indicates that EFTPOS systems are easier to introduce when reliance on credit is not widespread and in small countries, where integrated nationwide systems are the only realistic ones and bank cooperation is assured.

6.4 The Future Prospects of Hong Kong and Singapore

Both Hong Kong and Singapore have reached interesting stages in their development as financial centres. They are both major and mature international offshore centres and they face competition from newly established offshore centres in the Asia-Pacific region, such as Taiwan, Sydney and, most importantly, Tokyo. They still have more liberal tax regimes and less complex regulatory regimes than Tokyo but deregulation is probably far from complete in Japan and competition can only increase as the yen's importance as an international reserve currency increases, especially relative to the US$. Their future prospects have therefore been questioned. It is probably unrealistic to expect them to continue to grow at the pace of the 1970s and early 1980s but will they actually decline?

Such questions were first raised in connection with Hong Kong when the UK government entered into negotiations with the Chinese authorities, in 1983, over the prospects of the colony after the UK's lease expires in 1997. An agreement was reached in September 1984, following nearly two years of hard bargaining. Under the agreement sovereignty will revert to China in 1997 and Hong Kong will become a Special Administrative Region (SAR) of China. The SAR will remain a capitalist enclave but the question remained in the doubters' minds, for how long could China tolerate this arrangement? In terms of the number of foreign banks and financial institutions, but not in terms of quantitative measures such as volume of loans or deposits, Hong Kong was the third largest financial centre in the world in 1986. Its time zone position in relation to London and New York, along with its excellent telecommunications links, allow it to participate in the 24 hour trading of foreign exchange and gold and in the emerging global securities' markets.

Once under communist rule, however, will Taiwan and other countries, like South Korea and Indonesia, withdraw business and place it elsewhere? Taiwan may try to increase its share of the business by offering an alternative gateway to China. Tokyo would be an obvious beneficiary but so too would Singapore, which, like Hong Kong, seemed to have concluded, until 1982, that both centres could profitably co-exist, in a symbiotic relationship, by specialising. Singapore, which removed withholding taxes in 1968, had become the undisputed centre of the Asian dollar market whilst Hong Kong had taken the lead in fund management and loan syndication, drawing on Singapore's deposits. Then, in 1982, Hong Kong removed withholding tax from foreign currency deposits and, in 1983, as part of the currency rescue package, withholding tax was also removed from HK$ deposits. In response to these developments Singapore introduced further incentives to attract offshore business. They were designed to counter Hong Kong's attempt to attract more deposits and to attract fund management business to Singapore. Hong Kong's general level of taxation remains lower but the gap has been narrowing since 1978, when Singapore reduced tax on offshore profits from 40% to 10%. Singapore has traditionally been the more strictly regulated and supervised centre, but this difference has also diminished following the reforms of the supervisory system in Hong Kong, which came into force in 1986. The trend toward tighter regulation in Hong Kong is probably essential if the centre is to keep in step with the efforts of international bank supervisors in major centres. For offshore centres, however, the divide between over and under regulation has to be straddled. Under regulation can lead to a decline in reputation and a loss of business but the latter can also result from over-regulation. A further question, therefore, raised is: has Hong Kong, and Singapore for that matter, got the balance right? Given the discretion afforded to the supervisory authorities in both centres, there is considerable room for flexibility and pragmatism; but only time will tell. Hong Kong is also going to try to reduce tax avoidance and this might result in its simple low-tax regime becoming more complex and contradict the view that only income sourced in the Colony is taxed. If current tax proposals come into force the advantages of Hong Kong relative to Singapore and Tokyo may further decline.

It was the deadlock reached in the talks over the colony's future, in September 1983, that generated a panic reaction in the community. The result was a fall in property and stock market prices and a rapid depreciation of the HK$. The government responded rapidly by introducing the Currency Stabilisation Scheme and rescuing the Hang Lung Bank. The latter led to criticism of the bank supervisory system and led to its reform. Meanwhile the Commission for Securities and Commodities Trading was reviewing supervisory procedures in the Stock Exchanges following a series of scandals in the early 1980s.

Since 1984 the Hong Kong markets have remained sensitive to pronouncements from China about its future. There remain doubts about China's commitment to honouring the Sino-British agreement. In November 1985 Stock Exchange prices fell rapidly following a statement by the Chinese Premier. They have since recovered but further bouts of nervousness cannot be discounted as 1997 draws nearer. In January 1987, for example, there were significant changes in the Chinese Communist Party leadership which indicated that more conservative and isolationist approach to development might replace the previous policy of economic and political reform and modernisation. If this proves to be the case, the impact on confidence in Hong Kong could be serious.

In 1985 the head of Citibank HK claimed that offshore banking centres were an endangered species and in early 1986 Citibank's investment banking headquarters was moved from Hong Kong to Tokyo, again raising the spectre of Hong Kong's decline. Political uncertainty and a potentially tougher tax regime have clearly reduced its attractiveness. The tighter supervisory regime may also have this effect but could on balance be beneficial if it restores stability to the domestic banking market. The instability had inevitably affected the foreign banks operating in the domestic markets, although the damage to their positions was judged to be minor. Against these disadvantages, Hong Kong still has a well developed financial infrastructure, good telecommunications and travel links, and attractive urban facilities. Tokyo is probably less well placed geographically and still has a more complex tax regime and a tighter regulatory regime. The international banks are also more familiar with the British influenced legal and accounting systems in Hong Kong than those of Japan. They are also much more familiar with the English language.

In early 1986 there were 150 licensed banks and 313 DTCs operating in Hong Kong and the number was still rising, four Australian banks having recently arrived. These financial institutions accounted for a substantial proportion of the rapidly growing capital market business in the Asia-Pacific region. In 1985 the volume of business was twice that in 1984. The Japanese institutions were, however, the dominant lending force in the region and many feel that it is only a matter of time before they start arranging business from Tokyo.

Hong Kong's major geographical asset, apart from its proximity to the S.E. Asian countries, which Singapore shares whilst Tokyo doesn't, could yet turn out to be its proximity to and future absorption into China. Many judge it to be in China's interest to maintain Hong Kong as a financial centre, rather than simply a port and a manufacturing centre. As an international financial centre, organised as an SAR, it will have its own convertible currency and give the Chinese government access to financing for the country's development. China, with its massive population, is seen as a major export market of the future and a country that will have a voracious appetite for project finance. Because of its needs for project financing it is felt that China is unlikely to do anything to scare away foreign financial institutions. China is already a significant borrower and banks will want to be close at hand to win participations in major project financing deals. In the interim, domestic manufacturers are likely to continue to provide a reasonable amount of capital market business. Their tendency to turn away from the domestic banks and towards the capital markets is likely to further weaken those domestic institutions which are too small to follow the trend towards securitisation. The manufacturing sector is, however, likely to remain generally less demanding for the foreseeable future. Investment programmes have been curtailed because of the political uncertainty and falling export demand, especially for traditional products. A transition phase is in process as new hi-tech industries are developed to replace the declining industries and a lot depends on future world growth prospects. In 1986, however, industry benefited from the depreciation of the US dollar, to which the HK$ is pegged, against the other major currencies. This encouraged a substantial increase in exports worldwide, including the US. The US authorities have criticised Asian-Pacific countries for keeping their currencies artificially weak to help local exporters and an adjustment in the parity is to be expected.

The government proved sensitive to pressures from the offshore banking community by dropping proposals to tax interest on offshore funds in its 1986 budget. It, however, expressed its continuing concern about tax avoidance by international financial institutions. The February budget also eliminated stamp duty on certain lending instruments to encourage more local capital market activity. This move was welcomed by local banks.

Singapore's future as a financial centre also seemed to be at a crossroads in the mid 1980s. Local and regional markets were in a slump in 1985 and the government was considering ways of broadening the centre's appeal as a place for all kinds of financial transactions. The collapse of Pan Electric Industries, one of the island state's largest companies, in 1985, damaged the centre's reputation by forcing a three day closing of the Stock Exchange, to prevent a chain reaction, in November . The crisis was touched off by fraud and regulatory laxity and the MAS responded by assuming regulatory responsibility for the Stock Exchange. The growth prospects of the region were bleak because of its heavy dependence on commodity exports and the fall in commodity prices in the first half of the 1980s. Singapore in fact recorded negative growth in the year to mid 1986 and positive growth was not expected to resume until 1988. The financial sector has continued to grow, with 123 foreign banks represented by 1986, but bank profits have been hit by falling property prices. Singapore's problems are a result of the decline in growth in the ASEAN countries, particularly Indonesia and Malaysia, and in the US, its major trading partner. As in Hong Kong, traditional industries are judged to have limited potential and the government is trying to encourage the development of hi-tech industries. In an effort to identify areas of expansion and obstacles to growth a high level Economics Committee was established in 1985. It reported in February 1986, recommending reforms of the wage and tax systems, improved productivity and business efficiency; and promotion of the service industries, especially banking and finance. Key recommendations, adopted by the government, were a cut in the employers' contributon to the Central Provident Fund (CPF) from 25% of an employee's salary to 10%, wage restraint for two years and a number of tax concessions.

After a period of rapid growth in the early 1980s, the financial sector's growth slowed sharply in 1985. The Economics Committee nevertheless regarded it as the sector with the best growth potential. Whilst the export oriented manufacturing sector is largely at the mercy of world growth prospects, Singapore, like Hong Kong, enjoys geographical advantages as a financial centre. It has the infrastructural communications, legal, tax, accounting, urban facility and language advantages enjoyed by Hong Kong. The MAS has a reputation for strict supervision, which may have counted against it in the past but may be beneficial in the future if it can adopt a more pragmatic and less heavy handed approach. Given the government's decision to promote the financial sector, this seems likely and its high profile has anyway not discouraged the continued growth in the number of foreign institutions operating in Singapore. Its geographical advantages lie in its time zone position between London and New York and its proximity to the ASEAN countries. The latter, despite the problems experienced in the mid 1980s, have constituted a high growth region in the last decade and its long term prospects are generally regarded as being favourable.

Singapore grew into a centre for traditional loan business but with the trend toward securitisation this is no longer a growth area. The government has, therefore, been encouraging diversification into fee based business by revising the regulatory and tax systems. The Economic Committee (EC) supported this approach. It recommended, in particular, the development of business in the fields of risk and fund management and capital markets. The declared aim is to make Singapore the Switzerland of Asia. The government accepted in principle the recommendations of the EC. With regard to fund management, the EC felt that the tax regime was driving business overseas and encouraging tax avoidance. It felt that the government's monopoly over savings, caused by compulsory contributions to the CPF, should be reduced and a proportion of pensions should be allowed to be placed with private fund managers. It recommended that government institutions should raise funds by issuing tradeable debt, rather than by borrowing from the government, in order to encourage the development of debt securitisation markets. Towards the end of promoting the capital markets, the government announced plans to issue government securities in 1986. Although SIMEX was doing well, it recommended the addition of commodity futures contracts. In 1986 SIMEX was in fact aiming to double the number of futures contracts traded. To encourage the growth of trade financing and Singapore's role as an entrepôt port, it recommended that third country trade financing should be exempted from tax. With regard to the insurance market, it recommended the broadening of re-insurance operations. On the risk-management front it proposed that holding companies should be encouraged to establish on the island to attract regional treasury operations. Finally, it recommended the establishment of an unlisted securities' market and the development of Singapore as a centre for countertrade. The implementation of these recommendations will require a change of attitude by the authorities, especially the MAS which the EC recommended should adopt a developmental approach to regulating financial markets.

The three day Stock Exchange closure in December 1985 was Singapore's worst setback in the 20 years since it gained independence from Malaysia in 1965. Whilst the number of foreign banks continued to grow the 'big four' domestic banks and a number of foreign banks experienced falling profits. The property market collapse had reduced collateral and made a rise in bad debt provisions necessary. There was also a decline in trade related business and a reduction in interest rate margins. The foreign banks had lent to local brokers to fund forward share transactions. The fall in share prices following Pan Electric's default threatened the whole broking system and burnt the fingers of a number of banks. The banks were asked not to foreclose on their broking clients being experienced in 1986 because the loan recovery programme further weakened the Stock Exchange as share portfolios were liquidated. The property market also remained depressed in 1986.

Despite considerable doubts about the way the MAS had asserted control over the stock market following the crisis the action did restore confidence in 1986. The 'big four' banks took over stockbroking operations after the collapse of several securities firms and all now have seats on the exchange. They have taken over almost all of the stockbroking business from foreign brokers, even though they have not appeared as volume lenders to the market. A new set of market regulations were introduced in August 1986. They aim to add financial strength to broking firms and prevent a repeat fiasco. Previously brokers had relied heavily on bank loans to finance share transactions undertaken on their customers' behalf. When the market collapsed they could not collect on forward share contracts and were forced into liquidation by their banks. The new rules are similar to those applying to banks. They limit exposures to individual clients and securities, impose disclosure and other reporting and auditing requirements, and raise capital adequacy requirements. As a consequence, the brokers must raise more money and some fear that the MAS will regulate the life out of the market. The 'big four' local banks now dominate the stock exchange and seem keen to affirm their control. Consequently they are unlikely to provide the capital needed by the brokers. They also hoped to keep the big foreign securities houses out of the market. The MAS was, however, supporting foreign involvement in domestic securities firms to improve their capitalisation and the government's view seemed to be that the foreign securities houses should be admitted to the exchange if Singapore was to become a global financial centre. Consequently, in March 1986, broking rules were eased to allow foreign participation in local stockbroking firms with majority control being permitted in some cases. Also contributing to the stock market recovery were purchases of shares by government statutory boards, reduced tax and utility charges and the reduced contributions to the mandatory pension scheme, which increased corporate liquidity rapidly. Further stimulus was likely to come from the establishment of private pension schemes and regional economic recovery as commodity prices rose from what was judged to be their nadir. By the end of 1986 the 'big four' banks had been given seats on the exchange in reward for the funding assistance they had given to the MAS whilst it had attempted to prevent the collapse of the broking houses. Despite the rescue operation seven of the exchange's twenty-five members had gone out of business. In January 1987 Hoare Govett of the UK became the first foreign broking firm to buy a stake in a Singapore broking company. It bought the maximum permissible share of 49%. It is expected that this limit will be raised to allow majority participations in the future because the remaining brokers need to boost their capital to comply with the new Singapore Stock Exchange (SES) regulations which come into force in 1987. Other foreign institutions, including another UK broking firm, Morgan Grenfell, have also been seeking participations. A new second-tier stock market, the SES Automated Quotation market (Sesdaq), also opened in January 1987. In contrast to the SES, it is scripless and operates with a market maker system.

Plans to widen the Singapore dollar bond market were announced in July 1985. Previously the government had sold bonds to the CPF and the POSB when it needed to borrow. The POSB, with its favourable tax treatment [22] and the CPF, by virtue of the compulsory pensions scheme, captured a large proportion of domestic savings. This arrangement had stifled the growth of the bond market. The rundown of the CPF will allow the development of fund management, which is seen as perhaps the key to the centres' future prospects. The new market for government bonds, in which the 'big four' banks have primary dealerships, is planned to open in March 1987 and aims to establish a risk free benchmark for securities in order to encourage   the   development   of   non-equity   tradeable   securities' markets. The link-up of banks and brokers and the emergence of institutional investors, as private pension schemes develop, should reduce the dominance of the stock markets by individuals and private syndicates and help to attract offshore fund management. The MAS does seem to have changed its conservative attitude towards new financial products and has reduced regulatory impediments to the securitisation of debt whilst the government has introduced a series of incentives, which have significantly reduced the cost of operating in Singapore, to attract fund management and offshore business. [23] Hitherto, the MAS and the government have only sanctioned change that does not threaten the domestic financial system and has been unwilling to allow the Singapore dollar to become an international currency. Further changes or innovations are likely, therefore, to be permitted as long as the economy is not destabilised as a result.

It may well be that the position of the POSB will have to be considered further. It provides tough competition for the big four local banks because of its special tax exempt status. It has larger branch and ATM networks than any of the banks. The government has considered converting the POSB into a commercial bank. These plans were shelved in 1984 but the POSB was allowed to extend its services to include current account facilities and the issue of travellers' cheques. The POSB has in turn faced increased competition from higher interest paying offshore bank and finance company accounts. It nevertheless absorbs a large proportion of domestic savings and these may need to be freed, by removing its tax exempt status for example, to help stimulate the growth of the capital markets. The POSB could alternatively be encouraged to invest in marketed securities instead of buying bonds direct from the government and might play a useful role in this direction, at least until institutional investors are established.

Singapore's main target is Hong Kong's dominance of the discretionary fund management business in the area. The new internationalisation strategy has been exemplified by SIMEX from its outset. It is due to introduce its first home grown contract in 1987. The Singapore Stock Exchange Futures Contract will be comparable to contracts that have proved successful in the rival Hong Kong and Sydney exchanges. Because Singapore's domestic economy is small, SIMEX must, however, concentrate on international contracts. For similar reasons the financial centre must become increasingly international to survive.

Their concern about future prospects and the increasing reliance of both economies on their financial sectors as sources of growth have brought Hong Kong and Singapore increasingly into competition with each other and replaced their previously harmonious symbiotic relationship. Growing competition from Tokyo and other centres is likely to increase this tendency.

The increase in concentration in the Hong Kong banking system seems likely to be allowed, by the authorities, to continue. Many of the smaller family banks are seeking 'big brother' banks to take them over and more failures may be permitted now that the supervisory system has been strengthened and capital requirements have been increased so that the risk of panics and knock-on effects have been reduced. A deposit protection scheme would further reduce the risk of panic. The other major development in the domestic banking scene is the emergence of the Bank of China Group (BCG) as a potent domestic banking force. It controls approximately 20% of the domestic branch network and takes a similar proportion of deposits. It is competing aggressively to increase its market share on all fronts.

The future of the interest rate agreement under which the HKAB sets rates for all deposits below HK$500,000 continues to be questioned. The agreement was defended by the outgoing Financial Secretary in 1986 and has survived despite the pegging of the HK$ to the US$ in October 1983. Many felt that the need for interest rate flexibility to protect the exchange rate would break up the cartel, causing a squeeze on margins and further problems for the local banks. This appeared to be happening in 1986 as margins came under pressure as a result of a sharp rise in foreign currency deposits in response to interest rate differentials and speculation that the HK$ would be revalued against the US$. Even small depositors can easily find securities' investments offering a higher return than available on local deposits and proposals to introduce unit trusts in the fast developing capital markets pose a further threat. The banks will, therefore, have to offer higher rates to attract deposits and margins will be squeezed. The argument for the agreement is that it protects both small banks and small depositors, but a protection scheme could protect the latter and many believe that the cartel is more beneficial to the large banks, especially the HKSBC. The general manager of the HKSBC, who is also chairman of the HKAB, argues that the agreement is necessary because it is the only monetary tool controlling the relationship between the exchange rate and interest rates. Other bankers feel that a less crude method of interest rate control could be devised but the general expectation is that the cartel will remain. Its influence will, however, diminish as investment vehicles providing higher rates of return are allowed. The surviving local banks, in the face of weak domestic loan demand, will have to adapt themselves to succeed at a time when the global trend is towards securitisation.

Offshore centres proliferated as banks sought to circumvent restrictive regulations during the period of rapid internationalisation of banking in the 1970s. The emerging centres competed to attract foreign banks by offering tax incentives. During the 1980s, as financial deregulation has spread throughout the world, their raison d'étre has begun to disappear. They have also had to adapt to the process of securitisation which has tended to attract banks to capital market centres. The functional centres with stock exchanges, such as Singapore and Hong Kong, have begun to adapt to the new environment but many of the smaller functional centres and the paper centres may well decline in importance.

Singapore and Hong Kong also face the threat of growing competition from Tokyo. Nevertheless, because of their advantageous geographical positions and solid financial infrastructure, it seems likely that both Singapore and Hong Kong will remain as thriving international financial centres even if their relative advantages as offshore centres, with liberal regulatory and tax regimes, declines. The sovereign borrowers, such as Indonesia, Malaysia, and Thailand, have responded to the slump in commodity prices by cutting back rather than saddling themselves with debt problems. The regional demand for sovereign syndicated loans has declined and this has had an impact on Hong Kong, which has been the centre for such loans in the Asian region. Corporate demand for loans in Hong Kong has also declined in the wake of the 1983 crisis and the resulting uncertainty about the future and consequent postponement of investment projects. The process of securitisation has, however, generated a meteoric increase in the use of new instruments and bonds overtook syndicated loans as the main source of finance in the Asian regional market based in Hong Kong in 1984. The bond business has grown rapidly since the Mexican crisis in

1982 whilst syndicated loan business has slipped back. Hong Kong has, therefore, shown itself able to adapt to new trends. With domestic prospects uncertain, Hong Kong's future prospects are bound up with those of China and the South-east Asian countries, which are generally regarded as good in the medium to long term. It will also have to survive the transition to Chinese rule but the likelihood is that China will find it advantageous to have an international financial centre on its doorstep.

There is less uncertainty about Singapore's future, which is reliant primarily on the prospects of the ASEAN countries. It could, however, benefit from uncertainties surrounding Hong Kong's future. The Asian currency market has continued to grow despite the decline in regional growth during the mid 1980s. It remains the main source of the centre's growth. The volume of deposits from non-residents has been growing and so has volume of offshore interbank funds. It is attempting to adapt to the trend towards securitisation but issues of notes and bonds denominated in US$ were down in 1985. There has, however, been a growth in the use of new instruments such as Nifs and Rufs, [24] which made their debut in 1984. As centre of the Asian dollar market, Singapore has excelled in foreign exchange lending, offshore deposit taking and interbank lending and has provided much of the funding for Hong Kong's activities. The freer regulatory environment in the latter encouraged the growth of fund management, loan syndications and capital market activities. Singapore is now attempting to capture some of this business from Hong Kong through tax incentives and regulatory reform designed to encourage the introduction of new instruments that have taken hold in Hong Kong and elsewhere and through domestic reform designed to deepen the capital markets and encourage institutional investment with a view to winning fund management business. Hong Kong has, however, built up a significant lead in securities' business. Growth has been explosive in the mid 1980s and new instruments, such as certificates of deposit and commercial paper, have been introduced in rapid succession. The new Stock Exchange, formed by the merger of the four previously operating exchanges in 1986, has been booming and recording a rapid rise in turnover. The stock market seems to have recovered from the setbacks of 1983 and 1985 and benefited from an enhanced reputation, following its regulatory reform and the introduction of new technology. [25] The smaller Singapore exchange suffered its own, and more major, setback in 1985 and it too has been reformed. It is, however, starting the race towards the back of the starting grid in relation to Hong Kong whose capital markets have been given impetus by falling interest rates in 1985, which have reduced the cost of raising capital, and by the presence of underwriting bankers with experience in the Euromarket and especially in 'swaps'. New issues have been thriving, the secondary markets are in the process of development, and placement capacity is being developed, but at present a large proportion of the new issues remain on the books of the underwriters. Several banks have proposed unit trusts which will increase placement capacity and could further erode the deposit base. This will increase competition for funds and threaten the interest rate cartel. Hong Kong's futures' exchange has also been revamped and has introduced a series of innovations. SIMEX already has well developed international links, however, and could well hold its own in this area, although it is likely to face competition from Tokyo in the future. [26]

In the short term, as offshore centres, Singapore and Hong Kong will remain attractive relative to Tokyo's offshore banking facilities, which opened in December

1986, because of their relatively friendly regulatory and tax regimes. These advantages will probably be eroded in the medium term as Japan continues to deregulate. The Japanese financial surplus has so far been largely invested in US Treasury bills and equities and other instruments available in Europe and the US. If the Japanese switch their attention to the Asian-Pacific region in the future and the yen becomes a truly international trading and reserve currency, Tokyo's importance as a financial centre for the region, and particularly as the centre of the Asian yen market, will increase. Tokyo is, therefore, likely to become the major global financial centre for the region whilst Hong Kong and Singapore, drawn increasingly into closer competition, will remain as important regional centres for international financial business.

1) See Pecchioli (1983) for further discussion.
2) See McCarthy (1979).
3) See chapter 1.
4) See chapter 3.
5) See chapter 2.
6) See section 2.2iv.
7) See section 2.3iv.
8) See Bank for International Settlements (1986) and Committee on Banking Regulations and Supervisory Practices (1986).
9) Which operate in London, see section 1.2.
10) At a rate of US$1 to HK$7.80.
11) Discussed in section 6.4.
12) See section 3.4.
13) See Hirsch (1977) for further discussion.
14) See sections 3.4iv and 3.3iv.
15) See section 2.2iv.
16) See sections 1.3 and 1.4.
17) The Electronic Payment Services Company.
18) See section 1.2.
19) Its predecessor was established in 1938.
20) Discussed further in section 6.4.
21) i.e. 'letters of comfort'.
22) It enjoys tax exemption.
23) The 1986 budget lifted tax and other disincentives. As a result no tax is liable on either trading income or capital gains and tax exempt foreign participations in domestic equities were permitted.
24) Nifs are note issuance facilities and Rufs are revolving underwriting facilities, see Bank for International Settlements (1986) for descriptions.
25) The Stock Exchange computer system is not a dealing system. It provides an onscreen information system. Dealing is still done on the floor with negotiations over the telephone.
26) See section 2.3iv.

References

Aftab, M. (1986) 'Pakistan moves to Islamic Banking', *The Banker*, June, pp. 57-60.

Association of Yugoslav Banks (1977) 'Financial Institutions in Yugoslavia', *Jugoslovenska stvarnost*, Belgrade.

Balles, J.J. (1984) 'The Federal Reserve: The Role of the Reserve Banks', *Journal of Money Credit and Banking*, volume 16, number 1, February, pp. 110-117.

Bank for International Settlements (1985) *Fifty-Fifth Annual Report*, June, Basle, Switzerland.

Bank for International Settlements (1986a) *Recent Innovations in International Banking*, April, Basle, Switzerland.

Bank for International Settlements (1986b) *Fifty-Sixth Annual Report*, June, Basle, Switzerland.

Bank of England (1979) 'Monetary Base Control', *Bank of England Quarterly Bulletin*, pp. 149-159.

Bank of England (1980) 'The Measurement of Capital', *Bank of England Quarterly Bulletin*, pp. 324-329.

Bank of England (1981a) 'Monetary Control-Provisions', *Bank of England Quarterly Bulletin*, pp. 347-349.

Bank of England (1981b) 'Foreign Currency Exposure', *Bank of England Quarterly Bulletin*, pp. 235-237.

Bank of England (1982) 'The Measurement of Liquidity', *Bank of England Quarterly Bulletin*, pp. 399-402.

Bank of England (1985) 'The Future Structure of the Gilt-Edged Market: The Bank of England's Dealing and Supervisory Relationships with Certain Participants', *Bank of England*, April, London.

Bank of England (1986) 'Financial Change and Broad Money', *Bank of England Quarterly Bulletin*, pp. 499-507.

Bankers' Research Unit (1977) *Banking and Sources of Finance in Switzerland, Austria, Yugoslavia and Greece*, Financial Times Ltd, London.

Brimmer, A.F. (1972) 'Central Banking and Economic Development', *Journal of Money Credit and Banking*, volume 3, number 4, pp. 780-792.

Brown, R. (1982) *A Guide to Monetary Policy*, Bank Information Service, London.

Central Bank of Nigeria (1979) *Twenty Years of Central Banking in Nigeria: 1959-1979*, Research Department, Central Bank of Nigeria, Lagos.

Chrystal, K.A. (1984) 'International Banking Facilities', *Federal Reserve Bank of St. Louis Review*, volume 66, number 4, April, pp. 5-11.

Command Paper 7858 *Monetary Control*, 1980, HMSO.

Command Paper 8472 *Monopolies and Mergers Commission Report on the Proposed Merger Between the Hong Kong and Shanghai Bank and the Royal Bank of Scotland*, 1982, HMSO.

Command Paper 9125 *Review of Investor Protection*, Department of Trade and Industry, Part 1, Report (Gower Report), 1984, HMSO.

Command Paper 9695 *Banking Supervision*, 1985, HMSO.

Commission of the European Communities (1977) 'First Council Directive', OJ No L332, 17.12.1971, Brussels.

Commission of the European Communities (1983a) 'Council Directive of 13 June on Supervision of Credit Institutions on a Consolidated Basis', 83/350/EEC, Brussels.

Commission of the European Communities (1983b) 'Financial Integration', Com(83) 207 Final, 20 April, Brussels.

Commission of the European Communities (1985) 'Steps to European Unity', 5th Ed EC, Brussels.

Commission of the European Communities (1986) 'Programme for the Liberalisation of Capital Markets in the Community', Com (86) 292, Brussels.

Committee of Inquiry into Regulatory Arrangements at Lloyds (Neill Committee) (1987) Report, January, HMSO.

Committee on Banking Regulations and Supervisory Practices (1975) *The Basle Concordat*, Basle, Switzerland.

Committee on Banking Regulations and Supervisory Practices (1983) *Principles for the Supervision of Banks' Foreign Establishments*, Basle, Switzerland.

Committee on Banking Regulations and Supervisory Practices (1986) *The Management of Banks Off-Balance Sheet Risks*, Basle, Switzerland.

Committee on Finance and Industry (Macmillan Committee) (1931), *Report*, Command Paper 3897, HMSO, London.

Committee to Review the Functioning of Financial Institutions (Wilson Committee) (1980) *Report and Appendices*, Command Paper 7937, HMSO.

Corti, M.A. (1983) 'Switzerland: Banking, Money and Bond Markets', George-Giddy: *International Finance Handbook*, Section 4.6, volume 1, pp. 1-50, John Wiley and Sons Inc, New York.

Dale, R.S. (1984) 'Continental Illinois: The Lessons for Deposit Insurance', *The Banker*, July, pp.12-22 and 91.

Dorrance, G.S. (1969) 'The Role of Central Banks in Less Developed Countries', *Finance and Development*, volume 6, number 4, December, pp. 22-6.

Dunham, C.R. (1985) 'Recent Developments in Thrift Commercial Lending', *New England Economic Review*, Federal Reserve Bank of Boston, Nov/Dec, pp. 41-8.

Dunham, C.R. and Syron, R.F. (1984) 'Interstate Banking-PartII', *New England Economic Review*, Federal Reserve Bank of Boston, May/June, pp. 11-28.

European Communities (1977), see Commission of the European Communities.

European Economic Community (1973) 'Council Directive of 28 June 1973 on the abolition of restrictions on the freedom of establishment and the freedom to provide services in respect of self employed activities of banks and other financial institutions', (73/183/EEC).

Faith,N. (1982) *Safety in Numbers: The Mysterious World of Swiss Banking*, Hamish Hamilton, London.

Federal Reserve Bulletin (1984) *The Federal Reserve Position on Restructuring of Regulatory Responsibilities*, July, Washington D.C.

Fisher, J.L. (1953) *Report on the Desirability and Practicality of Establishing a Central Bank in Nigeria for Promoting the Economic Development of the Country*, Government Printers, Lagos.

Fraud Trials Committee (1986) *Report*, E.W.Roskill, January, HMSO.

Garvy, G. (1975) 'Post Reform Changes in Banking in Eastern Europe', *Banca Nazionale del Lavoro*, volume 28, number 115, pp. 370-86.

Garvy, G. (1977) 'Money, Financial Flows, and Credit in the Soviet Union', *National Bureau of Economic Research*, Chicago.

Goldsmith, R.W. (1975) 'The Financial Development of Yugoslavia', *Banca Nazionale del Lavoro*, volume 28, number 112, pp. 61-108.

Goode, R.M. (1985) *Electronic Banking: The Legal Implications*, Institute of Bankers, London.

Gorman, D. and Morales, J. (1985) 'Economic Adjustment in Latin America: An Overview of Policies', *Barclays Review*, February, pp. 5-11.

Grubel, H. (1984) *The International Monetary System*, Penguin Books, Harmondsworth, England.

Heaton, G.C. and Dunham, C.R. (1985) 'The Growing Competitiveness of Credit Unions', *New England Economic Review*, Federal Reserve Bank of Boston, May/June, pp 19-34.

Hirsch, F. (1969) *Money International*, Penguin Books, Harmondsworth, England.

Hirsch, F. (1977) *The Bagehot Problem*, The Manchester School of Economic and Social Science, volume XLV, number 3, September, pp. 241-57.

International Monetary Fund (1986) 'Switzerland's Role as an International Financial Centre', Occasional Paper number 4, Washington, D.C.

Kahn, M.S. (1986) *Islamic Interest Free Banking*, IMF Staff Papers, volume 33, number 1, March, pp. 1-27.

Karsten, I. (1982) 'Islam and Financial Intermediation', IMF Staff Papers, volume 29, number 1, March, pp. 108-142.

Kindleberger, C.P. (1984) *A Financial History of Western Europe*. George Allen and Unwin, London.

Kohli, U. and Rich, G. (1985) *Monetary Control: The Swiss Experiment*, Swiss National Bank, February 22, Zurich.

Kraft, J. (1984) *The Mexican Rescue*, Group of Thirty, New York.

Kuschpeta, O. (1978) *The Banking and Credit System of the USSR*, Tilburg Studies in Economics number 18, Martinus Nijhoff, Leiden.

Labour Party Financial Institutions Study Group (1982) *The City: A Socialist Approach*, The Labour Party, London.

Lever, H. and Huhne, C. (1985) *Debt and Danger*, Penguin Books, Harmondsworth, England.

Loynes, J.B. (1957) *Report on the Establishment of a Central Bank of Nigeria*, Government Printer, Lagos.

Luckett, D.G. (1984) *Money and Banking*, Third Edition, McGraw-Hill, New York.

Lydall, H. (1984) *Yugoslav Socialism: Theory and Practice*, Oxford University Press, Oxford.

Maisel, S.J. Ed. (1981) *Risk and Capital Adequacy in Commercial Banks*, National Bureau of Economic Research, University of Chicago Press, Chicago.

Mayer, T., Duesenberry, T.S., and Aliber, R.Z. (1981) *Money, Banking and the Economy*, W.W. Norton & Co, New York.

Members of the Bankers' Clearing House (1985) *Payment Clearing Systems: Review of Organisation, Membership and Control*, (Child Report), December, Bank information Service, London.

Mijovic, B. (1982) *The Banking System*, East European Economics, Volume XX, number 3-4, Spring-Summer, pp. 100-19.

Mullineux, A.W. (1987a) *UK Banking After Deregulation*, Croom Helm, Beckenham, England.

Mullineux, A.W. (1987b) *International Money and Banking: The Creation of a New Order*, Wheatsheaf, Brighton, England.

National Consumer Council (1983) *Banking Services and the Consumer*, Methuen, London.

Neill Report (1987), see Committee of Inquiry into Regulatory Arrangements at Lloyds (1987).

Nwankwo, G.O. (1980) *The Nigerian Financial System*, Macmillan, London.

Ojo, A.T. (1976) 'The Nigerian Financial System', Bangor Occasional Paper number 7, University of Wales Press, Bangor.

Ojo, A.T. and Adewunmi, W. (1982) *Banking and Finance in Nigeria*, Graham Burn, Leighton Buzzard, England.

Okigbo, P.N. (1982) *Nigeria's Financial System*, Longman, London.

Onoh, J.K. (1982) *Money and Banking in Africa*, Longman, London.

Osuntogun, A. and Adewunmi, W. (1983) *Rural Banking in Nigeria*, Longman, London.

Peat Marwick (1982) *Banking in France*, Peat Marwick Mitchell & Co, London.

Pecchioli, R.M. (1983) *The Internationalisation of Banking: The Policy Issues*, Organisation for Economic Cooperation and Development, Paris.

Perisin, I. (1982) 'The Monetary and Credit Systems of Yugoslavia: Reasons for its Frequent Change', *East European Economics*, volume XX, number 3-4, Spring-Summer, pp. 84-99.

Pindak, F. (1973) *The Post-War Trends in East European Banking*, Société Universitaire Européenne de Recherches Financières, Tilburg, Netherlands.

Price Commission (1978) 'Banks: Charges for Money Transmission Services', April, HMSO.

Prout, C. (1985) *Market Socialism in Yugoslavia*, Oxford University Press, Oxford.

Reid, M. (1982) *The Secondary Banking Crisis: 1973–1975*, Macmillan, London.

Roskill Committee (1986), see Fraud Trials Committee (1986).

Salomon Brothers (1986) *The Swiss Banks: Universal Banks Poised to Prosper as Global Deregulation Unfolds*, Salomon Bros Inc, Stock Research, June, New York.

Sayers, R.S. (1957) *Central Banking in Underdeveloped Countries*, Chapter 9 in *Central Banking after Bagehot*, Oxford University Press, Oxford.

Select Committee on Nationalised Industries (1976) *Seventh Report: The Bank of England*, HMSO, London.

Simpson, T.D. and Parkinson, P.M. (1984) *Some Implications of Financial Innovations in the United States*, Staff Studies 139, Board of Governors of the Federal Reserve System, Washington, D.C.

Syron, R.F. (1984) *The New England Experiment in Interstate Banking*, New England Economic Review, Federal Reserve Bank of Boston, March/April, pp. 5-17.

Terrell, H.S. and Mills, R.H. (1983) *International Banking Facilities and the Eurodollar Market'*, Staff Studies 124, Board of Governors of the Federal Reserve System, Washington, D.C.

Umoh (1984) 'Nigeria's Rural Banking Scheme: A Case Study in Financial Development', The Banker, September, pp. 74-81.

Uzuoga (1981) *Money and Banking in Nigeria*, Fourth Dimension Publishing, Enugu, Nigeria.

Wallich, H.C. (1984) 'US Banking Deregulation: The Case for Orderly Progress', *The Banker*, May, pp 25-8.

Welch, J. Ed. (1981) *The Regulation of Banks in the Member States of the EEC*, Second Edition, Martinus Nijhoff, The Hague.

White, B. and Vittas, D. (1986) 'Barriers in International Banking', *Lloyds Bank Review*, Number 161, July, pp. 19-31.

Wilczynski, J. (1978) *Comparative Monetary Economics*, Macmillan, London.

Index